# ABODE OF SNOW

# ABODE OF SNOW

A HISTORY OF HIMALAYAN EXPLORATION
AND MOUNTAINEERING FROM EARLIEST TIMES
TO THE ASCENT OF EVEREST

## Kenneth Mason

*Formerly Superintendent, Survey of India
and Professor of Geography in the University of Oxford, 1932–53*

DIADEM BOOKS, LONDON
THE MOUNTAINEERS, SEATTLE
1987

Published simultaneously in Great Britain and the United States
by Diadem Books Ltd., London and The Mountaineers, Seattle

Copyright © 1987 by Helen Mason

A photoreprint edition of the book first published in 1955
by Rupert Hart-Davis © Kenneth Mason

All trade enquiries in the U.K., Europe and Commonwealth (except Canada)
to Cordee, 3a De Montfort Street, Leicester, England

All trade enquiries in the U.S.A. and Canada to
The Mountaineers, 306 2nd Avenue West, Seattle, Washington 98119

British Library Cataloguing in Publication Data:
Mason, Kenneth, 1887-1976
    Abode of Snow
    1. Mountaineering – Himalaya
    – History
    I. Title
    796.5'22'0954      DS485.H6

ISBN 0-906371-91-0 (UK)
ISBN 0-89886-142-X (US)

Jacket illustrations: *(front)* Makalu and Everest from Kangchenjunga *Photo: Doug Scott*;
*(back)* An aerial view of K2 from the west *Photo: Dianne Roberts*

Printed in Great Britain by Oxford University Press
and Penshurst Press, Tunbridge Wells, Kent

ACKNOWLEDGEMENTS The copyright holder and the publishers wish to thank the
following for their help in producing this volume: Doug Scott for his Foreword and jacket
and text photographs; to Douglas Hughes, Lord Hunt, Trevor Braham, Audrey Salkeld,
Francis Mason, George Lowe, Geoff Milburn, Peter Hodgkiss, and John Boothe of Grafton
Books for general editorial advice or help; to the Royal Geographical Society and David
Warren for picture research and permission to use photographs; to other photographers and
organisations whose contributions have strengthened the pictures already in the Mason
collection – Dianne Roberts, Christoph Pollet, Mr and Mrs Scott Russell (the Finch
collection), the Wakefield collection, Brigadier Gordon Osmaston, Harish Kapadia, the Iwa
to Yuki archive, the Audrey Salkeld collection, the Tilman collection, Ian McNaught Davis,
Alfred Gregory, Richard Summerton, the Alison Chadwick Onychiewicz collection,
Captain John Noel and Ivan Urbanovic.

# Contents

PREFACE

## I
## The Mountains and Their Approaches

1. General Description of the Himalaya ... ... ... 3
2. Punjab Himalaya ... ... ... ... ... ... 11
3. Karakoram ... ... ... ... ... ... ... 16
4. Kumaun Himalaya ... ... ... ... ... ... 22
5. Nepal Himalaya ... ... ... ... ... ... 28
6. Sikkim Himalaya ... ... ... ... ... ... 37
7. Assam Himalaya ... ... ... ... ... ... 42
8. Weather in the Himalaya ... ... ... ... ... 45

## II
## Early History to 1885

1. Early Travellers and Adventurers to 1800 ... ... 55
2. Travels and Route Surveys 1800–1845 ... ... ... 63
3. Triangulation and Surveys 1845–1868 ... ... ... 71
4. Pundit Explorers and the Years 1865–1885 ... ... 84

## III
## 1885–1918

1. Opening Phase ... ... ... ... ... ... 99
2. Punjab Himalaya ... ... ... ... ... ... 106
3. Kumaun Himalaya ... ... ... ... ... ... 114
4. Nepal, Sikkim, and Assam Himalaya ... ... ... 122
5. Karakoram ... ... ... ... ... ... ... 131
6. Re-survey of Kashmir ... ... ... ... ... 142

## IV
## 1918–1928

1. Retrospect and Prospect 1919 ... ... ... ... 151
2. Everest 1921 ... ... ... ... ... ... ... 154
3. Everest 1922 ... ... ... ... ... ... ... 164

# CONTENTS

4. Everest 1924 ... ... ... ... ... ... 172
5. Karakoram ... ... ... ... ... ... ... 177
6. Kumaun Himalaya... ... ... ... ... ... 185
7. The Founding of the Himalayan Club ... ... ... 189

## V
### 1929–1939

1. Kangchenjunga 1929, 1930, 1931 ... ... ... ... 195
2. Kamet and Nanda Devi ... ... ... ... ... 202
3. Everest 1933–1938 ... ... ... ... ... ... 211
4. Nanga Parbat 1932, 1934 ... ... ... ... ... 225
5. Nanga Parbat 1937, 1938, 1939 ... ... ... ... 234
6. Karakoram Exploration ... ... ... ... ... 240
7. Gasherbrum, Saltoro, Masherbrum, and Rakaposhi ... 248
8. K2 ... ... ... ... ... ... ... ... 257
9. Kumaun Himalaya... ... ... ... ... ... 264
10. Sikkim and Assam Himalaya ... ... ... ... 274
11. The Inter-War Period ... ... ... ... ... 280

## VI
### 1939–1953

1. The Second World War and After ... ... ... 285
2. Kumaun Himalaya... ... ... ... ... ... 291
3. Karakoram ... ... ... ... ... ... ... 299
4. Conquest of Nanga Parbat ... ... ... ... 306
5. Nepal: Dhaulagiri and Annapurna ... ... ... 312
6. The Ascent of Everest ... ... ... ... ... 325

### EPILOGUE

1954 and the Future ... ... ... ... ... ... 343

APPENDIX A. Himalayan and Karakoram Peaks over 25,000
    feet ... ... ... ... ... ... 346
    B. On the Determination of Himalayan heights 348
    C. Chronological Summary ... ... ... 351
    D. Short Bibliography ... ... ... ... 355

INDEX ... ... ... ... ... ... ... ... 358

# Illustrations

All group photographs list personnel from left to right

*between pages 78 and 79*

1. Sir George Everest *Survey of India*
2. Rai Bahadur Kishen Singh – The Explorer A.K. *Mason collection*
3. The Explorer Kinthup *Sir Gerald Burrard*
4. Captain T. G. Montgomerie R.E. *Royal Geographical Society*
5. Younghusband's party crossing the Mustagh Pass in 1887
6. Captain H. H. Godwin Austen *Royal Geographical Society*
7. Sir Francis Younghusband *Mason collection*
8. Martin Conway *Mason collection*
9. General C. G. Bruce *Royal Geographical Society*
10. K2 and Broad Peak from Concordia *Ian McNaught Davis*
11. Chogolisa from the Kaberi Glacier *Christoph Pollet*
12. The 1902 Eckenstein K2 Expedition
13. The Duke of Abruzzi
14. Filippo de Fillipi
15. Vittorio Sella
16. K2 from Windy Gap *Vittorio Sella*
17. Nanga Parbat from above the Indus Valley *Mason collection*
18. Dr Norman Collie
19. A. F. Mummery
20. Nanga Parbat – the Diamirai (Diamir) Face *Mason collection*
21. The upper part of the Diamirai Face
22. Camp on the Zemu Glacier near Kangchenjunga *Vittorio Sella*
23. The East Face of Kangchenjunga *Paul Bauer*
24. Nanda Devi from the Bagini Pass *Eric Shipton*
25. Tom Longstaff
26. At the summit of Trisul
27. Haramukh in Kashmir from the air *A. Thoenes*
28. An Indo-Russian junction station *Mason collection*
29. Members of the Indo-Russian triangulation party, 1913 *Mason collection*
30. Opening the Khardung Pass north of Leh, Ladakh *Mason collection*
31. Mrs Fanny Bullock Workman and William Hunter Workman
32. C. F. Meade and Pierre Blanc
33. Dr Arthur Neve
34. Dr A. M. Kellas
35. Making blood observations at 17,000ft *Mason collection*
36. Mason's survey equipment *Mason collection*
37. The monsoon about to burst as seen from Mussourie *Mason collection*

*between pages 174 and 175*

38. The Rongbuk Valley and the North Face of Everest *George Finch*
39. The Kangshung faces of Everest and Lhotse *Royal Geographical Society*
40. Members of the 1921 Everest Expedition *Royal Geographical Society*
41. The North-East Ridge of Everest from the Lakpa La *Royal Geographical Society*
42. Makalu from the Kharta Valley *Royal Geographical Society*
43. Mallory and Norton at about 26,000ft on Everest *T. Howard Somervell*
44. George Finch and Geoffrey Bruce *Wakefield collection*
45. The North Face of Everest *Royal Geographical Society*
46. Members of the 1924 Everest expedition *Captain John Noel*
47. Frank Smythe *Mason collection*
48. Members of the 1925 Visser expedition

# ILLUSTRATIONS

49. Broad Peak, K2 and Skyang Kangri from the Tater La *Mason collection*
50. The Kyagar Glacier and the Shaksgam Valley *Mason collection*
51. Members of the 1926 Shaksgam expedition *Mason collection*
52. Nanda Devi and the Rishi Gorge from the west *Doug Scott*
53. The South Face of Nanda Devi *Harish Kapadia*
54. The North Face of Nanda Devi *Osmaston collection*
55. Hugh Ruttledge *Royal Geographical Society*
56. Eric Shipton and H. W. Tilman *Salkeld collection*
57. Ang Tharkay, Sen Tenzing and Pasang Bhotia *Tilman collection*
58. Fazil Elahi surveying above the Ramani Glacier *Osmaston collection*
59. Members of the 1936–37 Osmaston Garhwal/Almora survey team *Osmaston collection*
60. Changabang and Kalanka *Doug Scott*
61. Nanga Parbat – the ridge between Rakhiot Peak and the Silver Saddle
62. The Rakhiot Face of Nanga Parbat *Mason collection*
63. Members of the 1934 Nanga Parbat expedition
64. Karl Wien, Günther Hepp, Paul Bauer and Adi Göttner *Mason collection*
65. Gasherbrum 1 from Gasherbrum 3 *Alison Chadwick Onychiewicz*
66. Masherbrum from the north *Ian McNaught Davis*

*between pages 302 and 303*
67. K2 from the East *Iwa to Yuki*
68. Charles Houston
69. Fritz Wiessner
70. The North Face of Annapurna *Richard Summerton*
71. Maurice Herzog being carried back from Annapurna
72. The final section of the Rakhiot Route on Nanga Parbat *Ivan Urbanovic*
73. Hermann Buhl
74. Everest from the west *Alfred Gregory*
75. On the South Ridge of Everest, above the South Col *Royal Geographical Society*
76. On the 'Hillary Step' near the summit of Everest *Doug Scott*
77. Members of the 1953 Everest expedition *Royal Geographical Society*
78. Tenzing on the summit of Everest, 1953 *Royal Geographical Society*
79. Cho Oyu
80. Pasang Dawa Lama
81. Dhaulagiri from the north
82. André Roch

# Maps and Diagrams

| | | |
|---|---|---:|
| 1. | Section through the Great Himalaya from end to end | *page* 6 |
| 2. | Divisions of the Himalaya | 8 |
| 3. | The Karakoram | 18 |
| 4. | Kumaun Himalaya | 24 |
| 5. | Karnali Section, Nepal Himalaya | 30 |
| 6. | Gandaki Section, Nepal Himalaya | 32 |
| 7. | Kosi Section, Nepal Himalaya | 34 |
| 8. | Kangchenjunga and the Sikkim Himalaya | 38 |
| 9. | Ridges of Nanga Parbat | 108 |
| 10. | Ridges of Nun Kun | 110 |
| 11. | The Nanda Devi Sanctuary and its approaches | 116 |
| 12. | Glacier approaches to the Kamet group | 119 |
| 13. | K2 and the Baltoro Muztagh | 134 |
| 14. | Everest approaches | 158 |
| 15. | South-eastern approach to Masherbrum | 254 |
| 16. | Gangotri glacier | 265 |

# Foreword

by Doug Scott

With the publication of *Abode of Snow* in 1955 mountaineers, geographers and all others who had fallen under the spell of the Himalaya were given the opportunity to read an historical record of the greatest mountain range in the world. Thirty-two years later it remains the definitive work on the subject. No other author has emerged to continue where Kenneth Mason left off, and yet so thorough was his work that this book provides a solid basis for a continuation of the story.

In its way the format of the work, and Mason's division of the Himalaya is as significant to the region's history and geography as the Great Arc of the Meridian was to the mapping of India. As Hugh Ruttledge noted, '. . . the scope is vast: historically from the seventeenth century to the present, geographically from the Indus to the Brahmaputra. Clarity on this enormous canvas is achieved by an ingenious arrangement of chapters, in which time, place and sequence are in proportion and continuity is never lost'. Yet despite the vast amount of information the story is always highly readable and entertaining. If there is one problem the researcher might find when seeking information in these pages for an expedition or an article, it is the danger of becoming side-tracked, such is their wealth of interesting facts and comment. Thus it stands pre-eminent as a standard reference work for all of us who are interested in Himalayan climbing – a status blurred only by the book's rarity, as frequent pleas for me to acquire copies for friends abroad bear witness. This reprint is therefore long overdue.

Kenneth Mason was born in Sutton, Surrey, in 1887. Educated at Cheltenham College and the Royal Military Academy, Woolwich, he was commissioned in the Royal Engineers in 1906 and spent the next two years at SME, Chatham. His early work was concerned with the development of stereoplotting machines. In 1909 he sailed to Karachi where he was soon posted to the Survey of India, and

ix

between 1910 and 1912 he worked on the triangulation of Kashmir. After this he took over the final stages of work on linking up the Indian to the Russian triangulation in the region north of Hunza. Mason completed the project by August 1913 with such accuracy that when the surveys connected his team's final calculations differed from those of the Russians by a mere 1.5 metres.

Of particular interest to mountaineers was his work in the Karakoram, where he established the height and position of a number of peaks at the western end of the range which had been missed by the previous survey of the region 60 years earlier. Notable among these was Disteghil Sar (25,868ft), the highest peak west of K2. As a result future mountain explorers, such as Visser, Morris and Shipton were able to fill in the details between these fixed positions with greater accuracy. Mason was later to play an important role in the official naming of peaks, ranges and glaciers in the Karakoram.

It was this fortuitous sequence of events that put him in a unique position to write this book. Mason's detailed knowledge of the Karakoram formed the ideal basis from which to develop a profound understanding of the whole Himalayan range. It is unlikely that anyone will ever again acquire such a breadth of understanding about the Himalaya, its geography, its climate, the mountain people, the Gurkha porters, the surveyors, and the mountaineers themselves. He was the link between the older explorers such as Younghusband, Conway, Bruce and Longstaff and the inter-war explorer-mountaineers, such as De Filippi, Kingdon Ward, Stein, Bauer, Shipton, Tilman, Smythe and Hunt.

Although Mason's main theme is the exploration of the range, mountaineering – the sport – is intrinsically bound up with the story from the start. By his own admission, he was not a particularly skilful mountaineer. He did however join the Alpine Club in 1914, and though he had never climbed in the Alps, he had by that time travelled widely throughout Kashmir and the Karakoram. In fact it was in Kashmir that he first learned to climb, with a medical missionary, Ernest Neve, making the first ascent of the south peak of Kolahoi in 1911 and the main peak (17,799ft) the following year. These climbs were long and sustained, with much step cutting on the lower sections and passages of rock climbing on the final ridge of the main peak. During this period he achieved two other 'firsts': he was the first to bring a pair of skis to India and taught himself to ski there; he also took part in the first India Airmail flight from Allahabad, a bizarre event with Mason sitting on the mail bags, with the pilot of the Sommer biplane perched on his lap.

It was his love of adventure, and deep affection for the mountains without the obsessive need to reach the summits, that enabled Mason to travel widely throughout the Himalaya. Like so many of the other explorers and mountaineers of the time he spent his formative years at boarding school. Thus at an early age he had come to terms with being away from home and using his own resources, and in later life this enabled him to sustain long periods away in the mountains either climbing or on lonely surveys. It was while at preparatory school he read Younghusband's *Heart of a Continent* which first fired an interest in surveying and the Himalaya.

With the outbreak of war in 1914 Mason resumed his military career, serving on the Western Front (1914-15) and in Mesopotamia (1916-18). He was wounded at Loos, received the MC for his part in an action during the relief of Kut and was three times mentioned in despatches for activities as an intelligence officer.

He returned to his Indian survey work after the war. In 1921 he was invited to join the Mt. Everest Reconnaissance Expedition but his commanding officer, possibly piqued that Mason's invitation had preceded a formal request to the Survey, contrived to ensure that the two surveyors' places went to Moreshead and Wheeler. For some years Mason was involved in precise levelling, preparing for his most important project – the survey of the Shaksgam Valley and the Aghil ranges in 1926, a true "blank on the map". Such was the success and importance of this work he was awarded the Founder's Gold Medal of the Royal Geographical Society. With his wealth of surveying experience Mason fully understood the problems facing travellers in the region, particularly the need to maintain good relations with the local people through sympathetic employment and good organisation. His careful preparatory work did much to sustain the surveyors through the frustrations of route finding in the harsh terrain, during inclement weather and above all, to counter the debilitating effects of high altitude. Throughout his book it is obvious that Mason has been able to understand clearly the problems which confronted the first explorers to the Himalaya, and link those with his own experience to provide useful pointers for those who came later. But despite this thread of organisational wisdom perhaps the great strength of this book is in conveying to the reader Mason's own love of the Himalaya, his feel for the lie of the land, the weather, the mountain people, and the role of the porters and the mountaineers from Britain and Europe who were climbing the highest peaks. He also puts on record the little-known yet notable climbing achievements of the self-effacing Pundits and Indian surveyors who preceded him – an era epitomised in fiction by Kipling's *Kim*. We find that by 1862 they ascended thirty-seven summits above 20,000ft and five above 21,000ft. These climbs were accomplished with the lines of communication stretched to the limit, burdened with heavy survey equipment, and out in the field for months at a time.

Mason was able to make use of his survey work for the benefit of the next generation of mountaineers and geographers. In 1928 he helped found The Himalayan Club and one year later he launched *The Himalayan Journal* and edited the first twelve volumes, establishing a tradition of accuracy for which it has always been renowned.

In 1932, Mason, then a Lieutenant-Colonel and Deputy Director of Surveys, left the Survey of India to take up a newly created post, the Professorship of Geography at Oxford, which he held until 1953. Throughout the thirties and forties he also played an active role in the affairs of the Royal Geographical Society and was elected Vice President in 1937. He served on the Mt. Everest Committee during the thirties and played a part in team selection for the four expeditions during that period. Among his recommendations for the 1936 project was John Hunt (later to lead the successful Expedition) who was eventually rejected when pronounced unfit by the RAF Medical Board. During the Second World War Mason's geographical and military experience made him the ideal organiser for an Oxford-based group which produced a series of geographical handbooks for the Director of Naval Intelligence.

On retirement from Oxford Mason concentrated on the preparation of this book which was published two years later. Although it received enthusiastic reviews, its importance was perhaps eclipsed in the climbing world by the euphoria surrounding the first ascents of Everest and Kangchenjunga, and it was never reprinted. In his eighties Mason contributed to the BBC series *Plain Tales from the Raj*, his vivid recollections preserved by Charles Allen in eight hours of taped conversations. Allen pays tribute to Mason in his own book *A Mountain in Tibet*. There he notes, '. . . then almost ninety [he was] probably the last of the players in the Great Game'.

Here then is a book by one of the great experts of Himalayan exploration, which can be relied upon for factual accuracy and balance. It is to be hoped that the successor, if there is one, will achieve the same standard of excellence. Now, over thirty years later, the time must be right to continue the story, from the first ascents of the remaining unclimbed greats, such as Kangchenjunga and Makalu, through the climbing of the ridges, buttresses and faces of those peaks to the recent Alpine-like activity on the spectacular rock and ice spires in the Karakoram and Garhwal. Any new work would also make mention of the little known ranges of Bhutan and Arunachal Pradesh, where exploration is still in its infancy. If the mountains of Tibet and the Pamir were to be included, such a work would obviously run to several volumes.

*Abode of Snow* provides the basis from which to build, yet in itself it still has relevance, not only as a historical reminder, but in its thorough topographical commentary. It provides an immediate briefing and history, a framework on which to hang further knowledge. Now that improved organisation, equipment, more rapidly circulated information and cheap and speedy air travel is accelerating the pace of change, it is doubly important to have on record a reminder of the origins and traditions of the sport in the Himalaya. I found it a revelation when I discovered the book after several years of expeditioning, and learned of the activities of our predecessors, not just the comparatively recent activities of the last fifty years, but going back to Longstaff, Conway and earlier. It is a fund of history and inspiration for which I and others will be eternally grateful.

DOUG SCOTT
*Wigton, Cumbria, 1987*

# Preface

I WAS first asked to write a history of Himalayan exploration and mountaineering about thirty years ago. I had spent several years exploring and surveying in the Himalaya and had personally known many of those who had gone there for one reason or another during the previous forty or fifty years, among whom was Godwin-Austen who had surveyed in the Karakoram as long ago as 1861. Sir Sidney Burrard told me about the Himalaya before I was ten. I had read Younghusband's *The Heart of a Continent* before I was twelve, and a great deal of Himalayan literature both before and since I went to India. K2 came into my early dreams, as did Nanga Parbat and Kangchenjunga, long before I ever saw them. I had also browsed among the old historical files of the Great Trigonometrical Survey of India, then stored in the Clock Tower at Dehra Dun.

I was pressed again to write soon after we founded the Himalayan Club, but put it off, hoping that a better qualified mountaineer than I would set his hand to the task. Though I had been a member of the Alpine Club since 1914 I was never an expert climber in the modern sense. During the nineteen-thirties there was so much activity in the Himalaya that most of my spare time was taken up in editing *The Himalayan Journal*. Now in retirement I have been asked again. It would perhaps have been better to have left it to a younger man. These are my excuses for my shortcomings.

Nevertheless a mountain surveyor learns much about snow, ice, weather, and other things. He seeks advice from those who have gone before him and perhaps adds a little for those who come after. Certainly he learns to husband his strength and scanty resources, and with a definite task to perform within a given time he learns to make the utmost use of every daylight hour and to guard the health and welfare of every member of his camp, however humble, since success depends on them. He quickly learns the easiest way up a mountain, the amount of effort he can ask of his porters, where best to place his camps, what the weather is likely to be, the behaviour of ice and snow, when it is safe to travel light and to camp out. He has to become infinitely patient in bad weather. To be any use at his job he must develop a keen topographical sense, be able to recognize the same mountain feature from all directions, and guide his men almost instinctively through storm and blizzard. Their safety depends on him.

The early travellers had a harder time than those of to-day. There were no roads and fewer tracks; there were no maps; the people were often suspicious and superstitious, and sometimes hostile. They have been gradually weaned from their dread of the evil spirits that dwell among the mountains. The winning of their confidence has been the care of many travellers whose names do not appear in this book. The first men to go to the Himalaya had no mountain equipment, no ice-axes, crampons, pitons, no nylon ropes, wind-proof clothing or indestructible tents. They learnt about frostbite and snow-blindness the hard and painful way. They carried no oxygen and no Pervitine tablets to keep them going. But they blazed the trails for others to follow, and to go farther and higher. These are threads that run through Himalayan history.

The mountains of Asia are so vast that it is difficult to set limits in a history. I have felt bound to define my task by the Indus on the west and the Brahmaputra on the east, thereby omitting much fascinating exploration on the north-west frontier and on the confines of northern Burma. The exploration of the Hindu Kush, K'un-lun, the Pamirs, Chinese Turkestan, and Tibet, though partly interwoven with that of the Himalaya, is a series of separate stories and the reader will find little mention of them. Sir Aurel Stein and Sven Hedin do not therefore appear. Nor do Littledale, Bower, and Deasy, or more recent travellers in Central Asia such as Schomberg and Skrine. Kingdon Ward only touches the fringe in the extreme east.

There is enough to write about within the limits I have set in time and space. Man's efforts to reach the highest summits make an epic story. It has only been possible for me to outline it. Readers must go to the writings of those who set themselves against the mountains and overcame their problems, if they want the details. I have left out so much. At the same time so many people who have never visited the Himalaya are now interested in its problems that I have been persuaded to give a short outline of its geography and a summary of the weather conditions to be expected. But it must be remembered that this knowledge is the accumulation of experience and was not available to early travellers and mountaineers.

Geographical names have been spelt and heights have been given wherever possible from official Survey of India sources and maps; but in accounts of climbs the heights are often little more than estimates by the climbers themselves and are not wholly trustworthy.

The opening of Nepal, the closing of Tibet, the end of British rule in India, the emergence of Pakistan and India as separate States, all these almost coincide to mark the end of one era in Himalayan travel and the beginning of another. It seems wise to end the story with the ascent of Everest, and the events of 1954 are only summarized.

I am indebted to many who have told me of their travels and climbs, and to their books and letters. Most of all to Hugh Ruttledge, who has encouraged me. He has, I hope, prevented me from making any serious inaccuracies or omissions. My own memory as I get older is often at fault. I wish also to thank the Survey of India, the Royal Geographical Society, Eric Shipton, Sir Gerald Burrard, Paul Bauer and the *Deutsche Himalaja Stiftung,* for permission to reproduce certain illustrations; Miss Mary Potter for her excellent maps; and Mrs. D. Steer for her care in typing and preparing my manuscript for the press.

K. M.

*Oxford*
*December 1954*

PART ONE

# The Mountains and Their Approaches

, . . . Northwards soared
The stainless ramp of huge Himala's wall
Ranged in white ranks against the blue—untrod
Infinite, wonderful—whose uplands vast,
And lifted universe of crest and crag,
Shoulder and shelf, green slope and icy horn,
Riven ravine, and splintered precipice
Led climbing thought higher and higher, until
It seemed to stand in heaven and speak with Gods

\*　　\*　　\*

Beneath the snows dark forests spread, sharp-laced
With leaping cataracts and veiled with clouds:
Lower grew rose-oaks, and the great fir groves
Where echoed pheasant's call and panther's cry,
Clatter of wild sheep on the stones, and scream
Of circling eagles:—Under these the plain
Gleamed like a praying-carpet at the foot
Of those divinest altars

EDWIN ARNOLD *The Light of Asia*

# 1. General Description of the Himalaya

IN the beginning there were no mountains. Before time was, and before Man came, two great land-masses, separated by a shallowing sea, moved towards each other under the stress of elemental forces. The sediments of the sea were raised, first into gentle folds parallel to the land-mass edges, later into great mountain ranges. Molten mass welled into the primitive mountain arches, solidified, and altered the adjacent rocks; storm and rain, borne by the Indian monsoon, carved the southern ranges into their present complex forms, while the highest, the Great Himalaya, shielded the highland of Tibet, where are found, at over 20,000 feet above the sea to-day, the fossilized remains of life in the ancient sea.

Himalaya, the Abode of Snow, is properly speaking the mountain region that feeds the perennial rivers of the Ganges—Jumna, Ganges itself, Gogra, Gandaki and Kosi. The word is an ancient Sanscrit compound: *Himā,* snow, and *alāya,* abode. In Nepal the words *Himālā* or *Himāl* are given to many individual ranges and mountain groups. In the course of time the Sanscrit word has been extended to include the whole complex mountain system which stretches from the Indus near Gilgit in the west for some fifteen hundred miles to the Tsangpo or Brahmaputra bend in the east, and for over a hundred miles northwards from the plains of India to the highlands of Tibet; it is now used by Europeans, Indians and Pakistanis in its common Anglicized form; the accent is almost equal on the second and third syllables.[1]

[1] When the Himalayan Club was founded in 1928, Sir Geoffrey Corbett consulted in India a number of Northern Indian language experts. They concluded that the correct Sanscrit sounds were *Hi* as in 'him'; *ma* as in 'father'; *la* and *ya* as in 'fur.' In modern Hindi, the final 'a' is ordinarily not sounded, and the word is pronounced Himālay. Most other Indians stress equally the second and third syllables (*Himalayan Journal,* i (1929) 84). Brahmans sometimes use the expression Himāleh and Himāchal; Mr. Hugh Ruttledge tells me that a Hindu Brahman told him that the second part of this word is from *ānchal* (the resting-place for a child in its mother's arm).

Himalaya—or if one prefers it The Himalaya—is the greatest physical feature of the earth; in mass greater than all the mountains of Europe, including the Caucasus, put together. Set down its western end at London, and its eastern end would reach almost to Moscow. Plant the Jungfrau on the summit of Mont Blanc, or pile eight Snowdons one upon the other, and Everest overshadows all. In so vast a region man is humbled and insignificant.

Geographers, using the history of Himalayan rocks, have reduced the complexities of the ranges to a comparatively simple system. The gradual rise of the Himalaya took place in the form of a series of long parallel curvilinear folds whose general alignment and 'strike' is parallel to the edge of the old continental block of India to the south. Some of these folds have been overthrust and have become recumbent, lying on younger sedimentaries. Erosion through the ages, infinitely more powerful along the Indian-facing flanks than on the Tibetan Highland, because of the Indian monsoon, has carved the parallel folds and 'nappes' into their present shape.

To-day three major mountain zones between the Ganges plains and Tibet are recognized. First, the long low Siwalik range, youngest of all and a comparatively low feature, stretching from the Punjab to Assam, sometimes a single fold, sometimes double, and often with a broad plain or *Dun* beyond it, as at Dehra, from twenty to thirty miles wide. In Hindu mythology it is considered the edge of the roof of Siva's abode in the Himalaya. It extends from the Indus with remarkable unity for over 1500 miles to near the Brahmaputra in Assam, with one gap of 200 miles from the Kosi to the Manas of Bhutan, where the fierce erosion of the monsoon has destroyed it almost entirely.[1] Its greatest height above the Ganges plain is not more than 3000 feet. Often densely forested, it is the home of tiger, leopard, bear, and other wild animals.

Second, the Lesser Himalaya, a complex older zone, averaging perhaps sixty miles wide, with the same general 'strike' as the Siwaliks, but more contorted by uplift, occasionally forced to change direction, and intensely carved by erosion and mountain torrents: great limestone ridges, sometimes showing their original alignment and parallelism, but more often now appearing as spurs from a

[1] It is shown in heavy black in the foreground of fig. 1.

crystalline core of a range north of them. It is a zone where whole hillsides may crumble and disappear after heavy rain, destroying mountain paths and bridges. Dense tropical forests cover the lower slopes of these mountains in the east; westwards their place is increasingly taken by magnificent coniferous forests, pride of all being the deodar in Kashmir. On the outer fringe of the Lesser Himalaya, facing the Indian plains, are the man-made hill-stations, at altitudes of from 5000 to 7000 feet, Murree, Dalhousie, Simla, Mussoorie, Ranikhet, Almora and Naini Tal, and Darjeeling. The average height of mountain summits in this zone is perhaps 15,000 feet, with many higher, especially as the great range to the north is approached. The geologist J. B. Auden, who visited Nepal after the earthquake in January 1934, divides the Lesser Himalaya into two units, an outer one with ranges such as the Mahabharat Lekh, south of Katmandu, aligned from WNW to ESE, and an inner one with long ridges running in general from NNE to SSW from the Great Himalaya. This is a simplification which applies to much of the Lesser Himalaya.

Third, the Great Himalaya, axis and crystalline core of the whole system, composed fundamentally of intruded granites and gneisses, very occasionally capped still with the remnants of sedimentary rocks, aligned generally parallel to the Siwaliks, but by no means continuous throughout its length. This core has been—and is being—carved into giant blocks by the transverse head tributaries of the Ganges, which gather the waters of affluents lying in troughs, often on both sides of it. The crest of the Great Himalaya rarely falls below 18,000 feet except at the great river gorges and at well-known passes.

Within the axial zone of the Great Himalaya stand the highest massifs: Nanga Parbat, 26,620 feet, in the west, towering above the Indus; Nanda Devi, 25,645 feet, between the gorges of Alaknanda and Goriganga, tributaries of the Ganges, in Kumaun; Dhaulagiri, 26,795 feet, and Annapurna, 26,492 feet, separated by the gorge of the Kali Gandaki in Nepal; Mount Everest, 29,002 feet, and its neighbour Makalu, 27,790 feet, along the Tibet-Nepal frontier; Kangchenjunga, 28,146 feet, on the Nepal-Sikkim border; and Namcha Barwa, 25,445 feet, in the extreme east, towering above the

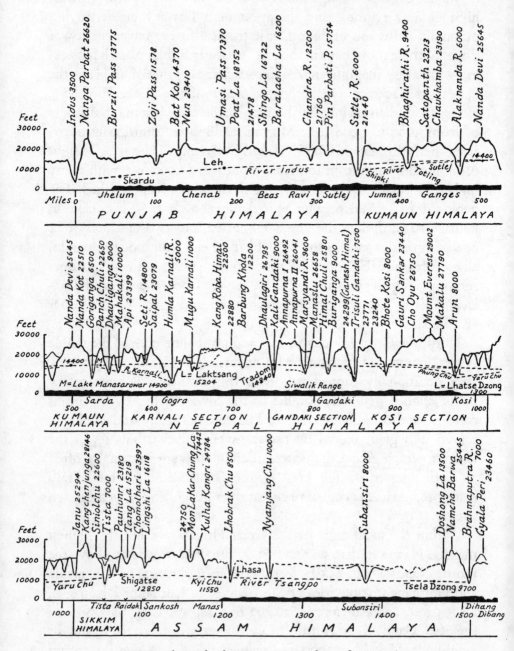

FIG. 1. *Section through the Great Himalaya from end to end.*

Tsangpo bend.[1] In this zone there are thirty-one peaks whose altitudes, all above 25,000 feet, are known with considerable accuracy, twelve of them over 26,000 feet; seven of the thirty-one have been climbed.[2] To reach them from India the mountaineer must traverse the whole breadth of the Lesser Himalaya on foot or pony-back, with human or animal transport, through winding valleys, over rivers (bridges may be swept away) and passes, often open for only a few months of the year, sometimes a caravan journey of nearly a month.

West of the Sutlej where monsoon erosion is less than in the east, the parallelism of the Lesser Himalayan ridges is more marked. The Indus, gathering its headwaters on the Tibet highland near Lake Manasarowar, flows parallel to and north of the Great Himalaya, forcing a passage round the great massif of Nanga Parbat. The chief sources of the Ganges also lie beyond the Great Himalayan crest-zone, and force a passage through it. Beyond the crests the monsoon penetrates to no great depth, and the landscape, often harsh and uninviting, is much less rugged. At some seasons of the year the fortunate mountaineer can stand on some high pass or peak, looking southwards into the cloud-filled forested valleys of the Lesser Himalaya and north into the clear semi-arid landscapes of Tibet. Flying high over the Ganges in the hot weather an airman to-day can see below him the sun-baked plains of India, the low Siwaliks, clad in forest and draped in cloud, with the giants of the Himalaya clear-cut against the purple distance of Tibet.

In the region of Manasarowar and Rakas Tal, sacred lakes in southern Tibet, with Gurla Mandhata south of them and holy Kailas to the north, three rivers of the first magnitude rise within a few miles of one another: the Indus, the Sutlej, and the Tsangpo. The first flows north-west behind the Great Himalaya into Ladakh and Baltistan, dividing the Himalaya proper from the Karakoram, and finds for itself a passage at 3500 feet above sea-level immediately west of Nanga Parbat; here a barrier of some 23,000 feet of rock and ice stands between the river bed and the summit. The Sutlej, rising

[1] These are the officially accepted heights in 1953. A list of known heights above 25,000 feet and their locations is given in Appendix A (page 346). A note on the problems of determining the exact heights follows the list as Appendix B (page 348).

[2] Kamet (1931), Nanda Devi (1936), Annapurna I (1950), Everest (1953), Nanga Parbat (1953), Cho Oyu (1954), Makalu II (1954).

7

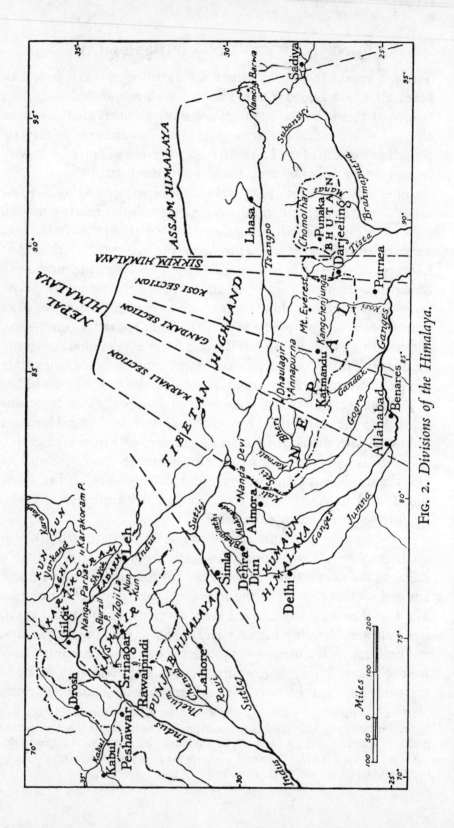

FIG. 2. Divisions of the Himalaya.

in Rakas Tal itself, passes through an arid gorge, breaks through the Great Himalaya at 6000 feet, and flowing westwards to the north of Simla enters the Indian plains to join the Indus in Pakistan. The Tsangpo, the broad and comparatively lazy river of southern Tibet, flows eastwards at some distance south of Lhasa and bursts through the eastern end of the Great Himalaya. East of its sentinel peak Namcha Barwa it is at about 7000 feet above sea-level; it is known as the Dihang in the unadministered country east of Bhutan, and is the Brahmaputra of Assam.

The highland of Tibet has now been crossed in many directions by travellers, but still offers much virgin land to the scientific explorer. It has always been difficult of access, physically and politically—perhaps more so now than ever—and its mountains are not of great interest to the climber. But at its western end, in Little Tibet, the lands of Ladakh and Baltistan, conquered between 1834 and 1842 by Zorawar Singh in the name of Gulab Singh, the Dogra ruler of Jammu, are much more rugged. North of the Indus is a series of trans-Himalayan ranges, more or less parallel to the Himalayan axis. They pass by various names—the Ladakh range, between the Indus and its tributary, the Shyok; the Karakoram Mountain system, as far north as the Shaksgam tributary of the Yarkand river, and the Aghil mountains between the Shaksgam and the Yarkand rivers. In the Karakoram are mighty peaks which have been the goal of many European mountaineers—among them K2, 28,250 feet, the second highest mountain in the world—and eighteen others above 25,000 feet, whose heights are known with considerable accuracy. Several of the longest glaciers outside sub-polar regions, such as the Hispar, Baltoro, and Siachen, drain the flanks of Karakoram.

Because of its great length it is convenient to divide the Himalaya into sections from west to east. Sir Sidney Burrard, in his standard work, *A Sketch of the Geography and Geology of the Himalaya Mountains and Tibet*, published in 1907, named these divisions the Punjab Himalaya, Kumaun Himalaya, Nepal Himalaya, and Assam Himalaya. Some travellers have preferred 'Kashmir Himalaya' and 'Bhutan Himalaya' for the first and last of Burrard's divisions, on the grounds that they are in Kashmir and Bhutan; with these travellers I used to agree, though now I am convinced that Burrard's names are best. The western division is drained by the great rivers of the Punjab and has been explored from bases in the Punjab province; though the greater part of the division falls within political Kashmir, the name Kashmir is really applicable only to one province of the dominions formerly held by the Maharaja of Jammu and Kashmir, while Ladakh and Baltistan were conquered from Jammu. It is however essential to include a small Sikkim division between the Nepal and Assam Himalaya, since the mountains here are neither in Nepal nor Assam, nor are they normally approached from these directions.

Thus we have the Punjab Himalaya on the west between the Indus and the Sutlej; it contains the mountain basins of the Jhelum, Chenab, Ravi, and Beas, and their glacier sources. The Kumaun Himalaya encloses the sources and tributaries of the Jumna and Ganges and reaches the western boundary of Nepal. The Nepal Himalaya, in the State of Nepal, is conveniently subdivided into three sections, embracing respectively the basins of the Karnali, Gandaki, and Kosi. Next is the narrow Sikkim Himalaya, most accessible of all, enclosing the Tista, with its great peak Kangchenjunga and satellites on the borders of Nepal. Lastly the Assam Himalaya, mostly in Bhutan and in the unadministered country between Bhutan and the Brahmaputra.

There are thus six main mountain regions each with special characteristics of varying interest to the explorer and mountaineer:

- (i) Punjab Himalaya
- (ii) Trans-Himalaya in Kashmir State, principally the Karakoram and its associate ranges
- (iii) Kumaun Himalaya
- (iv) Nepal Himalaya, with its three subdivisions, Karnali, Gandaki, and Kosi
- (v) Sikkim Himalaya

and (vi) Assam Himalaya.

In all except the second and fifth of these divisions there are the three zones, (a) Siwalik, (b) Lesser Himalaya, and (c) Great Himalaya.

This systematic arrangement is essential for any clear thinking about the Himalaya as a whole, in visualizing its similarities and contrasts, its physical and political problems, and in planning a journey to its great peaks.

# 2. Punjab Himalaya

THE Punjab Himalaya is a roughly rectangular mountain region, 300 miles long by 150 miles wide, lying between the Indus on the north-west and the Sutlej on the south-east, its north-eastern boundary being the Indus in its course through Ladakh and Baltistan. It contains the mountain basins of four of the five great rivers of the Punjab—Jhelum, Chenab, Ravi and Beas—as well as the left-bank tributaries of the Indus and the right-bank feeders of the Sutlej as this river passes through the district of Bashahr, north-east of Simla.

The Great Himalayan crest-zone extends from mighty Nanga Parbat (26,620) south-eastwards to the Nun Kun massif (lat. 34°, long. 76°) and thence to the Sutlej near Shipki close to the Tibetan border. North of it is the subsidiary Zaskar range (a branch leaving the Great Himalaya near the western boundary of Nepal) which carries some high peaks as it traverses the districts of Rupshu and Zaskar.

The two chief ranges of the Punjab Lesser Himalaya are the Pir Panjal and the Dhaula Dhar. The first of these leaves the Great Himalaya immediately north of the Sutlej between Chini and Shipki, and forms the watershed between the Chandra-Bhaga affluent of the Chenab and the Beas and Ravi on the south. After being pierced by the Chenab in Kishtwar it forms the serrated southern rim of the lovely Vale of Kashmir.

The Dhaula Dhar range, like the Zaskar a branch from the Great Himalaya far to the east, enters the eastern part of the region between Wangtu and Chini where it is cut through by the Sutlej; thence it passes near the source of the Ravi where its flanks almost merge with those of the Pir Panjal. It passes north-westwards through Kangra into the State of Jammu. It is pierced by the Beas between Larji and Pandoh, and by the Ravi south-west of Chamba town.

On the north-west the Jhelum drains the province and Vale of Kashmir, an ancient lake-basin eighty miles long by twenty miles broad, 'an emerald set in pearls,' which lies at 5000 feet above sea-level between the Great Himalaya and the Pir Panjal. Four tributaries, all important passages for travellers, join its right bank. The Kunhar, river of Khagan, and the Kishenganga, draining the Gurais district, both join the Jhelum near its acute bend at Muzaffarabad. The Sind and Liddar rivers join it in the broad Vale of Kashmir before it cuts a gorge through the Pir Panjal below Baramula. All have glacier sources and carry large volumes of water from melted snow in summer. A less important feeder is the Punch river, which drains the southern slopes of the Pir Panjal and joins the Jhelum near the foot of the Himalaya.

The Chenab has a basin nearly as large as the Jhelum and is the river of Jammu. Its two main tributaries, the Maru-Warwan and the Chandra-Bhaga also drain the trough between the Great Himalaya and the Pir Panjal, south-east of the Vale of Kashmir. The first is fed by the southern glaciers of Nun Kun. The Chenab leaves the Siwaliks near the city of Jammu.

The basins of the Ravi and Beas are much smaller. They drain the Dhaula Dhar and the southern slopes of the Pir Panjal, east of Jammu. Their glacier sources are smaller, but the heavy snowfall of winter and early spring, and the monsoon rains increase their volume considerably from May to September.

With the notable exceptions of Nanga Parbat and Nun Kun (23,410) the Punjab Great Himalaya carries no great peaks. The general level of its crest-zone is lower than in Kumaun or Nepal (fig. 1). No summits rise above 20,000 feet between these two mountains in Kashmir, though there are many between 16,000 and 19,000 feet, interesting to climbers, and easily accessible from Srinagar: Haramukh (16,872), Kolahoi (17,799), Koh-i-nur (16,725), and others up to 18,000 and 19,000 feet towards Nun Kun. Many have now been climbed.

This well-mapped section of the range is crossed by several famous routes: the Babusar pass (13,690), west of Nanga Parbat, takes the frontier road from Abbottabad to Chilas and Gilgit; the Kamri (13,368) and the Burzil (13,775), scenes of many an avalanche tragedy, take the direct 'Gilgit road' from Srinagar: both have witnessed the march of armies. The lowest notch in the range, Zoji La (11,578) is on the main caravan road from Srinagar to Dras, Leh, and Central Asia by the distant Karakoram pass, said to be one of the ways of Genghis Khan. The Bat Kol (or Lonvilad pass) is a deep notch at 14,370 feet between two peaks, 18,588 and 19,630, the pass on the direct route from Jammu by the Warwan valley to Suru and Leh. Though difficult, it is generally passable in summer and autumn for animals, and it was crossed by the Dogra general, Zorawar Singh, and his army in 1834.

South-east of Nun Kun the crest is less well known and there is only the map made from the old surveys of the eighteen-sixties. A few summits are known to reach 21,000 feet on the northern boundaries of Kishtwar, Chamba and Lahul. The two best-known passes across it are the Umasi La (17,370) leading into Zaskar and the Baralacha La (16,200) at the head of the Chandra-Bhaga.

The Zaskar range in this region is highest at its south-eastern end. Leo Pargial (22,280) rising immediately north of the Sutlej opposite Shipki, a neighbour (21,680) seven miles to the north, and Shilla (23,050) appear to be the highest. Little is known in detail of the crest-zone farther north-west as it traverses the districts of Rupshu and Zaskar, but several routes cross it to the Indus above and below Leh. Best known are the Parang La (18,300) linking Spiti with Rupshu, the Lachalung La and Marang La, both about 16,600 feet, which take the Baralacha La route on to Leh; the Nera La (15,966) between Zaskar and Khalatse on the Indus; and the Kungri La between Suru and Khalatse. These passes and valleys were for long the haunt of sportsmen in search of game, mostly burrhel, but mountaineers have climbed little among the peaks, though Leo Pargial and Shilla have both been conquered.

To a less extent the same applies to the Pir Panjal between the Sutlej and Kishtwar, though it is much more accessible and has been largely resurveyed since 1920, and it affords some first-class climbing. The lovely valley of the Beas in Kulu and its grimmer tributaries Malana, Parbati and Spin which join it from the east, are enclosed by many rocky and icy peaks (several of which rise above 20,000 feet) including the snow-dome of Deo Tiba, 20,410, visible from Simla, seventy-five miles distant.[1] At the head of the Beas, the Rohtang pass

---

[1] Reconnoitred but not climbed. (*Himalayan Journal* (*H.J.*) xvii (1952) 118.)

(13,050) takes a fairly easy track into Lahul; at the head of the Parbati is the Pin Parbati pass (15,754), leading into Spiti, not often crossed by Europeans. Kulu is easily reached by the motor-road from Pathankot, Baijnath, and Mandi, or from Simla by the suspension bridge over the Sutlej at Luhri; both routes are well supplied with rest-houses.[1]

West of Kulu many summits in the Pir Panjal rise above 19,000 feet, and the passes between the Ravi and the Chandra-Bhaga are mostly over 16,000 feet, with fair-sized glaciers on the northern side. In Kashmir the Pir Panjal is well known and has been frequented by climbers and skiers. Though lower than in Chamba it has a well-marked serrated crest, the highest peaks being between 15,000 and 16,000 feet. Barhma Sakil (15,440), Parasing (15,040), Tatakuti (15,560) and 'Sunset Peak' (15,567), near the Pir Panjal pass, have all been climbed more than once. They are pleasant holiday climbs from the *margs* or alps on their northern slopes, and can be reached from Srinagar in two days.

The passes over this part of the range are important. The best known are the Pir Panjal pass (11,462) which gives its name to the whole range, and the Banihal (8985). Until the construction of the Jhelum valley 'cart-road' in the eighties of last century, the Pir Panjal was the most frequented pass between the Punjab and Kashmir. It took the old road of the Mogul Emperors in the sixteenth and seventeenth centuries, and the traveller Bernier vividly described the imperial elephant-train negotiating the narrow track. Ruins of old Mogul *serais* are still to be seen at points along the route.

The motor-road over the Banihal pass has been constructed and metalled since 1910 and was opened for motors in 1922. It is the main road between the two capitals—Jammu and Srinagar.

The Dhaula Dhar is the densely wooded range of Kangra, drained and cut up by tributaries of the Beas and Ravi. It forms an imposing wall of precipitous rock north of Dharmsala, whose cantonments stand at 5000 feet on its southern flanks. It is easily accessible from Pathankot and Mandi, and many of its nearer mountains have been climbed by officers on short leave from nearby military stations.[2]

---

[1] *H.J.* v (1933) 75–89.
[2] J. W. Rundall: *Rambles and Scrambles in the Kangra Himalaya; H.J.* x (1938) 164; C. G. Bruce: *Twenty Years in the Himalaya.*

The two great massifs of the Punjab Great Himalaya are Nanga Parbat and Nun Kun. Nanga Parbat is one of the grandest mountains in the whole Himalaya. Seen from Gulmarg, the summer hill-station of the Pir Panjal across the Vale of Kashmir, it seems to float in heaven: watchers at dawn are spellbound. From the edge of the mountains of Gor, at 10,000 feet west of the Indus, the eye sees the river 6500 feet below and travels upwards to the summit at 26,620 feet in a distance of less than twenty miles (map page 108). There is more than 23,000 feet of precipice and ice. It is the cruellest and most vengeful of mountains and forgives no errors of judgement. A. F. Mummery and two Gurkhas were killed by an avalanche on its western flank in 1895; no fewer than eleven Germans and fifteen porters lie buried among the Rakhiot approaches on the north of it. After seven attempts its defences were conquered by an Austro-German expedition on 3 July 1953.

Kun and Nun, the twin summits of the Nun-Kun massif have also fallen to man. First visited by Majors Bruce and Lucas in 1898, and explored in more detail by Dr. A. Neve and Rev. C. E. Barton in 1902, the Dutch mountaineer H. Sillem reached a height of 21,000 feet on Nun in 1903;[1] they were followed by the Americans, Dr. and Mrs. Workman in 1906.[2] Count Calciati, an Italian, reached the summit of Kun (23,250), the highest rock peak, in 1914. It was not however until 1953, after some earlier attempts notably by Harrison and Waller in 1934, that the great snow-dome of Nun (23,410) was conquered by two members of a French expedition, Madame Claude Kogan, and the Swiss missionary in Ladakh, Pierre Vittos—a truly international mountain from first to last!

[1] H.J. vii. (1935) 65.
[2] The Workmans climbed 'Pinnacle Peak,' (east of Kun) to which they assigned a height of 23,300 feet. Actually the height by triangulation is 22,810 feet. See p. 111.

# 3. Karakoram

THE historic Karakoram pass to Central Asia has given its name to the mountains west of it which form the water-parting between the drainage to the Indian Ocean and that to the deserts of Central Asia. Loosely applied for many years, the name is now conventionally given to the whole mountain region between the lower Shyok and Indus rivers on the south and the Shaksgam tributary of the Yarkand river on the north. The region is bounded by the Ishkoman and Karumbar rivers on the west and by the upper Shyok on the east. Between the lower Shyok and upper Indus is the Ladakh range; beyond the Karumbar river on the west the mountains become known as the Hindu Kush; between the Shaksgam and the main upper course of the Yarkand river on the north are the Aghil mountains, discovered by Sir Francis Younghusband during his famous journey in 1887; east of the upper Shyok are the desolate plateaux and wastes of western Tibet.

The region is the most heavily glaciated outside sub-polar latitudes and, though remote, has become an almost international playground. Hardly a European nation has been unrepresented during its detailed exploration and survey. Here stands K2 (28,250), the second highest mountain in the world, first fixed in 1858 for position and height from survey stations in Kashmir.[1] Among other great mountains are the Gasherbrums, four of them 26,000 feet or over, Masherbrum (25,660), Rakaposhi (25,550) and Saltoro Kangri (25,400). There are nineteen heights above 25,000 feet, six of which are over 26,000 feet.

The Karakoram also contains some of the longest glaciers outside sub-polar regions: the Batura (thirty-six miles) and Hispar on the west, the latter combining with the Biafo to form one long passage of ice seventy-six miles long; the Baltoro (thirty-six miles) and the Siachen (forty-five miles), reaching up into the ice-world of K2,

[1] For the name K2, see pages 76, 78.

the Gasherbrums, and Apsarasas; and many others which feed these or descend to deep gashes in the mountains to swell the waters of the Indus.

On the west the gorge of the Hunza river drains the Pamir edge and collects the waters of the distant upper valleys of Hunza State: Chapursan, Khunjerab, Batura, Shimshal, and Hispar. In winter the traveller can take the valley floors, but in summer, the chocolate-coloured torrents drive him to the gorge-walls, where the track is made of stone and brushwood laid on pegs driven into the cliffs.

In the centre the Shigar river collects the waters of the Biafo, Panmah and Baltoro glaciers, and the Nubra is fed by the Siachen; there are few more exciting pastimes than shooting the rapids of the swollen Shigar on a skin raft surrounded by precious instruments and baggage, or more nauseating (to me at least) than crossing a long, frail rope-bridge, made of twisted twigs swaying in the wind, over one of these rivers, perhaps a hundred yards wide, in full flood.

The border river on the east, the upper Shyok, has its source in the Rimo glacier and the drier regions of western Tibet. This also has its excitements when a branch glacier, the Chong Kumdan, periodically plunges forward and blocks the valley, causing a lake to form above it ten miles long. When the ice-dam bursts the lake is released and cries havoc far down the valley of the Indus.

Much of the region is uninhabited, though crossed by old caravan and raiders' routes at chosen spots. But there are people living in the valleys, hardy and independent by nature in the west, Hunzakuts and Nagiris; rather more timid and suspicious in the centre, if taken far from their homes—the men of the upper Shigar and Braldoh, and particularly of Askole. In the past, before the Pax Britannica came to the valleys, the quarrelling rajahs of the petty states of Baltistan were an easy prey to raiders or conquerors from west or east.

As the Tibetan race-mixture gets stronger towards the east, the pure Ladakhi and his cross with traders from Turkestan are, in my experience, hardy, tough, and reliable. Being a polyandrous people, perhaps three brothers to one wife, they have to be! I have never met more sure-footed natural rock climbers than the men of Hunza, or more patient, long-suffering and reliable men than the Ladakhi on ice and snow, once their trust has been secured. But the polygamous men of Askole, whom I do not know, have a world reputation for unreliability.

Because of the lack of local names, geographers have had to group the mountains into some system and give names to many of them.

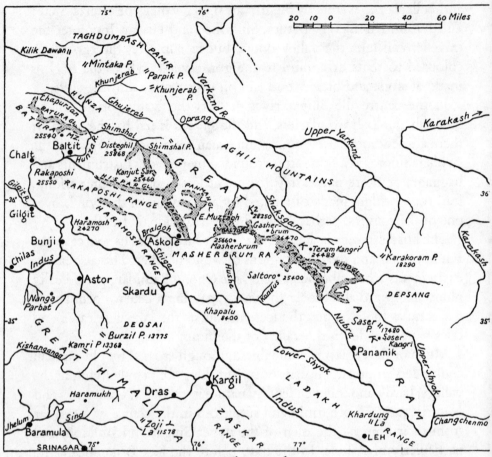

FIG. 3. *The Karakoram.*

At my request Sir Edward Tandy, Surveyor General in India in 1926, asked the Royal Geographical Society to call a conference to consider the problem of Karakoram nomenclature which was vexing geographers. Its report in 1936 was accepted by the Government of India and forms the basis of the present systematic naming of the mountains.[1]

[1] For the full report, see *Journal of the Royal Geographical Society* (G.J.) xci (1938) 128 or *H.J.* x (1938) 86.

The term 'Great Karakoram' is now given to the main crest-zone of the whole system from the ice-clad peaks at the head of the Batura glacier on the west, along the high serrated ridge south of this glacier, and north of the Hispar, Panmah, Baltoro, and Siachen glaciers; thence along the watershed range between the Nubra and upper Shyok rivers. It is divided into sections, known as *muztagh*,[1] a name given to almost all great ice-mountains by Turki traders who see them. These muztaghs are identified by the long glaciers which drain their slopes: thus the Hispar Muztagh is that section of the Great Karakoram from the Hunza gorge to the head basin of the Panmah. Each *muztagh* has its mountain groups, each named where possible from its chief summit and including several satellites. Two as yet unnamed peaks over 25,000 feet are found in the Batura Muztagh; Disteghil Sar (25,868) and Kanjut Sar (25,460) in the Hispar Muztagh; and the K2, Broad, and Gasherbrum groups in the Baltoro Muztagh, all with summits above 26,000 feet.

The Lesser Karakoram comprise the ranges of shorter alignment, though they too have mountain groups of great height: Rakaposhi, Haramosh, Masherbrum, and Saltoro ranges, the first three named from individual groups, the last from an old historic pass.

Mountaineering in the Karakoram is remote and expensive. Exploration and survey have been gradual. There are no rest-houses or supplies off the three main routes of approach: by Gilgit and Hunza on the west; by the Burzil pass or Zoji La and Skardu in the centre; or by the Zoji La, Leh, and the passes over the Ladakh range to the Nubra and the upper Shyok on the east. Numbers of transport animals or porters, who in a few weeks consume almost as much as they can carry, must be calculated with the utmost exactitude in order to get the best results. Constant consideration for the welfare of porters, combined with firmness and encouragement, is an essential attribute of the successful mountaineer in these parts, and a considerate party can be of the greatest value to mountaineers who follow after. I personally learnt much from my predecessors in these parts and benefited from their thoughtfulness.

Routes into the Karakoram were first described by such men as Alexander Gardner, Moorcroft, G. T. Vigne, the two Stracheys,

[1] *Muz* = ice; *tagh* = mountain.

Dr. Thomas Thomson, and Alexander Cunningham in the first half of the last century. The reconnaissance maps of the mountains were made in the early sixties by Godwin-Austen and his colleagues of the Survey of India. Francis Younghusband crossed the Muztagh pass over the Great Karakoram in 1887, and in 1892 Conway led the first climbing expedition to the Karakoram glaciers, Hispar, Biafo, and Baltoro. Since then much scientific work has been done by mountaineers from Europe, among whom should be mentioned in particular the Italian Duke of the Abruzzi, who first examined three sides of K2 in 1909, Sir Filippo De Filippi, who explored the Rimo glacier in 1914, and the Dutch explorer Dr. Ph. C. Visser and his wife, who added much to our knowledge of the northern side of the Hispar Muztagh in the west in 1925 and of the Saser Muztagh on the south-east in 1929 and later. Younghusband, Cockerill, and Bridges in the eighteen-eighties and nineties, and the indefatigable Longstaff before World War I, the Duke of Spoleto, Shipton, Tilman, Spender, and others between the two wars, all added greatly to our knowledge and improved the maps of these remote regions, often with the help of surveyors lent by the Survey of India.

De Filippi described K2 as

a quadrangular pyramid, the corners being formed by four main crests meeting at right angles—the south-west and north-east, the north-west and south-east. The first two are prolonged in long and powerful buttresses, proportionate in size to the mass which they sustain. The other two are cut off short and precipitously—one at the Savoia pass, the other at the shoulder of the mountain (map page 134).

This last ridge, which was climbed by the Duke to a height of over 21,000 feet, was chosen by the American Dr. Charles Houston on his brilliant reconnaissance in 1938 when he and Paul Petzoldt passed the shoulder at 25,354 feet and reached an altitude of about 26,000 feet. In the following year another American, Fritz Wiessner with the Sherpa porter Pasang Dawa Lama (Pasang Sherpa),[1] using the same route went about a thousand feet higher, at the sacrifice of the lives of one American and three Sherpa porters. Houston returned to the attack in 1953, but his party was caught in their camp above the shoulder by a violent blizzard which prevented all movement for

[1] Himalayan Club Register No. 139 ; see page 191.

a week and then forced them to descend with the loss of one American life.

In the present year (1954), the Italian Ardito Desio, Professor of Geology at the University of Milan, and a veteran of the Duke of Spoleto's expedition to the Karakoram in 1929, renews the attack. With his capacity for organization he should succeed.[1]

The Karakoram is the scene of a mountaineering Olympiad. Climbers from Austria, France, Italy, the Netherlands, Switzerland, the United States, and Britain have fought the elements and in friendly rivalry, passing on the lessons learnt to their successors. Some of the lesser peaks have been climbed. Gasherbrum, Masherbrum, Rakaposhi, and Saltoro Kangri have been unsuccessfully assaulted, but there is no such thing as an impossible mountain, since Everest fell.

[1] The above was written before the event. Desio's party was successful. See page 343.

# 4. Kumaun Himalaya

THE Kumaun Himalaya is bounded by the Sutlej on the west and north, and by the Kali (or Mahakali) on the east, which here forms the western boundary of the independent state of Nepal. In its passage through the Siwaliks at Tanakpur the Kali becomes the Sarda river of the Gangetic plain before joining the Gogra in the old province of Oudh. Left-bank tributaries of the Sutlej (chief of which is the Baspa) and right-bank tributaries of the Kali—Dhauliganga, Goriganga, and Ramganga—drain the two extremities of the region. Between them are the Himalayan basins of the Jumna—with its source near Bandarpunch, and its right-back affluent the Tons; of the mountain feeders of the sacred Ganges—Bhagirathi, Mandakini, Alaknanda, and Pindar; and of the small Ramganga, which drains the Lesser Himalaya in the districts of Almora and Naini Tal.

The Great Himalayan crest-zone passes south-eastwards in an almost straight line. From the gorge near Chini, where the Sutlej pierces it, it forms the northern watershed of the Baspa valley with at least two summits over 21,000 feet, then to the mountain groups of Satopanth (23,213) and Chaukhamba (23,420), at the head of the Gangotri glacier, through Nanda Devi (25,645), Nanda Kot (22,510), and Panch Chuli (22,650) to the extreme north-west corner of Nepal, within which lie the groups of Api and Nampa.

South of it is a second crest-zone of high mountains, identifiable as an eastern extension of the Dhaula Dhar of the Lesser Himalaya. It forms the southern watershed of the Baspa, passes through the mountain Bandarpunch (20,720), is cut through by the Bhagirathi below Harsil, and claims a ridge of high mountains: Srikanta (20,120), the Gangotri group (the highest 21,890), Thalayasagar (22,650), and Kedarnath (22,770), all south of the upper Bhagirathi river or Gangotri glacier, at the head of which it joins the Great Himalaya at the Chaukhamba massif.[1]

[1] These alignments differ slightly from those given by Sir Sidney Burrard before the detailed exploration and survey of the upper Gangotri.

North of the Great Himalaya crest-zone is the Zaskar range, already noticed in the Punjab Himalaya. It is generally regarded here as the boundary between India and Tibet, though this has never been demarcated, and the higher altitudes are not yet fully surveyed, particularly on the Tibetan side. The aspect is also much more Tibetan than Himalayan, and, though several mountains rise above 22,000 feet, there are few long glaciers east of the Dhauli tributary of the Alaknanda. There is however a high group close to the Tibetan border, between the sources of the Dhauli and Saraswati, which contains Kamet (25,447) and its satellites Abi Gamin (24,130) and Mana (23,860). South of Mana also on the watershed ridge between the two rivers there are several peaks rising well above 20,000 feet, chief among them being Mandir Parbat (21,520), Nilgiri Parbat (21,240), Rataban (20,230), Ghori Parbat (22,010), and Hathi Parbat (22,070). North of the Kamet group a few peaks exceed 20,000 feet, but there is much less snowfall: the whole aspect becomes more arid.

The troughs between the Zaskar range and the Great Himalaya are drained entirely by the Bhagirathi and by the Saraswati and Dhauli tributaries of the Alaknanda. Between the headwaters of the first two, a ridge of high summits rising to 22,000 feet separates the glacier basins on either side, but these belong to the Great Himalaya rather than to the Zaskar. Having collected the waters of these glaciers the Bhagirathi cuts through the Great Himalaya and Dhaula Dhar; the Alaknanda collects the Saraswati and Dhauli and plunges through the Great Himalaya south-east of the Chaukhamba mountain knot in a gorge between Joshimath and Chamoli. Along both the Bhagirathi and the Alaknanda there are pilgrim routes, the first leading to Gaumukh, 'the Cow's mouth' at the Gangotri glacier, and the second to holy Badrinath on the Saraswati. There are rest-houses or forest-bungalows and dispensaries along them.

From Harsil on the Bhagirathi a path leads over the Dhaula Dhar—by the Nela or Chhotkhaga pass, 16,900 feet, into the Baspa, but two of the best-known and most frequented passes lie at the sources of the Saraswati and Dhauli rivers: the Mana pass or Dungri La at 18,400 feet and the Niti pass at 16,628 feet. They are on the Zaskar crest-zone and take frequented tracks into Tibet. It was the Mana pass that was

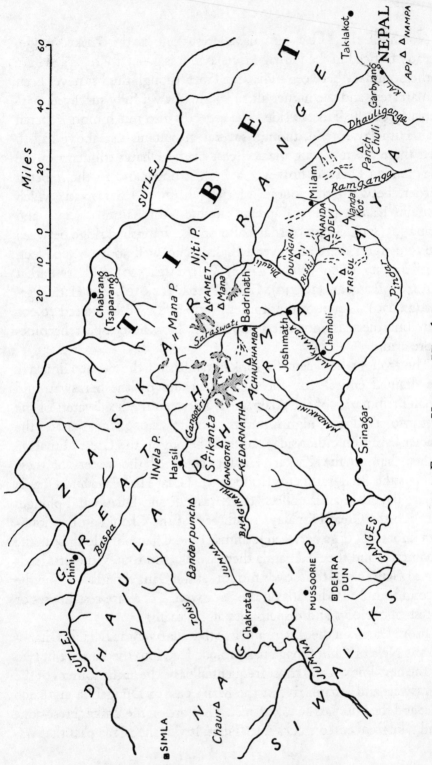

Fig. 4. *Kumaun Himalaya.*

used by the Portuguese Jesuits, Father Antonio de Andrade and Brother Manuel Marques in July 1624, on their missionary journey to Tsaparang on the Sutlej, the capital of Guge, then a prosperous little kingdom in Tibet, where they founded the first Christian church two years later.[1] No fewer than twelve missionaries crossed and recrossed this pass between 1624 and 1640.

The Lesser Himalaya south of the Dhaula Dhar is a maze of ridges deeply scored by torrents. An outer range, not always well defined, on the edge of which stands Simla, is known as Nag Tibba, from the hill 9913 feet high seen from Mussoorie across the Aglar valley. Its highest point is Chaur (11,966) on the boundary between the states of Sirmur and Jubbal, an important station of observation in the early survey. On the outer flanks of the Lesser Himalaya are the summer hill-stations of Simla, Chakrata, Mussoorie, Lansdowne, and the group of stations, Ranikhet, Almora, and Naini Tal, reached from the rail-heads at Ramnagar and Kathgodam. Two of the finest views of the distant snows are to be seen in October from Landour, near Mussoorie, and from China survey station near Naini Tal. From the former there is an unbroken view of snow mountains from Sargaroin (20,370) on the west to Nanda Devi on the east. From China the view extends from Kedarnath on the west to Api (23,399), just within the borders of Nepal, a total length of 120 miles; Nanda Devi, one of the nearest points on the distant range is seventy-five miles away.

Almost the whole of the Kumaun Himalaya is now well surveyed and some of the half-inch maps published by the Survey of India just before the Second World War are as accurate and attractively drawn as any modern mountain maps in the world. One of the least known and inaccessible parts until 1934 was the gorge of the Rishiganga and the immediate surroundings of Nanda Devi. The mountain stands in a vast ring of mountains seventy miles in circumference, the average height of which is about 20,000 feet (map page 116). On the ring are no fewer than nineteen peaks over 21,000 feet, and there is no known depression or break in the ring below 17,000 feet except on the west where the Rishiganga, rising from glaciers on either side of Nanda Devi and draining some 240 square

[1] See below, page 56.

miles of ice and snow, breaks through a stupendous gorge to the west. The early Indian surveyors in the middle of last century were unable to penetrate its fastnesses; W. W. Graham and two Swiss guides were defeated in 1883. After that no fewer than eight attempts were made to force a passage to the foot of the mountain within the 'inner sanctuary,' by such redoubtable mountaineers as Longstaff, with famous guides from Courmayeur, Bruce, Ruttledge, Wilson, and Somervell. Eric Shipton and H. W. Tilman with Sherpa porters forced an entrance through the Rishi gorge in 1934 and reconnoitred the approaches. On 29 August 1936 Tilman and N. E. Odell reached the summit.

During the thirties there was much activity in all parts of the Kumaun Himalaya. Trisul (23,360) had been climbed by Longstaff in 1907; after considerable reconnaissance by earlier parties Frank Smythe in 1931 led a party to the top of Kamet (25,447) and in 1937 climbed Mana (23,860). A Japanese party under Y. Hotta climbed Nanda Kot (22,510), east of the Nanda Devi group, in 1936, using the route reconnoitred by Longstaff thirty years before. In 1938 a German party led by Rudolf Schwarzgruber and based on the Gangotri glacier reached the tops of Bhagirathi II (21,364), Chandar Parbat (22,073) and an unnamed mountain (22,050). They also reconnoitred the Gangotri side of the Chaukhamba group. In 1939 a Swiss expedition under André Roch climbed Dunagiri (23,184) on the northern ring of Nanda Devi, and then Ghori Parbat (22,010) and Rataban (20,030) on the watershed between the Dhauli and the Saraswati. Disaster overtook them on an attempt to climb Chaukhamba from the east. All were swept away by an avalanche, and it was a miracle that no more than two of the porters lost their lives. In the same year a Polish party led by Jakub Bujak made the first ascent of Nanda Devi East (24,391). They later attempted the eastern of the Tirsuli peaks (23,210) on the Zaskar range at the head of the Milam glacier. They also met with disaster, the tent in which the two Poles, Karpinski and Bernadzikiewicz, were sleeping, being buried by an avalanche on the night of the 18th July.

During this period much scientific work was carried out. Survey of India parties under Major Gordon Osmaston made a detailed survey, between 1935 and 1938, of the Great Himalaya and Zaskar range, and of all the higher glaciers and mountains. Eric Shipton helped him in 1936 to reach the Nanda Devi basin and to complete the survey there by stereo-photogrammetry. J. B. Auden carried out several geological journeys, and Frank Smythe travelled among some of the beautiful valleys climbing many mountains, collecting flowers and taking magnificent photographs.

More recently, since the war, there have been several successful ascents. On 22 August 1950 an Anglo-Swiss party made the first ascent of Abi Gamin (24,130), north of Kamet, from the Tibetan side and J. T. M. Gibson led a party of young climbers up Bandarpunch (20,720). The following year a New Zealand party climbed Mukut Parbat (23,760) some three miles north-west of Kamet; and a French party lost two lives in attempting the traverse of the difficult arête between Nanda Devi and its eastern peak, which was climbed for the second time. In 1952 a small party from Oxford under John Tyson climbed Gangotri I (21,890) and III (21,578).

There are still many peaks of 22,000 and 23,000 feet to be climbed, particularly in the Gangotri region, which will test the skill and endurance of mountaineers for many years to come. The region is comparatively easy of access provided permission can be obtained to cross the 'Inner Line.'

# 5. Nepal Himalaya[1]

MOUNTAINEERS of to-day should be grateful to their fathers and grand-fathers for having left them so much to explore and map in the Nepal Himalaya. Much of its detail is still unknown to western geographers. Throughout the whole period of British rule in India the independent state of Nepal was closed to British surveyors and mountaineers, and the British Government respected the wishes of the rulers. Though the highest mountains were fixed a hundred years ago by accurate observations taken far to the south in British India, and though occasional travellers and British officers in Gurkha regiments were permitted to visit Katmandu and a few other places, mostly in the outer ranges, it was not until the years 1925-7 that India was allowed to send a party of surveyors into Nepal, and even then British officers were not permitted to supervise them. Special men, including some from Nepal, were selected and trained for the purpose, but they were not high-altitude mountaineers. The result was a satisfactory reconnaissance survey of the inhabited parts of the country on the quarter-inch scale, intended for publication on the smaller scale of eight miles to an inch. It was, however, published on the scale of survey. Too much reliability should not therefore be placed on the generalized topography of the higher regions, much of which could not be visited, and the spelling of some place-names could not be fully checked by experts in the language on the spot.

Since World War II the policy of exclusion has been relaxed and a limited number of parties are now allowed into Nepal each year; but they are chiefly bent on climbing individual mountain groups rather than surveying them; the chief points of interest are far apart; and it is not yet possible to give a fully trustworthy account of the geography or structure of the ranges.

[1] The substance of this account is from my papers in *H.J.* vi and vii (1934 and 1935).

The Great Himalaya in Nepal is drained by three large rivers, Karnali, Gandaki, and Kosi, with their tributaries; on the extreme west are also the left-bank tributaries of the Kali which forms the state boundary. It is convenient to divide the range into three sections with relation to the three rivers, all of which cut through it: from the massif of Api (23,399) on the west to Dhaulagiri (26,795) inclusive, near the Kali Gandaki gorge; from this gorge to the Ganesh Himal (24,299) inclusive, near the Trisuli Gandaki gorge; and from here to the Arun, exclusive of the great massif of Kangchenjunga, on the boundary with Sikkim, which has been till recently both politically and physically most easily approached through that country.

The range enters Nepal on the north-west immediately south of Garbyang on the Kali and rises at once to the Byas Rikhi Himal, which holds the two high peaks of Api and Nampa (22,162). North of it is a second crest-zone of high summits, here identifiable with the Zaskar range, which in places seems to come into contact or merge with the main crest, and elsewhere to remain distinct. Generally the Great Himalayan crest-zone is the higher; occasionally the northern carries higher summits than the southern. Many of the great rivers cut into the southern crest; some cut through it; a few only—the main courses of the Kali Gandaki, the Buri Gandaki (or Buriganga), the Trisuli Gandaki, the Sun Kosi (Po Chu in Tibet), and the Arun (Phung Chu and Yaru Chu are its Tibetan tributaries) drain areas behind both crest-zones. Parts of the northern are in Tibet, others are in Nepal, or form the boundary between the two, and little is known of its detailed topography. In the two crest-zones there are three known summits over 27,000 feet, Mount Everest, Lhotse, and Makalu, six others above 26,000 feet—Dhaulagiri, Cho Oyu, Manaslu, Annapurna I, Gosainthan (or Shisha Pangma), and Annapurna II —and fourteen more over 25,000 feet.

*Karnali Section*

In the western or Karnali section of the range, which is the least known, the Seti river has cut back into the Great Himalaya between the Api-Nampa group and Saipal (23,079), but not completely through it; both these mountains are probably most easily approached from the north, the latter from the trade-route along the Humla

Karnali between Simikot and the mart at Taklakot in Tibet. The trough between the two crests here is drained by the Humla Karnali; Gurla Mandhata (25,355) stands conspicuously on the northern crest about 40 miles north of Saipal. It was on Gurla Mandhata that Dr. Longstaff in 1905 descended 3000 feet in two minutes in an avalanche and survived the experience. Longstaff in 1905 was also the first mountaineer to examine the approaches to the Api-Nampa

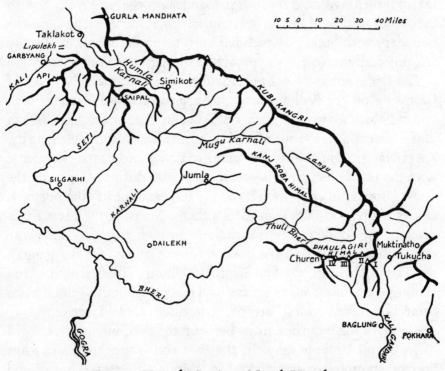

FIG. 5. *Karnali Section, Nepal Himalaya.*

group. It was not, however, until 1953 that W. H. Murray and John Tyson reconnoitred its northern approaches from the Kali river and its tributary the Tinkar Khola without discovering a feasible route.[1]

Farther east the trough is drained by the Mugu Karnali and its

---

[1] In 1954 an Italian party reached the summit. Of the successful three, two Italians lost their lives on the descent, and the only survivor was the Sherpa who brought one of the Italians down to the base camp. Another Italian lost his life earlier in the expedition when crossing the Kali. In the same year an Austrian expedition reconnoitred Saipal; details are not yet known.

head-stream the Langu, which rises far to the south-east, about forty miles north of Dhaulagiri. The two rivers Humla and Mugu Karnali, after collecting many affluents, pass separately through the axis of the Great Himalaya to unite on the southern side, making a much broader gap in the range than the rivers farther east.

East of the Karnali the Bheri and the Thuli Bheri (or Barbung Khola) cut back into and break the continuity of the Great Himalaya, which rises west of them to several summits over 22,000 feet, and on the east to the long section known as the Dhaulagiri Himal. This group has now been reconnoitred by two expeditions since the war: in 1950 by a French expedition led by Maurice Herzog, and in 1953 by a Swiss team, which after overcoming great technical difficulties reached an estimated height of over 25,000 feet before abandoning the attempt. Though the group is still not mapped in detail and the ridges shown on the existing maps are incorrect, the following summits on it have been fixed:

### DHAULAGIRI GROUP

|  | Height | Latitude | | | Longitude | | |
|---|---|---|---|---|---|---|---|
|  |  | ° | ′ | ″ | ° | ′ | ″ |
| Dhaulagiri I | 26,795[1] | 28 | 41 | 48 | 83 | 29 | 42 |
| II | 25,429 | 28 | 45 | 45 | 83 | 23 | 25 |
| III | 25,271 | 28 | 45 | 13 | 83 | 22 | 46 |
| IV | 25,064 | 28 | 44 | 07 | 83 | 18 | 53 |
| V | 24,885 | 28 | 44 | 03 | 83 | 21 | 51 |
| Churen Himal | 24,158 | 28 | 43 | 54 | 83 | 12 | 43 |
| Putha Hiunchuli | 23,750 | 28 | 44 | 50 | 83 | 08 | 55 |
| Sauwala | 23,539 | 28 | 40 | 20 | 83 | 16 | 40 |
| Tukucha | 22,688 | 28 | 44 | 40 | 83 | 33 | 42 |

There are also at least three peaks in the Mukut Himal north of Dhaulagiri which rise above 22,000 feet.

The northern flanks of this mass drain westwards into the Thuli Bheri; the southern into tributaries of the Kali Gandaki. The three rivers, Seti, Karnali, and Bheri pursue vagrant and independent

[1] The official height is 26,795. It is shown on some S. of I. maps as 26,810.

courses through the Lesser Himalaya; the Karnali, after forcing a tortuous passage through the Mahabharat range is then reinforced by the Seti; and their combined waters are joined in the *Dun* by the Bheri before piercing the Siwaliks to become the Gogra of the Indian plains.

## Gandaki Section

The central or Gandaki section of the Nepal Himalaya is drained by the Gandaki tributaries, chief of which are the Kali (or Krishna) Gandaki, the Seti Gandaki, the Marsyandi, the Buri Gandaki (or

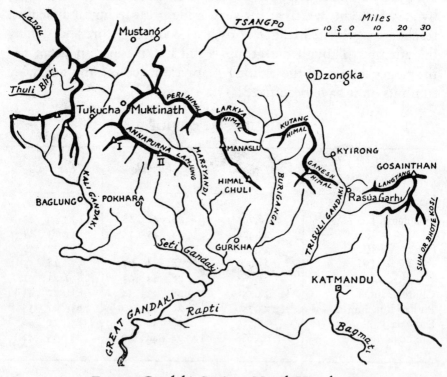

FIG. 6. *Gandaki Section, Nepal Himalaya.*

Buriganga), and the Trisuli Gandaki. All except the Seti cut through both crest-zones which are almost in contact with each other, so that the Great Himalaya here is a succession of mountain blocks separated by deep trenches. None drain large areas behind the range, the Kali Gandaki rising in a circle of mountains carved out of the northern slopes only twenty miles from the Tsangpo of Tibet. Between the Kali and the Marsyandi are the Annapurna Himal and the Lamjung Himal; between the Marsyandi and Buri Gandaki gorges, both at about 9000 feet, is the mountain block of Larkya Himal; between the Buri Gandaki and the Trisuli Gandaki, which cuts a passage at 7500 feet at the border village of Rasua Garhi, is the group of peaks known as Ganesh Himal, the highest of which is 24,299 feet.

Tracks passable for animals go through the Kali Gandaki and Trisuli Gandaki gorges, the first leading direct to the Tsangpo near Tra-dom (Tradun), that through the Trisuli leading to Kyirong and Dzongka. Along the first of these is the pilgrim route to Muktinath; thousands of pilgrims are said to visit its shrine high up in the cliffs of the Great Himalaya every year, since Muktinath ranks with Gosainthan, Pashpati, and Ridi as one of the four chief places of Hindu sanctity and sin-remission in Nepal. The route by the Trisuli Gandaki has been taken both by Tibetan and Nepalese armies in the invasion of each other's country.

Of the mountains the two highest in the Annapurna Himal are Annapurna I (26,492) and II (26,041), one at either end of it. Two others, III (24,858) and IV (24,688) stand between them. In 1950 Annapurna I was climbed by Maurice Herzog, who was also the first to reconnoitre Dhaulagiri from the east, and Annapurna IV was reconnoitred by H. W. Tilman whose party reached a point only 600 feet short of the summit.

Of the three chief summits of the Larkya Himal, Manaslu I (26,658), Manaslu II (25,705), and Himal Chuli (25,801), the first was attempted by a Japanese party in 1953 which reached a height of over 25,000 feet. The Japanese planned to return to the attack in 1954.[1]

## Kosi Section

The Kosi section of the Nepal Himalaya is dominated by the Mahalungur Himal and Everest (29,002), with Lhotse (27,890) standing on its southern buttress, and Makalu (27,790) twelve miles to the south-east. This section of the range is drained southwards by

[1] Latest reports (in 1954) are that the Japanese abandoned this attempt in favour of a reconnaissance of the Ganesh Himal to the east. No details are yet known.

the headwaters of the Bhote Kosi, Tamba Kosi, Dudh Kosi, Arun, and Tamur Kosi, and northwards into the Tibetan Phung Chu, tributary of the Arun.

The Bhote Kosi, as its name implies, rises in Tibet, where it is known as the Po Chu, passes the frontier village of Nyenam, and

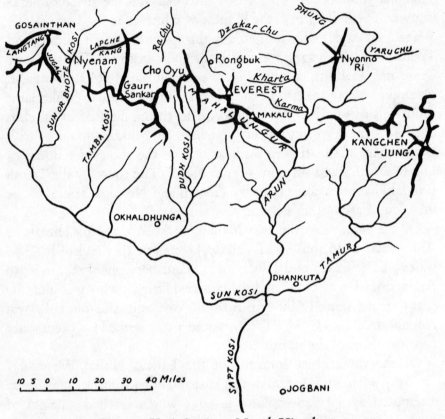

FIG. 7. *Kosi Section, Nepal Himalaya.*

breaks through the Great Himalaya east of the Jugal Himal. The Tamba Kosi (also known locally in northern Nepalese villages along its banks as the Bhote Kosi, for the same reason) likewise rises in Tibet, where it is called the Kang Chu. It is separated here from the Po Chu by the unexplored heights of Lapche Kang which rise above 23,000 feet. Its Tibetan basin is smaller than that of the Po Chu, but it also cuts a passage through the Great Himalaya.

The Dudh Kosi, famous now as the road to Everest, drains the southern flanks of that vast massif, with high difficult glacier sources such as the Khumbu and the 'Western Cwm.' Its westernmost head tributary is the third to be called the Bhote Kosi locally, which is rather misleading, since it drains no part of political Tibet, nor the Tibetan slopes of the range. Perhaps it is so named because at the head of it is a pass, the Nangpa La (19,050) which takes a trade-route over the watershed, by which Sherpa porters from Namche Bazar and Sola Khumbu have joined Everest expeditions in Tibet.

The Arun is the longest of all. It has an immense basin in Tibet north of the Himalaya, drained by the Phung Chu and Yaru Chu. The first of these is more than 120 miles long; it rises in the north-eastern slopes of Gosainthan (26,291) and flows eastwards along the whole length of the Kosi section, passing the Tibetan 'town' of Tingri and the 'Tingri Maidan,' from which the first expedition to Everest set out in 1921 to reconnoitre its northern approaches and seek 'the bottom rung.'

The Yaru Chu drains a similar trough to the east but is only half as long. Rising north-east of Sikkim it flows westwards and, after being deflected by the mountain Nyonno Ri (22,142), joins the Phung Chu, by which name the combined waters are known until they pierce the Great Himalaya in a tremendous gorge at the boundary with Nepal. The river is now the Arun; its twisting defile is bridged in a few places in north-eastern Nepal, but it is always difficult and in places quite inaccessible.

The Tamur Kosi is an important river fed from the western flanks of Kangchenjunga. Its headwaters break through the axis of the Great Himalaya, but drain no large area to the north, though they isolate the great mountain on the Sikkim border. In southern Nepal it joins the Arun a few miles downstream of the junction of the Arun and Sun Kosi and, as the Sapt Kosi, the waters of all three plunge through the Mahabharat range of the outer Himalaya to become the Kosi river of the Indian plains.

The courses of these rivers have been outlined because the heavy rainfall in this part of the Himalaya makes them considerable obstacles to travel. Most carrying has to be done on porters' backs and the most careful calculations and preparations must be made before an expedition can reach an objective in the Great Himalaya.

Of the chief mountains in the area, it is again easiest to define them as groups or *himals*, separated by the main rivers which pierce the range. On the west, between the Trisuli Gandaki and the Bhote Kosi (Po Chu) are the Langtang Himal and Jugal Himal, with many peaks over 21,000 feet, chief among them being Langtang Lirung (23,771) and Dorje Lakpa I (23,240). On the secondary crest-zone to the north is the massive Gosainthan (26,291), known in Tibet as Shisha Pangma, and its satellite (25,134); neither has been explored at close quarters, though Heinrich Harrer and Peter Aufschnaiter must have been tempted to do so during their long stay at Kyirong in 1944.

Between the Bhote Kosi (Po Chu) and the Tamba Kosi the range is in Tibet, but there are no known peaks above 20,000 feet; here again in the northern crest-zone, the Lapche Kang, is almost certainly higher, with peaks of up to 23,000 feet.

East of the Tamba, thanks to successive Everest expeditions, the range is well known. Gauri Sankar (23,440) on the Rowaling Himal is the highest before the great group that forms the Mahalungur Himal, on which stand from west to east Cho Oyu (26,750), Ngojumba Kang (25,730), Gyachung Kang (25,990), Everest (29,002), Lhotse (27,890), and Makalu (27,790)—and a host of others over 22,000 feet. It seems that the two crest-zones are now finally in contact, for many of the lesser heights are on the great buttress ridges to the north and south of Everest (map page 158).

Apart from Everest none of the other high mountains mentioned above has yet been climbed, though members of the Everest teams have reached the tops of several above 20,000 feet, either as acclimatization climbs or to console themselves in defeat. In 1952 Eric Shipton took a party to Cho Oyu and reached a height of 22,500 feet, but this was more of a practice climb for the attack on Everest in 1953, than a serious all-out assault on Cho Oyu.[1]

[1] Members of Sir Edmund Hillary's 1954 expedition reached the top of Baruntse (23,560) one of the three dominant peaks of the Barun glacier south-east of Everest. Makalu was attempted unsuccessfully in the same year by an American party led by Dr. William Siri. Since the above was written, Cho Oyu has been climbed in 1954 by an Austrian party.

# 6. Sikkim Himalaya

THE Sikkim Himalaya is the smallest of the five—so small that Sir Sidney Burrard preferred to include it in his Nepal Himalaya.[1] It has, however, so distinctive a character that it cannot rightly form part of the Nepal section. Kangchenjunga cannot, as Sir Sidney suggests, be regarded scientifically 'as the eastern peak of the Dhaulagiri-Mount Everest section.' Moreover, the Great Himalaya in Sikkim is less than fifty miles in a direct line from Darjeeling, which stands on the eastern extension of the Mahabharat range of the Lesser Himalaya, directly facing the plains, because of the absence of the Siwaliks. The axis of the Great Himalaya west and east of Kangchenjunga is not easy to follow: on the west it has been broken up by the Arun and by the Tamur Kosi; on the east by the Tista tributaries —Talung, Zemu, Lachen, and Lachung. Though Kangchenjunga is the highest mountain on this short section of the Himalaya running from west to east, it is buttressed north and south by long ridges which have mountains almost as high. Kangchenjunga is in fact unique, as pointed out by Frank Smythe, in that it is a mountain buttressed north, south, east, and west, so that there are four quadrants of approach; any one of the four faces and four ridges can be chosen for assault.[2]

On the ridge running from west to east are Janu (25,294), Kangbachen (25,782)—both in Nepal—Kangchenjunga I (28,146), Kangchenjunga II (27,803)[3], whence the ridge descends gradually to the Zemu Gap (19,275). East of this there are two fine mountains, the Simvu massif—the highest point of which is 22,360 feet—and the peerless Siniolchu (22,600)—to many who have seen it the most beautiful mountain in the world. 'Its ridges are as sharp as a knife-edge, its flanks, though incredibly steep, are mostly covered with

---

[1] Burrard: 2nd Edition, page 41.   [2] H.J. vii (1935) 66 ff.
[3] Survey of India triangulated height 27,803; Professor Garwood 27,820; Professor Finsterwalder, by stereo-photogrammetry, 27,888.

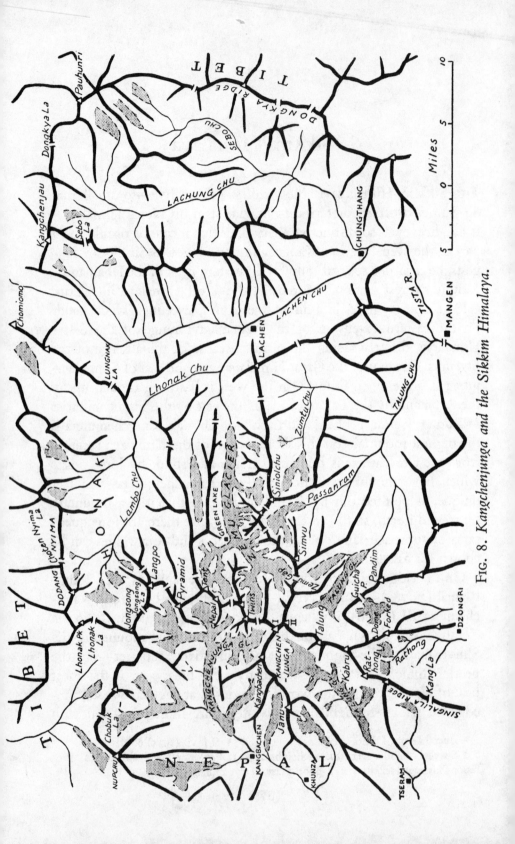

FIG. 8. *Kangchenjunga and the Sikkim Himalaya.*

ice and snow, furrowed with the ice-flutings so typical of the Himalaya. The crest of the cornice-crowned summit stands up like a thorn': so wrote Karl Wien, who with Adolf Göttner, both of Paul Bauer's party, reached the summit on 23 September 1936.[1]

The ridge running north from Kangchenjunga also carries some fine peaks, unofficially known to climbers as 'The Twins' (23,360), 'Nepal Peak' (23,560), 'Tent Peak' (24,089), 'The Pyramid' (23,400), 'Langpo Peak' (22,800), and 'Jongsong Peak' (24,344). Nepal Peak was first climbed by Schneider from the western side on 23 May 1930; it was climbed from the east by Wien and Göttner in September 1936. Tent Peak, first reconnoitred by Kellas in 1910, and attacked by Wien and Göttner in 1936, was climbed by Schmaderer, Paidar, and Grob in 1939. The Pyramid was reconnoitred from the Sphinx to the north of it by C. R. Cooke, Spencer Chapman, and J. B. Harrison in 1926 and attacked by Schmaderer, Paidar, and Grob in 1939. It was conquered by way of the Sphinx by René Dittert and the Grindelwald guide J. Pargätzi on 6 June 1949. Langpo Peak was climbed by Kellas on 14 September 1909 and again by him in May 1910, since when it has been climbed more than once. Jongsong Peak was ascended by two parties of four in June 1930, the first comprising Frank Smythe, Wood-Johnson, Hoerlin, and Schneider.

The Singalila ridge running south for fifty miles from Kangchenjunga also carries some fine peaks over 20,000 feet—Talung Peak (23,082), an unnamed summit (24,263), and Kabru (24,002). This section of the ridge separates the Yalung glacier in the south-west quadrant of Kangchenjunga from the Talung glacier in the south-east quadrant. The southern face of Kabru falls to the Rathong glacier by which C. R. Cooke made the first ascent on 18 November 1935—incidentally the first post-monsoon ascent to a summit in the Himalaya over 24,000 feet.[2]

East of this great group surrounding Kangchenjunga there is a

---

[1] In the same year, on 2 October, Bauer, Göttner, and Hepp climbed the western of the two north peaks of Simvu (21,473) (*H.J.* ix (1937) 58 ff.).

[2] *H.J.* viii (1936) 107. Kabru was first attempted by W. W. Graham in 1883. Maps were bad and doubt was cast on the authenticity of this climb (see below, page 94). The Norwegians Rubenson and Monrad Aas reached a point about a hundred feet from the top in 1907.

gap in the Great Himalaya. If the line of the highest peaks be taken the Himalayan axis passes out of Sikkim by Pauhunri (23,180) and the Lachen branch of the Tista cuts through it near the village of Lachen at about 8000 feet above the sea. The Lachung branch, which joins the Lachen river at Chungthang to form the Tista proper, cuts back into the range and almost through it near Kangchenjau (22,700).[1] Certainly the two head-streams, the Lachen Chu and its tributary the Lambo Chu as it passes through Lhonak, drain troughs north of the Great Himalayan axis in characteristically Tibetan country, while the aspect south of the Simvu-Siniolchu ridge is typically Himalayan.

On the east forming the boundary between Sikkim and Tibet is the Dongkya ridge, running south from Pauhunri. Unlike the Kangchenjunga ridges it carries no peaks above 20,000 feet, but it forms a marked water-parting between the Tista and the Amo Chu, one of the Raidak tributaries. The passes across it are of moderate height and afford easy access into the Chumbi valley. It was over the Jelep La (14,390) that the Younghusband mission entered Tibet in 1903, and the same route was taken by most of the expeditions which attacked Mount Everest from the north, though several members of different expeditions returned to Sikkim over the Dodang Nyima, a secondary range to the Great Himalaya which divides the waters of the Tista from those of the Yaru Chu tributary of the Arun.

The Sikkim Himalaya is the best known and the most easily accessible section of the Himalaya. Motors can go as far as Gangtok the capital whence four easy and beautiful marches take one to Lachen near the junction of the Zemu Chu with the Lachen Chu. Within a week from Calcutta the traveller can be among the high mountains, and many take advantage of the *Puja* holidays to do so. There is a good guide-book for the ordinary traveller, who will find comfortable and beautifully sited rest-houses along the main valleys, and the mountains themselves are worthy of the highest skill. It was Sir Joseph Hooker, the great naturalist of the mid-nineteenth century, who first opened western eyes to the beauty of Sikkim;

[1] The summit plateau of Kangchenjau was first reached by Dr. A. M. Kellas in August 1912.

Douglas Freshfield, who first called attention to the possibilities of climbing Kangchenjunga after his high-level circuit of the mountain in 1899; and Dr. A. M. Kellas who conquered a number of peaks and passes during the first twenty years of the present century before the modern climbers took up the task in earnest.[1]

Kangchenjunga has now been reconnoitred from all four sides. It is deemed impossible from the south-east by the Talung glacier. In 1905 a French party under Dr. Jacot-Guillarmod attacked it unsuccessfully from the south-west, one Frenchman and three porters losing their lives. Dyhrenfurth took an international party of climbers to the north-west quadrant in 1930 and could find no feasible route; the Sherpa porter Chettan was killed here by an avalanche. The nearest to success have been the German expeditions led by Paul Bauer, who in 1929 and 1931 attacked from the Zemu glacier in the north-eastern quadrant; on both occasions they ascended the great spur that projects eastwards from the northern ridge, and in 1931 were defeated at about 25,260 feet by the dangerous condition of the snow; the mountain claimed a sacrifice also from this party, Hermann Schaller and a porter being killed. The day will come when Kangchenjunga, like Everest, will be conquered by man.

[1] Hooker's *Himalayan Journals* and Freshfield's *Round Kangchenjunga* are standard works for the Sikkim mountaineer. Kellas' climbs are abstracted (from the modest accounts in the *A.J.*) by H. W. Tobin in *H.J.* ii (1930) 10 ff.

# 7. Assam Himalaya

VERY little is known of the high Himalaya in Assam. The western half is on the undemarcated frontier between Tibet and Bhutan, where European travellers have not been encouraged; the eastern half is either in Tibet or in the unadministered frontier tracts of Assam, which merge with Tibet. The country has never been accurately surveyed, except in a few places and along certain routes, in the first instance generally by survey officers pressed for time when accompanying small political or military missions.

A few political officers, with headquarters in Sikkim, such as Claude White at the end of the last and beginning of this century, F. M. Bailey and F. Williamson between the two world wars, and some experienced botanical explorers and naturalists such as Kingdon Ward, F. Ludlow, and George Sherriff have travelled in the remoter parts; but with the exception of Chomolhari (23,997), which was climbed by Spencer Chapman and Pasang Dawa Lama[1] on 21 May 1937; of the Kulha Kangri group (24,784) which was seen at close quarters by Claude White in 1906 and by Williamson in 1933; and of Namcha Barwa (25,445) in the extreme east, discovered by officers of the Survey of India in 1912, none of the higher mountains have been reconnoitred at close quarters.

The western part of the Assam Himalaya is drained by the Amo Chu (the upper Tibetan part of which is known as the Chumbi valley), by the Wong Chu or Raidak, and by the Sankosh, with their tributaries, which descend direct from the Great Himalaya through western Bhutan to the Duars and Brahmaputra in Assam, unrestricted by any outer Siwalik range.

Eastern Bhutan is formed by the basins of the four large tributaries of the Manas—Trongsa, Bumtang, Lhobrak, and Trashi Yangtse—which also have direct courses from north to south. The eastern half of the Assam Himalaya, comprising the Balipara and Sadiya frontier

[1] Or Pasang Sherpa: H.C. No. 139, Tiger's badge.

42

tracts of Assam, inhabited by Aka, Dafla, Miri, and Abor tribes, is drained by the small Bhareli and by the important Subansiri tributary of the Brahmaputra, which breaks through the Great Himalaya east of Chayul Dzong in the Charme district of Tibet.

For the greater part of Bhutan the rivers sweep down through the Lesser Himalaya in roughly parallel courses, so that the 'grain' of the country is from north to south. Each main valley has its administration centre and the journey from west to east ascends and descends each intervening ridge, all of which are densely forested; thus Punaka, the capital (5200), is separated from Paro Dzong on the west by a pass, Do-Kyong La (10,400).

The Great Himalaya enters on the west at Pauhunri (23,180); at the head of the Chumbi valley is the main route to Gyantse and Lhasa by the easy Tang La (15,219) over which pass the Young-husband mission took the road to Lhasa in 1903, and which was crossed by successive Everest expeditions between the two world wars. Chomolhari rises immediately east of it with its satellites. It is a sacred mountain to Tibetans and stands on the Tibet-Bhutan boundary as a sentinel.

East of Chomolhari the great range and upper valleys of the Punaka Chu (the Bhutanese name for the Sankosh) is almost totally unexplored, though the Tibetan side of the range was roughly surveyed in 1904-5 after the Tibet mission and by Major H. R. C. Meade in 1922. Several unnamed peaks rise above 20,000 feet, and there are probably two summits of 23,000. Two groups over 24,000 feet stand on the Great Himalaya near the sources of the Bumtang, one directly west of the difficult Mon La Kar Chung pass (17,442) with heights of 24,740, 24,660, and 23,750 feet, the other fifteen miles north-east of it, Kulha Kangri, the highest point of which is 24,784 feet. Both groups have been fixed for position and height, but their approaches are quite unexplored. The Mon La Kar Chung was crossed by Claude White in 1906 and by Williamson in 1933.

The headwaters of the Lhobrak and Trashi Yangtse in the Lhuntse and Trashigong Dzong districts of eastern Bhutan have been penetrated by Ludlow and Sherriff in 1933, but little is known of the great range to the north; both rivers have broken through the range and the crest barely reaches 21,000 feet. East of them the range and the passes over it are better known from the explorations of Kingdon Ward in 1933 and of Sherriff and Ludlow in 1934, 1936, and 1938, but the higher approaches to the mountains have not been surveyed and they are virtually unknown.[1]

At the eastern end of the Great Himalaya is Namcha Barwa, discovered first in 1912 by the observations of Captains Oakes and Field from the Abor country and by Captain Morshead from the Mishmi hills. The following year Morshead and Bailey saw it at close quarters, and discovered the mountain Gyala Peri (23,460) on the opposite side of the Tsangpo. Kingdon Ward does not consider the latter as being on the Great Himalaya, the extension of which beyond the river is still unsettled.

[1] *H.J.* viii (1936) 125 ff.; ix (1937) 145 ff.; x (1938) 1 ff.; xii (1940) 1 ff.

# 8. Weather in the Himalaya

MOUNTAINEERS often blame the weather for ill-success, and sometimes they have every reason to do so. At the same time there are seasons which are more favourable for climbing than others, and these may vary according to the altitude of the climb. The chief enemies in the Himalaya are violent blizzards, high winds, and intense cold. The first are rarely predictable and may cause disaster to the careless, but high winds and low temperatures follow more general rules and can be mitigated by choosing both the best season when their effects are least, and the right equipment and diet for withstanding them. Knowledge on these points has been gained by the analysis of experience in the Himalaya and Arctic regions, by the work of scientists in India and abroad, and by the co-operation of equipment and provision firms in England and continental countries.

The prevailing wind at high altitudes throughout the Himalaya and Tibet is westerly and strong, often blowing at gale force. It may be so strong at altitudes over 23,000 feet that it is impossible to advance against it or even to stand in one's steps. Climbers on the north-east ridge of Everest have estimated gusts of well over a hundred miles an hour, making the crossing of the north face at 27,000 feet impossible. Even at altitudes down to 19,000 feet or less on exposed mountains it may be strong enough to destroy a tent, and most mountaineers have at one time or another spent a sleepless night wondering whether they are going to be carried away into eternity.

India is a 'monsoon' land, and as such has two theoretical seasons governed by the south-west and the north-east monsoons. Because of the barriers of the eastern Himalaya and Burma, the north-east monsoon has little effect on India as a whole, and none in the north, where there are three marked seasons: the cold weather from the beginning of October to the end of February, the hot weather from

March to mid-June, and 'the rains' from mid-June to the end of September.

In Calcutta the cold weather is cool only in comparison with the rest of the year and the temperature rarely falls below 55° F.; in the Punjab there are frequent frosts at night. Snow falls in the outer Himalaya down to below 5000 feet in most years and roads to the hill-stations may be temporarily blocked. Passes become closed and inhabitants move down from the summer grazing-grounds to the valleys, and in some parts Gujars and other semi-nomad peoples take their flocks down to the foothills. Nevertheless, in some parts, deep in the heart of the Himalaya and Karakoram, there are advantages in winter travel. In Hunza and its side-valleys, for instance, where in late summer and autumn the traveller is driven high up the valley-walls, the river-beds and flood-plains become passable, and it is possible to explore regions that earlier in the year are inaccessible; but the cold is too great for high climbs.

Early in March the Indo-Gangetic plain begins to heat up and during April and May a low-pressure centre is formed. The moisture-laden monsoon strikes India late in May or early in June; heavy rain falls on the Western Ghats and that part which reaches the Bay of Bengal either strikes the Arakan Yomas of Burma or is drawn northwards into Bengal, Assam, and the Indo-Gangetic plains. The Lesser Himalaya in Eastern Nepal, Sikkim, and Western Bhutan receive its full impact and deflect the currents upwards and along the plains. During the four months from June to September Allahabad has thirty-three inches of rain out of an annual rainfall of thirty-eight inches; Delhi twenty-two out of twenty-six inches, and Rawalpindi twenty-one inches. As the currents rise and cool above the outer hills, they release an even greater rainfall. In the same four months Darjeeling has 102 inches out of an annual total of 122 inches; Simla forty-eight inches and Murree thirty-five inches.

The monsoon is due in Delhi about the 15th June; it 'bursts' with considerable violence, usually after a period of sweltering heat, and brings relief to the plainsman. From then until the beginning of September there may be 'breaks' in it, but fine days in the outer hills are not common and rainfall is heavy. At the height of the monsoon Darjeeling has forty-five wet days in July and August. Naini Tal and Mussoorie have more than twenty days in each of these months and Murree about fourteen. Rain is heavier and there are fewer fine days in the Sikkim and Nepal Himalaya than in the Kumaun and Punjab Himalaya, and the monsoon begins a little earlier and usually lasts longer.

The monsoon cloud-base is low, but as the currents rise they cool and cannot hold their moisture. Ranges such as the Mahabharat Lekh, Dhaula Dhar, and Pir Panjal standing directly across the path of the currents receive copious rain; but these outer ranges draw off only part of the moisture, and as the currents approach the spurs and crests of the Great Himalaya they are cooled still further. Being stronger in the east than in the Punjab their effect is greater on Kangchenjunga and Everest than on Nun Kun and Nanga Parbat; and in some places where there is a broad valley north of the outer hills, as the Vale of Kashmir, there is a marked drop in the rainfall. Srinagar, for instance, has only 2·3 inches on 5·2 wet days in August on the average, though I have known much wetter Augusts than this.[1]

There are few figures of rainfall beyond the Great Himalaya except in Kashmir, but the main axis is a climatic divide between India and Central Asia, particularly in the east. Tibet is not seriously affected by monsoon conditions, so that an approach to the Great Himalaya from the north can be most deceptive. On the northern slopes of the range the condition of the snow is affected by monsoon temperatures, and while the monsoon is establishing itself there may be a short period of three or four weeks when the high westerly winds are checked before bad weather sets in. It is this period of a month or less that is most favourable for an attempt on Everest from whichever side it is attacked.

Beyond the Great Himalaya in the west there are a few definite figures. Dras, beyond the Zoji La in Kashmir, has a negligible rainfall from July to November, and Leh, beyond the Zaskar range, has only three inches of precipitation in the year. Incursions of the monsoon are infrequent into the Karakoram and Gilgit on the west of it has an average of less than five inches in the year and only one inch in the four monsoon months. High mountains such as Rakaposhi and the peaks on the Great Karakoram get considerably more than this,

[1] For an analysis of weather west of Nepal see my paper in *H.J.* viii (1936) 86.

but there are often spells of a week's fine weather separated by shorter or longer periods when climbing may be interrupted. It is wiser then to descend, to be patient, and not to risk disaster.

About a fortnight or three weeks before the monsoon, usually late in May, there may be a short period, known as the *chhoti barsat,* when the weather is unsettled. It affects the outer hills and may have repercussions as far in as the Great Himalaya for short periods of a day or two, giving the climber the impression that the monsoon has arrived. But the onset of the monsoon in the plains is sudden; in India we speak of the 'burst' of the monsoon. Depending on the strength of the currents it may be sudden or gradual in its arrival at the main range, and it is then more continuous than the *chhoti barsat,* particularly in the east.

Its ending is much more gradual. Periods of bad weather in the mountains get shorter and the fine-weather spells longer. By October in the inner hills it is over, and this month and November are freer from rain and cloud than any other. Visibility, so essential for survey and photography, is nearly perfect, but for the high altitude climber, particularly in the north-west, there are two serious drawbacks. As the monsoon currents lessen in strength the high westerly winds are re-established. By November they again reach gale force and are much colder than in May. Also the days are shortening and the sun has little power to warm. On the other hand, streams which earlier in the year are unfordable from melting snow or monsoon rain are by November no obstacle to travel.

The months from December to February are ruled out for high climbing by the cold. Winter skiing became a popular pastime during the last twenty years of British rule in India at such places as Gulmarg (8700) on the northern slopes of the Pir Panjal in Kashmir and to a less extent in a few other places. But these have frequent bad-weather spells. Though the mountains are not affected by the north-east monsoon of the China Seas, the bitter cold allows the air to settle in the valleys and this is drawn out to the warmer plains of India in the form of northerly winds. Cyclonic disturbances from Persia, and probably from Iraq and the Mediterranean, affect the northern Punjab, Kashmir, and to a less extent the Kumaun and Nepal Himalaya. As they reach the cold valleys they bring a heavy precipitation, mostly in the form of snow. Srinagar may have snow in January and February and the surrounding hills are white almost to their foot. As late as April, its wettest month, Srinagar has an average of eight wet days; Sonamarg (8750) and Dras (10,150) on either side of the Zoji La, have fifteen and eleven wet days respectively in March, and nearly as much in April, when it generally snows. These western disturbances often affect the Punjab Himalaya as late as May, when bad weather on the passes is by no means so exceptional as many travellers seem to think. On a cloudless night in April or May after two fine days, the Zoji La offers an absolutely safe passage to a large caravan; by dawn or soon afterwards it may be dangerous. I warned a small party of Ladakhis not to cross by daylight on 17 May 1926; they took no heed and were swept away by an avalanche and killed, though two nights earlier I had taken over a party of 160 laden porters. Much the same applies to the Burzil, Kamri, and other passes. All have witnessed tragedy from avalanche and blizzard through fatalism, impatience, or carelessness.

Nanga Parbat, at the extreme western end of the Great Himalaya is affected by monsoon weather, though nothing like so much as Everest and Kangchenjunga. Mummery's exploration of the mountain took place in August 1895. Merkl began his attack in 1932 on 30 June, and carried on throughout July and the first half of August, though hampered by monsoon incursions, during the worst of which they descended to the lower camps. In 1934 Merkl began early in June. On 6 July almost the whole party were concentrated at Camp 8 (24,464) on the 'Silver Saddle'; the weather which had been perfect for several days suddenly broke, with disastrous results. In 1937, by sending out equipment over the passes the year before, Karl Wien was able to begin operations about 20 May. He encountered bad weather from the start. Almost the entire party was destroyed by an avalanche on the night of 14 June, that is some days before the monsoon reached the Punjab. In 1953 except for a few small spells of bad weather in June the weather was exceptionally fine throughout and the mountain was climbed on 3 July.

It is difficult to deduce from these events what is the best season in the Punjab Himalaya for such ventures. There is certainly little chance of long spells of fine weather in May or early June. Probably

July or August are the best months, or even September, but it is essential to be ready to retreat the moment a bad spell of weather intervenes.

Farther north, in the Karakoram, the monsoon has less effect. The predominant winds in Gilgit and on the Pamirs from the middle of May to the end of August are between north-west and west and they are interrupted only occasionally by monsoon incursions.[1] Campbell Secord had almost uninterruptedly fine weather on Rakaposhi in July 1938. The consensus of opinion of travellers to Hunza and Nagir is that the weather is fine throughout most of July and August. My own party, in 1913, having crossed the Burzil on the night of 1 May, carried out high triangulation through Hunza and on the Pamirs from 1 June until 22 August, when bad weather set in and lasted without interruption for a fortnight. This was the only serious monsoon weather in these parts that year, though cloud on the highest summits was often exasperating.

Farther east the Duke of the Abruzzi's explorations in 1909 in the upper Baltoro region were rarely upset by the weather during June and July, though there were occasional snowfalls. In 1938 Charles Houston for his reconnaissance on K2 had fine weather in early June, intermittent storms at the end of the month and in early July—not too bad to suspend operations—and a long fine spell in mid-July. Wiessner's expedition came to grief on the same mountain the following July when a similar fine-weather spell broke up. Houston's party in 1953 were also caught by a week's bad weather in their high camp early in August. There is little doubt, however, that the best season for climbing in the Karakoram is from late June to early August, but as in the Punjab Himalaya climbers must expect occasional violent interludes of storm.

The Kumaun Himalaya is more adversely affected by the monsoon. In 1934 Shipton and Tilman penetrated the 'inner sanctuary' of Nanda Devi in early June. Monsoon disturbances began about 24 June and though Shipton avoided the worst during July by exploring the Ganges watershed north of the main axis, the weather was still bad on the Badrinath–Kedarnath watershed in August. His party was back in the 'inner sanctuary' early in September and

[1] *Records of the Survey of India*, vi (1914) 96.

crossed the watershed out of it unhampered by the weather, though the cold was greater than in June. Nanda Devi was climbed by Tilman and Odell on 29 August 1936, after the monsoon had spent its force.

It is only since World War II that, with the exception of Everest, the Great Himalaya in Nepal has been attempted by climbers. Murray in 1950 explored Api near the western boundary of the State in June; he records that the monsoon broke on the 13th after which date activities at moderate altitudes were much hampered by the weather. In central Nepal Herzog's party in 1950 reconnoitred Dhaulagiri and Annapurna during the first fortnight of May; Herzog himself reached the summit of Annapurna on 3 June and was off the mountain before the monsoon reached it more than a week later. Without detailing the experience of early Everest expeditions, the sum of it is that there is a period between 15 May and 15 June when the high westerly winds are checked by air masses in front of the advancing monsoon and during that period there may be a spell of fine weather when the mountain may be climbed. Norton's expedition in 1924 had such a spell, but they were too exhausted and weakened by the loss of Mallory and Irvine to make use of it. Ruttledge in 1936 and Tilman in 1938 had no such chance; Lambert and Tenzing in 1952 had a similar spell of fine weather, which however deteriorated temporarily on 28 May, the day chosen for the final assault, after a bitterly cold night in their bivouac at 27,800 feet. No storm actually broke, more than a week of fine weather followed, and the monsoon did not arrive until 10 June. Sir John Hunt's plan was based on all this experience, gained from the earlier Everest attempts, and the mountain was conquered on 29 May 1953.

Reconnaissances of Everest by Shipton in 1937 and by the Swiss in 1952 hold out little hope of climbing the highest mountains after the monsoon. The cold is too intense at night and the days are too short. But Cooke's first ascent of Kabru (24,002) in 1935 as late as 18 November shows that lower mountains in the Sikkim Himalaya, and possibly in Nepal, may be attacked successfully after the monsoon. This part of the Himalaya is barely affected, if at all, by the early winter westerly depressions of the Punjab Himalaya and climbing on the lower mountains unaffected by the high westerly winds should be possible earlier than May.

Little is known of climbing in the Assam Himalaya, but conditions are probably very similar to those in Sikkim.

It may be worth mentioning here that at almost any season in the high Himalaya there is danger from avalanches. It is impossible to go into technicalities, but most European climbers are surprised at first by the distance travelled by Himalayan avalanches, and a much larger margin of safety is required in siting camps where these are likely to occur. In some parts of the Himalaya there is danger from thunderstorms. Surveyors who may have to camp for several days on or near the mountain tops are likely to suffer from them. My theodolite has been 'sparked' by mild lightning discharges, my observatory tent has emitted 'St. Elmo's Fires,' and some of my men as well as myself have received slight electric shocks. The camp of a surveyor in Kashmir was destroyed by lightning in 1912, and two men were killed. Dr. de Graaff Hunter designed a portable lightning-conductor which was effective, but on the whole I found by experience that it was pleasanter to come down. Storms arrive with great suddenness in the high Himalaya and their intensity can be frightening.

PART TWO

# Early History to 1885

'Who goes to the Hills goes to his mother.' They had crossed the Siwaliks and the half tropical Doon, left Mussoorie behind them, and headed north along the narrow hill-roads. Day after day they struck deeper into the huddled mountains, and day after day Kim watched the Lama return to a man's strength.

RUDYARD KIPLING *Kim*

# 1. Early Travellers and Adventurers to 1800

THE gathering of geographical and other scientific knowledge in so vast a region as the Himalaya is a slow process even when there is no lack of adventurous spirits. Every mountaineer owes a debt to his predecessors and as it were climbs on the shoulders of those who have gone before. There is an indescribable thrill in reaching an unknown pass and in setting eyes on unexplored land, in reconnoitring it and mapping it for the first time. Later travellers and surveyors with the knowledge so gained would not be worth their salt if they could not go farther and improve upon the first maps; and as science progresses more detailed maps on a larger scale are required.

Sir John Hunt pays a well-deserved tribute to the members of earlier Everest expeditions; an older generation of men such as Longstaff and Bruce praised the efforts of the early surveyors; and these in their turn worked on the knowledge gained by still earlier adventurers. Germans on Kangchenjunga planned from Douglas Freshfield and Professor Garwood, whose map improved upon the early surveys; Americans climbed the Abruzzi ridge on K2, gaining from the experience of the Italians in 1909 who based their plans on Martin Conway's in 1892, and so back to Godwin-Austen in 1861, and earlier travellers still. The modern climber is, in fact, rather like 'the man, all tattered and torn, that kissed the maiden all forlorn' in the house that Jack built.

There were great difficulties confronting early Himalayan travellers. Bases from which they set out were often far from the hills; there were no railways and few roads. Europeans were unknown to the men living among the mountains, many of whom were suspicious and unwilling to impart their knowledge of the passes, and who dreaded leaving the beaten track. These felt little urge to explore the inner recesses of the ice-clad regions—'the delighted spirit to bathe in fiery floods or to reside in thrilling regions of thick-ribbed ice.' For centuries men had crossed high passes for plunder or when forced to do so; but not for pleasure. Spirits dwelt among the high snows, and claimed victims from any bold enough to penetrate their mysteries; they must be propitiated. Hard-headed, sophisticated, sober Europeans have photographed the tracks of the *yeti*—the 'abominable snow-man'—though back in England scientists may smile and call him ape or bear, as no doubt he is; but spirits dwell in the high mountains, satanic and divine, malignant and benign, and mountaineers know them well, when they use their batteries of rock, bury the unwary under an avalanche of snow or graciously vouchsafe an unforgettable day. There can be purgatory as well as paradise among the high mountains. That is the fun of it all, when one is young. But the elements can be vengeful, and the rash and careless may deserve their fate.

The first knowledge of the Himalaya came to Europe through Alexander's invasion of India about 325 B.C. There is no record that his officers penetrated the Himalaya after the battle of Aornos on the Indus, but in the years that followed no doubt some adventurous Greeks from Bactria went there over the Pamirs, if lingering tradition is to be believed. The Mir of Hunza assured me in 1913 that he was a direct descendant of Alexander himself by a peri of the Hindu Kush; and certainly there is a small village called Sikanderabad in the Hunza valley to support his claim!

The earliest sketch-map of the Himalaya bearing some resemblance to the truth was drawn in 1590 by Father Anthony Monserrate, a Spanish member of the first Jesuit mission to Akbar's court in 1579. Benedict de Goes in 1603 travelled with trading caravans from Lahore to Peshawar and Kabul, and by the Pamirs to Yarkand, Turfan, and Suchow, where he died in 1607. The Himalaya was not crossed by him.

So far as I can discover, the first Europeans to penetrate and cross the whole breadth of the Himalaya were the intrepid Father Antonio de Andrade and Brother Manuel Marques, who set out from Agra on 30 March 1624 to search for a Christian community reported to be living in Tibet. Their route lay through Srinagar on the Alaknanda—not to be confused, as has often been done, with Srinagar in Kashmir—Badrinath and the Mana pass, 18,400 feet, on the crest of the Zaskar range, north of the Great Himalaya. Andrade's first attempt with two Indian Christians to cross the pass early in June failed when they were overtaken by a blizzard and frostbitten—a fact which he faithfully records: 'Our feet were frozen and frost-bitten, so much so that we did not feel it when later they touched a piece of red-hot iron.' The pass was crossed by Andrade and Marques on their second attempt probably at the end of July, with Tibetan guides, and they reached Tsaparang on the upper Sutlej, the capital of Guge, tributary to Leh in Ladakh, where they were hospitably received by the 'king.'

After a short stay the two Portuguese returned over the Mana pass to Agra, but they were back again in Tsaparang with a third missionary Gonzales de Sousa by July the following year. The first Christian church in Tibet was founded here on 12 April 1626, and for four years the mission flourished. The Alaknanda and the Saraswati, with the Mana pass, became the established route of the several Jesuit missionaries who travelled between Agra and Tsaparang during the next sixteen years.

The baptism of the king in 1630 led to a revolution. The church was sacked, four hundred converts were reduced to slavery and the king and two Jesuits were carried captive to Leh. This led to a daring journey by Francisco de Azevedo in 1631. Appointed Visitor to the Tsaparang church after the revolution, at the age of fifty-two he crossed the Mana pass in August and from Tsaparang undertook the journey to Leh across the high plateau north of the Sutlej. With him went John de Oliviera, who had been at Tsaparang for five years and spoke Tibetan. Passing through Hanle and Gya, they reached Leh on 25 October.

Their courage was rewarded and their mission successful. To avoid the journey back over the bleak Tibetan plateau, they set out from Leh in November direct for India via Kulu, crossing successively the Zaskar and Himalayan ranges by the Tagalaung La (17,500), Lacha-lung La (16,600), Baralacha La (16,200), and the Rohtang (13,050). They were the first Europeans to cross these passes, well-known to-day, though often closed at the season Azevedo took them long ago.

In spite of Azevedo's efforts the Tsaparang mission never fully recovered. Obstacles were put in the way of the five Jesuits who remained there until 1635, when Ambrosio Correa recommended its abandonment. The two who refused to leave, Manuel Marques and Nuno Coresma, were driven out soon afterwards. Four years later the Tibetan governor of Tsaparang invited the Jesuits to return, and in June 1640 Marques, with Father Stanislaus Malpichi, again crossed the Mana pass. Both were seized, and, though Malpichi escaped, Marques was imprisoned. He was alive late in 1641, but he never returned to India and his fate is unknown. With Father Andrade he had founded the mission; he never succumbed to depression or faltered in his faith. There is no record that the Mana pass was crossed again by Europeans until the nineteenth century, and not till 1912 was Tsaparang identified. In that year G. Mackworth Young of the Indian Civil Service made a study of its ruins.[1]

Two Jesuits of the same period, Stephen Cacella and John Cabral, crossed the western end of the Assam Himalaya. Leaving Hooghly on 2 August 1626 and Biar (now Cooch Behar) on 2 February the following year, they crossed the Duars and reached Paro Dzong by the Raidak valley on 25 March, where they were hospitably received. Both appear to have taken the Chumbi valley route and Tang La into Tibet, though separately, Cabral being the first to reach Shigatse on the Tsangpo in January 1628. On Cacella's arrival, Cabral returned to Hooghly through Nepal, though his exact route is not known, Cacella visiting Bhutan the following year. Cabral was back in Shigatse about the middle of 1631, and in a letter written from there in July, which reached Azevedo at Tsaparang before he left that place for Leh, Cabral records the death of Cacella at Shigatse on 6 March 1630. The efforts of the Jesuits in these parts came to an end when Cabral returned in 1631 to Hooghly.

Thirty years later two Jesuit missionaries, Johann Grueber, an Austrian, and Albert d'Orville, a Belgian, working at the Imperial Observatory in Peking, received a summons to return to Rome, and because of war with Holland resolved to journey overland. Leaving

[1] For a full account of the travels of these and other Jesuits, based on records in the possession of the Society of Jesus, see C. J. Wessels, S.J.: *Early Jesuit Travellers in Central Asia 1603–1721* (The Hague: Martinus Nijhoff, 1924). For an account of the Kingdom of Guge and the Tsaparang Mission see G. M. Young: 'A Journey to Toling and Tsaparang in Tibet' (*Journal of the Punjab Historical Society*, vii, Calcutta, 1919). Tsaparang is now represented by the insignificant hamlet of Chabrang.

Peking on 13 April 1661 they passed through Siningfu and reached Lhasa on 8 October. From there they appear to have passed through Kampa and Tingri, and to have taken the track by Nyenam and the Po Chu (Bhote Kosi), arriving in Katmandu in January and Agra in March 1662.

Fifty years later Ippolito Desideri was no less intrepid. From Delhi and Lahore, which he left on 19 October 1714, he crossed the Pir Panjal pass by the old Mogul imperial route and reached Srinagar on 10 November. Here he was forced to stay the winter. He crossed the Zoji La at the end of May—the first European to do so—and reaching Leh on 25 June, left on 17 August and

finally, two years and four months after I left Goa, and one year and a half since our departure from Delly, and ten whole months since leaving Kascimir, we arrived by the grace of God, on the 18th day of March 1716 at the city of Lhasa.

Desideri stayed in or near Lhasa for five years, until he heard that the mission-field of Tibet was to be handed over to the Capuchins. He resided in various monasteries during this period, conversed with the most learned lamas, and wrote a book in the Tibetan language refuting what he considered to be the errors of Lamaism and pressing the merits of Christian doctrine. His house became 'the scene of incessant comings and goings by all sorts of people, chiefly learned men and professors ... to apply for permission to see and read the book.'

Desideri left Lhasa on 25 April 1721. He travelled by the Kuti road to Nepal, reaching Katmandu in December. After a brief stay in the valley of Nepal he continued through India by Patna to Madras, whence he sailed for Europe. He died in Rome on 14 April 1733, aged forty-eight.[1]

These were romantic days in the Himalaya. Few of these old Jesuits were geographers; they were obsessed with their mission. Some took rough observations for latitude; Grueber and d'Orville alone had some astronomical training. But they were the first Europeans to force the Himalayan passes at almost any season of the

[1] An Account of Tibet: The Travels of Ippolito Desideri of Pistoia, S.J. Edited by Filippo De Filippi (London, 1932).

year, in the simple faith that they would arrive at their destination, like Desideri, 'by the grace of God.'

Throughout the middle part of the eighteenth century the only map of Tibet and the Himalaya which carried any weight was that prepared in Paris by the geographer d'Anville for his Atlas of China in forty-two sheets, which was a companion volume to Father du Halde's *Description de l'Empire de la Chine*. This atlas was published in Paris in 1735 and was compiled from maps sent home by the Jesuit Father Baptiste Regis of the observatory at Peking, some of which were from the surveys of the Jesuit missionaries in China themselves and based on astronomical observations made by them. Unfortunately the southern part of Tibet and the Himalaya was from the work of Chinese lamas sent out by the emperor Kang-Li between 1705 and 1717, and Regis felt obliged to accept it for fear of giving offence. D'Anville's map gives a fair representation of the general course of the Tsangpo in Tibet, and of the Tibetan courses of the Sutlej and Indus; but the latter, which is labelled 'Ganga,' is shown as sweeping round the western side of Kashmir to pass eastwards through the Lesser Himalaya, collecting the Sutlej and becoming 'Le Gange' of the Indian plains. The other rivers of the Himalaya and the mountains also bear little resemblance to fact.[1]

Very little additional knowledge was gained during the century. Clive, before leaving India, appointed Captain James Rennell the first Surveyor General of Bengal, but his task was primarily to map the Company's possessions in that presidency, and to collect material, mostly route surveys, made by officers attached to columns on active service.

A small expedition under Captain Kinloch in 1767, in answer to an appeal for aid from the Raja of Nepal, brought back sketches of a section of that country's southern border. In 1774 Warren Hastings

[1] The best critical and full account of the early maps of the Himalaya—in fact of all India—and of early surveys appears in *The Historical Records of the Survey of India*, by Colonel R. H. Phillimore. Volume I deals with the eighteenth century, Volume II with the years 1800 to 1815. Volumes III and IV are in the press. Phillimore has studied the old maps in the possession of the Survey of India and in the British Museum and Commonwealth Relations Libraries in England. He has sorted and studied some 700 volumes of manuscript correspondence dealing with early surveys of India. Many reproductions of the old maps appear in these volumes, which are invaluable to the historian.

sent one of the Company's civilians, George Bogle, on a trade mission to the Deb Raja of Bhutan and the Teshu Lama in Tibet. His route by Cooch Behar and Buxa through the Assam Himalaya to Tashi-cho Dzong and Paro Dzong in Bhutan, the Chumbi valley and over the Tang La to Gyantse and Shigatse was almost identical with that taken by the Jesuits Cacella and Cabral in 1626, though he did not know it. Bogle, in order not to prejudice the success of his mission, took no surveyor with him and brought back little but a bare description of his route. His journey back to Bengal from April to June 1775 followed his outward route.

After two minor missions in 1776 and 1777 to Punaka in Bhutan by Hamilton, who had accompanied Bogle as doctor in 1774, a second mission to Tibet in 1783 under Ensign Samuel Turner, an aide-de-camp and first cousin of Warren Hastings, was despatched to the Teshu Lama to congratulate him and acknowledge his reincarnation. This took the same route as Bogle, and the diversion taken by Hamilton to Punaka, the capital of Bhutan, where his surveyor, Samuel Davis, was unfortunately turned back.

In 1792 the Gurkhas again appealed to Calcutta for help in a minor war with Tibet. The result of this was a sketch-map of the route to Katmandu made by Ensign John Gerard who was in charge of the escort of the envoy William Kirkpatrick.

These six small missions are mentioned because they are the first penetrations into the hills from the south after Clive's victory at Plassey, and the only ones, so far as I know, which occurred in the eighteenth century. They were arduous, when it is considered that nothing was then known of the country, and they were moderately successful in their trade and political aspects, but they added very little to our geographical knowledge of the Himalaya, though both Bogle and Turner identified the Tsangpo of Tibet with the Brahmaputra of Assam, a fact which was accepted by Rennell but which much exercised the geographers of Europe at a later date.

Rennell, 'the Father of Indian Geography,' after his retirement in 1777 did for India what d'Anville had done for China. He set about compiling his great *Map of Hindoostan*, from every known source in India and England. His first edition (1782) was a great advance on d'Anville's *Carte de l'Inde* published thirty years earlier for the

French in their struggle for supremacy in India, since he had all the material collected during those years of early British rule, especially in Bengal, Bihar, and Assam; but for want of other material he was forced to accept d'Anville's map for the Himalaya in Nepal and west of it. A new and larger map appeared in 1788, with many alterations, and two further editions were published in 1792 and 1793 which had other important improvements. With them was a supplementary map entitled *The Countries situated between Delhi and Candahar*. In this Rennell corrected the middle course of the Ganges, but omitted the Bhagirathi, upper Alaknanda and Saraswati of which he had no information, and his knowledge of the Indus and its tributaries was much at fault.

# 2. Travels and Route Surveys 1800–1845

THIS was the state of our knowledge of the Himalaya when the nineteenth century opened. The next fifty years saw a remarkable change; most of the main valleys of the Kumaun and Punjab Himalaya had by then been penetrated, many of the high peaks had been fixed for position and height and regular surveys were about to begin throughout the western Himalaya.

Because of the rapid extension of the Company's possessions as a result of the wars in the south, a large amount of new country was crying out for survey all over India. At the same time the Directors in England were insisting on economy and retrenchment because of the high cost of the wars. Fortunately the Surveyor General of Bengal, Robert Colebrooke, was keenly interested in exploration and himself took the field as a surveyor and encouraged infantry officers to map any country they visited.

The first to survey in Nepal proper was Charles Crawford, who commanded the first Resident's escort in Katmandu from 1801 to 1803. Crawford brought back a large-scale map of the 'valley of Nepal' and the headwaters of the Bagmati, from his own observations and route surveys, and a smaller-scale map of the rest of Nepal from information he collected. He also surveyed in 1804 a small part of eastern Nepal where the Kosi breaks out of the hills, and was the first to announce the great height of the snowy range.

It was through Colebrooke's personal interest that the Ganges sources were at last made known. Much of the Kumaun Himalaya was at that time dominated by Nepal, the ruler of which refused to admit strangers. Colebrooke temporarily overcame his objections and obtained the support of the Governor General to a personal exploration of the sources. But shortly before starting he was taken ill and deputed an able young lieutenant, W. S. Webb, of the 10th Bengal N.I., who had been with him in Rohilkhand in 1807, to 'survey the Ganges from Hurdwar to Gungoutri (or the Cow's

Mouth) where the river is stated by Major Rennell to force its way through the Hymalaia Mountains by a Subterraneous Passage.'

Webb started early in 1808, accompanied by Captain F. V. Raper of his own regiment, and by a strange and adventurous character, Hyder Young Hearsey, who, after entering the Mahratta service in 1799, had served against the Mahrattas in command of irregular cavalry.

Webb reached Barahat on the upper Bhagirathi on 23 April, but could get no farther than Raithal just beyond Batwari, about thirty miles from Gangotri and forty miles from the glacier source at Gaumukh. He returned over the hills to the junction of the Bhagirathi and Alaknanda, surveying his route as he travelled, and then followed the course of the Alaknanda as far as Badrinath. On his return to Joshimath at the junction of the Alaknanda and Dhauli, he ascended the latter to Tapoban, struck south over the Kuari pass to Pana, and crossing the Birehi, Nandakini, and Pindar valleys made straight for Almora, which he was forced to avoid because of increasing Gurkha hostility.

It is a much travelled route to-day; at that time it was quite unknown to the Western World. Webb's route-maps were drawn on the one-inch scale; the journal kept by Raper was published in *Asiatic Researches* xi (1810) 446 ff. Webb was convinced that the Ganges had no distant Tibetan source in Manasarowar or Rakas Tal and that there was no tunnel under the Himalaya. That it rose north of the main axis of the Great Himalaya and cut through it he could not appreciate, since no alignment of the peaks or axis had yet been discovered, and he was travelling mostly in the valleys. His highest point was probably the Kuari pass, 12,140 feet, and he was the first European to cross it.

Colebrooke had already been impressed by the great height of the snowy range while surveying in the Ganges Doab and by Crawford's observations in Nepal in 1802. Webb took observations to some of the high peaks and after his return was surprised by the heights he obtained. In 1809–10 he again observed the position and height of Dhaulagiri from four survey stations in the plains and calculated the height to be 26,862 feet, though this figure was derided by geographers outside India where it was held that the Andes were the highest mountains in the world. Webb was not the 'discoverer' of Dhaulagiri, but he was certainly the first observer to place it on the map and to calculate its height within a thousand feet. The officially accepted height to-day is 26,795 feet, only 67 feet lower than Webb's figure.

Napoleon's threat to India in 1808 led to the despatch of British envoys to Persia, Afghanistan, Sind, and the Punjab. Ranjit Singh, the ambitious ruler of Lahore, was at the time causing concern among the Sikh rulers east of the Sutlej, who applied to the Company for protection. Charles Metcalfe, the British envoy to Lahore, negotiated a treaty with Ranjit Singh in April 1809, as a result of which the Company's influence was extended to the Sutlej. Much new country now came under its administration, and this required maps. At the same time the Company was obliged to take more interest in the hills to the north.

Colebrooke died of dysentery on 13 September 1808 and was succeeded as Surveyor General of Bengal by John Garstin. Between then and 1814 efforts were made to extend route surveys into the Dun and Lesser Himalaya of Garhwal. These efforts were frequently frustrated by opposition from the Gurkhas, whose advances south and west were being watched by the British authorities with increasing suspicion.

It was in these circumstances that William Moorcroft made his first daring journey through the mountains. Moorcroft was a surgeon of Liverpool who had studied veterinary science in France and had practised in London for some years before being appointed veterinary surgeon to the Bengal government in 1808, at the age of forty-three. Three years later, while superintendent of the Company's stud farm at Pusa near Patna, he obtained permission from the Agent to the Governor General at Fatehgarh to make a journey into the mountains in order to buy new strains for horse-breeding and to investigate the possibilities of wool trade with Tibet.

Moorcroft took Hearsey as his companion, and the two set out from Ramnagar, at the foot of the hills, in May 1812, before the Bengal Government, which disapproved of the venture, could intervene. Disguised as fakirs and under the assumed names of Mayapori and Hargiri, they followed the Ramganga to its source, struck the Alaknanda at Karnaprayag and reached Joshimath by Webb's route. They then explored the Dhauli, crossed the Niti pass (16,628), east of Kamet, into the Hundes province of Tibet. At the end of July they reached Manasarowar, being the first Europeans to get there since Desideri in 1715, and the first to cross the Niti pass.

They encountered much difficulty on the way back. Following the Sutlej west for a few days, they were detained by Tibetans at Daba (or Dapa) Dzong, where they were befriended by two Bhotia brothers, Bir Singh and Deb Singh, from the Milam district across the border. After this incident they recrossed the Niti pass, and were imprisoned by Gurkhas in Kumaun, though they succeeded in getting away and reached India in November with a herd of mountain goats.

Moorcroft's account appeared in *Asiatic Researches* with a reduction of Hearsey's map to the scale of ten miles to the inch. Neither was a surveyor, but their report and route-map aroused great interest, since they proved conclusively that no branch of the Ganges had any source so far north, while the Sutlej rose in Rakas Tal.

Before leaving, Moorcroft had despatched Saiyid Mir Izzet Ullah to reconnoitre routes through Kashmir to Turkestan and Bukhara, with a view to going there himself. The Saiyid left Attock on the lower Indus in August 1812, passed through Hazara and Kashmir, and crossed the Zoji La to Leh, the Digar La to the upper Shyok, and the Karakoram pass to Yarkand and Kashgar. He returned to India in December 1813, bringing detailed notes of his travels, stage by stage, which were later translated and published.[1]

A number of legends grew up at a later date regarding the fate of Moorcroft, one of which insisted that he reached and died at Lhasa or at Gartok on the way there or back.[2] This is incorrect. Between 1820 and 1825 he was constantly travelling. From headquarters in Leh he explored much of Ladakh, placed on his map the Karakoram and Saltoro passes, and correctly showed that the Yarkand

[1] The first translation appeared in the *Calcutta Quarterly Oriental Magazine*, iii (1823). A reprint with corrections will be found in *J.R.A.S.* vii (1842–3). A monograph entitled *Travels in Central Asia by Meer Izett Oolah in the years 1812–13*, translated from the Persian original by Captain Henderson of the Foreign Office in India appeared in 1872.

[2] See, for instance, C. G. Rawling: *The Great Plateau*, 4.

river rises on the northern slopes of the Karakoram.[1] His accurate records added much to the scanty knowledge of the western Himalaya, Karakoram, and the countries beyond the north-west frontier, about which very little was known. He died at Andkhui in northern Afghanistan, some 200 miles south of Bukhara, about the end of August 1825.

It was the Nepalese War of 1814-16, brought about by continued encroachment on the Company's territory and by attacks on frontier posts, that opened up the Kumaun Himalaya to further exploration. The four columns which advanced into Nepal had to rely almost entirely on the maps and reports of Crawford, Webb, Hearsey, and Moorcroft, of John Anthony Hodgson, who had completed a survey of the Dun and neighbouring hills in 1814, and of Joshua Pickersgill, who was surveying the southern boundary of Nepal when the war broke out. Hodgson and Pickersgill were with Marley's column which was to march from Dinapore to Katmandu. James Herbert, an energetic young subaltern of twenty-three, surveyed the route taken by Wood's column on the disputed Butwal frontier. Though neither column made much progress, both Hodgson and Herbert observed some of the great peaks of Nepal, the latter obtaining a height of 27,000 feet for Dhaulagiri.

The successes of the two columns under Gillespie and Ochterlony eventually finished the campaign. Hearsey, in command of irregulars, was wounded and made prisoner; Webb did a considerable amount of reconnaissance survey. In the treaty which followed, the western boundary of Nepal was fixed at the Kali. This opened up the whole of the Kumaun Himalaya to British administration. Henceforward there were no political objections to the exploration and survey of this area; difficulties were now the purely physical ones caused by the nature of the country. On the other hand the ruler of Nepal adopted the policy of excluding strangers within his established boundary, a policy respected by the British Government throughout the whole period of its rule in India.

A few favoured visitors since then have been invited to Katmandu, a British resident was stationed there, British officers in Gurkha regiments were allowed in certain parts for recruiting purposes; very

[1] Moorcroft's map, from the sketch by George Trebeck, was not published until 1841.

occasionally, as for instance in 1903, a selected British officer has been permitted to take observations for a specific purpose; but it was not until 1924 that the Prime Minister of Nepal invited the British to send a detachment to survey the country, and even then no British officer was permitted to accompany the party to superintend or check the work. It was this policy of exclusion that forced all expeditions to Everest up to World War II to make the long detour by the Chumbi valley and to attack the mountain from Tibetan territory, and only in certain years could permission to go there be extracted from the Tibetan Government. Since 1949 the policy of exclusion has at last been relaxed.

The opening up of the Kumaun Himalaya was a comparatively slow process, though the survey was begun in 1815 as soon as the Gurkhas were forced to evacuate the hills west of the Kali. In that year J. A. Hodgson was appointed 'Surveyor of the north-west mountain provinces.' In the summer of 1816 he explored the upper Sutlej. At his request Herbert was appointed to assist him, and in the following year joined him at Raithal, whence he explored the Gaumukh source of the Bhagirathi. The base for the survey of the hills was measured by Herbert with deodar staves, latitudes were fixed by the zenith distances of stars, and longitudes by observations of Jupiter's satellites. The scientific basis of the survey was probably sound enough for the purpose, but the detail mapped was scanty and comprised little more than the main rivers and routes. Hodgson suffered much from ill-health, 'terai-fever,' malaria, and rheumatism at this time and had to leave Herbert to complete the work, though both were engaged in 1819 in computing the heights of the main peaks of Kumaun. He became Surveyor General of India in 1821, but his appointment was not approved by the Directors in England, and in 1823 he handed over to Valentine Blacker, on whose death in 1826 he again became Surveyor General.

It would be tedious to describe the journeys of the new officers appointed to administer these parts, even if they had left accounts of them. Many did not do so and have left little trace. Mention must however be made of Captain Alexander Gerard and his brother, Dr. J. G. Gerard, nephews of John Gerard who was in charge of Kirkpatrick's escort to Katmandu in 1792. From 'the middling-sized village' of Simla, which they reached and described in 1817, they explored Bashahr, Spiti, and Kanawar, and between them crossed almost every pass from Simla into the Baspa valley. Another traveller of note was G. W. Traill, the first deputy commissioner of Kumaun, who, in the words of A. L. Mumm, 'exercised a benevolent and active despotism from 1817 to 1835.' In 1830 he crossed the Great Himalayan axis between Nanda Devi and Nanda Kot; from the Pindari glacier he reached Martoli in the Goriganga valley by a saddle at 17,700 feet—a difficult pass under certain conditions to-day and a notable achievement in his time; it is still known to mountaineers as 'Traill's Pass.' It was possibly crossed for the second time by the Schlagintweits about 1850; Ruttledge in 1926 was the first to cross it from the north.

The chief interest however at this period lies in the early journeys in Kashmir and Baltistan. Kashmir was then under the general control of Ranjit Singh of the Punjab who conquered it about 1817. Mention has already been made of Moorcroft's travels in the early twenties. With George Trebeck, a geologist and surveyor from Calcutta, he crossed the Baralacha La into Rupshu. Between them they explored much of Ladakh, including the lakes Tso Moriri and Pangong Tso, the Digar La and Chang La, passes over the Ladakh range, and the middle Shyok and lower Nubra.

In 1830, Alexander Gardner, one of several adventurers in the service of Ranjit Singh, crossed the Kadpo Ngonpo La close to the Karakoram pass on a journey from Yarkand to Kashmir, using almost the same route as Mir Izzett Ullah in the opposite direction by the upper Shyok and Chang La. From Srinagar he crossed the Burzil pass to Gilgit, being probably the first European to take this famous route. J. Henderson in 1834–5 also crossed the Baralacha La to Leh, and travelled down the Indus to Skardu, crossed the Alampi La to the Astor river and the Burzil pass to Srinagar. Farther north H. Falconer was probably the first to discover the Biafo glacier and cross the Skoro La in 1838.[1]

---

[1] The most exhaustive summary of the exploration of this region is Giotto Dainelli's *La Esplorazione della Regione fra l'Himalaja Occidentale e il Caracorum* (Bologna: Nicola Zanichelli) 1934. Dainelli gives sketch-maps of the routes of all the more important travellers.

Of the other travellers who added to our knowledge at this period, G. T. Vigne stands out from the rest. He made extensive journeys in Kashmir, Ladakh, and Baltistan in the years 1835–8, during the course of which he reached the snout of the Chogo Lungma glacier (1835) and ascended the Saltoro valley from Khapalu, in search of the Saltoro pass (1838). His book, *Travels in Kashmir, Ladak, Iskardo, the Countries adjoining the Mountain Course of the Indus, and the Himalaya North of the Punjab*, published in London in 1842, in two volumes, is a classic and was the first comprehensive account of this region, and it came at a time when it was perhaps most wanted, since it was available when the Great Trigonometrical Survey of India undertook the first survey of these parts a few years later.

In December 1840 or January 1841, the west side of the Lichar spur of Nanga Parbat, opposite Gor, was precipitated into the Indus by an earthquake. The waters were held back and formed a lake stretching to Gilgit nearly forty miles away. At the end of May or early June 1841 the dam gave way and the waters were liberated in a disastrous flood. No European at that time had been in this part of the Indus valley. It is interesting to study the views of those who best knew the Karakoram and who argued their theories in the pages of scientific journals. Falconer's theory, for instance, which placed the obstruction on the Indus above Skardu was accepted for several years.[1]

[1] *H.J.* i (1929) 15.

# 3. Triangulation and Surveys 1845–1868

GEORGE EVEREST came out to India as an artillery cadet in 1806. In 1818 he became chief assistant to William Lambton, the founder of the Great Trigonometrical Survey of India. On Lambton's death in 1823 Everest succeeded him and from 1830 until his retirement in 1843 he held the combined posts of Surveyor General of India and Superintendent of the Great Trigonometrical Survey.

During this period he conceived the 'gridiron' system of triangulation which now covers the whole of India and which forms a rigid framework for the detailed survey; in 1841 he completed his Great Arc of the Meridian, a stupendous achievement. He was a great organizer, a fine administrator, and a tireless worker.

The significance of Everest's work is often forgotten. By means of accurate observations he, with a very few assistants, measured the great meridional arc passing from Cape Comorin through the centre of India to the Himalaya. This arc forms the foundation on which was calculated the mathematical spheroid—Everest's spheroid—which most closely fits the figure of the earth, or geoid, in India. The positions and officially accepted heights of Himalayan mountains, and in fact of all places in India, are calculated on this spheroid. On the completion of his arc and the network of primary series of triangulation associated with it, it became possible to add by observation a framework of triangulation covering the Himalaya, and to fix with considerable accuracy the positions and heights of the highest summits without visiting them. No man before or since has done so much for the geography of Asia.

There is at present no more accurate method of computing the heights of the great peaks of the Himalaya than by taking very careful angles of elevation to them from a station whose height is accurately known and whose distance from the peaks observed has been calculated. Though such observers as Colebrook, Webb, and Herbert had taken such angles, their distances from the peaks were often at fault

71

and their calculated heights depended on the accuracy of the heights of their observation stations, which often depended on their barometers. Even to-day when aneroids carried by climbers are much superior to those of the past, heights recorded by them are rarely accurate within a few hundred feet, since they are dependent on the height of the base station at which they are set, and on a steady barometric pressure unaffected by the weather during a climb. Any worsening of the weather must invalidate the reading, as will any jar to the instrument. I have known my aneroid give a wrong altitude by over a thousand feet in adverse circumstances. It is for this reason that many climbers have over-estimated the height reached on a mountain when they turned back in deteriorating weather and with a 'falling barometer.'

The heights of the great peaks are not yet exact. They are as precise as scientific observation can make them, and on these values most of the topographical heights in distant parts of the Himalaya are based. Corrections were made for atmospheric refraction, but there are other uncertainties, such as the deflection of the plumb-line. The Survey of India has been investigating these uncertainties for over a hundred years and has wisely refused to alter the accepted heights until such time as the values are more or less final.[1]

Before Sir George Everest retired in 1843, he had initiated other meridional series of triangulation running from south to north, with connecting series from east to west and along both coasts. It was left to his right-hand man, Andrew Waugh, who succeeded him, to carry on his great work and to link up the northern ends by two primary series: the North-Eastern Himalaya series and the North-Western. These were observed between the years 1846 and 1855, and the work entailed considerable hardship which the Surveyor General shared with his officers, several of whom died of jungle fever and malaria in the deadly Terai tracts of marsh and jungle near the Himalayan foothills.

[1] A more technical note on this subject is given in Appendix B (page 348). See also the paper by Dr. J. de Graaff Hunter, F.R.S. 'Heights and Names of Mount Everest and other Peaks,' in *Occasional Notes of the Royal Astronomical Society*, No. 15, October 1953 (Vol. 3).

The mightiest of the Himalayan peaks are visible from the principal stations of the North-Eastern series and were fixed by precise measurements with the great theodolites. Seventy-nine of the highest, many of them in forbidden Nepal, were fixed, among them 'No. XV,' which on computation in 1852 took the place of Dhaulagiri (XLII) and Kangchenjunga (VIII) as the highest known mountain in the world.[1]

Up till then it had escaped notice, since from the south it appears merely as one of an array of summits some of which almost obscured it. Searching enquiries were made without finding any name for the mountain either in Nepal or Tibet.

The name *Mount Everest* was not given to this peak until 1865 when all efforts to find a local name had been fruitless. It was proposed by the Surveyor General, Sir Andrew Waugh, who was best able to assess the merits of his great predecessor, supported by Sir Roderick Murchison, President of the Royal Geographical Society, and it received the cordial approval of the Government of India. The name *Devadhunga* suggested in 1855 by Hodgson, a political officer in Nepal, was found to be spurious and unknown to the Nepalese. *Gauri Sankar,* suggested in the same year by Hermann Schlagintweit, was the name of another mountain mis-identified by him for Everest; the true Gauri Sankar, observed by the Great Trigonometrical Survey as Peak XX, has a height of 23,440 feet, and is thirty-six miles distant from Everest. Names found subsequently in Tibet, such as *Chomo Lungma, Chomolung* and *Chama-lung,* or in Nepal, such as *Mahalungur Himal,* refer to the district or range rather than to the peak itself. Tibetan scholars have found in sacred writings descriptive expressions for it, such as *Mi-thik Dgu-thik Bya-phur Long-nga,* or its variation *Mi-ti Gu-ti Cha-pu Long-nga* ('You cannot see the summit from near it, but you can see the summit from nine directions, and a bird which flies as high as the summit goes blind'), but no Tibetan would recognize these names. Surely after a hundred years the world should be content with 'Everest.'[2]

[1] The early designations of some of the highest peaks are given in Appendix A (page 346).

[2] Sir Sidney Burrard: *Mount Everest and its Tibetan Names* (Survey of India Prof. Paper No. 26) 1931; *Sketch of the Geography &c.,* 2nd Edition, 1933.

In the words of Sir Clements Markham, geographer to the India Office: Sir George Everest on his retirement

had completed one of the most stupendous works in the whole history of science. No scientific man ever had a grander monument to his memory than the Great Meridional Arc of India. Everest's was a creative genius. The whole conception of the survey, as it now exists, was the creation of his brain.[1]

A legend has grown up in recent years and has gained some currency in the popular press, particularly in India, that one day in 1852 the Bengali chief computer, Radhanath Sikhdar, rushed into the room of Sir Andrew Waugh and exclaimed breathlessly 'Sir, I have discovered the highest mountain in the world.' This story has been critically examined by Sir Sidney Burrard and is without foundation. He is supported by Dr. de Graaff Hunter, F.R.S., the past Director and by B. L. Gulatee, the present Director of the Geodetic and Training Circle in the Survey of India.[2] In any event the discovery was a joint enterprise by observers in the field and computers in the office.

With the completion of these two series of triangulation Sir Andrew Waugh turned his attention to the detailed survey of the mountains. The death of Ranjit Singh in 1839, the disaster at Kabul in 1841, the conquest of Sind two years later, and the Sikh Wars of 1845 and 1848, followed by the annexation of the Punjab, opened up a large tract of country to British administration, at a time when one of the greatest Governor Generals, Lord Dalhousie, was at the helm.

With the completion of the triangulation through the Punjab the scientific survey of Kashmir was taken up, and extended to Ladakh, Lahul, and Spiti. Chains of primary triangulation were observed across the Pir Panjal into the Vale of Kashmir, across the Great Himalaya to the Indus at Skardu and up the Indus to the borders of Tibet near Hanle; they were connected with other first-class work in the Kumaun Himalaya, and tied together by secondary and minor triangulation. A great number of subsidiary points were fixed and on these was based the detailed survey.

[1] Clements R. Markham, C.B., F.R.S.: *A Memoir on the Indian Surveys.* 2nd Edition (London, 1878), 94.
[2] B. L. Gulatee: 'Mount Everest—Its Name and Height.' *H.J.* xvii (1952) 135.

It must be remembered that mountaineering in the technical sense was unknown in India in those days, and was a very happy-go-lucky pursuit. The earlier travellers had blazed new trails, forced unknown passes and brought back sketches of their routes; they were explorers venturing into new country 'to see what lay beyond.' They did not go out of their way to climb high mountains, and I can find few, if any, of them who without a shadow of doubt went above 20,000 feet. Ice-axes, pitons, and alpine ropes were unknown.

During the new mountain survey, precision theodolites and other scientific instruments—heavier and more cumbersome than they are to-day—were carried up the mountains; huts and cairns were built on or near the summits; in some cases tracks were hewn out of the mountain-sides so that the great twelve-inch theodolite, carried by two men and slung on a pole between them, could reach the summit. Men were trained to carry the instruments with care so that they received no jar and remained in adjustment.

From the principal stations subsidiary observations were made deep into the more enclosed valleys and to higher peaks. By 1862 no fewer than thirty-seven mountains over 20,000 feet were climbed and observed from with the theodolite, and five above 21,000 feet. Many others, only identifiable by a close examination of the original field sheets, are known to have been climbed by the surveyors while reconnoitring for stations, or to complete the detail, and by native *khalasis,* trained and guided by European assistants. The world's altitude record, so far as we know, was held for about twenty years by one such *khalasi,* engaged by the Survey of India on a salary of six rupees a month (about twelve shillings), who carried a signal pole in 1860 to the top of Shilla in the Zaskar range east of Spiti, 23,050 feet above the sea. He did not know its height; and we do not know his name![1]

When the detailed topographical survey followed the triangulation, surveyors set up their plane-tables on the summits and shoulders of other mountains. More than fifty years afterwards, cairns and other traces of their work were found by later surveyors, though very few of the earlier ascents were recorded at the time.

[1] Dr. Longstaff in 1908 first called attention to this interesting record. The height has recently been disputed (*The Mountain World,* 1954, page 221).

Many devoted men were engaged on this work, but only a few can be mentioned here. Of these the most outstanding were two great men: Captain T. G. Montgomerie and Captain H. H. Godwin-Austen, both then in their prime.

Montgomerie, an Engineer officer, was the brain and organizer behind the whole survey of Kashmir, as well as a fine individual triangulator. He planned the network of stations that covered the mountains, and himself did much of the preliminary reconnaissance. At Haramukh, a mountain in Kashmir near the Great Himalaya, over 16,000 feet in height, he first saw in 1856 the giants of the distant Karakoram, and from the station on a lower summit of this mountain (16,001) G. Shelverton in 1857 took the first observations to them.[1] On this occasion Shelverton camped for a week at the station summit, waiting for the weather to clear. When I revisited his station in 1911 to repeat and add to his observations I found his raised platform, fourteen feet square, still intact, with his finely chiselled markstone firmly in position; nearby was a ruined stone shelter in the corner of which was a human skeleton.

Montgomerie and Shelverton recognized the great height of the Karakoram mountains and were struck by the immense pyramid of one which appeared to be the highest, but they could attach no names and did not know for certain whether they were within Kashmir territory or not. That they were in the Karakoram is proved by the entry in their angle-books by the designations K1, K2, K3, etc., up to K32. When the observations were computed in 1858, K2 was found to be the second highest mountain known—28,250 feet. It still retains that position.[2]

Godwin-Austen, an officer in the old 24th Foot (now the South Wales Borderers), had already seen service during the Burmese War in 1852, and was A.D.C. to General Reed in Peshawar in 1856 when he was recommended to assist Montgomerie. He joined the latter at

[1] Survey stations are not always placed on the highest point of a mountain, because of the difficulty of carrying up instruments. Montgomerie is believed to have climbed the highest peak, 16,872 feet, but the first *recorded* ascent of this was made by Dr. E. Neve and Mr. G. W. Millais in 1899; these were followed by C. G. Bruce and A. L. Mumm in 1907. All the five summits, 'Station,' 'Western,' 'Northern,' 'Middle,' and 'Eastern,' have since been climbed more than once.

[2] For a note on the height of K2 see Appendix B (page 348). See also frontispiece.

Manganwar, a survey station in Kashmir in 1857, that stormy year for India.

When the Mutiny broke out, the local authorities were at first inclined to refuse supplies to the surveyors, who were already in difficulties. Sir John Lawrence, the wise Governor of the Punjab, advised Montgomerie to carry on as long as possible, to show the aged Maharaja Gulab Singh that the outcome of the Mutiny was not in doubt. Montgomerie became an unofficial political adviser to the Maharaja until the crisis had passed, and at the same time supervised the survey. When Gulab Singh died on 2 August 1857 Montgomerie won over Ranbir Singh who succeeded and, in spite of occasional alarms caused by bands of marauding rebels who entered Kashmir, the survey was not seriously interrupted, largely through Montgomerie's personal influence. Because of his loyalty to the British Raj, Ranbir Singh was confirmed in his position after the Mutiny.

During these exciting events Godwin-Austen was surveying the Kaj Nag range not far from the Wular Lake and the Pir Panjal in southern Kashmir. He was the first to put Gulmarg, the well-known summer resort of later years, on the map. In 1858 and 1859 he was in eastern Kashmir and Jammu, and was then ordered to rejoin his regiment in England. Probably he never did so, for he was in Kashmir in 1860 when he surveyed the Shigar and Saltoro valleys of the Lesser Karakoram.

By this time the position and great height of K2 were known. In 1861 Godwin-Austen crossed the Skoro La (16,644) to the Braldoh valley, explored and mapped the great glacier region comprising the Chogo Lungma, Kero Lungma (which he ascended to the Nushik La and so discovered the Hispar glacier), Biafo, Panmah, and Baltoro. He was the first to ascend most of these glaciers, to discover the Baltoro approaches to K2, and to sketch its topography.[1]

Godwin-Austen was ideally built for this survey, though he had no knowledge of technical mountaineering: he carried no rope except as an aid to crossing streams and had no ice-axe. Slight and extremely hardy, with little weight to carry, he had immense endurance and great enthusiasm; he was also an artist of considerable talent. His original survey of these regions is a beautiful example of

[1] S. of I. Synoptical Vol. VII (Dehra Dun, 1877).

the surveyor's art of those days, though it lost much in reproduction. Fifty years later he told me that he had learnt from studying the topographical drawings of the old French School, and that he drew the topography as true to nature as possible. 'I was always mapping with a geological eye,' he said, 'and that makes a man look well at the country.'

In 1862 and 1863 Godwin-Austen sketched the upper Chang-chenmo and northern border of the Pangong district in eastern Ladakh, up to the Tibetan frontier near Rudok. He was often over 20,000 feet during these years. His journal for 1863 was printed by the Government of India and included a valuable physical description of lake Pangong and its basin. Before the close of the year, however, he was sent to the other end of the Himalaya to survey the country between Darjeeling and Punaka and elsewhere with the Bhutan Field Force; he also made some rapid but useful reconnaissances on the north-east frontier among the then unvisited Dafla tribes. Fever contracted on these surveys undermined his health and caused his premature retirement. Though a sick man when he left India, he recovered completely, worked on many branches of the natural sciences, was elected to the Royal Society, and died in 1924 at the age of ninety.

Godwin-Austen was a great explorer and probably the greatest mountaineer of his day. In 1888 at a meeting of the Royal Geographical Society in London, General J. T. Walker proposed that the name Godwin-Austen should be given to the mountain K2. But he did not discover it, as has often been stated; and for this reason and because successive Surveyor Generals and the Government of India have been unwilling to label natural features with the names of individuals, Walker's proposal was never accepted in India nor by the Royal Geographical Society in England. Mountaineers should be grateful for this policy and that these magnificent mountains are not plastered with exotic personal names. Everest is the only exception.[1]

There were other surveyors and triangulators who ought to be mentioned if space allowed: E. C. Ryall, for instance, who in 1861 surveyed in the Saltoro and other regions adjacent to Godwin-Austen, and several who worked in the Kumaun Himalaya.

[1] *Proc. R.G.S.* x (1888) 516.

1   Sir George Everest, C.B., F.R.S.
Superintendent Great Trigonometrical Survey of India 1823 – 1843;
Surveyor General of India 1830 – 1843

2 Rai Bahadur Kishen Singh
– The Explorer A.K.

3 The Explorer Kinthup.

4 Captain T. G. Montgomerie R.E.

5 Younghusband's party crossing the Mustagh Pass in 1887.

6 Captain H. H. Godwin Austen.

7 Sir Francis Younghusband.

8  Martin Conway.  9  General C. G. Bruce.

10 (large photo) K2 and Broad Peak from Concordia – the junction of the Baltoro and Godwin Austen glaciers. 11 (inset) Chogolisa, or Bride Peak, from the Kaberi Glacier.

The first climbers to attempt K2:

12 (above) The 1902 Eckenstein Expedition that attempted the North-East Ridge – V. Wesseley, Oscar Eckenstein, Dr. Jacot Guillarmod, Aleister Crowley, Hans Pfannl and Gu Knowles.

13 (left) The Duke of Abruzzi, leader the 1909 expedition that reconnoitred, surveyed and photographed the surrounding glaciers and all possible routes on the mountain from the Balto approach, before attempting the Eckenstein route (the diagonal foreground ridge in photo 16).

14  15  16
Members of the
Abruzzi party – Filippo
de Fillipi and Vittorio
Sella (insets) and
Sella's celebrated
photograph of K2
from Windy Gap.

17   The Rakhiot flank of Nanga Parbat
from above the Indus Valley.
18   (inset left) Dr. Norman Collie.
19   (inset right) A. F. Mummery.

The 1895 Mummery/
Hastings/Collie Nanga
Parbat Expedition:

20 21 The Diamirai
Face of Nanga Parbat.
Mummery and Raghobir
Thapa reached the top of
the faint rib leading
between the two hanging
glaciers on the upper
photo. The upper section
of the face is shown in
the smaller picture.

22 Freshfield's Zemu Glacier camp during his circuit of the Kangchenjunga group in 1899.

23 Kangchenjunga from the east – the 1929 and 1931 expeditions tackled the right-hand ridge.

24   Nanda Devi from the Bagani Pass – guarded by the Sanctuary Wall (inner curtain).

25   (left) Tom Longstaff.   26   (right) Longstaff's photo of Alexis and Henri Brocherel and Subadar Kabir nearing the summit of Trisul after their 6000ft summit push in 1907.

27 (above) Haramukh in Kashmir from the air.

28 (left) An Indo-Russian junction station, Sar-bulak, Tagablumbash Pamir, 1913.

29  Members of the Survey of India party that competed the India part of the
Indo–Russian triangulation of 1913: Lt. R. W. G. Hingston, V. D. E. Collins,
Lt. Kenneth Mason, C. S. McInnes.

30   Opening the Khardung Pass with yaks north of Leh, Ladakh.

31   Mrs. Fanny Bullock Workman and her
husband, William Hunter Workman.

32   C. F. Meade and Pierre Blanc with
unknown porters.

33   Dr. Arthur Neve.

34   Dr. A. M. Kellas.

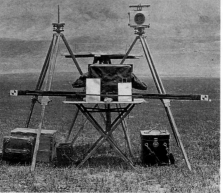

35 Making blood observations at 1,700ft, 1912.

36 (inset) Mason's survey equipment.

37 (overleaf) The monsoon about to burst as seen from Mussoorie.

An interesting example of the difficulties in the Kumaun Himalaya, when little was known of the vagaries of the climate, is the connexion between the surveys of the upper Bhagirathi and Baspa valleys, that is, between the headwaters of the Jumna and the upper Sutlej. In the early summer of 1853, J. Dyer, an assistant in the Survey, observed from several high stations in the upper Bhagirathi, but failed to ascend or take his survey across the Great Himalaya near the Nela pass. A second attempt after the monsoon was made in October from both sides of the watershed, by Mulheran from the Bhagirathi side, and by Shelverton and Dyer from the Baspa. Low temperatures and early winter snow thwarted them. A third effort in May 1854 was successful when W. H. Johnson, one of the most active of survey assistants, placed a triangulation station on the Great Himalaya at 19,069 feet, a quarter of a mile east of the Nela pass.

Weather is the ultimate deciding factor of all successful high-altitude observations, since the surveyor has not merely to reconnoitre and choose the best stations, and climb them with his instruments, but he must often camp on or near them for several days in bad weather, in order to seize a fleeting chance when his station is clear of cloud and when there are no clouds on the neighbouring stations and peaks which he wishes to observe. In unsettled weather many fruitless and exasperating climbs are made before success is won, and such work requires endurance and infinite patience.

Johnson had an exceptionally interesting career, even among his contemporaries in the Himalaya. Born and educated in India, the son of English parents, he had already attracted notice in the Great Trigonometrical Survey before completing the work described above. He was the most indefatigable of observers during the triangulation of Kashmir from 1857 till 1863. His work was in the most difficult parts of the country and more than once he was detached to help other observers in difficulties. In 1861 two of his stations were above 20,000 feet; in 1862, seven. For sixty years four of his stations were the highest triangulation stations in the world.

Unfortunately his excess of zeal was his undoing. He had already crossed the Karakoram pass in 1864 and returned from Suget when he applied for permission to explore farther into Central Asia. Hearing privately that his request was likely to be refused, because of the disturbed state of Chinese Turkestan, he secretly borrowed 15,000 rupees in 1865, crossed the K'un-lun range into Chinese Turkestan and reached Khotan, where he stayed with the rebel ruler Habibullah. He had difficulty in leaving and getting back to India. The adventurous spirit behind this exploit was wholly admirable, but unfortunately his survey work was faulty. General J. T. Walker, then Superintendent of the Great Trigonometrical Survey, did his best to overlook the matter and successfully persuaded the Government to pay Johnson's debts and ransom to the extent of 16,400 rupees (over £1,500). Johnson expected greater recognition and reward, and unwisely resented the very mild rebuke that he 'ought not to have crossed the frontiers of India without the permission of the Government.' He resigned from the Great Trigonometrical Survey and accepted the more remunerative post of Governor of Ladakh. He was assassinated while holding that post.

Among Johnson's claims on his return from Khotan was one that he had climbed E61, 23,890 feet, a mountain of the K'un-lun range south of Khotan. The claim was disallowed and suppressed by General Walker after a careful examination of Johnson's survey; but it received considerable support among mountaineers in England, among them Douglas Freshfield, Godwin-Austen, and Norman Collie, who did not know all the facts. There is no doubt whatever that General Walker was correct and that Johnson was mistaken in his claim to have climbed E61, the summit of which is still untrodden. He was a brilliant triangulator and impervious to hardship and danger, but his detailed survey both on this journey and in the previous year in the neighbourhood of the Karakoram pass was much below his previous standard.[1]

The opening up of the Himalaya after the Sikh Wars led to other journeys of importance. Henry Strachey reached Manasarowar and Rakas Tal in 1846. Alexander Cunningham travelled extensively as Commissioner appointed to examine the boundaries of Gulab Singh's dominions, including his recent conquests in Ladakh, with the newly

---

[1] *Alpine Journals* xii (1884–6) 58–60; xix (1899–1900) 49. See also my paper 'Johnson's "Suppressed Ascent" of E61' and Sir Aurel Stein's supplementary note in *A.J.* xxxiv (1921). Also Wood: *Explorations in the Eastern Karakoram and the Upper Yarkand Valley* (Dehra Dun, 1922) pages 28 ff.

acquired British territories and with Tibet. With him in 1847 and 1848 were Henry Strachey and Dr. Thomas Thomson, surgeon to the commission and a keen naturalist. Together they covered much of Zaskar, almost the whole of Rupshu and eastern Ladakh, and much of Baltistan. Cunningham was the first to note the continuity of the Zaskar range and to distinguish it from the axis of the Great Himalaya; Strachey discovered the Siachen glacier at the head of the Nubra, but though he ascended it for about two miles, he failed to realize its great length; Thomson was the first European to cross the Saser pass (17,480) between the Nubra and the upper Shyok, and to reach, though he did not cross, the Karakoram pass (18,605). All were close observers; their writings have been the basis of much subsequent work, and considerable help to their successors. Henry Strachey's brother Richard also visited the Kumaun Himalaya and reached the Tibetan lakes. His interests were mainly geological and botanical; of the 2000 species of plants collected, thirty-two, discovered for the first time, bear his name.[1]

Of the growing number of Himalayan travellers of this period certainly the most important in the eastern Himalaya was Joseph Hooker, the great botanist and naturalist. To him we owe a debt for opening the delights of travel in Sikkim, for he spent most of the years 1848 and 1849 there and left a charming and vivid account of his travels in his *Himalayan Journals*. He encountered many political and transport difficulties, overcame most of them, but with his companion, Dr. Campbell, then superintendent at Darjeeling, was seized and detained as a prisoner at Tumlong under the orders of Namgay, the chief minister of Sikkim. As a result of this outrage on a British official the part of Sikkim south of the Great Rangit river, including the Terai from the Mechi to the Tista—afterwards a district of fertile tea-gardens—was annexed by the East India Company. This district had been taken from Sikkim by the Nepalese but had been restored on British insistence after the Nepalese war of 1814-16, in return for the cession of Darjeeling. Hooker was not a

---

[1] Cunningham, A.: *Ladak, Physical, statistical, and historical*, with *Notices of the surrounding Countries* (London, 1854); Thomson, T.: *Western Himalaya and Tibet* (London, 1852); Strachey, H.: *J.R.G.S.* xxiii (1853) 'Physical Geography of Western Tibet'; Strachey, R.: *J.R.G.S.* (1851) 'Physical Geography of Kumaon and Garhwal in the Himalaya Mountains, and of the adjoining parts of Tibet.'

surveyor, but his small sketch-map remained in use until it was supplanted by that of T. T. Carter, a young Engineer lieutenant attached to Colonel J. C. Gawler's force in 1861.

The Himalayan journeys of the three Schlagintweit brothers, Adolf, Hermann, and Robert, between 1854 and 1858, under the general direction of the East India Company, cannot be easily summarized. Many, if not most, of their routes had been taken earlier by other travellers, and their deductions were not always correct; but the scope of their investigations was so wide that in some matters they laid the foundations of future research. Their studies included geology, climatology, ethnology, magnetology; they took astronomical observations, investigated the meaning of Tibetan words, and observed some of the great peaks. Between them they added to our knowledge of the extreme north-eastern corner of Ladakh, Adolf crossing the desolate plains of Lingzitang and Aksaichin to the Karakash river, and thence to Yarkand. He was murdered at Kashgar on 26 August 1857.

Both Richard Strachey and the Schlagintweits made interesting explorations in the Kumaun Himalaya before the regular topographical surveys reached the region. The Kamet group lies to the north of the Great Himalayan axis in the extreme north of Garhwal and on the watershed between the upper Saraswati and Dhauli rivers, not far from the Tibetan border (map page 119). Richard Strachey first determined their approximate heights in 1848.[1] The Schlagintweits named them Western, Central, and Eastern Ibi Gamin and Mana. These are identifiable on modern maps from Major Osmaston's surveys of 1936-8 as Mukut Parbat (23,760), Kamet (25,447), Abi Gamin (24,130), and Mana (23,860). The Schlagintweits claim to have reached a height of over 22,000 feet, probably on Abi Gamin;[2] but little was known of the higher topography until the Survey of India under E. C. Ryall worked there in 1874-7, when I. S. Pocock set up his plane-table at 22,040 feet on the eastern slopes of Abi Gamin.[3]

[1] J.A.S.B. xix (1850); J.R.G.S. xxiii (1853) 25.
[2] A.J. xxxiii (1920-21) 72; G.J. xxxi (1908) 363.
[3] S. of I. Syn. Vol. XXXV, page xxxiv; Survey of India: General Report, 1874-5; A.J. xxv (1910-11) 401; A.J. xxxiii (1920-21) 72.

From now onwards more and more travellers went into the Himalaya for sport or science, and it becomes less easy to select those who added to our knowledge. The results of the Survey of India labours were published in the 'Indian Atlas' series on the scale of four miles to the inch. The mountains were shown by hachures. The publication of these sheets was hailed as a magnificent achievement, as indeed it was, but it must always be remembered that many of the surveyors were expressly instructed not to spend too much time exploring uninhabited wastes and higher altitudes, so that the more inaccessible regions were not rigorously surveyed. All the more important mountains had, however, been precisely fixed for position and height, and these were the only maps available for mountaineers when serious climbing began in the Himalaya about twenty years later. There is another even more lasting heritage from the old travellers: they laid down a tradition of sympathy, fair-dealing and trust among Himalayan peoples which has been an inestimable boon to their successors.

# 4. Pundit Explorers and the Years 1865–1885

BY 1864 the surveys west of Nepal had reached the confines of Tibet and China, and British surveyors and travellers were forbidden to cross the frontiers. But the years 1865 to 1885 are no less romantic in exploration than the years before. Our trans-frontier maps were either a blank or based on d'Anville and travellers' tales. Gilgit, Chilas and Chitral on the north-west were unexplored; Yarkand though visited, was a hundred miles out of position on the map; Central Tibet was quite unknown; the position of Lhasa was largely conjectural in longitude; only one point on the Tsangpo, Shigatse, had been charted with any approach to accuracy.[1]

Geographers speculated on these matters and wanted to know more; travellers ached to find out. On the other hand Chinese Turkestan was still in a turmoil after the Tungan rebellion which had broken out in 1863; Tibet was more than ever exclusive, aloof, and watchful on her frontiers; the border states on the north and west were openly predatory; Nepal was barred against intrusion; Sikkim was suspicious and sulky; Bhutan unhelpful and un-cooperative. Far away to the north-west was Russia, between whom and Britain 'the Great Game in Asia' was in full play.

Walker and Montgomerie of the Great Trigonometrical Survey now set about to train Indian explorers who might lift the veil. Through Major E. Smyth, the British Education Officer in Kumaun, a great traveller in his district, Montgomerie selected two Bhotias, Nain Singh and his cousin Mani Singh,[2] of the village of Milam, north-east of Nanda Devi. They were nephew and son of Deb Singh,

---

[1] By Samuel Turner in 1783 (page 61).

[2] Mani Singh, 'GM' or the 'Second Pundit' was enlisted as the brother of Nain Singh, and Montgomerie refers to him as a younger brother in the report on Nain Singh's first journey. I am convinced that Nain Singh was the son of Lata Budha and Kalian Singh was his brother; Kishen Singh and Mani Singh were the sons of Deb or Devi Singh. All four were the grandsons of Dhamu. The word *bhai* covers all.

who with Bir Singh had befriended Moorcroft and Hearsey in 1812 at Daba (or Dapa) Dzong in Tibet. Both had travelled with the Schlagintweits, and were known to be resourceful and intelligent. At the time Nain Singh was recruited into the Survey he held the post of headmaster of the small vernacular school at Milam, and was probably about thirty-five years of age.[1]

The two men were brought to Dehra Dun, given nearly two years' training in practical reconnaissance and route survey, taught the use of the sextant and pocket compass, how to recognize the stars and observe them, to take heights by boiling water, to count and record their paces and to keep accurate notes of routes. Being of hardy Bhotia stock and living not far from the Tibetan border, they were closely allied to the Tibetans in race, custom, and speech. Their village Milam, about 11,200 feet above the sea, was a mart to which Tibetan traders came each year in August and September.

Nain Singh and Mani Singh were first despatched through Kumaun towards the end of 1864, but failed to pass the Tibetan border, since they were too well known. They then tried through Nepal whence, after months of disappointment and trying various disguises, Nain Singh succeeded in crossing into Tibet. Mani Singh was unsuccessful and returned through Nepal (map page 32).

Nain Singh passed through the Great Himalaya to Rasua Garhi, where the Tibetan frontier now is, reached Kyirong (Kerun Shahr), crossed into the head of the Buri Gandaki, and over the Tsangpo watershed by the No La, 16,600 feet. At Tra-dom he joined a caravan going to Lhasa, and reached that place on 10 January 1866, having surreptitiously paced his route all the way and observed latitudes with his sextant. After three months he left with the caravan westwards, repacing his route to Tra-dom and on to Manasarowar, whence he crossed into Kumaun, having left his sick servant Chumbel and his watch in pawn with the caravan to be recovered later. Nain Singh's journey of 1200 miles was full of interest and incident, and he brought back details for a map of the southern trade-route of

[1] Accounts of the more important journeys of the 'Pundits' appeared in *General Reports* of the Survey of India and other official papers. They were collected and republished in *Records of the Survey of India*, viii, 2 vols. (Dehra Dun, 1915). There was also a considerable amount of unpublished material and correspondence about the 'pundits' in Dehra Dun which I examined in 1920.

Tibet, and of the Tsangpo's course for 600 miles, besides a most valuable report.

Meanwhile other Indians, Himalayan by birth, were being trained. Collectively they became known to the outside world as 'the Pundits,' though as time went on all were by no means Hindus or Buddhists. Some elected the guise of traders, some went as pilgrims or lamas, others as Moslem holy men. They were taught the rudimentary use of drugs and simple remedies; sometimes the 'mullahs' carried special compasses that pointed to Mecca. 'Lamas' carried rosaries and prayer-wheels. The survey-pattern rosary had a hundred beads instead of the usual Tibetan number, a hundred and eight; every tenth bead was slightly larger than the others; a bead was counted after a hundred paces, the larger ones recording a thousand. With due piety the lama murmured the Buddhist prayer, *Om mani padme hum*—'Oh Jewel of the Lotus'—turned his prayer wheel, dropped a bead to count his distance, and was safe from interruption. His notes were kept within the prayer wheel.

To my generation the story of Kim is fascinating. Kipling has completely caught the spirit of the pundit period, when Hurree Babu, the Pathan horse-dealer, and the Indian Civilian were real and adventurous characters, when the Great Game in Asia was on, and when the frontier mists were almost impenetrable. These characters are not overdrawn, and Kim himself is a type of youth born in India, adventurous, loyal and devoted, who learnt to do great things.

Nain Singh, the first and greatest of the pundit explorers, helped in the training of others, among whom was his cousin Kishen Singh, son of Deb Singh, later to become famous as AK.

Their explorations were secret. During the period of their travels they never used their own names and were known by numbers, designations, or initials; where initials were used they were generally, but not always, the last sounded letter and the first. Nain Singh was 'No. 1,' or 'the chief pundit,' or simply 'The Pundit'; his brother Kalian Singh was GK, and his cousin Kishen Singh, enlisted as Krishna became AK. Kishen Singh's brother Mani Singh was GM. It was a famous family.[1] Among the Moslem explorers, Ata

[1] A descendant is in the Survey of India at the present time.

Muhammad was known as 'the Mullah'; Mirza Shuja as 'the Mirza'; Abdul Subhan as NA or 'the Munshi.'

One of the Hindu pundits, Hari Ram, 'No. 9' or MH, made the first circuit of the Everest group in 1871. Starting from Darjeeling, he crossed the Singalila ridge to Taplejung just above the Tamur Kosi, followed that river to its source, partly by the route taken by Hooker in 1848. In August he crossed the main Himalayan axis by the Tipta La, 16,740 feet, and reached Tashirakha, where he was suspected and stopped. Luck favoured him, because, though totally ignorant of medicine, he chanced his arm, and to his own surprise effected a miraculous cure of a notable's wife, thereby earning protection and permission to proceed. Hari Ram then made a secret route traverse to Shigatse over unknown ground; and from there came south-westward to Sakya Dzong, explored and mapped the Phung Chu to Tingri Dzong, and crossed the Thong La (17,981) into the head of the Po Chu, the Bhote Kosi branch of the Sun Kosi. From Nyenam in October he followed the difficult course of this river through the Great Himalaya to Katmandu and reached India before the end of the year.

Montgomerie who had despatched Hari Ram had urged on him the importance of finding out local names for mountains. Hari Ram found no name for Everest anywhere in Tibet and reported that 'neither the Bhotias (i.e. Tibetans) nor the Gurkhas seem to have specific names for remarkable peaks,' though in a few cases they gave the name of the nearest village. The only exception was Kangchenjunga, which the Gurkhas of the Tamur Kosi called 'Kumbhkaran Lungur,' a name later found by the surveyors in Nepal in 1925 to belong more correctly to the section of the Great Himalaya on which stands Makalu.[1]

Hari Ram's next contribution to geography was a journey he made in 1873, when from Pithoragarh in Kumaun he crossed the Kali into Nepal at Bargaon and traversed northern Nepal from west to east as far as the Kali Gandaki near Muktinath; from there he turned north

[1] This problem of names is a very difficult one for surveyors and travellers. In many parts of Nepal, Gurkhas, when asked the name of a distant mountain, will with confidence reply *Dhaulagiri*, meaning 'white mountain.' In the early days of the nineteenth century several of the observations to *Dhaulagiri* were to different mountains. The true Dhaulagiri Himal is west of the Kali Gandaki.

to Tra-dom, where he connected his survey with Nain Singh's traverse of 1865–6. Returning to the Kali Gandaki he traced this river southwards till it emerged from the mountains and reached the Gangetic plain.

Personally I have always considered Kishen Singh, AK, to be as great and bold an explorer as Nain Singh, his cousin and teacher. I pass over his first important journey in 1872, when from Shigatse he made a route traverse north of the Tsangpo, round the shores of Tengri Nor and reached Lhasa from the north. In 1873 and 1874 he was with Forsyth's mission to Yarkand, mention of which is made later. His last great journey began at Darjeeling in April 1878. After reaching Lhasa, he started northwards for Mongolia; he met with desperate hardships in Chang-tang where he was robbed and stripped by bandits. With his faithful servant Chumbel—the same man who had been with Nain Singh in 1865–6—he pushed on and reached the extreme north-west confines of the Chinese province of Kansu, carrying out a route survey all the way. Four years after his departure, when hope of his return had been abandoned, he arrived back in India, worn out, but with complete details of all his travels.

Both the Pundit and AK received honours from the Geographical Societies of Europe, and Nain Singh became a Companion of the Indian Empire. The Indian Government made them generous grants of land. Years afterwards when looking through their files in Dehra Dun I came across a terse remark by the Surveyor General of the time referring to AK: 'accurate, truthful, brave, and highly efficient.' That testimony has been fully endorsed by time.[1]

Though much of their most valuable work was in Tibet and so beyond the scope of this book, no account of Himalayan exploration would be complete without some mention of them, for they set a

[1] In 1933 I received a letter from Captain F. Kingdon Ward from Zayul in eastern Tibet dated 25.5.1933. In it he wrote: 'AK came up here from Rima to Shinden Gompa exactly fifty years ago; but no white man preceded us. AK's report and route survey, however, are excellent. It is hard to find a mistake. I have checked and identified every village he mentions; and it is remarkable how little the valley has changed even in fifty years—the villages even have the same number of houses that they had then. The names, the marches, all are the same . . . We have found AK's work invaluable.'

Some travellers in recent years who have found fault with the 'pundits'' travels should remember that all communities are not so unchanging.

high standard for later generations of fine Indian surveyors, such as Lal Singh and Ram Singh who accompanied Sir Aurel Stein in Central Asia, Sher Jang, a great frontier surveyor, and more recently Afraz Gul Khan who has accompanied a number of travellers to the Karakoram and is probably responsible for a larger area of detailed survey in high mountains than any other surveyor in the world.

The Mohammedan explorers who surveyed mostly on the North-west Frontier and beyond also deserve mention, especially as their work was even more difficult politically. Ata Muhammad, 'the Mullah,' a well-educated Punjabi of Peshawar, versed in Arabic, was the brother of a sapper murdered in Swat in 1869. He was the first to explore the wild gorges of the Indus from the Indian plains to Bunji —the 'route of the hanging chains' recorded by ancient Buddhist pilgrims; he also gave us our first map of Swat in the extreme north-west, the reconnaissance of which he completed in the guise of a timber-merchant. His map was not superseded until after World War I.

Mirza Shuja, 'the Mirza,' had served as a lad under Eldred Pottinger in the siege of Herat. To him we owe the first rough map of northern Afghanistan and the Pamirs. While still employed by the Survey of India he became tutor to the sons of Sher Ali, ruler of Afghanistan. With his son-in-law he was afterwards murdered in Bukhara.

One last story of these men. Though Bogle and Turner had identified the Tsangpo of Tibet with the Brahmaputra of Assam, and almost every explorer, including AK, who had reached Shigatse or Lhasa had brought back similar information; though this was accepted by Montgomerie and other great surveyors in India, doubt was thrown on the matter by geographers in Europe, some holding that the Tsangpo flowed into the Irrawaddy of Burma or the Salween. A Chinese lama of the Darjeeling district was trained as an explorer by Captain H. J. Harman of the Survey of India. He was sent into Tibet in 1880 and told to follow the Tsangpo as far as possible downstream, and then to mark and throw logs into the river. Meanwhile Harman had men posted in Assam to watch for the arrival of the logs. None arrived and after two years the watch was abandoned. In

November 1884 a hill native of Sikkim, Kinthup,[1] who had been an assistant of the lama, returned to India and asked for Captain Harman. Probably because of Harman's death, Kinthup's story attracted no attention for two years, when it was taken down and translated. He told how after visiting Lhasa with the lama, they had followed the Tsangpo down to Gyala, and at Tong-juk Dzong in May 1881 the lama had broken faith, sold him into slavery, and gone to China. Kinthup claimed to have escaped into Pemakoi-chen and to have traced the Tsangpo down to the monastery of Marpung on the Dihang. Here he took refuge from his pursuers, worked for the lamas, and on the pretence of visiting holy places made several journeys of exploration. On one of these he reached Olon, in the Abor country. He had followed the left bank of the river to within about thirty-five miles of the plains of Assam, but was forced to return through Pemakoi-chen and Tibet.

Kinthup was not a trained explorer, and he was illiterate. He enumerated the places he had passed, relying on his memory; a map to illustrate his account was compiled by Colonel Tanner, who believed the man's story, partly because of his description of a rainbow seen at the foot of a great waterfall. It was also accepted by the Surveyor General, though not generally credited outside the Survey of India. Some thirty years later Morshead and Bailey explored the great bend of the Tsangpo gorge and proved the story true. Hardly a place had been forgotten by Kinthup. Sir Sidney Burrard, the Surveyor General, brought Kinthup up to Simla, where he was suitably honoured by the Viceroy for his courage and determination of bygone days.[2]

Captain Harman, mentioned above, began the regular survey of the Sikkim Himalaya in 1878 and penetrated several of its valleys, though he met with considerable opposition from the inhabitants. Surveyors cannot often pick the best seasons for their work; his survey in the moist steamy valleys undermined his health and in 1881 when trying to reach the foot of Kangchenjunga he was forced to

[1] Kinthup had already in 1878 accompanied the explorer GMN, a lama of Pemayangtse monastery in Sikkim, whom Harman had employed as a *munshi* to teach him Tibetan. On this journey they had followed the Tsangpo down to Gyala.

[2] Kinthup acted as 'guide' and chief porter on several of L. A. Waddell's journeys in Sikkim between 1886 and 1896.

give up and take sick leave. It was his departure from India this year that caused the watch for the Tsangpo logs to be abandoned. His successor, H. C. B. Tanner, was responsible for much fine work in this area as triangulator, organizer, and trainer of topographical assistants and explorers, among whom may be mentioned SCD, UG, and RN.

Sarat Chandra Das, 'the Babu' or SCD of Survey of India records and perhaps, as there is some reason to think, one element in the make-up of Kipling's 'Hurree Babu,' worked from 1879 to 1881 between northern Sikkim and Lhasa which he reached in 1881. Ugyen Gyatso of Pemayangtse monastery and a Darjeeling school-master, 'the lama' or UG of the records, travelled by the Tista and Lachung route and the Dongkya La to reach Lhasa by a different route in 1883, south-east of which he made extensive explorations. Rinzin Namgyal, RN, explored several side-valleys in Sikkim and crossed the Kang La into Nepal, where he sketched the Yalung glacier and followed SCD's footsteps to the Jongsong La. He was the first surveyor to map the circuit of Kangchenjunga. These journeys were in the nature of reconnaissances, but rough maps were made from them, and where they were not superseded by the regular surveys by Tanner and his assistant Robert, they were fitted on to them.[1] RN also made considerable additions to our knowledge of Bhutan in 1885-6.

Meanwhile in the Kumaun and Punjab Himalaya travellers and sportsmen began to take advantage of more settled conditions brought about by direct British administration and by advisers posted to help local rulers.

Several journeys of importance took place in the outlying parts of Kashmir. F. Drew, during a residence of nearly nine years in that country, from 1862 to 1871, travelled extensively and described it in great detail.[2] In 1868 Lieutenant G. W. Hayward crossed the Lingzi-tang plains and followed the Karakash valley to Shahidulla. He reached Yarkand and the following year explored the sources of the

---

[1] UG and RN were uncles of Sirdar Bahadur Laden La, a well-known police officer and a keen supporter of the Himalayan Club in its early days. Rai Bahadur Lama Ugyen Gvatso collected while in Lhasa a number of ancient Tibetan fables which I believe were published, though I have been unable to trace them.

[2] *The Jummoo and Kashmir Territories* (London, 1875).

Yarkand river near the Karakoram pass. He was murdered in Yasin in 1870 in an attempt to reach the Darkot pass in order to explore the Pamirs and the Oxus sources.

Robert B. Shaw also reached Yarkand and Kashgar in 1869. He was with Douglas Forsyth's first mission to Kashgar in 1870, succeeded Dr. H. Cayley, who also travelled extensively, as British Joint Commissioner at Leh in 1871, and added greatly to our knowledge of these parts. Forsyth's second mission in 1873-4 was a more elaborate affair. With him were Colonel T. E. Gordon as second-in-command, Captain H. Trotter of the Great Trigonometrical Survey, Captains J. Biddulph and E. F. Chapman, both of whom were given some elementary survey training before leaving, and four Indian surveyors or explorers, including two of the most promising 'pundits,' Kishen Singh and Abdul Subhan (NA or 'the Munshi'). Dr. H. Bellew went as doctor and naturalist, and Dr. F. Stolicza, who had already studied the geology of Kashmir, as geologist. It might truly be said that this was the father of several future expeditions which combined a comprehensive programme of scientific investigation with exploration pure and simple.

Most of the work of this expedition lay beyond the mountains dealt/with here, but it may be mentioned that our knowledge of the Pamirs and of Chinese Turkestan benefited greatly from the travels of its various members, and much information was collected about the routes across the K'un-lun and mountains east of the Karakoram pass. All members contributed to the growing literature of the Karakoram, as did other travellers, such as G. Henderson and A. O. Hume.

It is tempting to describe the work of British officers and surveyors (such as Sir Thomas Holdich, who had an almost unbroken service on the N.W. Frontier from 1878 till 1898) who with British columns in small frontier campaigns and in the more important Afghan wars gradually surveyed this borderland beyond the Indus. Many of their exploits were in the nature of 'tip-and-run' surveys and had little sanction from above. Holdich could not bear to see a blank on his map in these parts. Very little was made public at the time and only occasionally did the world outside hear of the further doings of men like Abdul Subhan, NA, who after serving with Holdich during the siege of Sherpur took service with the Amir at Kabul, or William Watts McNair who in 1883 penetrated Kafiristan disguised as a Moslem doctor. Such men were not encouraged to write or talk of their deeds.

W. W. Graham was the first traveller to come out from England with the main object of climbing mountains 'more for sport and adventures than for the advancement of scientific knowledge' as he admitted on his return to the Royal Geographical Society in 1884.[1] Graham took with him Joseph Imboden, a Swiss guide from St. Niklaus, and first visited Sikkim in March 1883. From Dzongri which he reached on 28 March he crossed the Singalila ridge by the Kang La into Nepal, climbed a peak 'rather over 20,000 feet' on 30 March, was back at Dzongri on the 31st, and crossed the Guicha La to the Talung glacier on 1 April; from here he reckoned that the circuit of Kangchenjunga could be completed within nine days, involving 'one pass of 16,000 feet, one double one of 16,000 and 17,000 feet, and one of nearly 20,000 feet.' After this early venture Imboden went sick with fever and had to go back to Switzerland; Graham replaced him by Emil Boss of Grindelwald and the guide Ulrich Kauffmann for his summer journey which followed (map page 38).

With these two Graham was at Joshimath in the Kumaun Himalaya by 6 July. He made a gallant attempt to penetrate the Rishiganga gorge with the intention of climbing Nanda Devi; the difficulties he encountered forced him to withdraw. He then attempted to climb Dunagiri (23,184), and estimated that he reached a height of about 22,700 feet. He was forced to retreat by bad weather, having suffered little from the height (map page 116).

He next claims to have ascended A21, now known as Changabang (22,520), with no great difficulty, but his description of this mountain is so utterly at variance with its true form, that there is very little doubt that he was mistaken. His altitudes of other points are much greater than the true heights, and it would have been quite impossible for him to reach Changabang from Dibrugheta in the time stated, even if he had crossed the Ramani glacier, of which he makes no

[1] *Proc. R.G.S.* vi (1884) 429. See also *A.J.* xi (1882-4) 402; xii (1884-6) 25. A fuller account appeared in *Good Words,* Jan., Feb., and March 1884.

mention. It is more likely that the summit he reached was on the southern or Hanuman ridge of Dunagiri, possibly that shown on the latest maps at 19,210 feet.[1]

After this campaign in the Nanda Devi region, he was back at Naini Tal (a '150-mile tramp') on 12 August, at Darjeeling on 25th, and at Dzongri on 2 September. From here he explored Pandim from all sides, climbed Jubonu on 1 October, and from a camp at an estimated height of 18,500 feet claimed to have climbed Kabru, 24,002 feet, on 8 October 'with no great difficulty,' apparently by the south-east face in three days!

Great doubt has been thrown on the validity of this last claim. Colonel Tanner of the Survey of India and Robert his assistant were both emphatic that Graham had mistaken the mountain he climbed for another, a view supported by Sir Martin Conway and others in England. Douglas Freshfield, Norman Collie, Professor Garwood, and L. A. Waddell have argued for or against the claim; some more generous than others, especially Dr. T. G. Longstaff, who in reality was probably the first to reach an altitude of 24,000 feet some years later, as well as Rubenson and Monrad Aas, who made an attempt from the Rathong glen on the south side of Kabru in October 1907, have been inclined to give Graham at any rate the benefit of the doubt. Harold Raeburn, in 1920, suggested Graham might have climbed the 'Forked Peak' (20,340) in mistake for Kabru.

My own considered opinion, as a mountain surveyor, for what it is worth, is that Graham did not climb Kabru, any more than he climbed Changabang in the Kumaun Himalaya. No one need accept my view. I have studied his casual account critically with modern maps and discussed it with men who know the region well; and I have examined the remarks of such restrained critics as Tanner and Waddell. Graham is hopelessly at fault in some of his statements; he frequently mixes up his points of the compass; more than once he mis-reads his map for his position, mistakes Siniolchu for Simvu, mis-identifies Everest, speaks of the north-west of Kangchenjunga as seen

[1] For a full discussion on this claim see A. L. Mumm in *Five Months in the Himalaya* (London, 1909), 103–14. Mumm, Bruce, and Longstaff explored and mapped this area in 1907. Graham's account should be re-read with the new half-inch maps, 53 N/NE and 53 N/SE, published in 1946.

from the Yalung glacier; his almost casual claim to have climbed Kabru from the south-east with little reaction to altitude fatigue from a camp at 18,000 feet, that is, from below the ice-fall of the Kabru glacier of which he makes no mention, is to me inconceivable, and I find it easier to agree with Raeburn's suggestion.[1] But as Sir Martin Conway said: 'All this implies no attack upon Mr. Graham's veracity. He carried no instruments and made no observations for position. He merely believed that the peak climbed was Kabru. Nothing is easier than to make a mistake in such a case.' I may add that, in the Himalaya, he would be neither the first nor the last to do so.

By 1885 a change was coming over the Himalaya. Roads were being improved and the mountains were becoming more accessible. On the west the Jhelum valley cart-road to Srinagar was begun. Political advisers, collectors and deputy commissioners, road contractors, public works engineers, and forest officers were touring their districts; missionaries and sportsmen in search of game were already in remote places. But hardly anyone yet climbed for pleasure. It was still the period of passes, rather than of peaks. The lower valleys were well known and well enough mapped for administrative purposes and the high peaks were correctly placed upon the map. But the upper reaches of the glaciers were *terra incognita* and the topography of the high peaks and their satellites unknown. No one, I am convinced, had yet reached 24,000 feet. It was still a long way to the top of Everest.

---

[1] For the views of L. A. Waddell see *Among the Himalayas* (London, 1899) 389 ff.: for Longstaff's see G.J. xxxi (1908) 363.

PART THREE

# 1885–1918

'Now needs thy best of man,' so spake my guide
'For not on downy plumes, nor under shade
Of canopy reposing, fame is won
Without which whosoe'er consumes his days,
Leaveth such vestige of himself on earth,
As smoke in air or foam upon the wave.
Thou therefore rise: vanquish thy weariness
By the mind's effort in each struggle formed
To vanquish, if she suffer not the weight
Of her corporeal frame to crush her down.
A longer ladder yet remains to scale.
From these to have escaped sufficeth not,
If well thou note me, profit by my words.'

*Vision of Dante. Hell (Canto xxiv. 71)*

# 1. Opening Phase

THE period of Himalayan mountaineering that begins about 1885 opens with the journeys of Francis Younghusband, the establishment of the Gilgit Agency, and the first exploration of the border states of Hunza and Nagir. Under the more settled conditions that followed, climbers from Europe and men stationed in India began the technical reconnaissance of some of the highest mountains. It is the period of such men as Martin Conway, A. F. Mummery, Norman Collie, Douglas Freshfield, Charles Bruce, and Tom Longstaff, who with professional Alpine guides helped to gain the confidence of villagers and tribesmen and wean them from their instinctive terror of the hills. Englishmen living in the hills added much to our knowledge; the Neves, Arthur and Ernest, already established in their mission hospital in Kashmir, travelled extensively during the period, and to them and to such men in other parts of the Himalaya the new-comer went for advice and guidance.

Gilgit was important strategically to Kashmir and British India since it commands several important routes: the Dorah pass route through Chitral on the west, the Darkot pass route through Yasin on the north and the Hunza valley on the east with Irshad, Wakhjir, Kilik, and Mintaka passes at its head. By the eighties Russia had absorbed the Central Asian states and was at the northern foot of the Hindu Kush. In 1885 an Anglo-Russian Boundary Commission had settled the north-west frontier of Afghanistan, but east of this, on the Pamirs, the boundaries were unsettled between Russia, China, Afghanistan, and Hunza, the latter nominally paying tribute both to China and Kashmir.

At this time Gilgit was under Kashmir by the sovereignty of conquest. It had been visited occasionally by adventurous British officers such as Hayward, and during Lord Lytton's viceroyalty (1876–80) Major Biddulph had been stationed there as Agent for a year or two. Now there was a small garrison of Dogra troops badly officered and equipped, short of supplies, and quite incapable of dealing with its barbarous neighbours. The Hunzakuts raided far and wide—over the passes to north and east where they depopulated the head valleys of the Yarkand river carrying the people into captivity, and southwards towards Gilgit, where often the corrupt Kashmir officials were in league with them, selling Dogras and Gilgitis indiscriminately into slavery. Hunza was, in fact, a kind of slave-trade entrepôt for Central Asia. The Indus valley tribes in Chilas were equally lawless and raided over the Mazeno pass into Astor where they destroyed villages and crops.

It was to investigate the cause of a minor war between Kashmir and the Hunza and Nagir states that Algernon Durand was sent to Gilgit in 1888. The outcome of his report was the establishment of a permanent Gilgit Agency to help control the situation, to advise on measures to make peace, and to restore order. Two British officers successfully carried through this difficult task.[1]

Meanwhile, in 1887, after an adventurous journey across the Gobi desert to Yarkand, Francis Younghusband, then a young lieutenant in the King's Dragoon Guards,[2] made a daring crossing of the Great Karakoram by the Muztagh pass (c. 18,000) to the Baltoro glacier and to Baltistan and Kashmir. The route was entirely unknown and though it had apparently been in use many years previously there were only the vaguest reports of it. In the course of this journey Younghusband discovered the Aghil mountains, the Shaksgam or Oprang tributary of the Yarkand river, and the Sarpo Laggo glacier, the first of the northern glaciers of the Great Karakoram to be discovered; he was also the first white man to set eyes on the northern flanks of K2. His crossing of the Muztagh glacier pass, with no technical mountaineering knowledge, and without tents or equipment, was an amazing feat, especially as he had to sleep in the open without daring to light a fire for fear of being seen by Hunza raiders (map page 134).[3]

Younghusband was sent on a second mission in 1889 to the same area, primarily to investigate recent Hunza raids on caravans crossing

[1] A. G. Durand: *The Making of a Frontier* (London, 1900).
[2] Afterwards Sir Francis Younghusband, K.S.C.I., K.C.I.E.
[3] F. E. Younghusband: *The Heart of a Continent* (London, 1896).

the Karakoram pass, and to search for other passes across the main range. There were rumours of an old pass, the Saltoro, which led into Baltistan, and though it was fully realized that no large force could attack India over such a pass, there was some fear that in the event of a clash between Britain and Russia a diversion here might cause considerable trouble.

On this occasion Younghusband had a small escort of men from the 5th Gurkha Rifles, the first occasion, I believe, when such men were employed on purely mountain exploration. Charles Bruce was a subaltern of the regiment at the time and was already beginning the work of training his riflemen to be disciplined mountaineers. From a base at Shahidulla Younghusband carried his supplies on ponies over the Aghil pass into the Shaksgam, discovered the Gasherbrum and Urdok glaciers, and explored the latter to its head, though he was unable in bad weather to reach a col over the main range.[1] He then followed the Shaksgam down to the Sarpo Laggo stream, and explored a large tributary glacier which drains the Great Karakoram north of the Panmah Muztagh. This glacier, called by him 'Crevasse glacier,' is now known as the 'Skamri glacier,' from the group of mountains near its head.[2]

Though it was the beginning of October and at fords the river was well up to his ponies' backs, Younghusband was able to follow the Shaksgam from here for about eighty miles to its junction with the Yarkand river, visiting on the way the Shimshal pass, which was manned by Hunza watchmen, and discovering the Braldu glacier, though he did not ascend it. One march down the valley of the combined Yarkand and Shaksgam rivers he met the Russian Captain Grombchevsky, and a German naturalist Herr Conrad, who were bent on the exploration of the Yarkand headwaters and passes into India from the Pamir side.

Younghusband reached the Taghdumbash Pamir by the Ili-su pass, and, after visiting Tashkurghan, crossed the Mintaka pass (15,450) into northern Hunza, whence he followed the Hunza valley

[1] 'Younghusband's Col,' now Indira Col, 18,950 feet, a possible pass leading to the head of the Siachen glacier, but not yet crossed.
[2] It was fully explored and mapped for the first time by Eric Shipton's expedition in 1937.

to near Gilgit. In the Hunza valley he was on ground traversed rapidly by Lockhart's mission in 1885-6, and also penetrated by Grombchevsky and his Cossacks earlier in 1888. At Tashkurghan he had met Major Cumberland, Lieutenant Bower, and the Frenchman M. Dauvergne, who had been exploring the northern foothills of the K'un-lun. It is a curious commentary on the political state of affairs at this time that in this no-man's land a Russian, a Frenchman, a German, and no less than three Britishers should meet as friendly, if rival, explorers without an official passport of any kind.

Younghusband's next journey, in 1890, when with George Macartney, afterwards British Consul-General at Kashgar, he wintered at that place and explored the Pamirs the following year, is beyond the scope of this book. Passing mention must however be made of the Hunza-Nagir campaign of 1891, brought about by the continued intransigence of the two robber rulers, if only because it led to a great improvement of the Gilgit road, now being built under contract by an energetic British engineer, Spedding, who also constructed the greater part of the road through the Chaichar gorge to Chalt. Several of the old rope-bridges made of twisted twigs were also replaced by floating or telegraph-wire suspension bridges designed and built by Frederick Aylmer, a young sapper officer who, with Manners-Smith and Boisragon, won the Victoria Cross at the storming of Nilt,[1] the decisive action of this brilliant campaign.

The immediate result of peace on this borderland was the exploration and rapid reconnaissance survey of the great lateral valleys of Hunza. The task was entrusted to Lieutenant George Cockerill,[2] whose orders were to explore and map the western Karakoram and eastern Hindu Kush, an area of about 12,000 square miles of some of the most difficult country in the world. Cockerill, during the winter of 1892, explored the Shimshal gorge and valley as far as the Shimshal pass, discovering the Momhil, Mulungutti, Yazghil, Khurdopin, and Virjerab glaciers, and the great peak Disteghil Sar (25,868), the highest in the Karakoram west of the K2 group; he

---

[1] For accounts of this campaign see A. G. Durand, *op. cit.*, and E. F. Knight: *Where Three Empires Meet* (London, 1895).

[2] Afterwards Brig.-General Sir George Kynaston Cockerill, C.B., M.P. for Reigate.

next explored the Khunjerab and Chapursan valleys in northern Hunza and other valleys and routes in the Hindu Kush. It was a fine piece of exploration, though not made public at the time.[1]

The pacification of the country was also the opportunity for the first major expedition organized from England to explore and climb in the Himalaya, and the first Himalayan venture to receive financial support from the Royal Society and Royal Geographical Society. It was organized and led by Martin Conway, a well-known and experienced traveller and mountaineer.[2] The party included the artist A. D. McCormick, J. H. Roudebush, O. Eckenstein, Lieut. Charles G. Bruce and four men from his regiment, the 5th Gurkhas, whose headquarters were at Abbottabad. It had played a conspicuous part in the recent campaign in Nagir and had a detachment at Gilgit. The guide Mattias Zurbriggen of Macugnaga on the Italian side of Monte Rosa, and Colonel Lloyd-Dickin, who was to collect birds during the first part of the expedition, completed the party.

After crossing the Burzil pass on 24 April 1892 they were at Gilgit on 5 May and during the second half of the month explored the Bagrot valley, which is fed by glaciers descending from the south-eastern flanks of Rakaposhi (25,550); it enters the left bank of the Gilgit river about fourteen miles below the town. The party again left Gilgit on 8 June, visited Nagir and Baltit, the capitals of the two states, and explored two side-valleys, the Samaiyar and Barpu, which contain glaciers descending from the northern flanks of the Rakaposhi range.[3]

The greater part of July was spent in exploring and mapping the Hispar and Biafo glaciers. On 3 July Bruce, Eckenstein, two Gurkhas, Amar Singh and Karbir, and about eight Nagir porters crossed the Nushik La (17,300) into the Kero Lungma glacier which they followed down to Arandu. The pass had been reached from the south by Godwin-Austen in September 1861 and was later visited by a Major Cunningham, but neither had crossed to the Hispar.

---

[1] For a summary account see *H.J.* xi (1939) 15 ff.

[2] Afterwards Lord Conway of Allington. President of the Alpine Club 1902-4.

[3] W. M. Conway: *Climbing and Exploration in the Karakoram Himalayas* (London, 1894).

Zurbriggen and Roudebush also crossed the pass with laden Nagir porters ten days later, the former returning over it to rejoin Conway on the Hispar, for the first crossing of the Hispar pass on 18 July and the exploration of the Biafo.

Eckenstein now returned to England. At Askole Bruce rejoined the party by way of the Skoro La (16,644) for the exploration of the Baltoro glacier. Conway discovered the head glaciers, which he named 'Godwin-Austen' and 'Vigne' and the head of the Baltoro glacier rising in the south-west between the Chogolisa and Gasherbrum groups. From a camp near Doksam he climbed a peak of about 19,400 feet ('Crystal Peak') and on 23 August made an attempt on Baltoro Kangri ('Golden Throne'), 23,390 feet; with Bruce, Zurbriggen, and the two Gurkhas, Harkbir and Karbir, he reached a peak ('Pioneer Peak') 22,600 feet, but found it separated from the summit of Baltoro Kangri by a depression too deep to cross.[1]

Conway's expedition was of great interest. Though the actual climbing feats would not be considered very important to-day, he kept a very detailed day-to-day account of every aspect of the journey: the effects of altitude and diet, the rates of pulse-beats, wear and tear on equipment. He was the first to bring Whymper and Mummery tents to the Himalaya, and almost the first to use crampons. He made a detailed reconnaissance map on the scale of one inch to two miles (1 : 126,720) which was published by the Royal Geographical Society in two sheets. He claimed no great accuracy for the detail of side-glaciers and was often unable to get clear views of the very few points fixed by the Survey of India; but the map and Conway's detailed account were the basis of the great expedition of the Duke of Abruzzi some sixteen years later.

Conway said afterwards that he planned his expedition after consultation with Godwin-Austen and Younghusband, and modelled his ideas and equipment on the experience of Whymper's Andes expedition of 1879-80. A lasting result of Conway's expedition was

[1] Conway's 'Crystal Peak' is south of the crest, not on the crest as shown later on Abruzzi's and Spoleto's surveys of 1909 and 1929 with the heights of 20,587 feet and 6237 metres (20,460 feet). The two points are not the same. Conway's heights must be considered approximate, being calculated from barometric readings in variable weather.

the experience gained by the four Gurkhas by their association with Zurbriggen. Bruce was then a young officer of twenty-eight, who had already seen three years' active service in Burma and on the north-west frontier; he already knew that Gurkhas and other local men living in the mountains were natural mountaineers, and that with practice and confidence many could become first-class climbers and mountain porters. He himself was a great load-carrier; Conway described him as the 'goods-train plus engine' of his expedition! For the next fifteen years Bruce roamed the Himalaya with selected Gurkhas, whenever he could get leave from his frontier duties, gaining an unrivalled experience of the mountains and the people, learning their languages and their customs and winning their confidence and trust. His laugh was a tonic throughout the Himalaya; he was worshipped by his Gurkhas who would follow him anywhere; he was the first to plan an expedition to Mount Everest in 1907, though the project had to be abandoned for political reasons; he was primarily responsible for the choice of Sherpas as porters for the early Mount Everest expeditions; and he was chosen to lead the reconnaissance and first two assaults on the mountain in 1921, 1922, and 1924, though he was unable to accept leadership of the first.

In 1896 the rest of Russia's southern boundary on the Pamirs was demarcated. On the principle that the boundaries of Russian and British interests should not touch, a small finger of Afghan territory in Wakhan was extended eastwards to touch the province of Chinese Turkestan (Sinkiang) on the Taghdumbash Pamir. Colonel T. H. Holdich and Major R. A. Wahab mapped the country along the new boundary.[1] Thereafter the halcyon days of 'go where you will and don't worry about Governments' were over, and the Russian Pamirs became more difficult of access to British mountaineers and sportsmen.

[1] *Report on the Proceedings of the Pamir Boundary Commission 1896* (Calcutta, 1897).

# 2. Punjab Himalaya

THE massif of Nanga Parbat stands in the angle formed by the Indus on the north, flowing south and then west at about 3500 feet, and by the Astor river on the east, flowing north and then north-west into the Indus at Ramghat. Its western boundary is the Bunar Gah, a northward flowing left-bank tributary of the Indus; on the south is the glacier-fed Rupal Gah, a left-bank feeder of the Astor river. At the head of the last-named are two passes, the Thoshe (16,820) and the Mazeno (17,640), tiresome but not difficult, which Chilasi tribesmen used until 1892 to harry the Astor villagers (fig. 9).

The great ridge of Nanga Parbat rises steeply from the Mazeno pass to its highest summit, 26,620 feet.[1] curves north-eastwards through Rakhiot Peak (23,210) and the three Chongra peaks (21,090, 21,150, and 22,390) and ends in the north at the Hattu Pir spur overlooking the Astor-Indus confluence.

The southern and south-eastern faces of this ridge, from the Mazeno pass to the Chongra peaks, are precipitous and in places vertical, the rise in height from the Rupal bed to the summit being 14,000 feet in a horizontal distance of about 5000 yards.

On the north-western side this wall of rock is buttressed by a north-west ridge on which stand the North Peak or Nanga Parbat II (25,572) and Ganalo (21,680), a shoulder peak with two narrow buttress ridges descending gradually northwards and westwards for about twelve miles before falling ten thousand feet to the Indus below; they are known as the Jalipur and Ganalo ridges. The north-western face of Nanga Parbat is clad with the hanging ice of the upper Diamirai glacier, lying between the main and Ganalo ridges; the northern face thunders down ice-avalanches to feed the upper reaches of the Rakhiot glacier.

[1] The official triangulation heights, given to Sir Sidney Burrard in 1933 by the Survey of India, are Nanga Parbat I, 26,620 feet, Nanga Parbat II, 25,572 feet. On the Survey of India sheet 43 I (1934) the heights are shown as 26,660 and 25,620 feet. See note on heights in Appendix B.

Before 1892 very few Europeans had been up the Rupal *nala*; Dr. Arthur Neve, the medical missionary who had come to Kashmir in 1882, was one of the first to visit the hamlet of Tarshing in 1887. It was then none too safe from prowling Chilasi raiders. Sir George Robertson's bold and brilliant campaign against Chilas in 1892 brought order and security, and sportsmen in search of game were able to cross the Mazeno pass in safety.

In 1895 A. F. Mummery, G. Hastings, and Professor J. Norman Collie, probably the most experienced team of amateur Alpine climbers of the day, came out to India to reconnoitre and, if possible, to climb Nanga Parbat.

After establishing a temporary base camp at Tarshing in the Rupal nala and ruling out the southern wall as impracticable, they made a rapid crossing of the Mazeno pass to see whether the Diamirai side would offer better prospects of success. They were joined in the Rupal in July by Bruce with two Gurkhas from his regiment, Raghobir Thapa, who had been with Bruce in Chitral in 1892–3, and Gaman Singh, a younger and less experienced man. After some practice climbing for the Gurkhas under Mummery, the party again crossed the Mazeno pass on 31 July and established a main base camp by the terminal moraine of the Diamirai glacier, whence Bruce had to return to Abbottabad as his month's leave was nearly at an end.

The first half of August was spent in climbing subsidiary points and reconnoitring in detail the Diamirai face. Light camps were pushed up the Diamirai glacier; on 18 August the first of these was occupied by Collie, Mummery, and Raghobir, but Collie, unaccustomed to the rough food, became unwell, and Mummery and Raghobir alone were available for the main effort.

These two climbed an extremely difficult rock rib in the centre of the face, while avalanches fell on either side of them, and spent two nights and three days above it examining and climbing the upper reaches. Above 20,000 feet Raghobir was also taken ill, mainly through lack of sufficient food, and the attempt had to be abandoned, though Mummery recorded his opinion that the technical difficulties had been overcome, and that with one more night on the mountain they should have reached the summit. From what is now known of climbing between 20,000 and 26,000 feet, and in

Bruce's opinion at the time, there is little doubt that this was too optimistic a view.

It was now decided that Collie and Hastings should move the base camp round to the north and examine the Rakhiot face; they were to take the lower route by the Indus valley while Mummery decided to try and cross, with the two Gurkhas, the high shoulder

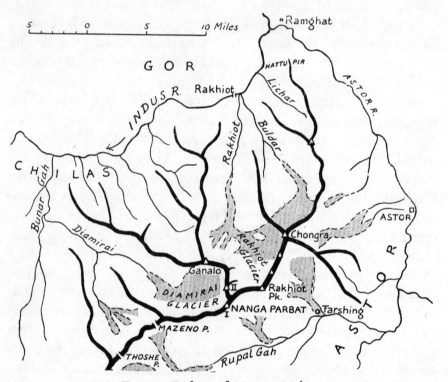

FIG. 9. *Ridges of Nanga Parbat.*

ridge between Nanga Parbat II and Ganalo at a col since measured at 20,430 feet. Mummery started on 23 August with two porters to carry extra provisions. These two returned the following day having made a depot for the climbers for use in the event of failure.

Collie and Hastings reached the Rakhiot valley and waited. They at once realized that there was no way down from Mummery's col, even if he reached it from the south, and they expected him to retreat and follow their camp by the lower route. When it was clear that this was not so, Hastings returned to the Diamirai glacier, found the food depot untouched, but no sign of the climbers. His belief was that during the ascent to the col they were destroyed by one of the many avalanches that rake this route. 'A slip is out of the question,' wrote Bruce commenting on the accident afterwards, 'for Mummery was one of the most accomplished amateurs there has ever been, and both the Gurkhas were first-rate on their legs.'

So ended in tragedy the first brilliant but desperate attempt to climb a Himalayan giant. Years later Bruce wrote that the climbing on the Diamirai face was still 'some of the most daring mountaineering that has even been accomplished,' though there had also been, he thought, an element of recklessness. He maintained that one lesson could be learnt from the tragedy: that suitable and sufficient food was essential for prolonged effort at 20,000 feet, since Collie's illness had been caused by unsuitable food, and Raghobir's by insufficient. In 1910 he wrote: 'I wonder whether Nanga Parbat will ever be climbed; it is probably as difficult a mountain as there is to tackle. . . . At present it seems beyond the strength of man.'[1]

No serious attack was again made on the mountain for thirty-seven years after the death of Mummery. Twenty-one years after that it was conquered.

On Nun Kun, the other great group of the Punjab Himalaya, there was also much activity and reconnaissance. The old maps of the higher reaches were faulty, and had to be corrected before the main peaks could be tackled. The massif stands on the Great Himalayan axis immediately south of Tongul at the bend in the Suru river which joins the Shingo tributary of the Indus about five miles below Kargil. Its three highest peaks are Nun (23,410), Kun (23,250) and 'Pinnacle Peak' (22,810), the last-named being on the north-east ridge of Kun.[2] Between Nun and Kun is a high névé plateau ending in a broken ice-fall and then forming an eastern branch of the Parkachik glacier, of which the main trunk descends from the western ridge of Nun (fig. 10). The south-eastern and eastern slopes of Pinnacle Peak drain eastwards into the Shafat glacier whose

[1] J. N. Collie: *Climbing on the Himalaya* (Edinburgh, 1902); C. G. Bruce: *Twenty Years in the Himalaya* (London, 1910). For Bruce's story written later in life see *H.J.* iii (1931).

[2] Nun is sometimes known as Nana or Ser; Kun, as Kana or Mer. Pinnacle Peak has no official name; its Survey of India number is Pk. 6/52 B.

waters join the Suru river on the north. The southern glaciers of Nun drain into the head of the Fariabad river which passes southwards through Kishtwar. The main west ridge of Nun, after enclosing the head of the Parkachik glacier continues west-north-west at a high level for about ten miles, and on it stand three unnamed peaks, the positions of which were fixed by triangulation during the early survey of Kashmir, but not their heights. From east to west they were designated D41, D42, and Snowy Peak No. 10.[1]

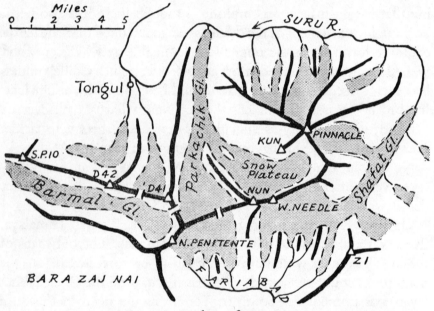

FIG. 10. *Ridges of Nun Kun.*

Their approximate heights are 19,938, 17,183, and 19,830 feet respectively. South of them the long Barmal glacier flows westwards into the head of the Bat Kol tributary of the Warwan river.

This topography was incorrectly shown on the old maps in 1898, when Bruce, with a brother officer, Major F. G. Lucas, took a party of sixteen Gurkhas to Suru for training in mountain exploration and climbing, under two experienced Gurkha officers, Subadars Karbir Burathoki and Harkbir Thapa. Both had been on Conway's expedition in 1892; both had been with Bruce and Conway on Pioneer

[1] Their Survey of India peak numbers are Pk. 12/43O, Pk. 11/43O and Pk. 39/43N.

Peak on that expedition; Harkbir had been with Conway in the Swiss Alps; both had been awarded the Indian Order of Merit for great gallantry in Frontier campaigns, and were fine natural mountaineers, now fully trained in Alpine technique.

This expedition carried out the preliminary reconnaissance of the group, and at the end of it ascended the small Sentik glacier from the north, crossed the Sentik La between D41 and D42, and followed the Barmal glacier down to the Bat Kol.

In 1902 Dr. Arthur Neve and the Rev. C. E. Barton ascended the Shafat glacier on the east of the group, examined the eastern flanks of Nun, and repeated, without knowing it at the time, Bruce's crossing of the Sentik La to the Barmal glacier. Neve visited the region again in 1904, made a small sketch of the topography correcting the old map, and sent it in to the Survey of India authorities at Dehra Dun.

Dr. H. Sillem explored the region in 1905, discovering and photographing the névé plateau between Nun and Kun. The following year Dr. and Mrs. Bullock Workman visited it, claimed to have discovered Dr. Sillem's plateau, and made a complete tour of the mountain knot. Unfortunately they had a poor sense of topographical direction, failed to connect their sketch-map to the points whose positions were fixed beyond doubt, and strongly criticized the corrections made by Dr. Neve. Mrs. Bullock Workman also claimed to have reached the summit of 'Pinnacle Peak' to which she gave the height of 23,300 feet, instead of 22,810, and persisted in stating that it was higher than Kun. The map produced in her book, *Peaks and Glaciers of Nun Kun*, is faulty in so many respects that it could not be accepted by the Survey of India.[1]

Dr. Neve again visited the region in 1910 and with the Rev. M. E. Wigram climbed D41. He took observations with a clinometer lent him by the Survey of India, which were computed at Dehra Dun, where his photographs were also examined, and the following year I observed the peaks of the group with a theodolite from high

[1] C. G. Bruce: *Twenty Years in the Himalaya*, Ch. v; A. Neve: *Thirty Years in Kashmir*, 172–98; see also my paper 'A Note on the Topography of the Nun Kun Massif in Ladakh' in *G.J.* lvi (1920) 124. Captain Ralph James has since shown that the Workmans' map south of Nun is also at fault (*H.J.* xiv (1947) 32).

stations in Kashmir. The topography as described above rests on the work of Bruce, Neve, and mountaineers who have visited the region more recently, but I believe the group has never been rigorously surveyed. There is no doubt however that Dr. Neve's reading of the topography was correct.

In 1914 the Italian Count Calciati reached the summit of Kun, the second highest of the group. In all this exploration Neve and Bruce placed their knowledge at the disposal of later comers, who not always acknowledged their debt to the pioneers. Nun was unconquered until 1953.

It is not possible to detail the many journeys to other parts of the Punjab Himalaya that took place during the thirty years following 1885. The two brothers, Drs. Arthur and Ernest Neve, visited between them almost every valley in Kashmir, Baltistan, and Ladakh in the course of their medical missionary work, and were sometimes joined by climbing friends. Both climbed most of the higher peaks of the Kashmir Pir Panjal, including the four highest— 'Sunset Peak,' Tatakuti, Barhma Sakil, and Parasing, all over 15,000 feet; most of these summits can now be reached in two days from Srinagar. Between them they climbed all five peaks of the Haramukh group which is prominent near the mouth of the Sind valley; Ernest Neve, with G. W. Millais, climbed the highest 'East Peak' of the group (16,872) in 1899. Ernest also visited and explored the Kolahoi group on six occasions between 1900 and 1910, being twice turned back by bad weather when within measurable distance of the top of the highest peak. In 1911 he and I were the first to climb the south peak and the following year we climbed the highest (17,799).[1]

Bruce also made many first ascents of the Kashmir peaks with his Gurkhas. After his first reconnaissance of Nun Kun in 1898 he divided his party of Gurkhas into two, under Karbir and Harkbir, and from the Bat Kol traversed two of the Koh-i-nur (or Kunyir-hayan) peaks which look down on the lake of Shisha (or Shishram) Nag in the East Liddar valley. Bruce went with Harkbir's party which traversed the northern peak (15,736); Karbir traversed the

[1] E. F. Neve: *Beyond the Pir Panjal*, Chaps. iii, x, xi; A. Neve: *Thirty Years in Kashmir*.

southern and highest (16,852).[1] Bruce returned to Abbottabad with his Gurkhas by way of the Kishenganga and the Khagan valley, through which flows the Kunhar tributary of the Jhelum. He had already almost made this valley his own, having visited it and climbed many of its peaks when training his Gurkhas in 1890, 1894, 1895, and 1896. On this occasion, 1898, when traversing the group known as Raji Borjees from Tod Gali to the Shikara valley, the party was caught in a thunderstorm and four Gurkhas were struck by lightning, though not seriously hurt.

There were many other travellers. During this period, the whole country was divided into 'game blocks,' some of the mountain streams were stocked with trout, and licences to shoot or fish were issued. Many officers and civilians on leave from their regiments in the plains, with their wives, took advantage of these facilities. Hardly a regimental mess in India was, by 1910, without some Himalayan trophies of barasingh, bear, burrhel, ovis ammon, ibex, markhor, and even Tibetan antelope from beyond the Great Himalaya and ovis poli from the Pamirs. To many there was no more delightful and satisfying way of spending a holiday than wandering in some remote valley in Kashmir or exploring some group of mountains— minor peaks, perhaps, compared with the giants, but affording plenty of thrills and adventure.

[1] C. G. Bruce: *Twenty Years in the Himalaya,* Chap. vi. The central peak (16,725) was first climbed by J. B. Corry, R. D. Squires, Kulbahadur Gurung, and myself on 29 June 1911.

# 3. Kumaun Himalaya

THE great mountain of the Kumaun Himalaya is Nanda Devi, 25,645 feet, surrounded by its vast outer ring and cut off from an approach from the west by its two curtain ridges which bar access to the 'inner sanctuary.'[1] With its southern ring peaks, Maiktoli (22,320), Mrigthuni (22,490), Trisul (23,360) and Nanda Ghunti (20,700)[2] it forms the centrepiece of the imposing panorama of the snows seen from China or any other prominent viewpoint on the outer hills near Naini Tal—an irresistible magnet to the eye of a mountaineer. But there are other notable groups farther to the north near the Jumna and Ganges sources—Chaukhamba, Kamet, Panch Chuli and their satellites—which have tested the skill and daring of modern climbers and will do so for many years to come before all their defences are subdued.

It was, I believe, the experiences of W. W. Graham and his two Swiss guides, Boss and Kauffmann, in the Rishiganga in 1883 that first drew Dr. T. G. Longstaff to the Himalaya, and, like Bruce and the Neves, he fell to their fascination.[3] He, too, became an oracle to whom no subsequent traveller has ever turned for advice in vain.

Longstaff's first journey to the Himalaya was in 1905 when, at the age of thirty, he visited the Kumaun Himalaya with the brothers Alexis and Henri Brocherel, Alpine guides of Courmayeur, to explore the eastern approaches of Nanda Devi. On 27 May he pitched camp near the hamlet of Pachhu (*Panchu*) in the Goriganga valley about three miles south of Milam, the old home of Rai Bahadur Kishen Singh, who now lived in retirement at Mansiari.

Longstaff first explored the Pachhu glacier to its head, directly under the north-east ridge of Nanda Devi East (24,391), and on 2 June

[1] Page 25.
[2] The first three are the east, centre, and west peaks of Trisul, the trident of Siva.
[3] Page 93.

114

crossed a difficult snow pass (17,750 a)[1] into the Lawan (*Lwanl*) valley to Naspanpatti grazing-ground (13,400), and to his main camp in the Goriganga valley.

He next explored the whole of the Lawan valley to its head, and on 8 June reached a col (19,390) on the Goriganga–Rishiganga watershed, at one of the few points where Nanda Devi's protecting ring sinks below 20,000 feet. From here, where he spent the night, he overlooked Nanda Devi's south face and the southern glaciers of the 'inner sanctuary.' He also reconnoitred the south ridge of Nanda Devi East, but had insufficient food for an all-out assault.

Back in the Lawan valley he attacked Nanda Kot (22,510), but had to turn back at about 21,000 feet because of the dangerous condition of the snow. He followed this attempt by exploring the Shalang (*S'halung*) glen and glacier, east of Nanda Kot, crossed a difficult glacier pass (18,000 a) to the Poting (*Ponting*) glacier and followed its valley back to the Goriganga.[2]

Longstaff then accompanied Mr. C. A. Sherring, I.C.S., the deputy commissioner at Almora on a long tour into Tibet, during which he crossed the Kali at Garbyang and took a rapid look at the Tinkar valley and the northern approaches of the Api–Nampa group in the extreme north-west corner of Nepal. After crossing the Lipu Lekh pass (16,750) to Taklakot, he reconnoitred the western approaches of Gurla Mandhata (25,355) late in July, probably reaching an altitude of about 24,000 feet. He visited the Tibetan lakes, Manasarowar and Rakas Tal, accompanied Sherring to Gartok, and crossed back into Garhwal by the Shalshal pass (16,390) on 25 August.

Following the wild valley of the Dhauli to Tapoban, Longstaff late in September reached Gwaldam by the Kuari route and explored the south and west approaches to Trisul (23,360). The existing map at this time was incorrect at the head of the Kail Ganga, and, as he discovered, the grazing-ground of Kurumtoli and its streams do not

[1] The spelling of names and heights given in this account are from the modern half-inch maps of the Survey of India, 53 N/SE (1946) and 62 B/SW (1944), drawn from detailed surveys made under Major Gordon Osmaston in 1936–8. Longstaff's names are in italics, and his aneroid heights are shown thus (17,750 a). His full accounts in *A.J.* xxiii (1906), *G.J.* xxviii (1907), and *G.J.* xxix (1907) can be followed very closely on these modern maps.

[2] *G.J.* xxix (1907); *A.J.* xxiii (1906).

lead to Trisul. From his camp at Mulket he explored the glacier shown on modern maps as the Bidalgwar, which rises from the high ridge of the Nanda Devi 'ring-wall' between Mrigthuni (22,490) and Trisul. Longstaff's corrections to the old map were all sound and his account is completely illustrated by the modern surveys.

And yet Longstaff wrote generously of the efforts of the old surveyors, and of the accounts written by the two Stracheys, who had visited the Tibetan lakes nearly sixty years before.

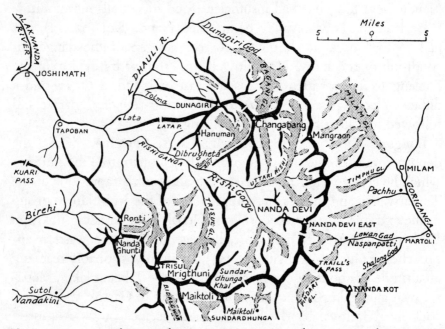

FIG. 11. *The Nanda Devi Sanctuary and its approaches.*

The next notable addition to our knowledge of the Kumaun Himalaya came two years later. In 1907, after their project for a reconnaissance of Everest had been turned down by the India Office in London when all preparations had been made, Bruce, Longstaff, and A. L. Mumm decided to revisit Nanda Devi and if possible to climb it. Bruce was now aged forty-one, Longstaff thirty-two, and Mumm, the veteran of the party, had more than twenty years' experience of climbing in the Alps. It was a strong party: Mumm brought with him Moritz Inderbinen of Zermatt, Longstaff the two

Brocherels of Courmayeur, and Bruce added Subadar Karbir Burathoki and eight other Gurkhas from his regiment, including Havildar Daman Singh, who was a trained plane-table surveyor. Though the 'inner sanctuary' was not penetrated, it was a very successful venture.[1]

Taking the Kuari pass, still under snow, they reached Tapoban on the Dhauli by 5 May. This was too late to force an entry into the lower Rishiganga gorge because of the volume of melting snow water, and too early to take porters over the Lata 'back-door' route, used occasionally by Tolma shepherds, because of the depth of snow. This route had been taken by the single surveyor who had entered the lower Rishiganga valley in 1874, by W. W. Graham in 1883, and by a few determined sportsmen in search of game.

The party therefore explored the Dunagiri Gad, which enters the Dhauli about twenty miles above Tapoban, and the Bagani (*Bagini*) glacier; on 22 May Longstaff, Bruce, the two Brocherels, and four Gurkhas made a pass over the ridge between Dunagiri and Changa-bang to the Ramani glacier, a feeder of the Rishiganga. Once again the old map was incorrect, the inner curtain ridge which cut them off from the base of Nanda Devi having been omitted. From here they traversed the spurs of the Hanuman ridge, which runs south from Dunagiri, to Dibrugheta and crossed back to the Dhauli valley by the Lata track.

Longstaff was back with Mumm, the three guides and four Gurkhas at Dibrugheta on 2 June. He explored the Trisul glacier, which enters the Rishiganga valley from the south about two miles below the Ramani. From a camp on this glacier at 17,400 feet, Longstaff, the two Brocherels, and Karbir reached the summit of Trisul, 23,360 feet, on the 12th. This was the highest summit actually reached at that time, the height of which was accurately known, and about the ascent of which there was no doubt.

Longstaff's conclusions as the result of this climb are interesting. They were that the effect of low atmospheric pressure depended on

---

[1] It is interesting to record that Mumm took with him some small pneumatogen oxygen cartridges prepared by Siebe Gorman & Co. This was the first suggestion of using oxygen in the high Himalaya, but the other members of the party treated it rather as a joke!

the strength and condition of the climber, much more than on the actual altitude reached; that the idea of acclimatization to low pressures was fallacious; and that the ill-effects of high altitudes are cumulative. These views seemed to be borne out by the fact that the fittest of the party had reached the top and that 'rush tactics' had been used for the last 6000 feet which had been climbed in ten hours. It must however be remembered that the party had, by the date of this climb, already been at heights of over 15,000 feet for most of the previous month, and had in fact already spent two nights, 7 and 8 June, at over 20,000 feet.; they had thereby reached some measure of acclimatization to that altitude, and on that occasion some of them at least had suffered from its effects. Later experience has shown that acclimatization can be attained up to about 23,000 feet and that it is only above that altitude that the cumulative effects become harmful and rapid deterioration may set in. But it was a long road to this knowledge.[1]

After this brilliant success Longstaff with the Gurkhas Kulbahadur and Pahal Singh tried to force a way through the upper Rishiganga gorge to the 'inner sanctuary' of Nanda Devi, but they were unable to find a practicable route in the time available. The whole party reassembled at their base in the Dhauli valley on 18 June.

The next objective was Kamet, which was farther from the effects of the monsoon. Leaving the route to the Niti pass north of Siunti, Longstaff ascended the Raikana valley and glacier, and on 30 June from the East or Purbi Kamet glacier climbed to a point over 20,000 feet on the flanks of the ridge extending south-east from Abi Gamin, which from the faulty map appeared to lead to Kamet. Longstaff recorded that the upper part of the Purbi Kamet glacier was raked by ice-avalanches and that there was no safe route by which it could be attacked from this side. Then, sending the main camp with Karbir into the Alaknanda by way of the Dhauli valley and Joshimath, Bruce, Longstaff, and Mumm crossed the Bhiundhar pass (16,700), which is on the watershed between the two peaks Nilgiri Parbat (21,240) and Rataban (20,230),[2] into the Bhiundhar valley, one of

[1] G.J. xxxi (1908); A.J. xxiv (1908-9). Mumm's account of this expedition appears in *Five Months in the Himalaya* (London, 1909).

[2] The highest point, 20,230 feet, is about 400 yards south-west of the triangulated summit (20,100).

the loveliest natural flower gardens in this part of the Himalaya. According to Longstaff, the Bhiundhar pass had probably been crossed by Richard Strachey about 1848 and by Colonel Edmund Smyth on 31 October 1862.[1] The party then crossed the Khunt Khal (14,520) to Hanuman Chatti on the pilgrim road to Badrinath on the Alaknanda, and between them they reconnoitred the western approaches to Kamet, the junction of the Bhagirath Kharak and

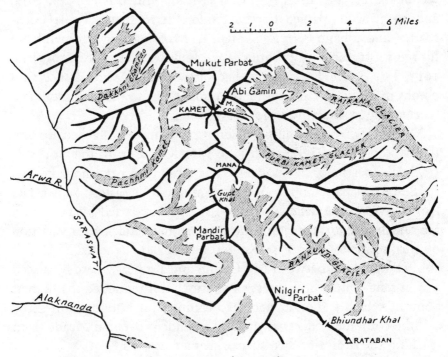

FIG. 12. *Glacier approaches to the Kamet group.*

Satopanth glaciers—the latter descending from the great Chau-khamba group (23,420)—and the Mana pass, famous for its old Jesuit associations (map page 265).

The weather was far from good and on 23 July a bad spell of an unusually strong monsoon put an end to further exploration, and the party broke up. Bruce and Mumm left for Kashmir where they climbed Haramukh and went on to Khagan. Longstaff spent August in completing his reconnaissance of the western and southern faces

[1] Smyth's account of the passage is given in Macintyre's *Hindu-Koh*, page 384.

of the three Trisul peaks from Sutol in the Nandakini valley and from Sundardhunga and Maiktoli in a branch tributary of the Pindar river. He made valuable corrections to the faulty maps of the topography at the head of the glaciers which descend from the Trisul group. Longstaff's accounts should be read in conjunction with the new map, 53 N/SE, made from the surveys of 1936–8.

Kamet was the scene of considerable activity after Longstaff's reconnaissance just described. C. F. Meade visited it in 1910, 1912, and 1913, accompanied by the guides Pierre Blanc, Franz Lochmatter, and Johann Perren; Captain A. M. Slingsby with men from his regiment, the 56th Frontier Force Rifles, attacked it in 1911 and 1913; Dr. A. M. Kellas, who had already made several successful climbs in Sikkim, visited it in 1911 and 1914, so that the mountain received unusual attention for five years in succession.

Meade opened the campaign in 1910. Slingsby attacked it from the west in 1911. In May and June 1912 Meade from the same side reached a height of 23,000 feet, after ascending a col now known as 'Slingsby's pass,' and in August examined the eastern approaches from the Raikana valley, and the route already tried by Longstaff. He returned in 1913, made a most determined attack by a variation of this route by the East Kamet glacier and reached 'Meade's col,' (23,420 feet) between Abi Gamin and Kamet, where he placed a light tent. Until the Everest expeditions this remained the highest point at which a mountaineer had camped for a night. Soft snow and the combined effects of sun and altitude prevented Meade from reaching the summit when success seemed assured.

Slingsby attacked it again in the same year from the west, reached a point over 23,000 feet but was then defeated by bad weather.[1] Kellas's first visit in 1911 was not pushed home; his second attempt in 1914 which had as its special object the scientific investigation of the effects of high altitude on the human body, rather than an assault on the summit, was cut short by the outbreak of war. The outcome of these attacks was that a practicable route had been found, but it was not until 1931 that the summit was won by that route.

Most travellers in the Kumaun Himalaya acknowledge their debt to the deputy commissioners of Garhwal, Almora, and Naini Tal,

[1] A.J. xxvii 326.

who were accustomed to travel widely.[1] Many of the valleys of Garhwal are a botanist's paradise, and naturalists travelled and collected in many parts at this period. It was, I think, about 1906 that officers of the Geological Survey of India, following a suggestion made the year before by Douglas Freshfield on behalf of the *Commission Internationale des Glaciers*, began to record the positions of the snouts of Himalayan glaciers. Among the first to be examined and marked in the Kumaun Himalaya were the Pindari, Milam, Shankalpa, and Poting.[2] It is not possible to do more than mention these activities, nor to describe the travels of sportsmen and others to the valleys and passes of the Lesser Himalaya. But to climbers of this period the lesser hills here seem to have been less alluring than those of the Punjab Himalaya. Perhaps the attractions of Simla and Mussoorie were too great to be easily by-passed!

[1] C. Sherring: *Western Tibet and the British Borderlands* (London, 1906).
[2] For a complete list, see *Records, Geological Survey of India*, xxxv.

# 4. Nepal, Sikkim, and Assam Himalaya

THE Nepal Himalaya was almost closed to British mountaineers from 1885 to 1918; but not quite. The occasional traveller ventured over the Kang La into the western approaches of Kangchenjunga or in the reverse direction, the most notable being Douglas Freshfield in 1899. Captain Henry Wood of the Survey of India was permitted to enter Nepal in 1903 for the special purpose of observing the principal peaks and to discover and check their names. In 1905 a small mountaineering party crossed the Singalila ridge into Nepal to attack Kangchenjunga from the Yalung glacier.

In 1907 a single surveyor, Natha Singh, unaccompanied by a European, was allowed to make a hurried visit to the upper Dudh Kosi to sketch the southern slopes of Everest; with no technical knowledge he could hardly be expected to ascend the Khumbu glacier or use a plane-table in the 'Western Cwm'; but he did in fact delineate roughly the southern end of the glacier. It was poor consolation to those who had hoped to see a reconnaissance of the mountain by Bruce and Longstaff in that year after all preparations had been made. In 1908 the Prime Minister of Nepal and the British Resident at Katmandu, Major J. Manners-Smith, V.C., of Hunza-Nagir fame, discussed a project for a joint Anglo-Nepalese expedition to Everest, and in 1909 the Nepalese Durbar actually were prepared to permit it. At the last moment the British Government judged it to be inexpedient and preparations were abandoned.

There were of course British Residents at Katmandu throughout this time, but even they and their visitors were limited in their movements. The Nepalese Durbar was unwilling to alter its policy of exclusion, and the British Government very rightly respected the terms of the treaty, still intact after eighty years. Gurkha officers were allowed to visit specific places, and among them Bruce saw as much as any of them.

In Sikkim it was the reverse. After the campaign in the sixties and the reconnaissance surveys under Harman and Tanner, which were completed in the seventies, the country soon became open to travellers and explorers to the more distant parts. Several names are prominent. Between 1888 and 1896 Major L. A. Waddell, of the Indian Army Medical Corps (later known as the Indian Medical Service), made several journeys, including one to the Yalung glacier over the Kang La. His book is of more interest to ethnologists and folk-lore enthusiasts, since he was mostly travelling over ground that had been already traversed. He was accompanied by Kinthup, who has been mentioned in connexion with the survey of the Tsangpo.[1] His contribution to the discussion of Graham's 'ascent' of Kabru is of interest to-day.[2]

Claude White also travelled extensively in Sikkim and Bhutan. He first visited Sikkim in 1887, was Assistant Political Officer with the expeditionary force in the Sikkim-Tibet campaign of 1888, and then became the first Political Officer to be appointed to Sikkim, a post he held for twenty years. He also was more interested in the people and their customs than in routes to the high mountains. He was, however, mainly responsible for opening up communications and for the construction of roads and bridges, which made access easier for later comers. In 1890 he crossed the Guicha La from Dzongri to the Talung glacier south-east of Kangchenjunga and followed the Talung valley to the Tista, being probably the first European to investigate the gorges between Pandim and the Simvu group (map page 38).

On another occasion during the monsoon he ascended the Zemu glacier to about 17,500 feet but was forced by bad weather to return. He crossed the Lungnak La into Lhonak in 1891 but it was not until 1902, when on the Sikkim-Tibet boundary commission, that he visited the whole of Lhonak, which till then was claimed by the Dzongpön of Kampa Dzong as being part of Tibet. On this occasion he visited the Choten Nyima La.

White's Bhutan journeys are of greater interest, for here he was on ground that is still very little known to-day. He was on two

[1] Page 90.
[2] L. A. Waddell: *Among the Himalayas* (London, 1899).

official missions to that country, in 1905 and 1907, but in 1906 also explored the eastern parts of the country.[1]

Waddell and White were handicapped by the lack of guides among the local people. The former in 1898 stated that the natives were not good on the hillsides, and 'there are no professional guides, as no natives of these regions are climbers.'

This was to some extent remedied the following year when Douglas Freshfield with Professor Garwood, the brothers Sella as guides, and Rinzin Namgyal (who as RN had already explored part of the route) made their 'high-level tour' of Kangchenjunga.[2]

Freshfield chose the post-monsoon period as likely to afford the best weather. His party left Darjeeling on 5 September and on the 20th camped east of 'Green Lake' by the Zemu glacier at about 15,000 feet. His plan was to ascend the glacier and climb some accessible peak over 20,000 feet in order to examine the possibility of the Nepal Gap (20,670) and the northern approaches to the Zemu Gap (19,275),[3] the first of these over the main northern ridge of Kangchenjunga, the other over the eastern ridge immediately west of the Simvu massif. Unfortunately they were foiled by bad weather, a late continuation of the monsoon. He therefore crossed into Lhonak by White's route of 1891, and with some difficulty, because of the new snow, crossed the Jongsong La (20,080) on 6 October. The descent of the Kangchenjunga glacier was arduous for the first three days, but the hamlet of Kangbachen (13,150) in Nepal was reached on the 10th; on the way he made a careful examination of the western sides of the main peaks of the northern ridge—'Pyramid,' 'Tent,' and 'Nepal.'

From Kangbachen the party passed through the small Nepalese village of Khunza (or Ghunsa), crossed the Senon La (Chunjerma) and the upper Yalung valley past Tseram (Chairam); they crossed back into Sikkim by the Kang La to Dzongri, whence they visited the Guicha La.

Freshfield's book recording this journey is of great interest to

[1] J. Claude White: *Sikkim and Bhutan: Twenty-one years on the North-east Frontier, 1887–1908* (London, 1909).

[2] Douglas Freshfield: *Round Kangchenjunga* (London, 1903).

[3] Unofficial heights from the map made by Paul Bauer's 2nd Expedition, 1931. Otherwise from Marcel Kurz's map of 1930.

mountaineers who visit Sikkim, and Garwood's map which accompanied it was a great improvement on the one compiled from earlier route surveys. Chapter IX gives Freshfield's views as regards the best method and route for tackling the mountain, but he did not examine the eastern approaches very closely. He gives an accurate description of the southern head of the Kangchenjunga glacier which descends the north-west side of the mountain and draws special attention to the great ice-terrace lying directly under the highest peak at about 27,000 feet; he also records his opinion that this glacier affords the only direct route to Kangchenjunga which is not impracticable.

Perhaps Freshfield did not altogether appreciate the contribution made to the success of his expedition by his porters; this was Bruce's opinion. But he was handicapped, as so many visitors from Europe are handicapped, by not being able to communicate directly with them or to understand fully their point of view. Confidence and training alone were lacking in pre-Everest days.

Younghusband's Tibet mission of 1903–4, with its lines of communications through Sikkim, the Chumbi valley and Gyantse resulted in a detailed survey of these parts and of Tibet south of Lhasa. A strong party of surveyors under Captain C. H. D. Ryder and including Captains H. Wood and H. McC. Cowie accompanied the mission. After Younghusband signed the treaty at Lhasa on 5 September 1904 a mission was despatched to Gartok in western Tibet, and thence to Simla by the Shipki route. In the course of this Ryder and Wood fixed by triangulation the positions and heights of a large number of peaks in southern Tibet and on the northern flanks of the Great Himalaya. The whole course of the Tsangpo from Shigatse to its source, the two lakes Manasarowar and Rakas Tal, the course of the Indus as far as Gartok, and that of the Sutlej from Rakas Tal to Shipki were surveyed by plane-table. For want of time the surveyors were unfortunately unable to make a close reconnaissance of the northern approaches to the Makalu, Everest, Gauri Sankar, Annapurna or Dhaulagiri groups.

It was the wise moderation of Younghusband's treaty, by no means fully appreciated in England at the time, which not only made this survey possible but sowed the seeds of the friendly relations between Britain and Tibet and led to permission for the approach to Everest through Tibet being obtained seventeen years later.

The year after Younghusband's mission, in August 1905, a mixed French, Swiss and British party of mountaineers came out to Sikkim to climb Kangchenjunga. It comprised Dr. Jacot-Guillarmod, MM. Reymond, Pache, and de Righi, and Aleister Crowley. It was not a well conceived expedition either in plan or composition. After crossing the Singalila ridge to the Yalung glacier in the south-west quadrant, the party tackled the steep ice-slopes below the south-west face of the mountain. With the aid of untrained Darjeeling porters a light camp was established on 1 September at an estimated height of 20,500 feet. In the afternoon Guillarmod, Pache, and de Righi with three porters, all apparently on one rope, started to descend to a lower camp. While traversing the ice-slope a porter in the middle slipped, pulled a second out of his steps, and the two dragged the whole party down the slope, starting an avalanche which buried Pache and the three porters. Hearing their shouts Reymond in the upper camp descended and assisted Guillarmod and de Righi in attempts at rescue, but it was three days before the bodies were recovered, buried under ten feet of snow. The attempt naturally ended with this disaster.[1]

A better planned but less ambitious climb was undertaken in 1907 when two Norwegians, C. W. Rubenson and Monrad Aas, made an attempt to climb Kabru, the peak on the Singalila ridge about seven miles south of Kangchenjunga, which Graham claimed to have climbed in 1883.[2] Starting after the monsoon on 6 October from the Rathong Chu, which is fed by the east Rathong glacier and its northern branch, the Kabru glacier, they skirted the 'Forked Peak' (20,340) and the 'Dome' by their western flanks. Their first high camp was placed at about 19,500 feet near the foot of the ice-fall on the Kabru glacier which descends from the eastern face of the snow ridge separating the two summits of Kabru. This ice-fall is very heavily crevassed and it was five days before the party reached the easier slopes above it. At about 21,500 feet a light camp was

[1] A.J. xxiii (1906–7) 51.
[2] Page 94.

established just below the connecting ridge—the 'snow flat' seen from Darjeeling between the two peaks—and from here a first attempt was made to climb the north-eastern summit (24,002). Because of the bitter cold the start was postponed and the attempt failed.

Camp was now pushed forward to about 22,000 feet and a second attack was made on 20 October. Once again intense cold delayed the start until 8.30 a.m., and it was not till 6 p.m. that the two climbers reached an estimated altitude of 23,900 feet. There was then only a final short snow-slope of about a hundred feet between them and the summit. But the wind was so violent that it almost swept them from the ridge and the cold so intense that at this late hour it was unwise to go on. Monrad Aas, the stronger climber of the two, was also beginning to lose sensation in his feet, and therefore led during the descent. Suddenly Rubenson, who was behind, slipped and shot down past his companion. Monrad Aas managed to check the fall, but Rubenson's life literally hung by a thread, five of the six strands of the rope breaking under the strain. On arrival in camp it was found that the toes of Monrad Aas were badly frostbitten.

Though success was not achieved, this climb taught several valuable lessons. Both climbers were high in their praise for the Sherpa porters who accompanied them. The fact that they had spent no fewer than thirteen days and nights at 19,500 feet or over, including three over 21,500 feet, without any signs of cumulative physical deterioration, and indeed with apparent acclimatization at least to that altitude, was curiously at variance with the experience of Longstaff during the same year on Trisul.[1] Longstaff's summit, 23,360 feet, had been reached by 'rush tactics' at the rate of 600 feet an hour for ten hours. Rubenson's and Monrad Aas' speed was 200 feet an hour in a slightly shorter time. Undoubtedly the intense cold and high wind, as well, perhaps, as Rubenson's climbing inexperience, were factors against a high rate of climbing, but the difficulties of the Kabru ice-fall would have precluded rush tactics from below 20,000 feet in any case.

Perhaps no climber has enjoyed himself more among the Sikkim Himalaya than Dr. A. M. Kellas of Glasgow, though he published

[1] Page 118.

very few details of his climbs.[1] He first visited Sikkim in 1907 and returned in 1909, 1910, 1912, 1920, and 1921. His visits to the Kumaun Himalaya in 1911 and 1914 have already been mentioned.[2]

In 1907 he concentrated on the Zemu glacier region and in September with Alpine guides made three vain attempts to climb Simvu (22,360), all of which failed because of fresh snow and bad weather. In the same year he twice tried to reach the Nepal Gap (20,670), on the great northern ridge of Kangchenjunga between 'the Twins' and 'Nepal Peak'; the first failed because of mist and bad visibility on the Nepal Gap glacier at about 18,000 feet; the second about a thousand feet higher because of open and impassable crevasses.

He returned in 1909 and attempted to climb Pauhunri (23,180) in the extreme north-east of Sikkim. In August he and his two porters were driven back at about 21,700 feet by storm and snow. He tried again after the monsoon in October, reached a height only 200 feet from the summit but exhaustion and failing light, deep snow, and the violent and bitter wind prevented him from finishing the ascent.

Meanwhile in early September he visited the Langpo and Kangchenjunga glaciers in the extreme north-west of Sikkim, crossed the Jongsong La from Lhonak, reached an altitude of about 22,000 feet on the west ridge of Jongsong peak (24,344) and climbed the Langpo Peak (22,800) from the west on 14 September. He also made his third attempt to reach the Nepal Gap, which he had twice tried in 1907, but was defeated at about 20,000 feet by a heavy snowstorm.

Kellas next visited Sikkim in May 1910, intending to examine the snow and weather conditions in the pre-monsoon period. From the Zemu glacier he visited the Simvu Saddle (18,110) and Zemu Gap (19,275), but did not cross them. In the same month he attacked the Nepal Gap for a fourth time and conquered it, except for a small rock wall at the summit. He then crossed the difficult 'Lhonak pass' (19,500) into Lhonak, and again climbed Langpo Peak to 22,500 feet to reconnoitre the summit of Jongsong Peak; next he crossed the Choten Nyima La, reached the top of 'Sentinel Peak' (21,240)

[1] Brief summaries are given in A.J. xxvi 52, 113; xxvii 125; xxxiv 408; also by H. W. Tobin in H.J. ii (1930) 10-12.
[2] Page 120.

east of it, and then dashed off to north-eastern Sikkim. Here he climbed Pauhunri (23,180) on a five-day struggle from 13 to 17 June and finished a most successful season in July by climbing Chomiomo (22,430) after reconnoitring several different approaches.

Kellas again visited Sikkim in August 1912 and on this occasion explored the approaches to Kangchenjau (Kangchima, 22,700) and reached the summit plateau from the north. Throughout most of his Sikkim climbs Kellas made observations on his physiological reactions to altitude, and wrote valuable accounts on these aspects. Except on his first expedition in 1907 he was unaccompanied by Alpine guides and relied entirely on local men and porters engaged at Darjeeling.

Our knowledge of the mountains in Bhutan was very little advanced during the early years of the present century. In the extreme east of the Assam Himalaya a great deal of survey work was done between 1911 and 1913, as part of a concerted programme of exploration for which four detachments of the Survey of India were formed. The immediate cause was the murder of Mr. Noel Williamson, the Assistant Political Officer of Sadiya, and his party in March 1911 by Minyong Abors in Komsing village. Williamson had already made a journey in 1909 up the right bank of the Dihang from Pasighat to Kebang, taking with him Partab Singh of the Survey of India. His murder decided the Government of India to send a small expedition to punish the Minyong Abors and the opportunity was taken to send a survey detachment with it, and others into the neighbouring tracts. The two parties under Major C. P. Gunter and Captain E. B. Cardew which explored and mapped the Mishmi country east of the Dihang, mainly in the basins of the two great tributaries of the Brahmaputra, the Luhit, and the Dibang, and the Hkamti Long country in the upper Irrawaddy basin are outside the scope of this book; but towards the close of the survey in the Mishmi country in 1913 Captains F. M. Bailey and H. T. Morshead crossed the Dibang–Dihang watershed into the country known as Pemakoi-chen, in the valley of the Dihang north of the Abors.[1]

---

[1] 'Dihang' is the accepted name for that portion of the Tsangpo on the Indian side of the Great Himalaya as far as its junction with the Dibang and Luhit rivers. Thereafter it becomes the Brahmaputra. Strictly speaking the name is only used by

The other two survey detachments were those which accompanied the Abor expedition under Captain O. H. B. Trenchard, and which visited the Dafla and Miri country in the basin of the Subansiri under Lieut. C. G. Lewis. With Trenchard's detachments were Lieuts. G. F. T. Oakes, J. A. Field, and P. G. Huddleston, Khan Bahadur Sher Jang, four surveyors and a computor. It was a strong party, but the country is extremely difficult to penetrate, being densely forested up to the snowline. Those hills that did not reach so high were useless for triangulation stations until their tops had been cleared of jungle and trees. Though these tops were generally rounded the flanks were precipitous, and immense labour was spent in clearing paths and hill-tops before the observers could get to work. A second season was required before the surveys were completed satisfactorily. Among the results was the fixing for position and height of a number of peaks on the Great Himalayan range near the source of the Subansiri on and both sides of the Dihang, including Namcha Barwa (25,445) the highest peak of the range east of Kangchenjunga. It had been seen by the pundit explorer Nem Singh in 1879, by Kinthup in 1881, by Captain C. L. Robertson in 1900, but none were in a position to fix it with any accuracy. Morshead with Bailey in their journey of exploration in 1913 surveyed the Dihang in Pemakoi-chen and saw it from close quarters; the main geographical result of their work was the survey of the Tsangpo gorge east of it, which showed that the river made a great loop some sixty miles east of the position previously shown on maps. Much of the topography of the Subansiri basin was for the first time correctly surveyed by Lewis and his detachment.[1] It is tragic to record that no fewer than four officers who took part in these surveys were killed in France during the 1914-18 war.

the local Miris near the junction of the three rivers. The Abors call it the Siang. In northern Pemakoi-chen the inhabitants use the Tibetan name Tsangpo.

[1] *Records of the Survey of India*, Vol. IV (Explorations on the North-Eastern Frontier during 1911-12-13) (Calcutta, 1914). The difficulties are much minimized in this account. Captain H. T. Morshead: *Report on an Exploration on the North-East Frontier, 1913*.

# 5. Karakoram

CONWAY's expedition of 1892 has already been describe᷈ ᷈ The results of it focused attention on the Karakoram, on its great ᷈orld of ice and on its mighty peaks. Among those who took a ᷈on-spicuous part in their exploration were the American couple, ᷈ ᷈s. Bullock Workman and her husband, Dr. Hunter Workman, w᷈ ᷈ visited the Karakoram no less then seven times between 1898 an᷈ 1912. In 1898 they were in Ladakh and reached the Karakoram pass; the following year they crossed the Deosai to Skardu and the Skoro La to the Braldoh valley, and then with Conway's old guide Zurbriggen ascended the Biafo glacier. In 1902, with Dr. Oestreich as topographer and Zurbriggen again as guide, they explored the Chogo Lungma glacier from Arandu, repeating the journey in 1903 with Joseph Petigax, a guide from Courmayeur, when they also visited the Nushik La from the Hoh Lumba glacier. In 1906 they made a circuit of the Nun Kun massif in the Punjab Himalaya,[2] and in 1908 followed in Conway's steps from Gilgit and Nagir over the Hispar pass and down the Biafo glacier to Askole. During these journeys they made a number of minor ascents. Their two later expeditions in 1911 and 1912, when they visited the Hushe, Kondus, and Siachen glaciers are mentioned later.[3]

It is difficult to assess even now how much all this activity added to our accurate knowledge of the Karakoram; certainly not as much as it should have done, since a great deal of the ground traversed in their first five journeys had been visited and described before, though the Workmans often lacked the grace to acknowledge it. When they did refer to the work of their predecessors it was in too carping and controversial a manner. Probably from an excess of zeal and enthusiasm the Workmans were, on their journeys, the victims of their own faults. They were too impatient and rarely tried to understand the mentality of their porters and so did not get the best out of them;

[1] Page 103 ff.          [2] Page 111.          [3] Page 139.

and they left too much, without supervision, in the hands of their Kashmiri and down-country servants, who can be harsh and unscrupulous with local men. Some of the trouble experienced by later travellers can be traced to this unsympathetic attitude of the Workmans. They had good European guides and ample funds, but money will not buy willing co-operation in the mountains, even from simple, superstitious, and unsophisticated hill-men.

Balti porters are patient and susceptible to firmness, if coupled with kindness and persuasion, but they are stubborn under threats. This is easily understandable. 'What,' asks Bruce on another occasion, 'would have happened a hundred years ago in Switzerland, if a whole village had been ordered to send every available man with some unknown Englishman and to stay with him for a fortnight above the snow-line?' This is what the explorer in the Karakoram has to ask of the Balti villages.

The many books resulting from the Workmans' travels are still useful, particularly for their fine illustrations; the attractive maps are deceptive and not always reliable. The Workmans lacked a sense of topography; their surveyors were too much hustled; they often misidentified the fixed points on which their maps should have been based, so that their statements led to controversy at the time and have since been disproved.[1]

In 1902 a mixed party under the leadership of O. Eckenstein, who had been with Conway ten years earlier, visited the Baltoro glacier to explore the approaches to K2, and if possible to climb it. Besides Eckenstein there were two other Englishmen, A. E. Crowley and G. Knowles; two Austrians, H. Pfannl and V. Wesseley; and a Swiss doctor, J. Jacot-Guillarmod. The climbing programme was much hampered by bad weather, but the exploration of the 'Godwin–Austen' glacier was a valuable contribution to knowledge and two members of the party, Guillarmod and Wesseley, reached an altitude of about 21,400 feet on the north-east ridge of K2. Too much reliance should not be placed on Guillarmod's sketch-map

[1] Errors made in the Nun Kun region have already been mentioned (page 111). Their topography and heights in the Chogo Lungma and Hispar regions have been often criticized. Shipton, Tilman, and Spender found major errors in their map of the glaciers south-west of the Biafo (*H.J.* x (1938) 35, 36).

which appeared with his book, nor on the heights given in the narrative and shown on his map, all of which are too great.[1] Dr. Pfannl's sketch-map in his account shows the topography more correctly than Guillarmod's.[2]

Of several other travellers and sportsmen who visited the Karakoram between 1900 and 1909 mention should be made of A. C. Ferber and E. Honigmann, who in September 1903 visited the Muztagh pass which had been crossed by Younghusband in the opposite direction in 1887. They found the ascent from the Baltoro and Muztagh glaciers too difficult for laden porters, but their account is of interest for the evidence they found of an old route over it, abandoned because of glacier changes.[3]

The year 1909 saw great activity in the Karakoram. The first great Italian expedition under the leadership of the Duke of the Abruzzi reconnoitred K2. He had with him Filippo De Filippi as aide, physician and naturalist; F. Negrotto, a very capable topographer; Vittorio Sella, a magnificent mountain photographer; and no fewer than seven Italian guides and porters from Courmayeur: Joseph and Laurenzo Petigax, father and son, who had been with the Duke on his Ruwenzori expedition and with the Workmans on the Chogo Lungma glacier in 1903; the Brocherel brothers, Alexis and Henri, who had been with Longstaff in the Kumaun Himalaya in 1905 and 1907 and had reached with him the summit of Trisul; and the porters Emil Brocherel, Albert Savoie and Ernest Bareux. Sella took with him as assistant photographer, Erminio Botta, who acted also as his guide and porter. On account of the bad weather generally experienced by Eckenstein's and the Workmans' expeditions from mid-June to August the Duke planned to reach the Baltoro glacier about the middle of May and to use the expected month of fine weather before the monsoon for his reconnaissance

---

[1] J. Jacot-Guillarmod: Six mois dans l'Himalaya (Neuchâtel, 1903). The latest height values are Mitre, 20,462 feet (Negrotto); Broad Peak, 26,414 feet (S. of I.); Skyang Kangri, 24,750 feet (S. of I.). Guillarmod's heights for these are Mitre, 24,600 feet; Broad Peak, 28,000 feet; Skyang Kangri, 26,250 feet. The height reached, 21,400 feet, is an estimate by Filippo De Filippi from Negrotto's map some distance below a point fixed by him.

[2] Zeit, des deutsch. u. oest. Alpenver. xxv (1904).

[3] G.J. xxx (1907) 630.

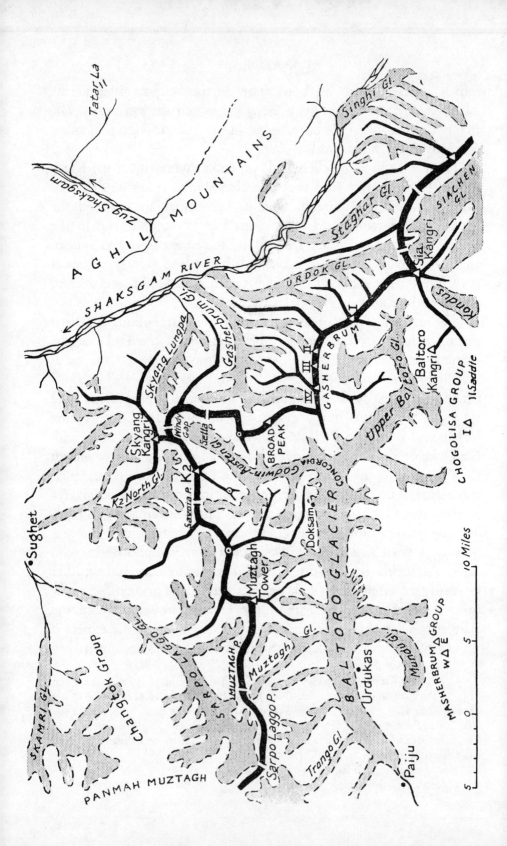

and climb. Sir Francis Younghusband, then Resident in Kashmir, took great interest in the enterprise and entrusted all transport arrangements to the glacier to A. C. Baines, who was an expert in such matters and had travelled much in remote parts of Kashmir.

On 24 May the party reached 'Concordia,' the meeting-place of the Godwin-Austen glacier which descends from K2, and of the upper Baltoro and Vigne glaciers. The next two months were spent exploring the approaches to K2, attempting to climb it, photographing it from all sides except the north, mapping the whole region on a large scale, including the great Broad, Gasherbrum, and Chogolisa groups. With Baines at Urdukas (Rdokass), lower down the Baltoro, to look after his supply-line, the Duke was able to concentrate on his exploration.

From an advanced base at about 16,500 feet near the south foot of K2 the Duke reconnoitred all four ridges which unite to form the apex of the pyramid.[1] He first attacked the rib (now known as the 'Abruzzi ridge') that descends steeply to the south from the 25,354-foot shoulder, but abandoned the climb as too difficult for laden porters, after reaching a height of about 22,000 feet. The south-west ridge being quite impracticable, he took his party up the western (Savoia) glacier, examined the western face of K2, and on 7 June reached the col at the head of the glacier on the north-west ridge (21,870), only to find that this ridge offered little prospect of success. Finally he returned by his advanced base to the Godwin-Austen glacier, ascended this to its head by Guillarmod's route and reached Windy Gap, from which rises the southern arête of Skyang Kangri (24,750). The north-east ridge of K2 was reconnoitred and ruled out as impracticable also, but a height of about 21,650 feet was reached on Skyang Kangri. An ascent was made to a col[2] on the east side of the Godwin-Austen glacier, between Broad Peak and Windy Gap. From here at about 20,000 feet the east face, the north-east and south-east ridges are best seen, and it was deemed that the summit might be gained if the great shoulder at 25,354 feet could be reached.

[1] See page 20.
[2] This col, named by the Duke 'Sella pass,' is wrongly shown on the latest Survey of India quarter-inch map 52A (1946) by the name 'Windy Gap' which should be closer to Skyang Kangri at the head of the Skyang Lungpa glacier.

The photographs taken by Sella at this point are superb, and illustrate in profile the route to the shoulder eventually pioneered in 1938 by Charles Houston.

De Filippi in his account of these explorations writes: 'After weeks of examination, after hours of contemplation and search for the secret of the mountain, the Duke was finally obliged to yield to the conviction that K2 was not to be climbed.'[1] In actual fact he had, though he did not know it, solved the problem.

From his exploration of K2 the Duke now turned to the upper Baltoro and made a determined assault on the great snow-clad mass of Chogolisa I, the 'Bride Peak' of Conway, 25,110 feet. From a base camp (16,640) at the northern foot of the mountain, it took him eight days, hampered as he was by bad weather, to establish a camp on the Chogolisa saddle on 10 July at 20,784 feet. To this point his Balti porters carried full loads and kept him supplied for eight days. With three guides he made two attacks on the peak by the east ridge. On the 12th they reached a height of 23,458 feet, but were driven back to the saddle and imprisoned there for four days by bad weather. On the second attempt on 18 July from a shelter tent at 22,483 feet they reached a height of 24,600 feet having overcome all the technical difficulties of the climb by one o'clock. After waiting two hours shrouded in mist and cloud at this point they were forced to descend to the saddle, which they reached after $14\frac{1}{4}$ hours of hard going at 8 p.m. It was a fine achievement, and but for the weather the last long snow ridge must have been won.

Throughout this expedition a period of more than five consecutive fine days was rare. It is usual in this region to have longer spells of fine weather, though these are interrupted by four or five days of storm. In spite of the poor weather the Duke's altitude on Chogolisa was a record and the height at which he spent the night of 17 July was second only to Longstaff's at about 23,000 feet on Gurla Mandhata in 1905. Negrotto's map from photographic measurements, carefully based on fixed points, was a great advance on those of his predecessors, and Sella's photographs have enabled subsequent climbers to examine every detail of the topography.

In the same year, 1909, Longstaff made a great contribution to our

[1] F. De Filippi: *Karakoram and Western Himalaya* (London, 1912) 279.

knowledge of the southern and eastern Karakoram. Because of the difficulties of penetrating the upper Nubra in summer and the narrow gorge of the lower Siachen glacier, the old survey here was sketched by E. C. Ryall in 1862 from a great distance, and the glacier was in fact shown not longer than twelve miles. Beyond that point Ryall's map was blank. The Saltoro group, fixed as K10 and K11 by triangulation, and the Saltoro pass were believed to stand on the watershed of the Shaksgam river, discovered by Younghusband in 1887. The error in the map was made after Younghusband's explorations in 1889, partly because of the misconception of the position of the Saltoro pass which it was believed Younghusband had seen from the Urdok glacier, so that his Urdok glacier was stretched southwards to fill the blank north of Ryall's work. It is easy to be wise after the event, but it seems to me quite unjustifiable that the compiler of the map in the Survey of India should have distorted Younghusband's work to such an extent, when it was quite adequately controlled by his observations for latitude.

Longstaff with Arthur Neve and A. M. Slingsby set out in June from Khapalu in the lower Shyok to search for the Saltoro pass over the watershed. They reached the pass (18,200), at the head of the Bilafond glacier, the northern of the four glaciers which feed the Saltoro, crossed it, and discovered a great glacier on the far side. On this they camped at 15,875 feet, and one of their men followed it south-eastwards for seven miles. To the north of the glacier they discovered the group of peaks, which they named 'Teram Kangri,' Teram being the name of the glacier given to Longstaff by his porters from Khapalu. As no peaks had then been triangulated in that area by the Survey of India and the topography was unknown, Sir Sidney Burrard had suggested it as a likely spot for an unknown mountain of the first magnitude. Longstaff's estimate of its height was about 25,000 feet; but to make sure, he measured a short base as best he could and took observations from each end with compass and clinometer. When the observations were worked out at Dehra Dun there was great excitement, since it appeared to be nearly 30,000 feet and therefore higher than Everest!

But Longstaff was twelve miles from the mountain; his base was short and his long rays to it intersected at a very acute angle. The smallest errors in the measurement of his base, or in the angles measured with his small instruments, and therefore in his distance to the peak, would cause a considerable error in the height. Longstaff's own estimate of 25,000 feet was not far wrong, as it turned out afterwards. Its accepted height now is 24,489 feet.

Longstaff, still believing that he had crossed the main watershed, on to a glacier draining northwards into the Shaksgam, returned over the Saltoro pass, and, after exploring and mapping the Chumik and Rgyong glaciers, crossed the Chulung La southwards to the Shyok and ascended the Nubra valley to Panamik. From here he reconnoitred the approaches to the Saser group, the highest peak of which is the old K22, now Saser Kangri, 25,170 feet. On 30 July he camped at 18,200 feet on the north Phukpoche (Popache) glacier, but a spell of bad weather set in and drove him back to Panamik.

Slingsby now had to leave him and he was joined by D. G. Oliver, British Joint Commissioner in Ladakh, who had the year before with Arthur Neve been prevented from reaching and exploring the Siachen glacier by flood-water in the Nubra. Longstaff had already come to suspect that his Teram glacier was none other than the upper part of the Siachen glacier and that this was very much longer than shown on Ryall's map.

It was now mid-August and there was still too much water coming down the river. Longstaff therefore spent the next four weeks with Oliver examining the Yarkand trade-route as far as the Karakoram pass. The Saser pass and the Kumdan glaciers of the upper Shyok render this route difficult and Oliver was intent on choosing a better line and constructing a new road in the upper Shyok, if a good line could be found. Longstaff's observations on the Kumdan glaciers are of considerable interest to glaciologists.

On his return to Panamik in the middle of September he and Oliver were able to reach the Siachen glacier and Longstaff ascended the glacier for some ten miles. From the farthest point he reached he was able to see right up the Siachen glacier, past the point at which he had camped with Neve and Slingsby on 17 June, to its head near 'Younghusband's saddle.' The total length of the glacier was about forty-seven miles.

Longstaff's modest account of this fine piece of exploration gives almost too much credit to others.[1] His map, made with very few fixed points to work from, completely altered the topography as shown on older maps. It only remained for others to follow up his discoveries and improve on what he had accomplished in this short season of four months.

The discovery of Teram Kangri led the Survey of India in 1911 to send out two men, V. D. B. Collins and C. S. McInnes, to fix it for position and height. The group was observed by Collins from four stations which he tied to the old Kashmir triangulation observed by C. J. Neuville in 1861: Collins' stations were Ningstet (18,365), Wusak (19,571), Tiggur (19,385), and Stongstet (19,730), all on the mountains of Nubra. He had a difficult task to get his instruments up to these stations and to Spanpuk (20,288) south of the Shyok, where the weather was not too good. Altogether Collins climbed sixteen peaks over 19,000 feet to fix the position and height of Teram Kangri before he was fully satisfied. His observations gave a height of 24,489 feet for Teram Kangri I, and 24,218 feet for the summit now known as Teram Kangri III. A third summit Teram Kangri II, 24,300 feet, was fixed by Grant Peterkin the following year.

In 1911 and 1912 the Workmans visited and explored the whole of the Siachen glacier. They had with them trained Alpine guides and surveyors: Grant Peterkin who carried out the triangulation and Surjan Singh, lent by the Survey of India to map the detail. The results of this expedition are in an entirely different category to those of the Workmans' earlier ventures. They followed Longstaff's route over the Saltoro pass, explored the Teram Shehr affluent which enters from the east, and near the head of the Siachen reached two cols, the 'Indira' and the 'Turkestan,' on the watershed of the Shaksgam. From near the head of the glacier they crossed a pass, Sia La (c. 18,700), into the head of the Kondus glacier, under the southern flanks of Baltoro Kangri ('Golden Throne'), and made a rapid reconnaissance of this area. The great peak of Saltoro Kangri (25,400) was examined at close quarters, both from its north-eastern and south-western sides and a height of about 20,000 feet was reached. From Grant Peterkin's triangulation, which was based on the fixed points of the Survey of India, including Collins' work of the previous

[1] G.J. xxxv (1910) 622 ff.

year, the heights of all prominent peaks along the Shaksgam watershed were fixed for position and height. This was a fine achievement. Peterkin recorded excellent weather throughout the period from 24 June to 27 August, eighty per cent of the days being suitable for observations to high peaks. Surjan Singh's plane-table survey was also very satisfactory, though no great claim to accuracy was made for the sketch-map of the Kondus, which was not visited by him or Peterkin.

The last expedition before the outbreak of World War I was led by the Italian Filippo De Filippi, who was with the Duke of the Abruzzi in 1909, into the area east of the Siachen. It was highly and scientifically organized, and arrived in Kashmir in two parts. The first comprised De Filippi, Commander A. Alessio, Professors G. Abetti and G. Dainelli, Marchese Ginori, A. Antilli, and the guide G. Petigax; it reached Srinagar in the autumn of 1913 and wintered at Skardu in Baltistan. The second part included a Survey of India detachment under Major H. Wood, as well as O. Marinelli, C. Alessandri, and A. J. Spranger, who came out from Europe. They crossed the Zoji La on 13 April 1914 and met the first party at Leh at the end of the month.

The programme was the largest and most comprehensive of any previous expedition to the Karakoram. It included geodesy and geophysics (Alessio and Abetti), geology (Dainelli and Marinelli), meteorology and climatology (Ginori and Alessandri), and photography (Antilli). For the survey Wood had with him Jamna Prasad and surveyor Shib Lal, as well as Spranger, who was a trained topographer. The expedition had the support of the King of Italy, of scientific bodies in Italy and England, and of the Government of India, which contributed to the cost.

Only a brief summary of the geographical work can be given here, but the activities of the specialized scientists were no less important in their own line. It is of particular interest to record that in these early days of wireless, special time-signals were sent out from Lahore and picked up simultaneously by Alessio's portable receiver in the Karakoram and by Dr. de Graaff Hunter in the Survey of India observatory at Dehra Dun, so that the difference of longitude between Alessio's station and the Dehra Dun meridian could be found with accuracy. It was the first time the method was employed in India.

During the winter of 1913 much work was done by the specialists. It was not until 1914 that the geographical exploration was begun. The whole expedition left Leh on 15 May, crossed the Ladakh range by the Chang La and ascended the upper Shyok to the Depsang by Oliver's new road. Here a depot was made and the expedition settled down to work. Wood and the topographers made a complete survey of the Depsang plateau based on triangulation, Wood fixing a number of new peaks to the west for the subsequent exploration of the Rimo glacier.

By 1 July the work was completed and De Filippi, with Alessio, Abetti, Antilli, Petigax, and Jamna Prasad left for the exploration of this great glacier, the main source of the Shyok. Its end had only been roughly sketched by Johnson in 1864, and Robert Shaw in 1869 was the first to realize its size. Alessio fixed additional points by triangulation and the whole glacier and its feeders were accurately mapped to its head, thereby connecting with Peterkin's Siachen survey of 1912.[1]

Meanwhile Wood, with Spranger and Shib Lal, set off to explore the headwaters of the Yarkand river where the map was either a blank or based on a sketch-map made by Johnson in 1864. Wood made a complete reconnaissance of the various head-streams, which feed 'Hayward's' branch of the river. During the course of this exploration he reached a pass 'G' and descended the valley 'H' leading from it for about a mile, without realizing at the time that he was in the easternmost head of the Shaksgam. It was hoped to carry out the exploration of this valley at a later stage of the expedition, but on his return to the depot on the Depsang in August, news of the outbreak of World War I was received and the expedition began to break up. Those who remained, including De Filippi, Wood, Abetti, and the surveyors, crossed the Karakoram once more on 19 August, surveyed the side tributaries of the Yarkand river which Wood had already visited, and from the main branch of the river crossed the western K'un Lun to Yarkand and Kashgar. Unfortunately they had to abandon the exploration of the Shaksgam, as had been planned. They returned to Europe by way of Tashkent and Bucharest.

[1] G.J. xlvi (1915) 85 ff.

# 6. Re-Survey of Kashmir

ABOUT 1906 it was decided that the time had come to re-survey the whole of India on the one-inch scale with contours at a normal interval of a hundred feet. This was a vast undertaking for a small department such as the Survey of India, but it was hoped to complete the whole programme in about twenty-five years. Sir Sidney Burrard, Superintendent of the Great Trigonometrical Survey, and Surveyor General from 1910 to 1919, himself an enthusiastic Himalayan geodesist and geographer, ordered the re-survey of Kashmir to begin in 1910.

With three other officers I was fortunate to be sent on this work, first as a triangulator and then in charge of detail surveyors. Previous to this none of us had climbed on snow or ice, and I alone had done some climbing on a rope on rock. Ice-axes and other mountaineering equipment were unobtainable in India, and until these arrived from England we were dependent on what the Neves could lend us.

During the next three years we learnt by experience and trained a number of surveyors in the use of axe and rope. I spent some most enjoyable 'busman's holidays' with Ernest Neve and other climbers more experienced than myself—S. G. Dunn of Allahabad University, J. B. Corry and R. D. Squires of the Alpine Club. Bruce kindly attached two first-class Gurkhas from his regiment, Kulbahadur and Logbahadur Gurung, to my camp, ostensibly to learn, but in fact they taught me more than I taught them, since they had both already been trained by him. Kulbahadur had also been with Longstaff on his Rishiganga exploration of 1907.

Our work took us to a number of Montgomerie's old stations as well as to new ones, and with Ernest Neve or the Gurkhas I climbed many of the peaks between the Sind, Liddar, and Warwan valleys, including almost all of the Kolahoi group, sometimes with Ernest Neve, generally with my *shikari*, Abdulla Bhat, who had had some mountaineering experience with the Neves and had been with the

Eckenstein and Abruzzi expeditions to K2 in 1902 and 1909. They are only practice climbs to-day, but the old hachured maps showed little of their detail, and it was easy to appreciate the difficulty men like Graham who were not surveyors must have had in locating the mountain they were on.

It was all great fun. The lower mountains of the Punjab Himalaya are both a climber's and a sportsman's paradise. There are none of the difficulties of the Assam Himalaya caused by dense jungle, and none of the purgatory of the bitter blasts and severe cold of the giants. It is possible to break one's neck, but there is no need to do so. I sent to England for skis, took them to my survey stations, and learnt the art by trial and error and with the help of Caulfield's book *How to Ski*. I was, I believe, the first to use ski in the Himalaya, and though never an expert, I afterwards found them most useful; but I always regretted that I never climbed with expert Alpine guides. My longest day was a climb of 5000 feet to a station, five hours waiting and observing on the summit, a descent of the same amount and a march of thirty-two miles; it was a full twenty-four hour day, but I carried no pack.

At this time the political situation in Asia was favourable for an extension of the survey northwards. The Anglo-Russian Agreement of 1907 led to a proposal the following year at the International Union of Geodesy at Potsdam that 'in the interests of science the triangulation of India and Russia in Asia should be joined together.' The proposal was approved in London and St. Petersburg, and plans were made by the Indian and Russian survey authorities to carry it out.

The triangulation on the Indian side was begun in 1909 by Dr. J. de Graaff Hunter, who based his work on a side of the geodetic North-West Himalaya Series near Rawalpindi. The work was to be of the highest order of accuracy. Observations were made to heliographs placed on station mark-stones, a process which necessitates very careful training of signallers both in mountaineering and in technical ability. Nothing is more exasperating to an observer, who has placed his signallers on distant mountains which he has to observe, than to reach his own station and find one of those signallers has for some reason disappeared. Considerable patience, discipline, and endurance are required on the part of all.

Hunter was in charge of the observations in 1909 and 1910, by which time they had reached the neighbourhood of Shardi. Lieutenant H. G. Bell succeeded Hunter in 1911 and took the observations forward to Gilgit. The difficulties were great with snow lying as low as 8000 feet during the reconnaissance; Bell then reconnoitred forward into Yasin, hoping to observe from stations on either side of the Darkot pass and across the Afghan pamir to join with the Russians in the neighbourhood of Lake Victoria, but found the physical difficulties too great. Though he climbed several peaks he was unable to take men laden with instruments up them. He visited Garmush, 20,564 feet, but was turned back by avalanches; crossed the Darkot-Ashkuman pass; examined the mountains of the Karumbar valley, and again found the difficulties insuperable. His assistant Wainright meanwhile examined the Hunza valley and reported that a series could probably be taken as far as Misgar, some distance short of the Kilik pass.

Meanwhile the Russians brought their triangulation from a measured base at Osh southwards over the Russian pamirs to the neighbourhood of Pamirski Post. Bell was again in charge of the Indian work in 1912 and had with him as his two assistants V. D. B. Collins and C. S. McInnes, who had in 1911 been on the Teram Kangri triangulation in the Nubra. Collins was to begin observations from the stations near Gilgit, while Bell and McInnes went forward to the Russian stations. It was a season of ill-fortune. One of Collins' camps on Yashochish (16,231) south of Gilgit was destroyed by lightning. One man was killed, another died later of shock and burns, and the others were more or less incapacitated for the rest of the year. Bell reached the Russian stations and had a friendly reception from Colonel Tcheikine, the senior Russian observer. He then carried out preliminary observations at three stations on the pamirs, but was taken ill with acute appendicitis on Lup Gaz (17,695), north of the Mintaka pass on 19 July and died six days later. These losses crippled the work, it was too late in the year to strengthen the party, and observations were abandoned.

Bell was a hardy mountaineer whose reconnaissances greatly lightened my task when I was put in charge of the work after his death. Sir Gerald Lenox-Conyngham, then Superintendent of the

Great Trigonometrical Survey, gave me a free hand; Bruce again lent me two of his Gurkhas, Kulbir and Hastabir Rana; Army Headquarters deputed Captain R. W. G. Hingston, I.M.S., whom I had already met travelling in Kashmir, as naturalist, physiologist, and doctor; and after considerable persuasion I was allowed six signallers from the 9th Gurkhas. After some practice training in Kashmir, the whole party crossed the Burzil pass by night early in May 1913, reached Gilgit on the 11th, and began work a week later.

I adopted Bell's plan: Collins observed from the stations in the south on either side of the Hunza gorge; I went forward to the Russian stations Kukhtek (17,031) and Sar-bulak (17,284) on the Russo-Chinese boundary and worked southwards over the Taghdumbash Pamir, with stations on the peaks on either side of the Kilik pass; McInnes reconnoitred the difficult country between us and observed from some of the stations. All observations were made to signal lamps and helios, a process which necessitated putting the Gurkhas and other trained men on their mountain stations and leaving them there with a week's supplies until the observers could signal them to descend and 'rendez-vous' elsewhere. Our success was largely due to the discipline, training, and cheerful co-operation of the Gurkhas who never failed us, and to the tough Hunza men who were sure-footed and agile on difficult ground, and carried our heavy instruments.

As surveyors with a task to finish in a specified time before bad weather or winter set in we did not attempt difficult climbs if an easier ascent was possible; but during the work we fixed the position and height of a number of peaks in the Western Karakoram which had been missed by the surveyors sixty years before from stations in Kashmir. Among them was the great double-headed Disteghil Sar (25,868) from which descends the Mulungutti Yaz to the Shimshal valley; this had been first seen by Cockerill in 1892. It is the highest peak of the Great Karakoram west of K2 and a magnificent peak for some future climber. Other peaks fixed by us have enabled later mountain-explorers—the Vissers in 1925, Montagnier and Morris in 1927, and above all the indefatigable Shipton and his colleagues more recently—to map these mountains and their glaciers in detail. The main object was to connect the triangulation frameworks of

India and Russia in Asia. This was attained by the end of August. The length of the junction side Kukhtek–Sar-bulak as found by the Russians (7134·9 metres) differed from our value (7133·4 metres) by only a metre and a half.[1]

More as an experiment than for any other reason we took with us field equipment, including fixed-focus box cameras, for a stereo-photogrammetric survey of the Taghdumbash Pamir. The pairs of photographs taken on extended bases were developed on the pamirs at night and plotted in 1914 on our return to Dehra Dun in the semi-automatic stereo-plotter designed by Captain Vivian Thompson. It was the first time stereoscopic photography had been used in exploration and proved itself to be most useful. The resulting map has so far been sufficiently accurate to escape criticism.

Hingston's services as a doctor were not required by any member of the party, but his skill contributed to the friendly relations maintained with the Hunza people and on the pamirs where our lower camps were visited by nomads even from long distances, with all kinds of illness, mostly eye-troubles. He also collected zoological, geological, and botanical specimens, which were classified after our return. The physiological tests made on various members of the party, on visitors to our camps, and even on occasional animals were not so popular. I was the principal victim of his acclimatization experiments; on arrival at my stations and before leaving them, as well as in camp, he counted the increase of my red blood corpuscles per cubic millimetre in a microscope. I only hope the blood he drew from me contributed to the scientific knowledge that eventually led to the conquest of Everest, as Hingston assured me, even in those early days, it would.

It would be wrong to give the impression that this country is easy to triangulate with accuracy. Even in fine weather a single cloud may obscure the reflected sun in a helio. We often worked long hours and camped high. When observations were finished we came down, packed camp, marched and climbed again, always in the fear that the weather might turn against us. My chief recollections now are of the high and bitter wind and the cheerful way our Gurkhas and other

[1] *Records of the Survey of India*, Vol. VI (1914). 'Completion of the Link connecting the Triangulations of India and Russia 1913.'

men put up with it. The secret of this cheerfulness was good food and plenty of it. No one can plan and work hard under these conditions on an empty stomach; and it is astonishing how much one can eat once the body has become acclimatized to altitude. Food helps to keep out the cold.

The re-survey of the Punjab Himalaya was progressing throughout this time. A fine programme of Himalayan exploration and survey was in prospect when war broke out in August 1914. Almost all of the younger officers of the Survey volunteered at once to return to military duty, and many of these were in France by the end of the year. On a much modified scale Himalayan surveys continued throughout the war, but many of the more energetic and skilled mountain surveyors were required elsewhere.

## PART FOUR

# 1918–1928

'Why partest from me, O my strength?'
So with myself, I communed, for I felt
My o'ertoil'd sinews slacken. We had reached
The summit, and were fix'd like to a bark
Arrived at land . . .
    And waiting a short space,
If aught should meet mine ear in that new round,
Then to my guide I turn'd and said:
                        'Loved sir!
'Declare what guilt is on this circle purged
'If our feet rest, no need thy speech should pause.'

*Vision of Dante. Purgatory (Canto. xvii 72)*

# 1. Retrospect and Prospect 1919

WORLD WAR I marked the end of an era in Himalayan adventure. The old friendliness of the mountain brotherhood had received a shock. Men who had met among the mountains of the world had fought as enemies and had learned to hate; men's names had been expunged from the membership of their Alpine clubs. Friends had been killed or maimed, especially those in the prime of life.

In 1914 for many of us there had been a vista ahead of happy days among the mountains. We had talked of founding an Alpine Club in India, of training hill-men to become guides in the Alpine sense, Bruce, with his knowledge, thought it could and ought to be done; the Neves, Arthur and Ernest, were equally sure. Most mountaineers from Europe had brought professional guides from the Alps with them; these paid tribute to the best of the Himalayan porters. We loved the mountains and travel among them. Those of us with work to do, surveyors, forest officers, district officers, deputy commissioners, geologists, and the rest worked and revelled in our surroundings and the grandeur of the hills.

In a vague kind of way we had discussed the possibility of climbing Everest; not with any knowledge of the problem, because Tibet and Nepal were closed, but just in case one of them opened a door. We had no idea whether it would be difficult to climb. Ideas on acclimatization were vague and contradictory: Longstaff had spoken of deterioration at high altitudes; Abruzzi had shown that men could live at over 17,000 feet for two months without deteriorating. Both had camped well over 22,000 feet, Longstaff probably at 23,000 feet. But the altitude record had only been lifted from 23,050 feet in 1860 to 24,600 feet in 1909. How much higher could man go? Trisul (23,360) was the highest summit yet reached by man, about which there could be no doubt. Most of us believed, as Longstaff did, in rush tactics before deterioration set in, though we thought fit men could probably acclimatize up to 20,000 feet, as Abruzzi seemed to have done.

Oxygen, as an aid to climbing, was not discussed in India, except possibly by one or two doctors and physiologists. The surgeon-mountaineer Clinton Dent in the nineties had propounded the theory that distress from mountain-sickness resulted from lack of oxygen; that it could be relieved by acclimatization; that acclimatization required time, and therefore could not be achieved in a rapid climb or in a balloon ascent. He had stated, even in those early days, his belief that Everest could be climbed. That some had faith in oxygen is shown by the fact that Mumm had consulted Messrs. Siebe, Gorman & Co. about it when the expedition to Everest was being planned for 1907. Mumm took with him in that year pneumatogen cartridges to the Kumaun Himalaya as a precaution. Furthermore, acclimatization experiments, mostly on the oxygen-carrying red corpuscles of the blood and on pulse-rates, had been carried out by Kellas in Sikkim and by Hingston on the Pamirs in 1913. Scientists had also made experiments in pressure-chambers; but none of the results had told us much, except through inference, about acclimatization above 20,000 feet.

Experience had been gained about the best seasons for climbing in various parts of the Himalaya and Karakoram; but weather varies from year to year, and it is difficult to generalize from conflicting evidence. Our equipment in India, especially as regards tents, though excellent for valley and down-country travel, was unsuitable for high altitudes. The special equipment brought out by the Duke was thought by many to be superfluous; the many are sometimes wrong.

We had had plenty to talk about over our camp-fires. In the Punjab Himalaya Bruce had reconnoitred Nanga Parbat on the Mummery expedition; both he and Arthur Neve had been to Nun Kun. In the Karakoram K2 had been written off the 'list of possibles' by Abruzzi. The problem of Everest was not how to climb it, but how to get there, and then 'the bottom rung,' as Longstaff put it; Kangchenjunga we left to those who liked wallowing in the mists of the eastern Himalaya.

When war came we had asked to be sent to Europe at once. We had been afraid it might end before we reached France, and that we should miss it. The Himalaya could wait till later. We had had our way and several of us had been in the thick of it before the end of 1914.

By 1918 the Survey of India had lost several officers with valuable Himalayan experience: E. B. Cardew, P. G. Huddleston, J. A. Field, and G. F. T. Oakes, all of whom had been on surveys in the Assam Himalaya; R. L. Almond and H. M. McKay, who in 1913 had attempted unsuccessfully to place a survey observation pole on Bandarpunch in the Kumaun Himalaya; A. A. Chase, who had been on the Kashmir survey in 1911, and V. D. B. Collins who had observed Teram Kangri and had been with me on the Indo-Russian triangulation in 1913.[1] Among others killed were A. M. Slingsby, who had reconnoitred Kamet and explored with Longstaff in the Karakoram; C. G. Rawling, who had done fine exploration in Western Tibet in 1903 and had been with Ryder across southern Tibet after Younghusband's Mission in 1904; and J. B. Corry and R. D. Squires with whom I had spent happy days in Kashmir. Arthur Neve had died as a result of his labours for the wounded.

Bruce, severely wounded in the Dardanelles, had laughed at his doctors and always remained ready to climb Everest; he was now fifty-three. Longstaff, as a territorial officer in the Hampshires, had found himself in his element as Assistant Commandant of the Gilgit Scouts. Most of the rest of us had been hit and had had our fill of adventure for the time being.

We went back to an India that had changed. The cost of everything had risen, political agitation and restlessness were upsetting loyalties, and, coupled with retrenchment, were hampering science and scientific departments. Sir Sidney Burrard, the mainspring of Himalayan surveys, retired in 1919, and the programme was cut down. For the private individual also mountain travel had become more difficult. Passports and visas were now required and scrutinized. The Russian revolution and the aftermath in Russia had killed the friendly relations between Britain and Russia, so that the British and Indian Governments were less willing to give permits for travel on the frontiers.

[1] *Killed in action*: Cardew, on Hill 70 (25 September 1915); Huddleston, in the Ypres salient (25 March 1916); Field, on the Somme (13 July 1915); Oakes, on the Somme (15 July 1916); Almond, at Neuve Chapelle (28 October 1914); McKay, near Sailly (13 November 1914); Chase, on the Somme (11 March 1917); Collins, near Richebourg (17 December 1914). *Records of the Survey of India*, Vol. xx (The War Record 1914-1920).

# 2. Everest 1921

No one can claim to be the first to have thought of climbing Everest. The mountain was built before man was born. Mallory, when asked why anyone wanted to climb it, spoke the simple truth: 'Because it is there.' This is a concise summary of an indefinable urge in the spirit of man. The attitude of mind is no more easy to analyse than the mental process of one who tries to hit an expensive and exasperating little ball into a tiny hole in fewer strokes than those of a phantom colonel.

Bruce, eminently sane, suggested to Younghusband in Chitral in 1893 that they should cross Tibet and climb Everest. Mumm, Bruce, and Longstaff made preparations to attack it in 1907. C. G. Rawling a few years later had planned an expedition, but was prevented from pursuing his preparations by the outbreak of war.

Soon after the armistice the matter was revived on 10 March 1919 at a lecture given by Captain J. B. L. Noel when he spoke of a journey he had made in 1913 and of Rawling's plans.[1] Freshfield, President of the Royal Geographical Society, J. P. Farrar, President of the Alpine Club, Younghusband, and Kellas were present at the meeting and spoke in support of it. But it was too early. The Government were not prepared to forward a request to Tibet for permission.

When Younghusband became President of the Royal Geographical Society later in the year he again took up the matter with the President of the Alpine Club. At an Expedition Committee meeting of the Society held on 26 April 1920, among a number of resolutions, it was decided that the Society should be responsible for all negotiations with the British, Indian, and Tibetan Governments; that permission should be sought for a two years' permit, the first year to be devoted to reconnaissance, the second to the assault; that the co-operation of the Survey of India be asked for through the Indian Government;

[1] G.J. liii (1919) 289.

and that the reconnaissance party should include experienced Alpine climbers to examine the technical difficulties of the ascent. The Secretary of State for India was to be asked to receive a deputation and a Joint Committee of the Alpine Club and the Society was to be formed as soon as necessary for the organization and direction of the enterprise. Colonel Howard-Bury was to be invited to go to India and seek the support of the Indian Government.

Assured of the support of the Secretary of State, Howard-Bury went to India and explained the plan to the Viceroy, who was sympathetic. Charles Bell, Political Agent in Sikkim, was in Lhasa and was instructed to seek permission from the Dalai Lama, with whom he was on friendly terms. The Tibetan Government gave its sanction and the news was received in London early in January 1921.

A joint Everest Committee of the Royal Geographical Society and Alpine Club was now formed, with three members from each body, under Younghusband's chairmanship. Much preparatory work had already been done, and it was at once decided to carry out the reconnaissance in 1921 and the assault in 1922. Of the £10,000 estimated, about £6,000 was raised by members and fellows of the two bodies. His Majesty King George V, the Prince of Wales, and the Viceroy of India, Lord Reading, gave generous donations, and the balance was found later by selling the rights of publication of despatches and photographs to *The Times*, the *Graphic*, and the *Philadelphia Ledger*.

Bruce was the obvious man to lead, but he was unable to accept for military reasons. Howard-Bury, who had done so much of the preliminary negotiation, was then selected. The four experienced climbers chosen were Harold Raeburn, A. M. Kellas, George Leigh Mallory, and George Finch, the first two, veterans in climbing, to supply the Himalayan experience, while Mallory and Finch ranked among the best Alpinists in England. At the last moment Finch had to decline through illness and his place was taken by G. H. Bullock of the Consular Service, who was also a fine climber. A. F. R. Wollaston was chosen as doctor and naturalist.[1]

In India several of us were keen to go. I was invited, and was bitterly disappointed when leave was refused. Major H. T. Morshead, a friend of long standing, was appointed by the Surveyor General to

[1] Howard-Bury: *Mount Everest: The Reconnaissance 1921* (London, 1922).

lead the survey party, with Major E. O. Wheeler as his assistant. No better choices could have been made. Morshead had explored the Tsangpo with Bailey in 1913, had roamed the Himalaya, and had reached 23,420 feet with Kellas on Kamet in 1920;[1] Wheeler, who joined the Survey of India after the war, was a Canadian who had climbed much in the Rockies and had experience of the Canadian method of photographic survey. Dr. A. M. Heron of the Geological Survey of India was lent by the Indian Government as geologist.

During the Tibet mission of 1903–4 the Survey of India detachment under Ryder had surveyed southern Tibet westwards to Tengkye or Tinki Dzong in about longitude 88°, but in his journey up the Tsangpo Ryder had only been able to survey a short distance south of the river. An area of about 13,000 square miles, between the Tsangpo watershed and the Great Himalaya, which here forms the Nepal-Tibet boundary, was still unsurveyed, and indeed almost unknown, except for the route-sketches made by the explorer Hari Ram (MH) in 1871–2 and 1885. Ryder, who was now Surveyor General, decided to take the opportunity to strengthen Morshead's detachment both to revise the quarter-inch map of Sikkim and to survey the blank area west of longitude 88° and north of Everest, through which the expedition was to pass. The whole of the cost of the surveys was borne by the Government of India. All stores and equipment for the Expedition were granted freedom from Customs duties and the Darjeeling Railway gave the Expedition a free pass for all members and stores.

Morshead's detachment, including three Indian surveyors and an Indian photographic assistant, assembled at Darjeeling early in April, and began the revision of the Sikkim survey soon afterwards. They completed some 2500 square miles of this work before the arrival of the main party from England about six weeks later. After meeting Howard-Bury, Morshead finally left Darjeeling on 13 May, picked up his surveyors, and took his detachment by the direct road through Sikkim northwards to Kampa Dzong in Tibet, which he reached on the 28th.

Howard-Bury had meanwhile planned his approach by the Chumbi valley route, which is longer but more suitable for baggage

[1] See below, page 186.

animals. He engaged about forty Sherpas and Bhotias at Darjeeling to act as porters for the expedition. Sherpas are of Tibetan stock, born and bred in the uppermost reaches of the Dudh Kosi tributaries, the best of them from villages, such as Namche Bazar, in the Sola Khumbu district of Nepal, within a few miles of Everest, and are accustomed from birth to high altitudes and cold. They are adventurous, light-hearted, courageous, and splendid material for the making of first-class mountaineers with technical training. They first came to Darjeeling about 1902 to trade, and finding they could earn good wages, stayed to work as rickshaw-wallahs and to do coolie work during the summer season. They were first engaged on mountain expeditions with Kellas and with the Norwegians, Rubenson and Monrad Aas. Bhotias are Tibetans who for much the same reasons come to Sikkim; the best of them also make good porters, and are hardy and reliable if properly looked after.

The main transport for the approach to the Chumbi valley was composed of about a hundred mules belonging to the Supply and Transport Corps and lent by the Commander-in-Chief. They saved the expedition much expense, but were not up to the hard marches through Sikkim and Chumbi at this season, when the *chhoti barsat*, precursor of the monsoon, was particularly heavy and troublesome. Since the camping-grounds in Sikkim are small, the main body of the expedition went in two parts, the first leaving Darjeeling on 18 May, the second the following day. They took the road by Kalimpong, Gnatong, and the Jelep La (14,390) to the Chumbi valley, where the whole expedition assembled and marched on together with yak transport via Phari, and the Tang La (15,200) to Kampa Dzong, which was reached on 5 June, and where Morshead's detachment was already assembled.

Just before reaching Kampa Dzong, Dr. Kellas died of heart failure. He had been ailing since the march through the Chumbi valley. He had strained his heart during the previous year on Kamet and Narsing (19,128) and in the early spring of 1921 in camps over 20,000 feet on Kabru. The country between Phari and Kampa Dzong, mostly above 16,000 feet, was now too severe for him. He was buried on 6 June on the slopes of the hills south of Kampa Dzong facing the mountains of Sikkim, which he alone had climbed.

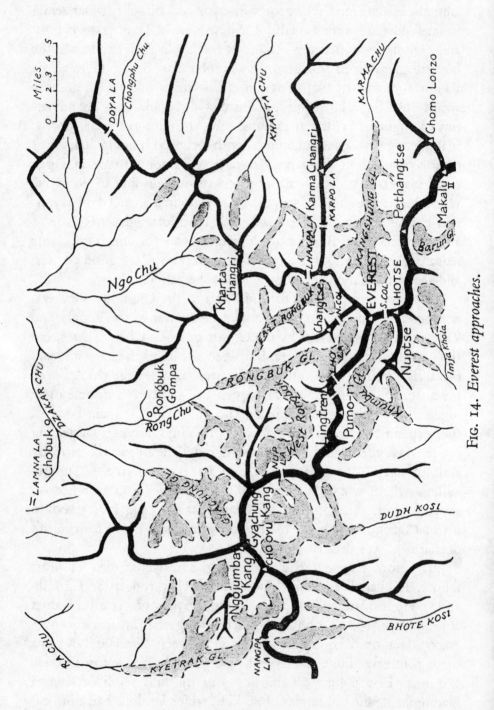

FIG. 14. *Everest approaches.*

Raeburn also was found to be suffering from a strained heart and Wollaston decided it would be unwise for him to continue. Howard-Bury therefore sent him back under Wollaston's care direct to Lachen where he could be looked after by the lady missionaries in that place. The loss of these two was a severe blow to the expedition, for they were the two most experienced Himalayan mountaineers of the party and Kellas was the only authority on the physiological effects of altitude.

Kampa Dzong was quitted on 8 June. Beyond the Tengkye La it was unmapped country and Morshead and his surveyors were at work all the time, though views to the south were hampered by cloud. The first base of the expedition was made at Tingri on 18 June, Wollaston rejoining on the 22nd after escorting Raeburn back to Lachen. Bullock and Mallory left to reconnoitre the northern side of Everest on the 23rd and two days later Wheeler and Heron went off to begin the photographic and geological surveys. Morshead allotted the smaller-scale topographical work in the area north of the mountain to his surveyors.

On the way across Tibet, after crossing the Tang La near Phari, the expedition had been in the basin of the Yaru Chu, the westward flowing head tributary of the Arun, until about two marches west of the Tengkye La. Here the Yaru Chu meets the Phung Chu which drains a large region of the Great Himalaya from beyond Tingri, and it was the course of this river the expedition took to that place. After the meeting of the Yaru Chu and Phung Chu the combined waters break south-westwards and then south, receiving successively three right-bank tributaries, the Dzakar Chu, the Kharta Chu, and the Karma Chu, before forcing a passage through the Great Himalaya in the Arun gorge. The three tributaries flow eastwards from the direction of Everest.

At Tingri a large tributary, the Ra Chu, enters the Phung Chu from the south and is fed by the Kyetrak glacier which descends from Cho Oyu (26,750) and Ngojumba Kang (25,730), peaks of the Great Himalaya about eighteen miles west-north-west of Everest. At the southern head of the Kyetrak glacier is the Nangpa La (19,050), a pass used occasionally by Sherpas for trade with Tibet in fine weather from mid-May to October.

East of Ngojumba Kang which sends off a long high ridge northwards is the Gyachung glacier, lying between that ridge and a
similar ridge thrown off north-eastwards by Gyachung Kang
(25,990), the next peak of the Everest group. The south ridge of this
peak forms the crest-line of the Nepal–Tibet watershed, falls steeply
to the Nup La, a col at the head of the West Rongbuk glacier, and
then bends eastwards carrying the peaks Pumo-ri (23,190) and
Lingtren (21,730), with the 'north-east col of Pumo-ri' between
them. From Lingtren a south-east ridge falls steeply to the Lho La,
about 19,250 feet, and from this point the great west ridge of Everest
rises steeply to the summit.

The northern face of Everest and of its western ridge falls precipitously to the Rongbuk glacier, which is joined by the West Rongbuk
glacier after about five miles and continues northwards after the
junction for the same distance to feed the Rong Chu. Ten miles
farther down it is joined by the Gyachung Chu, fed by the glacier
from Ngojumba Kang, and the combined river, the Dzakar Chu,
flows north-east and then east, parallel to the Phung Chu and about
fifteen miles to the south of it.

It was these upper glaciers of the Kyetrak and Dzakar rivers, all
utterly unknown, that Bullock and Mallory set out to explore and
if possible reconnoitre for a possible route to the summit, while
Wheeler and Heron had the task of making a photographic survey
of the region and of examining its geology.

Bullock and Mallory, accompanied by sixteen porters, discovered
the Dzakar Chu near the hamlet of Chobuk, turned south up
the Rong Chu, and from near the Rongbuk monastery had the
first complete view of Everest's stupendous northern face, 10,000
feet from top to bottom, the summit pyramid lying back fore-
shortened by the angle of sight and supported by its two ridges, the
north-east ridge and the west ridge. The crest of the north-east ridge
falls gently for some 1500 feet to a shoulder (27,510) from which a
rib is detached to form a north buttress or ridge. This drops to the
North Col at 22,900 feet and then rises again to the North Peak,
'Changtse' (24,730). The west ridge has no shoulder but falls very
steeply to the Lho La, some four miles distant.

From 27 June until 25 July, generally in bad weather, Mallory and Bullock explored the Rongbuk and West Rongbuk glaciers in great detail, climbing a number of heights over 20,000 feet. During the course of this they reached two cols overlooking Nepal, Pumo-ri's north-east col, and the Lho La. From them they had a view down to the head of the Khumbu glacier and its great broken ice-fall enclosed by the south face of Everest's west ridge and the north face of Nuptse.

A complete reconnaissance was made of Everest's north face and of all possible approaches from the west and north. The conclusion reached was that from this side the only feasible route to the summit was from the North Col by the north ridge to the north-east shoulder, and thence by the north-east ridge to the summit. An ascent from the Rongbuk glacier to the North Col would be difficult, but not impossible: and this line should be taken only as a last resort.

Meanwhile in the same bad conditions Wheeler had been carrying on the photographic survey, often climbing heights only to find the views obscured by storm. Having done all he could on the Kyetrak glacier he worked on the lower Rongbuk. During the course of his work he ascended a small stream which joins the Rongbuk glacier from the east about four miles above its snout and discovered that this issued from a large glacier, afterwards known as the East Rongbuk glacier. This he explored for a considerable distance to the south, discovering that the medial moraines afforded a comparatively easy line of approach up the glacier. This was a secret which had eluded Bullock and Mallory. Wheeler closed his work in the Rongbuk region on 21 August, and set off to join the rest in the Kharta valley.

Meanwhile Morshead, Heron, and Wollaston had been carrying out their surveys farther afield, all covering large areas of unknown ground. Howard-Bury, after visiting the various camps, crossed the Doya La to the Arun, and selected his second base in the Kharta valley for the exploration of the eastern approaches by way of the Kharta and Karma valleys. It was hoped to find a route from one of them which would give access to the North Col from the east.

By the end of July all stores had been brought over the Doya La to Kharta and during the first half of August Bullock, Mallory, and Howard-Bury explored the two valleys. From the Karma valley they had magnificent views of Everest's east face, and the north-east and south ridges, the latter dipping to the 'South Col' between the summit and Lhotse, the South Peak.

From Lhotse (27,890) the main crest of the Great Himalaya continues eastwards through Pethangtse (22,060) and then south-east to Makalu II (25,120) and Makalu I (27,790), all of which show fluted ice-clad faces impossible to approach. The east face of Everest was examined from vantage points over 20,000 feet and reckoned to be quite inaccessible, and it was recognized that there was no way up from the Karma valley to the north-east ridge by which the shoulder could be reached. The alternative was to explore the head of the Kharta valley and see whether this led to the North Col. On 18 August the riddle was solved by an ascent of the Lhakpa La (22,200) at the head of the Kharta valley. By this time a note from Howard-Bury had reached the two climbers telling them of Wheeler's discovery of the East Rongbuk glacier.

From the Lhakpa La it was seen that the descent to the head of the East Rongbuk glacier was easy, but clouds obscured the North Col and the route from it to the shoulder. The reconnaissance was therefore incomplete until the North Col had been actually reached and the route beyond it to the shoulder examined. It was also determined to see what altitude could be reached by the now well-acclimatized party. Mallory and Bullock returned after this reconnaissance to the base in the Kharta valley where the party was now collecting for the final effort. They were unexpectedly rejoined by Raeburn towards the end of the month.

Early in September the whole expedition were in occupation of their advanced base in the Kharta valley, but not until the 19th did the weather clear. The following day Mallory, Bullock, Morshead, and Wheeler with fourteen Sherpas went up to the Lhakpa La, and for the first time had a clear view of the problem beyond. From the head basin of the East Rongbuk glacier, to which they must descend about 1200 feet, the North Col slopes rose 2000 feet at a steep angle and its face was split by a series of long crevasses. It could be climbed, but not without a camp at its base, and a strong party of climbers would be required to prepare a route before laden porters could ascend it and place a camp on the col.

On the 22nd all except Raeburn went up to the Lhakpa La with twenty-six laden porters and spent the night there at 22,000 feet. Next morning only ten porters were fit to continue; this meant that only three climbers could reconnoitre the North Col. Howard-Bury, Morshead, and Wollaston turned back, while Mallory, Bullock, and Wheeler descended to the basin and pitched camp below the North Col.

After a disturbed and squally night the three climbers with three unladen Sherpas stamped a track to the North Col. Only once did they have to use the axe to cut steps. They took the final steep slope in one long zig-zag and reached the col by mid-day.

They were met by the bitter blast of the west wind sweeping across the face of Everest and over the col, and were forced to take shelter. But they had seen enough. On this day, 24 September, it was believed that the secret of the ascent of Everest had been found, provided that there were no insuperable physiological difficulties to be overcome. From the North Col the north ridge was rounded and appeared easy and free from danger at least as far as the shoulder.

The party returned to the camp at the foot of the col and there spent the night. Mallory now had to decide whether to make an attack. The weather was worsening, the wind increasing, and porters and climbers alike were worn out after their exertions of the last three months. There was no reserve of energy for a crisis and therefore no choice but to return. Mallory withdrew over the Lhakpa La on the 26th and camps were struck in the Kharta valley. The return through Tibet was begun on 5 October.

# 3. Everest 1922

THE expeditions of 1921 and 1922 were one operation. It was the task of Howard-Bury's party to explore and survey the approach to Everest and to 'find the bottom rung' without entering forbidden Nepal. This had been done. All were agreed that the only route to the summit from the north, where the technical difficulties were not insuperable, had been found. Much had been learnt also about acclimatization and high-altitude snow conditions in the Everest region during and after the monsoon; wind, except on the North Col in September, had not been excessive—in Mallory's words: 'never an enemy to be feared during the whole period of the monsoon.' Snowstorms, 'though they prevented more than one expedition, never turned us back.' These were hopeful, if unexpected, signs.

Climbers and porters, when acclimatized, had spent a night at the North Col, at almost 23,000 feet. Nothing was yet known about acclimatization at higher altitudes, or whether the human system could stand the strain of 25,000 feet; but it was recognized that very severe technical difficulties at or above that height would spell defeat. One or perhaps two camps would have to be carried up and pitched on the north ridge before the assault could be pressed, and it was uncertain whether suitable sites would be found, or that porters could carry at that altitude. In concluding the summary of his account Mallory wrote:[1]

Another sort of difficulty will jeopardize the chances of success. It might be possible for two men to struggle somehow to the summit, disregarding every other consideration. It is a different matter to climb the mountain as mountaineers would have it climbed. Principles, time-honoured in the Alpine Club, must of course be respected in the ascent of Mount Everest. The party must keep a margin of safety. It is not to be a mad enterprise rashly pushed on regardless of danger. The ill-considered acceptance of

[1] Howard-Bury: *Mount Everest: The Reconnaissance 1921* (London, 1922), 278.

any and every risk has no part in the essence of persevering courage. A mountaineering enterprise may keep sanity and sound judgment and remain an adventure. And of all principles by which we hold the first is mutual help. What is to be done for a man who is sick or abnormally exhausted at these high altitudes? His companions must see to it that he is taken down at the first opportunity and with an adequate escort: and the obligation is the same whether he be Sahib or coolie: if we ask a man to carry our loads up the mountain we must care for his welfare at need. It may be taken for granted that such need will arise and will interfere very seriously with any organization however ingeniously and carefully it may be arranged.

In all it may be said that one factor beyond all others is required for success. Too many chances are against the climbers; too many contingencies may turn against them. Anything like a breakdown of the transport will be fatal: soft snow on the mountain will be an impregnable defence; a big wind will send back the strongest; even so small a matter as a boot fitting a shade too tight may endanger one man's foot and involve the whole party in retreat. The climbers must have above all things, if they are to win through, good fortune, and the greatest good fortune of all for mountaineers, some constant spirit of kindness in Mount Everest itself, the forgetfulness for long enough of its more cruel moods: for we must remember that the highest of mountains is capable of severity, a severity so awful and so fatal that the wiser sort of men will do well to think and tremble even on the threshold of their high endeavour.

Before the reconnaissance party returned to England preparations for the assault in 1922 were under way. It was a principle established by the early Everest Committees that three elements in the party were required: sound organization by an experienced leader, Alpine knowledge of the highest quality among the climbers, any one of whom must be technically capable of making the final climb, and experience of Himalayan ice and snow conditions which differ in many respects from those in the Alps. No man combined all these qualities. Bruce had a vast experience of Himalayan organization, travel, and climbing in all its aspects; he knew the Himalaya almost from end to end, and understood its people as none other has ever done; but though thirty years old at heart, he was now fifty-six years of age. Longstaff had been higher and had the greater technical knowledge—almost an instinctive knowledge—of climbing and of snow and ice conditions at great altitudes; he had explored and climbed in the Himalaya, Caucasus, the Rockies, and the Alps; he was now forty-seven. Colonel E. L. Strutt, aged forty-eight, was an Alpinist of great experience. It was obvious from the first that all these should go; Bruce as the ideal leader and organizer, Longstaff as chief medical and technical adviser, and Strutt as second-in-command. It was essential that the friendliest relations should be maintained with the Tibetan people, and that the organization of this, the first attack on the summit, should be as perfect as possible. None of these three were expected to go higher than the North Col.

The assault party comprised younger men, each technically capable of reaching the summit, Mallory, George I. Finch, Dr. T. Howard Somervell, Major E. F. Norton, and Dr. A. W. Wakefield. Of these Norton was the eldest at thirty-eight, Mallory thirty-seven; these alone at that time had Himalayan experience. Finch, who had been unable to go on the reconnaissance, was an authority on the use of oxygen and its apparatus. Five others were chosen as supports, and for transport and photography: Morshead (now forty), C. G. Crawford, C. J. Morris, J. G. Bruce, and J. B. Noel, all about thirty-two. There were therefore fifteen British members of the party. No professional guides were included. Sherpas would act as porters, and they were not yet trained.[1]

Bruce planned to establish his base at the snout of the Rongbuk glacier by the end of April, so that he could have a probable six weeks to place the intermediate camps, acclimatize his party and make the assault. There were two reasons for not starting earlier; Bruce contended that the cold of an earlier approach through Tibet would be a severe strain on the health of the party, and that a longer campaign than six weeks at a high altitude would lead to a deterioration of physical and mental powers. He intended a methodical advance to the North Col, with gradual acclimatization to that altitude, after which he had an open mind. Though much has been learnt since, there is no doubt even now that his reasoning and plan were sound.

[1] Bruce: *The Assault on Mount Everest, 1922* (London, 1923).

The expedition, using yak transport, crossed southern Tibet according to plan, the weather becoming more spring-like every day, and it reached its base camp site on 1 May. A hundred Tibetans had been engaged to carry equipment and stores to the lower camps in order to conserve the energies of the fifty Sherpas who would be required higher.

On 4 May Strutt, Longstaff, Morshead and Norton reconnoitred the route up the glacier; they reached the foot of the North Col at 21,000 feet and returned to the base camp on the 9th with a full report. Camp I (17,800) at the snout of the East Rongbuk glacier Camp II (19,800) two and a half miles up it on its left bank, Camp III (21,000) a further three miles and below the North Col slopes, were now established and stocked with supplies.

Camp III was set up by Mallory and Somervell on 12 May. The weather was fine and on the following day with one Sherpa they reconnoitred the route to the North Col. As was to be expected the detail of the ice-slopes had changed since the previous year, the ice was more bare and the crevasses more open; but having fixed a rope at one difficult pitch they forced a route to the col. Here they were greeted by the west wind, strong but of less intensity than in September 1921. As yet unacclimatized, both suffered from the altitude, and they rested in Camp III for three days.

On 16 May they were joined by Strutt, Morshead, and Norton. Finch should have accompanied Strutt, but had been delayed at base camp with stomach trouble, and the oxygen apparatus was with him. Bruce's plan was to make two attempts: the first with Mallory and Somervell, the second with Finch and Norton using oxygen. Strutt, at Camp III, had authority to select the dates for the attacks, and to vary the plan according to his judgement on the spot.

At this point the weather played false. Though it remained fine in Camp III, a party which visited the Rapiu La overlooking the Karma valley saw grey clouds boiling up from Nepal; the bogey of an early monsoon decided Strutt and his party to act at once. It is probable that in the absence of Kellas the length of time required for acclimatization was not fully appreciated, since all felt fit and were anxious to start. It must be remembered that in those days there were no radio reports of the weather, and the climbers at Camp III had to forecast from the signs they saw.

Mallory was in favour of a party of four for the assault in preference to one of two. Strutt decided therefore to make the first assault with the four climbers available, Mallory, Somervell, Morshead, and Norton. On 17 May these moved up to the North Col (22,900) with ten Sherpas, each carrying thirty pounds, and rested there in Camp IV for two nights. On the 19th they returned to Camp III and brought up the remaining loads for stocking Camp IV and for the assault. Five tents were pitched on a shelf below the col out of the wind. The monsoon threat had vanished; the night of the 19th was clear and starlit; hopes were high.

Bruce's original plan had been to have two camps above the North Col, as advocated by Mallory, who was convinced that the final assault should start from no lower than 27,000 feet. This plan needed an intermediate camp at between 25,000 and 26,000, but it was compromised by the decision to double the number of climbers without increasing the number of porters, who were not available; it had to be modified by the sacrifice of one camp. It was hoped to place Camp V at 26,000 feet or higher, and to make the assault from there. Loads and supplies were cut to a minimum—four loads each of twenty pounds to be shared between nine porters taking them in turn.

On the morning of the 20th five of the nine porters were mountain-sick and out of action. The rest started with Morshead leading the first of three ropes, and carrying a load. During the climb the wind rose and it became colder. By half-past twelve the whole party sheltered in the lee of the crest at about 25,000 feet. Mallory had intended to go a thousand feet higher, but the wind was still rising and for the safety of the porters it was essential to give them an ample margin of time to descend. The two small tents were pitched on built-up platforms at three o'clock, the porters were sent down, and the four climbers went to bed. Morshead's fingers and toes, Mallory's finger-tips, and one of Norton's ears had been frostbitten; there was little sleep for any of them, but they remained hopeful.

Morning brought a slight snowfall, but at 6.30 the weather

improved, and the four started at eight o'clock. Morshead, feeling himself a drag on the others, returned to the tent almost at once. The rest ascended the ridge to within about seven hundred feet of the shoulder, probably to 26,800 feet, and turned back at half-past two. Tired though they were, they reached Camp V in an hour and a half. Here they picked up Morshead and started down for the North Col. Mallory's skill was well illustrated on the descent, when the third climber on the rope slipped and dragged the fourth and second off the ridge. Mallory, in the lead, instinctively drove the pick of his axe deep in the snow, hitched the rope round its head and threw the whole of his weight on the axe to hold it down. By a miracle the pick and the rope held all three men who had fallen.

They were exhausted when they reached Camp IV in the dark. On the morning of the 22nd they descended to Camp III where Wakefield took charge of them and evacuated them to the Base Camp.

On the way down to Camp III they passed Finch and J. G. Bruce going up to the North Col to try out the oxygen apparatus for the second attempt. Defects had been found in the apparatus, caused by the long journey across Tibet. Finch had remedied these, and the party, which included several Sherpas, reached the col in three hours.

On the 24th Finch, Bruce, Noel, and the Gurkha Tejbir, using oxygen, went up to the col for the second assault. The following day they reached a height of 25,000 feet but were forced by the rising wind and deteriorating weather to halt, pitch camp, and send the Sherpas back with Noel, before retiring to their sleeping-bags. At sunset the storm reached gale force, and lasted for eighteen hours with only occasional lulls, during which one or other of the three would have to venture out and re-anchor the tent. At about 1 p.m. on the 26th the wind at last began to drop and at Finch's suggestion they decided to risk a second night at this altitude, though short of food, and if the weather was kind to make an assault on the morrow. As they were turning in at 6 o'clock six Sherpas from the North Col arrived to help them down. As soon as the storm had abated, these six had devotedly made the ascent of their own accord and had brought thermos flasks of hot beef-tea to the climbers.

Having sent the Sherpas back reassured, the three climbers spent their second night at 25,500 feet, surviving it with the aid of oxygen. At 6.30 on the morning of the 27th they started for the shoulder, Finch and Bruce each carrying forty pounds, Tejbir fifty, all using oxygen. Within five hundred feet Tejbir could go no farther and descended to Camp V. At 26,500 feet, in a still rising wind they left the ridge and struck across the north face which seemed easier going. It was here that they first encountered the difficulty caused by Everest's formation, the rock strata on the face dipping down at an average angle of thirty-five degrees like the slates of a roof. Climbing diagonally they reached 27,000 feet, half-way across the face. Three hundred feet higher Bruce's oxygen supply suddenly failed. Finch immediately connected his supply to Bruce in order to give him relief while he repaired the damage.

The effects of their two nights at 25,500 feet with insufficient food had, however, reduced them to such weakness that they realized it would be folly to struggle on. They had reached about 27,300 feet. After regaining the north ridge they followed it down to Camp V, and as a relief party of Sherpas was arriving they passed on down to the North Col, and after an hour's rest descended to Camp III. The following morning both were suffering from frostbitten feet and were evacuated to the base.

The two planned attempts had failed. All now were resting at the Base Camp. Strutt and Norton had dilated hearts; J. G. Bruce and Morshead were frostbitten and unable to walk, and General Bruce decided to send them back under Longstaff's care to Darjeeling. By 3 June Mallory, Finch, and Somervell were rested, and though there were signs of an early monsoon they determined to make a third attack.

The party was made up of these three, with Wakefield and Crawford, and they started for Camp I the same day. It was felt that Finch's previous attempt had failed only from shortage of food at the high camp and he was ready to try again. But it was only six days since his gruelling two nights at 25,500 feet, and at Camp I he realized he was unfit for a further effort and returned to base.

Heavy snow fell at Camp I and lasted throughout the 4th. The west wind had been absent for two days and the temperature had risen. But the morning of the 5th was fine and the party went on to Camp III to find the stores buried and the tents half-filled by wet snow. The night was fine and the next morning sunny. The west wind had risen again and was blowing the snow off the west ridge. With one more day of these conditions it was considered safe.

At 8 a.m. on the 7th the party of seventeen started. They mounted the slopes on four ropes, Somervell leading Mallory, a Sherpa and Crawford on the first, and the thirteen remaining Sherpas on the three ropes behind. About six hundred feet below the crest of the col the snow avalanched and all four ropes were swept away. When the snow stopped the eight men on the first two ropes were able to extricate themselves, but the last two ropes had been carried by the snow into the broad crevasse below. Two only of the nine were brought out alive; six of the seven bodies were found. One of the two rescued was Lewa, who later become one of the best-known Sherpa guides. He had been with the 1921 Expedition, went again to Everest in 1924 and 1933, to Kamet in 1931, and Nanga Parbat in 1934.

So ended in tragedy the third attempt of the first assault on Everest. It is easy to be wise when the lesson has been learnt. No Himalayan climber, except perhaps Longstaff, had, at that time, sufficient knowledge of snow on ice under early monsoon conditions, how it packed in the lee of the wind; and in 1922 the monsoon was early and deceptively hesitant.

In other respects the expedition of 1922 was the most notable of any that had yet visited the Himalaya. Four men had spent a night at 25,000 feet; three had reached about 26,800 feet, more than two thousand feet higher than the Duke's record in 1909. Two had camped at 25,500 feet, 2000 feet higher than Meade in 1913, and after two gruelling nights at that height had reached 27,300 feet with oxygen. In both cases wind, weather, and insufficient food had, it was thought, prevented success. Above all, the best of the Sherpas had shown themselves devoted, disciplined, and reliable at great heights, and capable of carrying loads to 25,500 feet.

# 4. Everest 1924

THE Tibetan Government sanctioned a third expedition to Everest in 1924. This gave time for a full appreciation of the lessons of 1922. It was realized that the difficulties above the North Col had been underestimated, that at least two camps above it must be established, and that not more than two men should attempt the summit at the same time, though they must be closely supported. Views differed on the value of oxygen, some maintaining that the relief gained from it was offset by the extra weight to be carried, and by the danger from its failure. Much had been learnt about equipment, and improvements had been made.

The party for 1924 was stronger for the knowledge and experience gained. General Bruce was again chosen to lead; Mallory, Somervell, Norton, J. G. Bruce, and Noel had all been to Everest in 1922; Bentley Beetham, J. de V. Hazard, N. E. Odell, and Andrew Irvine, the latter only twenty-two years of age, were all new-comers, but the first three had much climbing experience elsewhere. R. W. G. Hingston, with Himalayan experience, was doctor, physiologist, and naturalist; E. O. Shebbeare of the Indian Forest Service went as transport officer.[1]

General Bruce's plan, as before, was to reach his base at the end of April, but early on the march he went sick with malaria and had to return. He was succeeded by Norton, who, in consultation with the rest of the party, decided to make the attempt early in May.

The detailed plan was as follows: A hundred and fifty Tibetans were engaged to stock Camps I and II, leaving fifty-five Sherpas to establish Camps III and IV, carry between these two camps and establish Camps V, VI, and VII. These last three were to be at approximately 25,500, 26,500, and 27,200 feet. On the eve of the assault two climbers would occupy Camp VII (one tent), with two at Camp VI (one tent), and four at Camp V (four tents). The two

[1] Norton: *The Fight for Everest, 1924* (London, 1925).

pairs in Camps VI and VII were to attempt the climb the following day, one pair with oxygen, the other without. If they failed, the supporting four men in Camp V would pass through them, occupy the two high camps and make a second attempt. There were thus four chances for two men to reach the top.

This most promising plan was wrecked at the outset by a fearful blizzard which routed the porters while Camp III was being established. They were badly shaken, two lives were lost, and all had to be brought back to the base to recover. Not until 19 May were the three camps re-established and occupied. More than a fortnight had been lost, and the bogey of an early monsoon once more reared its ugly head.

All the climbers had had a most exhausting time and now had to prepare the route up to the col in haste and in severe conditions. Norton, Mallory, Somervell, and Odell completed this on the 20th, and the following day Hazard with twelve porters established Camp IV. Bruce and Odell were to join him on the 21st. Once more the weather made this impossible, and on the evening of the 23rd Hazard came down to Camp III, but with only eight of the twelve porters; two with frostbite and two others too scared to descend had returned to Camp IV during the early part of the descent.

A tremendous responsibility now rested on Norton, who, with Mallory and Somervell, both of whom were suffering from sore throats, had to reach the marooned men and bring them down to safety. With the greatest difficulty and in very dangerous conditions the men were rescued, but the strain on the climbers during this operation and the three previous weeks of storm had been intense, while the morale of the porters had suffered severely. Only fifteen of the fifty-five Sherpas were any longer reliable for work above Camp III.

A new plan had to be improvised with the carrying power available. Camp VI of the original plan had to be cut out, oxygen had to be left behind, two attempts only could now be made, each by single pairs from the highest camp, the second attempt following the day after the first. The first pair was to be Mallory and Bruce, the second Norton and Somervell. The first pair were to establish Camp V at 25,500 feet and Camp VI at 27,200 feet, with the aid of the strongest available porters. Odell and Irvine would support both parties from the North Col.

The weather now cleared and it became cloudless. On 31 May Mallory and Bruce with nine porters camped on the North Col and next day set up Camp V at 25,200 feet on the north ridge, Though fine, a strong wind prevented them from reaching three hundred feet higher as planned. Three porters were chosen to remain with them for the night and the rest sent down. When the morning of the 2nd dawned, however, two of the three were sick and there was nothing for it but to return for reinforcements.

On the way down they passed Norton and Somervell ascending to Camp V with the remaining six porters. These kept with them four porters for the night, Nurbu Yishi, Lhakpa Chedi, Semchumbi, and Lobsang Tashi. On the 3rd Lobsang was sick, but Norton's force of personality and persuasion, coupled with another fine day, induced the other three to carry a tent to 26,800 feet, about 700 feet below the shoulder. A platform was made for it and the porters were sent down. Norton spent an unexpectedly comfortable night, but Somervell's throat was giving him trouble.

On the morning of the 4th they continued across the face, gradually making height by the 'yellow band,' until Somervell was forced to give in at about 27,700 feet. Norton went on, crossed the remainder of the face alone, and reached the great couloir, leading up the side of the summit pyramid; he crossed it, but found it too dangerous for a single climber to ascend because fine powder-snow was lying on the steep slabs. He was also suffering from double vision, caused by the extreme altitude. His height, measured afterwards by theodolite, relative to the summit (29,002), was 28,126 feet. Those who like to add a hundred and forty feet to the official height, must add the same amount to Norton's 'record.'

Norton regained the anxious Somervell at 2 p.m. and they reached their tent, collapsed it and made their way down to the North Col, where they were guided into Camp IV by Mallory and Odell. Norton was suffering from acute snow-blindness, which lasted for three days.

One more attempt was made and it ended in tragedy. After a day's rest at the North Col, during which the oxygen apparatus was

38   The view up the Rongbuk Valley to North Face of Everest.

The 1921 Everest
Reconnaissance
Expedition:

39 (above) From a
well-positioned camp
above the Kharta
Valley the climbers
had this magnificent
view of the East
(Kangshung) Face of
Everest and the
North-East Face of
Lhotse and Lhotse
Sar (left). Also in view
is the South Col
(centre) and the upper
part of the North-East
Ridge with its steps
(right).

40 (left) Members of
the expedition: (back
row) Dr. A. F. R.
Wollaston, Lt. Col.
C. K. Howard Bury,
Rand Heron, Harold
Raeburn; (seated)
George Leigh Mallory,
Major E. O. Wheeler,
G. H. Bullock, Major
H. T. Morshead.

41  The 1921 party left the Kharta Valley, crossed the Lakpa La and descended below the North-East Ridge of Everest (above) to establish a camp on the East Rongbuk Glacier. From there they reached the North Col below the profiled sunlit ridge on the right.

42  The northern flank of Makalu from the camp above the Kharta Valley.

The 1922 Everest Expedition:
43    (inset) Mallory and Norton at about 26,800ft.
44    George Finch and Geoffrey Bruce setting out from the
North Col on their oxygen–assisted attempt.

45 (above) The upper part of the North Face – the scene of the ill-fated 1924 attempt when Mallory and Irvine disappeared during their summit bid. The first and second steps are marked 1 and 2 and x indicates the point where the ice axe was found in 1933. 46 (inset) Members of the 1924 expedition – back row: Andrew Irvine, Mallory, Major E. F. Norton, N. E. Odell, John MacDonald; seated: E. O. Shebbeare, Geoffrey Bruce, Dr. T. Howard Somervell, Bentley Beetham.

47 F. S. Smythe who took part in the 1930 Kangchenjunga Expedition and the 1933, 36 and 38 Everest Expeditions. He also led the successful 1931 Kamet expedition.

48 The 1925 Visser expedition that surveyed various Karakoram glacier systems north-west of Hunza – seated: Khan Sahib Afraz Gul Khan (Survey of India), Dr. Ph. C. Visser, Mrs. Jenny Visser Hooft, Baron B. Ph. van Harinxma thoe Slooten; standing: four Indian survey assistants and the guides Franz Lochmatter and Johann Perren. The Vissers also conducted successful survey expeditions in the eastern Karakoram in 1922, 1929–30 and 1935.

The 1926 Shaksgam Exploration. 49 (above) A panorama of the great Karakor

50 The Shaksgam valley in 1926, blocked by the four-mile wide Kyagar Glacier with its 200–300ft ice pinnacles. Two similar glaciers blocked the lower valley. The Gasherburm group, Broad Peak and K2 can be seen in the distance, some forty miles away.

from the Tater La – Broad Peak (left), K2 (centre right) and Skyang Kangri.

51 Members of the Shaksgam survey team: Captain F. O. Cave, Major Kenneth Mason, Major R. C. Clifford and Major H. D. Minchinton.

The Nanda Devi Sanctuary:

52 (top left) Nanda Devi and the Rishi Gorge.

53 (lower left) The South Face of the mountain with the distinctive slanting ramp of the Coxcomb Ridge.

54 (near left) The great northern precipices of Nanda Devi.

55 (top) Hugh Ruttledge.

56 (above) Eric Shipton and H. W. Tilman who led the first party to penetrate the Inner Sanctuary.

57 (left) The sherpas – Ang Tharkay (Angtharkay), Sen Tenzing and Pasang Bhotia – who accompanied Tilman and Shipton on many of their expeditions.

58 (lower left) Fazil Elahi mapping the Ramani Glacier during the 1936 Garhwal survey. Changabang is prominent in the background.

59 Major Gordon Osmaston with his survey team that mapped the Garhwal–Almora region in 1936 and 1937. Osmaston kneels on the left and Fazil Elahi is seated in front of the tent.

60 (lower right) Changabang and Kalanka – two fine peaks on the Nanda Devi Sanctuary Wall. Shipton's Col is on the right and the valley on the left leads to the Bagini Pass.

The German Nanga Parbat expeditions of the thirties were dogged by appalling disasters:
61   (above) A view from Rakhiot Peak to the Silver Saddle. In 1934 nine men died during a
desperate retreat along this ridge in blizzard conditions.

62　(above) The route up the Rakhiot Face to Rakhiot Peak showing camps 3 to 6.
In 1936, sixteen men died when an avalanche engulfed Camp 4.

63　Members of the 1934 expedition – front row: Erwin Schneider, Willy Welzenbach,
Peter Aschenbrenner, Willy Merkl, Kapp, Peter Mullritter and Kuhn; back row: Willy Bernard,
Uli Wieland, R. A. K. Sangster (UK), Hans Hieronimus and Fritz Bechtold.

64  Karl Wien, Günther Hepp, Paul Bauer and Adi Göttner – the team that climbed Siniolchu in 1936 by Alpine methods, with two bivouacs. All except Bauer later died in the 1937 Nanga Parbat tragedy. Bauer led the 1938 Nanga Parbat attempt which though unsuccessful was completed without further loss of life.

65  66  Gasherbrum 1 (Hidden Peak) and Masherbrum, two major Karakoram peaks that saw determined attempts by (respectively) French and British teams in 1936 and 1938.

brought up and tested, Mallory and Irvine went up with six porters to Camp V on 6 June, and Norton was escorted down to Camp III. The following day the two climbers, using oxygen, reached Camp VI and sent down the last of their porters to Odell, who had moved up to Camp V, where he spent the night alone.

On the morning of the 8th there was a light wind which swept mist-banks across the face of Everest. Conditions seemed favourable for a successful climb by Mallory and Irvine. Odell decided to climb up to Camp VI. At 12.30 the mist cleared from the ridge for a short time; before it came back, Odell saw two figures, about six hundred yards from him on a snow-slope directly under one of the two steps on the north-east ridge. From the position of the ice-axe discovered in 1933, it is almost certain that this was the 'first step,' the base of which is at 27,950 feet. At 2 o'clock Odell reached Camp VI in worsening weather, and for two hours there was a snowstorm: then the weather cleared.[1]

Having satisfied himself that the two climbers were not within immediate range of Camp VI, Odell returned to Camp IV, according to Mallory's instructions. There he waited in growing anxiety with Hazard, who had come up in support. Two days later Odell was back alone at Camp VI, and spent two hours searching the slabs for any trace of the two climbers. The Camp was exactly as he had left it on the 8th. No man could survive a night on the north face at this altitude.

Odell's feat was astonishing; he had been very slow to acclimatize; but once acclimatized, he had spent eleven nights at 23,000 feet or above, and had twice made the ascent during that time to about 27,000 feet.[2] He was still fit to search the north face had there been any hope of the climbers' survival. Norton from Camp III wisely recalled him from his quest.

---

[1] Odell *thought* the climbers were at the 'second step.' This, he admits, was impossible. Some believe he was mistaken altogether and that it was some kind of hallucination. I cannot conceive this possible at a range of six hundred yards, since Odell's belief that he saw them is unshaken. To me it seems that having failed at the second step they were returning to camp for the night, possibly intending to renew the attack on the morrow.

[2] I venture to suggest that this was in accordance with the theory of Kellas: 'the slower the acclimatization the longer deterioration is delayed.'

The loss of Mallory and Irvine was a tragedy which cast gloom over the expedition and for a time obscured their achievements. When in 1933 Wyn Harris and Wager found an ice-axe belonging either to Mallory or Irvine on the face of Everest at about 27,600 feet, there could be no reasonable doubt that it marked the point where one of them had slipped on the steeply sloping slabs, and had dragged his companion with him to death.

On 15 June the expedition left the base for its journey back. They left an Everest which mocked them; the monsoon had not yet arrived.

The casualties of these first three expeditions had been heavy: Kellas died in 1921; seven porters—Lhakpa, Nurbu, Pasang, Pema, Sange, Dorje, and Temba—were killed in the avalanche of 7 June 1922; the Gurkha Shamsher and the porter Manbahadur died from exposure and frostbite caused by the great blizzard of early May 1924; Mallory and Irvine. A cairn by the site of the Base Camp bears their names.

But there was no longer any doubt that Everest could and would be climbed. That Norton should have been within a thousand feet of the summit without oxygen, after the strain of the blizzard and North Col rescue operations, and that Somervell was not far behind —all this coupled with Odell's feat—seemed to point the lesson that with acclimatization fit men, if placed at 27,000 feet with all their powers unstrained by crises, would reach the summit. Norton at 28,126 feet was not at the limit of human endurance, but he could not go on alone.

No expedition went to Everest again until 1933. For eight years permission from the Tibetan Government was sought in vain.

# 5. Karakoram

ONE of the first mountaineers to visit the Karakoram after the war was Dr. Ph. C. Visser, who with his wife began in 1922 the first of their four journeys of exploration. Both were experienced climbers. Their first journey, wisely unambitious, was by the Nubra and the trade-route to the Saser pass, up the Thulambuti valley (map page 18). Arthur Neve and D. G. Oliver had in 1907 explored the large Mamostong glacier which descends from Mamostong Kangri (24,690) in the Kumdan group of the Saser Muztagh and enters the valley from the north.[1] The Vissers, with two Swiss guides, Franz Lochmatter[2] and Johann Brantschen, both from St. Niklaus, visited the six small glaciers, which drain the Saser group northwards into the valley, during July. The following month they reconnoitred Saser Kangri (25,170) from the west, approaching it by the south Phukpoche (Popache) glacier, as suggested by Longstaff in 1909. Like him they had bad weather and were unable to get farther than the glacier head at about 20,000 feet.

For their next journey in 1925 they chose the main tributaries of the Hunza river in the western Karakoram, for which the Surveyor General lent them the services of Khan Sahib Afraz Gul Khan, a Pathan who had already seen service with Sir Aurel Stein in central Asia. He was an accomplished surveyor, feared nothing, and had an extraordinarily well-developed sense of topography.

The two main eastern valleys of Hunza, the Khunjerab and the Shimshal, had been sketched as long ago as 1892 by Sir George Cockerill, but the country between them, including the Ghujerab, a large and inaccessible tributary which joins the Khunjerab in a precipitous gorge, had not been penetrated. Nor had the glaciers

---

[1] Mamostong Kangri is the old K32 of the early observations. Saser Kangri is the old K22.

[2] Franz Lochmatter, considered by C. F. Meade to be one of the finest guides of his time, had been with him to Kamet in 1912.

descending the northern flanks of the Hispar Muztagh been mapped. The Mulungutti glacier had been visited and sketched by Cockerill, and others discovered by him which had blocked the river in 1908 had been visited by Bridges of the Gilgit agency, but very little was known of any of them. There were now a few more fixed points to work from than in Cockerill's day, though there were none in the Ghujerab region.

Besides the Vissers and the Khan Sahib, the party comprised Baron B. Ph. van Harinxma thoe Slooten and two Swiss guides, Franz Lochmatter and Johann Perren. Like Lochmatter, Perren had been with Meade on Kamet. This strong party reached Gilgit on 16 May. In early June from the Hunza valley they surveyed the Pasu glacier, which descends from two peaks of the Pasu group, 23,897 and 24,970 feet, on the crest of the Batura Muztagh. Then, crossing the Batura glacier near its snout, the party left the main track to the Pamirs between the villages of Gircha and Misgar and entered the Khunjerab.

Like most Himalayan rivers, those of Hunza bring down an immense volume of water in summer from the melting ice and snow. They are particularly troublesome in the less inhabited parts of the Karakoram, since there are very few bridges, even of the twig-rope variety, and in the Khunjerab there are none. Constant fording is often dangerous, especially late in the day. Hunza men are courageous and strong at this pastime and their judgement is sound; they seem able to pick the best places to ford by instinct and are very sure-footed.

The two head valleys of the Khunjerab were explored and mapped, the Parpik (19,532) and Khunjerab (16,188) passes, which lead to the southern head of the Tagdumbash pamir, being reached. From Kuksel, near the head of the Khunjerab, the Vissers next crossed the Chapjingal pass (16,900) into the open but unknown head of the Ghujerab. This was surveyed by Afraz Gul to a pass leading to an unknown feeder of the Oprang (lower Shaksgam); the survey was also taken some distance down the Ghujerab. The whole party then crossed the Boesam pass into the Zardigarben tributary of the Shimshal, where they were on known ground. Shimshal village was reached on 14 July.

More explorations were to follow: the magnificent and pinnacled Khurdopin glacier, which even Lochmatter was unable to cross, thirty-two miles long; the moraine-covered, ugly Virjerab, twenty-five miles long; and the fissured Yazghil—all four descending from the mountain groups of the Hispar Muztagh, with Kanjut Sar (25,460) the highest peak and many others well over 20,000 feet. The Mulungutti Yaz, descending the giant Disteghil Sar (25,868), was explored and mapped and the three smaller glaciers which feed the Shimshal lower down. As if this were not enough, after returning over the Karun Pir (15,988) to the Hunza valley, some three weeks were devoted to the exploration and survey of the Batura glacier at the end of August and first half of September. Its whole length of thirty-seven miles was traversed, including its two head branches, the weather remaining favourable throughout. Few mountain expeditions have brought back so rich a harvest in so short a time.[1]

The war had put an end to De Filippi's expedition before its programme was finished. The upper Shaksgam had not been entered or explored and there was a large gap between Wood's surveys and Younghusband's routes of 1887 and 1889.

For three years after the armistice De Filippi and Wood pressed for permission to go; when De Filippi gave up in despair in 1921, Wood persevered. Early in 1923 he received permission, made his plans, bought his supplies, and was having his transport collected at Leh, when a telegram from the India Office cancelled his permit. It was a repetition of what had happened to the Everest project of 1907, but with less excuse.

De Filippi had invited me to join him in 1914, but with the Indo-Russian work to complete I had had to decline. With his and Wood's blessing I became heir to their plans in 1923, and, being familiar with the literature, knew what a tender subject this frontier had always been. After Wood had received permission he had rather unwisely suggested that he might be caught by the flooded Oprang river and might then have to return by Turkestan and the Pamirs. This had been his mistake: it is never wise for an applicant to suggest

[1] Mrs. Visser-Hooft's account appeared in English in *Among the Kara-Korum Glaciers* (London, 1926). See also *G.J.* lxviii (1926) 457.

complications to the official mind. Its instinct is to say 'No' without any further encouragement.

In one of the old native reports the place-name 'Shakhs Kambo' seemed to be identical with the 'Oprang or Shaksgam valley,' of Younghusband. He had crossed 'the Shaksgam' in 1887; two years later he had followed the same valley down to its junction with the Yarkand river. In this lower course it is known as 'the Oprang.' Thereafter Younghusband had generally referred to the whole river as the Oprang, and the problem of the watershed and of fitting in his route and the Urdok glacier became the 'problem of the Oprang.' By his discovery of the great length of the Siachen glacier and Teram Kangri in 1909, Longstaff had half solved this problem. It was part of De Filippi's project to enter 'the Oprang' in 1914. The valley remained 'the Oprang' in Wood's mind until 1923.

What had happened to the Shaksgam? I proposed to look for it. The problem became 'the problem of the Shaksgam.'[1] The India Office acquiesced and became helpful and understanding, and my plans were made. The Oprang was forgotten and permission was granted in November 1925 to explore the Shaksgam in the following year. The Government of India gave me a substantial grant towards the cost, Army Headquarters at Simla lent me the services of Hingston, who had been with me on the Pamirs in 1913 and on the Everest expedition of 1924, of Captain F. O. Cave of the Rifle Brigade, of Major H. D. Minchinton, of the 1st Gurkhas (a member of the Alpine Club) and of three men from his regiment. At the last moment Hingston had to withdraw through illness, and his place was taken by Major R. C. Clifford, I.M.S. The party was completed by Khan Sahib Afraz Gul Khan, of the Survey of India.

The real problem of exploration in this area is one of organization. In most parts of the Himalaya and Karakoram a small amount of local supplies can be counted upon and local porters enrolled. Beyond the Great Karakoram, the Shaksgam and upper Yarkand valleys are uninhabited, and even fuel and grass are often absent. From Panamik, the last village where there are limited supplies of flour, to the point where we hoped to enter the Shaksgam was a march of fourteen

[1] *G.J.* lxviii (1926) 225. 'The Problem of the Shaksgam' (Sir Francis Younghusband).

days. We planned to be away from Panamik from 20 June to 7 October, about 110 days. I needed twenty-one baggage ponies and twenty-four Ladakhi porters for work in the Shaksgam for eighty-two days. For the carriage of our equipment and for fodder and food we required 137 more baggage ponies with forty-six pony-men to look after them for the fourteen days' march to the Shaksgam; these had to be rationed for twenty-eight days; and their food and fodder had to be carried by other animals. The modern word for this is 'logistics': to me it is synonymous with 'headache.'

We crossed the Saser pass on 25 June, spent the night of the 27th at De Filippi's old depot-site on the Depsang, and reached the 'amphitheatre' discovered by Hayward in 1868 and mapped by Wood in 1914, on the 29th. Three days later we crossed Wood's 'Pass G' into the head of the Shaksgam, within two days of the date planned fifteen months before, and pitched our depot camp about ten miles down the valley. The caravan had done wonders; but over much of the route there is no grass, the going was exhausting for laden animals at this time of year, and fifteen ponies out of our two hundred had died from exposure, altitude or other causes. After a medical examination the hired pony-men were paid off and sent back, Ali of Hondar, one of the best of them, having agreed to return for us after eighty-four days. We were left with our picked Ladakhi porters under a trusted man named Kunchuk, who had been with Oliver on several journeys. We had now eighteen ponies of the twenty-one which I had bought (three had died), and their four pony-men. Unexpectedly there was very little grass in any of the valleys we visited, though lower down the Shaksgam Younghusband had found enough for his ponies in 1889.

Six miles below our depot came our first surprise. We were held up by a large lake dammed by a glacier which poured down from the Apsarasas and Teram Kangri groups of the Siachen Muztagh. Its wall of ice facing us was over 200 feet high, and above that towered great ice-pinnacles. We explored its snout in a canvas boat and found it piled up against the marble cliff. We climbed the hill overlooking it. Its breadth at the snout was about four miles and its surface for a distance of seven miles was a chaos of crevasses and ice-pinnacles, some of them between 200 and 300 feet high. From survey stations which I made on the high ridge east of the glacier we had a magnificent view down the broad open Shaksgam valley below this, the Kyagar glacier, where two more glaciers, afterwards named the Singhi and the Staghar, also appeared to block the valley at distances from us of fourteen and twenty-four miles. At the far end of the valley, beyond the Staghar glacier, where it changed direction to the north-west, dominating all, stood the giants of the Karakoram, K2 (28,250), forty-two miles distant but showing 5000 feet of its eastern face, Broad Peak (26,414), and the four Gasherbrums, all over 26,000 feet. Gasherbrum I was less than twenty-five miles away. In the clean atmosphere we could see every detail (map page 134). While I was making stations for the photographic survey, Minchinton and Cave could find no route across the glacier, though Minchinton thought we might get over it with difficulty in a week.

In view of what we had seen, and with the prospect of two more glaciers equally uncertain lower down, we felt we could not spare the time to cross it. It was already certain that Younghusband's route was in the valley before us.[1]

Minchinton, Afraz Gul, and I now crossed the watershed north of the Shaksgam by a glacier pass (Marpo La, 18,500), while Cave and Clifford took the ponies and base back by the 'amphitheatre' to meet us in the head of Wood's 'valley I.' From here we explored and surveyed a large area of unknown country to the north and north-west, fixing our position by K2 and the Gasherbrums, and by additional points which I triangulated and computed at night. One problem we left unsolved. We explored a valley, which we called the Zug-Shaksgam, down to an altitude of below 12,500 feet, fifty feet lower than the height shown on our maps for the junction of the Surukwat and the Yarkand river. Though it seemed hardly possible, since rivers do not flow uphill—almost anything can happen to rivers here—it appeared therefore that it must join the Shaksgam, and so it was dotted in, but with a caution. This problem was finally solved in 1937 by Eric Shipton, when he linked his survey with mine. The Zug-Shaksgam enters the Surukwat at 11,270 feet. The old height, 12,550 feet, found by De Filippi by aneroid, was nearly 1,300 feet too high.

[1] *Records of the Survey of India*, Vol. xxii; *G.J.* lxix (1927) 289 ff.

During the expedition, Clifford was threatened with appendicitis. Competent surgeon that he was, we managed to dissuade him from operating on himself. We were interested in the wide open spaces, not in the inside works of man. We had one serious accident on almost the last day in the Yarkand river. Tilak Bahadur, one of our Gurkhas, fell when climbing and fractured his skull. We brought him back on a stretcher and thanks to Clifford's skill he completely recovered.

I had long been interested in survey by photography, as a method of saving time when mountains are only clear of cloud for short intervals, and especially in the plotting of photographs by stereoscopy. I had not convinced the Survey of India of the usefulness of the method which I had used on the Pamirs in 1913. During World War I, the design of the automatic plotting-machines had been revolutionized on the Continent, and the method was already in use for large-scale detailed surveys. The Royal Geographical Society, with the strong support of its Secretary, Arthur Hinks, purchased and lent me the field equipment designed by Heinrich Wild of Switzerland. With this I took many pairs of photographs from high stations, sometimes as much as half a mile apart, developing them at night. Hinks and I plotted these in Switzerland in 1927, and were able to extend the plane-table survey of the Khan Sahib.[1] The value of the method was well proved and has since been used by most of the larger and more important scientific expeditions to the Pamirs, Karakoram, and Himalaya.[2]

A fine piece of exploration was completed the following year by H. F. Montagnier and C. J. Morris. The latter had been on the Everest expedition of 1922. They had planned and had obtained permission to visit Hunza, to cross the Shimshal pass into the Oprang, and to follow the Shaksgam valley upstream to the Kyagar glacier, discovered by us the year before. To their disappointment, when all arrangements had been made, and when they had passed through Hunza and over the Karun Pir into the Shimshal valley, they received

[1] G.J. lxx (1927) 342.

[2] German Expedition to Pamirs 1928; Duke of Spoleto's Karakoram Expedition (Baltoro glacier) 1929; Karl Wien's survey of Zemu glacier and Kangchenjunga on Bauer's Expedition, 1931; Finsterwalder's map of Nanga Parbat, 1934; Michael Spender's map of Everest with the 1935 Expedition.

a telegram at the village of Shimshal cancelling their permit and forbidding them to cross the Shimshal pass.[1]

They had with them Torabaz Khan, a surveyor lent by the Surveyor General, and decided to try and survey the blank left in the Ghujerab valley by the Vissers in 1925. They crossed into the valley by the route the Vissers had used, and then explored and surveyed the whole valley to its junction with the Khunjerab, Morris and Torabaz Khan climbing and surveying from several high points. Morris records that in many years this route would not be passable, and that they were fortunate in having cloudy weather which checked the melting of the snow. Even so, they had great difficulty in penetrating the gorge, and Morris pays a tribute to the capacity of his Shimshali porters, who proved themselves 'to be mountaineers of the very first order.' Two of them cut steps across the rock of the gorge, as though it were of ice. Montagnier, a veteran mountaineer, described the passage of the gorge as the most extraordinary performance in his whole experience.

Morris, on their return to the Hunza valley, with Torabaz Khan completed the survey of the Chapursan valley to the head of the two glaciers at its source, the Yashkuk and Beskiyenj, thereby completing the detailed survey of upper Hunza.

[1] G.J. lxxi (1928) 513.

# 6. Kumaun Himalaya

KELLAS's physiological experiments had been interrupted in 1914 by the outbreak of war. In view of the possibility of an Everest expedition, the Royal Geographical Society persuaded him to visit Kamet in 1920 to continue his practical experiments at high altitudes, and arranged for the loan of oxygen apparatus through the Medical Research Council in England. The Survey of India were asked to co-operate by lending an officer to go with Kellas and assist him with the experiments. The Surveyor General decided to take the opportunity of resurveying the eastern approaches to the mountain and deputed Major H. T. Morshead to go with Kellas, with Laltan Khan as his assistant.

Kellas intended to study the problem of gradual acclimatization as well as the physiological effects of high altitudes on the acclimatized human body, both with and without the aid of oxygen; and he was to experiment with two types of apparatus. The first comprised three oxylith portable sets, each consisting of a large rubber bag holding sufficient oxygen for from fifteen to twenty minutes' consumption, the oxygen being generated by the chemical reaction of oxylith and water. The other comprised a number of oxygen cylinders, each weighing fifteen pounds when charged and holding 280 litres of gas under pressure. The cylinders were designed for use in pairs and were to be carried on the back by belts and straps, and there was a meter for regulating the flow of oxygen to the face-mask at one, two, or three litres a minute. The apparatus was due to arrive in June, so that experiments could be made during a march to Niti by easy stages in July and during an attempt to be made to climb Kamet late in August.

This programme was spoilt by delays in the arrival of the apparatus, caused by the shipping company classifying the cargo as 'high explosives,' presumably under the impression that Kellas was about to start a private war. In consequence it was not until 8 August that it reached Kathgodam, six weeks late. It had then to be repacked for coolie transport, the journey had to be rushed, and Niti was reached on 27 August.

Kellas and Morshead followed Longstaff's route of 1907 up the Raikana and Purbi Kamet glaciers (map page 119). Like him, they recorded frequent ice-avalanches in the upper part of the latter, but avoided them by hugging its northern side, deliberately taking several days over the journey and halting in order to acclimatize and make tests. An incident of interest was the disappearance of two live sheep down a crevasse. Two and a half days later one of the porters was lowered into the crevasse on forty feet of rope, and after an hour's work with an ice-axe brought them up to the surface, one of them little the worse—or at any rate alive—the other reduced to frozen mutton. This was an accidental and unintentional test of endurance!

By following Meade's route of 1913 they eventually reached 'Meade's col' on 19 September with considerable difficulty, because of shortage of supplies and fuel, and the breakdown at one stage of their communications. Both felt that the summit was within their powers, had they been able to induce the Bhotia porters to carry a tent to the col.

Morshead gave two contributory causes to their failure; the lateness of the season and the inefficiency of their camp and cooking equipment. It had been part of Kellas's plan not to carry loads in order to save themselves for the final effort and for the purpose of the physiological experiments. He wished both to acclimatize gradually; this they succeeded in doing. Kellas found that the Bhotia porters, even though their homes were at over 11,000 feet and they were already acclimatized at that altitude, suffered more discomfort above 18,000 feet than he did and took longer to acclimatize: he attributed this to the greater effort of load-carrying. Morshead found that Garhwali coolies, who had been fitted with boots and warm clothing on a lavish scale, suffered more than the Bhotias of Niti, for whom he had nothing but praise. To quote his words: 'On rock they can climb like goats, while on ice they readily learn step-cutting. It appears very doubtful if the present-day expense of importing Alpine guides can ever justify their employment in future Himalayan exploration.' He concluded that a party of four Europeans with Bhotia porters could reach the summit of Kamet if they attempted it earlier in the year.

The experiments carried out by Kellas were valuable for the design of equipment and had an important bearing on the use of oxygen on the early Everest expeditions; but there is little doubt that Kellas wore himself out and to some extent strained his heart on Kamet. He was then over fifty years of age.

Two journeys to the Kumaun Himalaya in 1926 and 1927 are worthy of record. Both were due to Hugh Ruttledge, who was now Deputy Commissioner at Almora and like Sherring in 1905 intended to know every part of his mountain dominion. In 1926 with Colonel R. C. Wilson and Howard Somervell, all ardent mountaineers, he reconnoitred Nanda Devi's ring of mountains from the north-east, with the object of trying to find a route into the inner sanctuary from the Bhotia village of Milam and the Timphu glacier. Though not fully equipped to press the reconnaissance home, they saw enough to justify the opinion that a very detailed examination would be necessary before it would be possible to force a pass over the ring with laden porters (map page 116).

Ruttledge, his wife, and Wilson then visited Tibet to investigate trade matters. The party took the same route as Sherring and Longstaff had taken, over the Lipu Lekh pass, and crossed on 10 July to Taklakot. While in Tibet they made a complete circuit of the holy mountain Kailas, north of Manasarowar, and were thus the first Europeans to complete the *parikarma* or sacred pilgrimage.[1]

On the return journey the party made the first recorded crossing of Traill's pass (17,700), which is on the ridge between Nanda Devi and Nanda Kot, from the north.[2]

An innovation on this journey, hardly noticed at the time, but a direct result of the Everest expeditions, was the selection by Somervell of the Sherpa porter Chettan to go with this expedition. Chettan had been Finch's personal servant on the 1922 Everest expedition, and Finch had then taught him the use of rope and axe. On that

[1] Wilson and Chettan, during the *parikarma*, made a bold and difficult reconnaissance of the S., SW., and W. faces of Kailas; and reported that the E. ridge is probably climbable.

[2] Page 69.

occasion he went to Camp V (25,500) with Finch and J. G. Bruce and returned to them after the first night. He went again to Everest in 1924, did remarkably well and was chosen by Hingston to help bring down the snow-blind Norton from the North Col. On this 1926 expedition he impressed both Ruttledge and Wilson with his steadiness and judgement.

In May 1927 the Ruttledges paid a second visit to Nanda Devi's outer defences with Longstaff. They approached by the Nandakini valley and reconnoitred its two main glaciers; at the head of the northern they reached a col from which they overlooked the Ronti (Rinti) glacier, descending from a trough north-west of Trisul, and draining into the lower Rishiganga.

On this occasion Ruttledge had again engaged Chettan and five more Sherpas from Darjeeling; among them was Lewa, who had been on all three Everest expeditions, and who was one of the two porters rescued alive from the avalanche on the North Col in 1922. These six and two riflemen from the 3rd Gurkhas were the only porters used by the expedition after the glaciers were reached. Longstaff paid them a high tribute. Both Chettan and Lewa were already on the way to becoming the first Himalayan guides.

# 7. The Founding of the Himalayan Club

AN event which had a far-reaching effect on Himalayan mountaineering was the founding of the Himalayan Club in 1927–8. It was no new idea. Some association of the kind had been formally suggested to the Asiatic Society of Bengal by W. H. Johnson of the Survey of India and by Mr. F. Drew, the Kashmir traveller, as long ago as 1866; Douglas Freshfield made a similar proposal when writing in the *Alpine Journal* in 1884; in the decade before World War I, the formation of a club was in the minds of many who worked and travelled in Kashmir. We discussed it again in Simla in 1925. Among mountaineers stationed in Bengal, with Kangchenjunga on their horizon, the idea recurred to many. But for one reason or another the idea had never taken shape, not because a Club was not wanted, possibly because we had no fixed objective; perhaps, as Sir Geoffrey Corbett excused us, 'because in this land of endlessness it is only now and then that the two or three are gathered together.'[1]

And then two Clubs were born, independently and almost simultaneously: The Mountain Club of India in Calcutta on 23 September 1927, the Himalayan Club at Simla eleven days later. It was when the preliminary steps were being taken to inform Himalayan mountaineers scattered about the world that the moving spirits of the two Clubs became aware of each other, and agreed to establish both clubs on a sure foundation in a spirit of co-operation and goodwill, and with the same single objective in view. Bruce became first President of the Mountain Club of India, Field-Marshal Sir William Birdwood, Commander-in-Chief in India, who had strongly supported us from the beginning, became President of the Himalayan Club. The Viceroy (Lord Irwin), the Governor of the Punjab (Sir Malcolm Hailey), the Chief of the General Staff (Sir Walter Kirke), the G.O.C. Northern Army (Sir Alexander Cobbe), the Surveyor General (Sir Edward Tandy), the Director of the Geological Survey (Sir Edwin Pascoe),

[1] *H.J.* i (1929) 1.

the Army Secretary (G. Mackworth Young), the Deputy Foreign Secretary (J. G. Acheson), among others, promised their support and became Founder Members of the Club.

To about a hundred Himalayan mountaineers of note and experience we made known our intentions by letter. From all over India and beyond came replies welcoming the Club and making valuable suggestions. Almost everyone who replied became a Founder Member, many who had left India became Life Members and gave generously to our Foundation Fund. Among them were Sir Francis Younghusband, Sir Martin Conway, Norman Collie, Douglas Freshfield, Bruce, Longstaff, Neve, Howard-Bury, Norton, Ruttledge, and every member of the Everest expeditions. Many of us in our enthusiasm became members of both clubs. For this close co-operation and fair start the Himalayan Club now owes an immense debt of gratitude to the two wise Honorary Secretaries, Sir Geoffrey Corbett and W. Allsup, who were the moving spirits in those days. We owed much also to the Alpine Club, especially to Colonel E. L. Strutt, editor of *The Alpine Journal*, and Sydney Spencer, Honorary Secretary. Basing our objects on the famous definition in its Rules, we declared our intention: 'To encourage and assist Himalayan travel and exploration and to extend knowledge of the Himalaya and adjoining mountain ranges through science, art, literature and sport.'

By the end of 1928 the two clubs had agreed to amalgamate, 'for the benefit of the common aims,' as one strong and united organization and under the title 'The Himalayan Club.'

Among the first steps taken was the appointment of Honorary Local Secretaries in Himalayan districts who could assist and advise members in all matters relating to travel in their district, including transport, equipment, supplies, and costs. They were first appointed in Kashmir, Chamba, Simla, Almora, and Darjeeling, and included Ernest Neve, Hugh Ruttledge, and Colonel H. W. Tobin; an additional one, G. B. Gourlay, was appointed in Calcutta to co-operate with Tobin at Darjeeling and to deal with the Assam Himalaya.

Local Correspondents were nominated in many of the Indian stations, e.g., on the north-west frontier, Quetta, Waziristan, Peshawar, and at Rawalpindi, Meerut, and Lahore. Later these were augmented, and there were correspondents in London and some cities on the Continent. Specialists in various branches of knowledge, e.g. archæology, botany, entomology, geodesy, geology, meteorology, zoology, ornithology, photography, maps, fishing, shooting, folklore, who had travelled in the Himalaya, became correspondents to whom would-be travellers with a particular bent might apply to find out both what had been done and where were the gaps. We knew that there were many magnets in the Himalaya that drew men and women from the discomforts of modern civilization, and many distinguished men helped to direct their steps to the high hills.

The Club soon proved its worth. Expeditions from abroad were helped in their early arrangements, and with their transport; where a party had no knowledge of the language or country, a member of the Club would assist it and, if he could spare the time, sometimes go with it. This practice in fact became common with larger expeditions from Europe, the Government of India sometimes making it a condition of permission. It was a safeguard to the Himalayan people and an encouragement to the best of them; it was a guarantee to them against underpayment, and a protection to the expedition against exploitation.

The most lasting results of these plans were due to the enthusiasm and energy of members in the Eastern Section of the Club, primarily composed of the old members of the Mountain Club of India, such as W. Allsup, G. B. Gourlay, H. W. Tobin, E. O. Shebbeare, and Mrs. Townend. Gradually a list of the best Sherpa porters who had been employed on expeditions was compiled. In the 1924 Everest expedition the fifteen porters, who were fit and ready after the disastrous storms to go high to the North Col and above, had been nicknamed 'Tigers.' These were among the first to be registered, though it was some time before they were given numbers. Gradually the list of competent and reliable porters grew, a register was made and the steadiest and best trained became eligible for the distinction of a 'Tiger's Badge.' Among those who gained it were Lewa (No. 46), Ang Tenzing II (No. 3), Ang Tsering III, nicknamed 'Pansy' (No. 51), Dawa Thondup (No. 49), Ang Tharkay (No. 19), Pasang Dawa Lama, sometimes known as Pasang Sherpa (No. 139), and Tenzing Bhutia or Tenzing Khumjung (No. 48),[1] all of whom, from

[1] Now famous as Tenzing Norkhay Sherpa, G.M., one of the victors of Everest.

a 'coolie status' rose to be fine mountaineers and colleagues under the training of skilled European Alpinists, the last-named and youngest of those mentioned having attained the summit of his ambition and of the world with Hillary.

Many of these men climb now for the joy of climbing, but since they must eat to live they have to be paid, and the best can command a wage in accordance with their talents. Much of their training and trust is due to the British expeditions to Everest, the German expeditions to Kangchenjunga, and to Swiss expeditions to Nepal more recently. The Himalayan Club promulgates rules for the guidance of expeditions employing them, the porters know them and though the rules have no official or legal authority, expeditions are advised to keep them. Rates of pay, questions of food and equipment are unofficially laid down, and advice on these matters is obtainable through the Honorary Local Secretary of the Club at Darjeeling. At the instigation of the Club official rates of compensation payable for injury or death were introduced in August 1950 by the Political Officer in Sikkim.

*The Himalayan Journal*, which began publication in 1929, was patterned closely on *The Alpine Journal*. It records Himalayan activity in many fields of adventure. Sir Geoffrey Corbett in his introduction to the first volume, briefly describing the founding of the Club, concluded:

And so the Himalayan Club is founded, and we hope great things of it: the geographer that the blank spaces on his map may be filled in; the scientist that our knowledge of the Himalaya, its rocks and glaciers, its animals and plants, its peoples and their way of living, may continually expand. The mountaineer may dream of the first ascent of a thousand unclimbed peaks, the *shikari* of record heads shot in nalas yet unknown. My own hope is that it may help to rear a breed of men in India, hard and self-reliant, who will know how to enjoy life on the high hills.

PART FIVE

# 1929–1939

He who thinks of Himachal, though he should not behold him, is greater than he who performs all worship in Kashi. And he who thinks of Himachal shall have pardon for all sins, and all things that die on Himachal and all things that in dying think of his snows are freed from sin. In a hundred ages of the gods I could not tell thee of the glories of Himachal where Siva lived and where the Ganges falls from the foot of Vishnu like the slender thread of the lotus flower.

*Hindu text*

# 1. Kangchenjunga 1929, 1930, 1931

WITHIN a year of its founding, the Himalayan Club received a request from the veteran Heligolander Rickmer Rickmers to help a young Bavarian Paul Bauer who planned to bring a party of climbers to the Himalaya: 'They want to test themselves against something difficult,' wrote Rickmers, 'some mountain that will call out everything they've got in them of courage, perseverance, and endurance.'

World War I had brought an aftermath of misery to Europe. Young men brought up to believe in an invincible Germany were shattered by defeat, without aim and leaderless. A few sought solace in their mountains and took stock of the future. Paul Bauer tells how in those early joyless days he found hope again in the mountains; 'Years passed in which we spent every free day among them and in many a night watch we probed nature's deepest secrets.' With companions he learnt to master their own mountains under every condition, in wind and storm, snow and darkness, until a goal was reached.

Bauer brought with him eight other climbers: E. Allwein, Peter Aufschnaiter, E. Beigel, J. Brenner, W. Fendt, K. von Kraus, J. Leupold, and A. Thoenes. Bauer and Beigel had already been to the Caucasus in 1928; Allwein had made the first ascent of Peak Lenin, 23,360 feet, in the Pamirs the same year. All were members of the *Akademischen Alpenverein* of Munich, and of the German and Austrian Alpine Club. By a curious coincidence, Bauer and I had fought each other in the trenches a hundred yards apart in France in 1915. The mountains have drawn us together since and we remain close friends.

We met Bauer and his party on their arrival in Calcutta at the end of July, and three days later they were in Darjeeling, where Colonel H. W. Tobin and E. O. Shebbeare of the Himalayan Club had made arrangements for the journey to the Zemu glacier. In the first week of August they left Darjeeling with ninety porters, among whom were fifteen who had been to Everest in the early twenties. Accompanied by Tobin they established their base (Camp III) on the Zemu glacier at 14,340 feet (map page 38).

On 14 August, less than three weeks after landing in India, they began their reconnaissance of Kangchenjunga's north-east quadrant. About a mile north of the summit and half-way between it and the Twins, the north ridge of Kangchenjunga is supported by the north-east spur projecting eastwards for four miles.[1] It separates the Twins glacier from the upper Zemu glacier which descends from the east face of the mountain and which is fed by avalanches from the high south-east ridge descending to the Zemu Gap. Reconnaissances were made of the Zemu Gap to examine the possibility of a route by the south-east ridge, of the Twins glacier, and of the northern and southern faces of the north-east spur; but the only practicable route was by the last, though all approaches were swept by avalanches and could be reached only with extreme care.

Camp VI (17,300) was established at the foot of the eastern end of the north-east spur on 28 August and a week was spent in finding a safe way up the 650-foot ice-fall above the camp and a route to the crest of the north-east spur. On 6 September they reached the crest, but a violent blizzard drove them back again to Camp VI and much effort was lost. Not until the 16th did Bauer, Beigel, and Kraus regain the crest and occupy Camp VII—'the Eagle's Eyrie,' at 19,128 feet. From here the going was exceptionally difficult, days being spent in hacking a way through the great ice-pinnacles which crowned the ridge. Camp VIII at 20,570 feet, Camp IX at 21,550 feet, Camp X at about 22,700 feet were slowly established, each being formed by roomy caves carved out of the ice. While the route was being made safe for porters the stocking of the camps continued.

On the evening of 3 October six Germans (Bauer, Beigel, Allwein, Aufschnaiter, Kraus, and Thoenes) and four porters (Chettan, Lewa, Ila Kitar, and Pasang Anju) were in the ice-cave at Camp X ready for the move higher. Supports were at Camps VI and VIII. On the previous day Allwein and Kraus had reconnoitred ahead to 24,250 feet, and though the snow had been soft the two had

[1] For the ridges of Kangchenjunga, see pages 37–9.

averaged 300 feet an hour. Hopes were high; they felt that the worst difficulties had been overcome.

During the night the weather worsened, and a heavy blizzard struck the ridge. It lasted for three days. To conserve supplies, strengthen the supports, and remain safe the high party had to be reduced. Kraus, Thoenes, Chettan, and Lewa retreated to Camp VIII on the 4th to help Brenner and Fendt. Beigel and Aufschnaiter started back on the 6th, leaving Bauer, Allwein, Kitar, and Pasang to take a chance on the weather improving. These four during a break on the 7th reconnoitred upwards, but found the snow too deep for them to make much headway. On the 8th they also began the descent.

The retreat was carried out methodically but under great difficulties. The danger spots had been carefully noted and avalanches were deliberately broken away from the crest. The climbers ploughed through lanes of snow nearly the height of a man. The first party of four reached Camp VIII in one day and withdrew with Brenner and Fendt to Camp VII. Aufschnaiter and Beigel in appalling weather took three days; avalanches carried away their packs and obliterated the route, so that they were forced to spend a night in the snow without shelter. Beigel with frostbitten feet guided Aufschnaiter who was snow-blind into Camp VII. Bauer's rearguard of four, after jettisoning their packs over the crest to the Zemu glacier below, reached Camp VII after two gruelling days, and brought the whole party safely down to Camp VI. During this period attempts to reach Camp VII from below had failed because of the treacherous snow. The whole expedition now regained their base at Camp III in fine weather.

So ended Bauer's first 'reconnaissance in force.' He had been unable to choose his season, or even his objective before leaving Germany; and much of the reconnaissance had been carried out during the monsoon. His closely-knit party had rapidly gained the confidence of the porters, who had behaved staunchly throughout and gained much technical experience. Bauer's highest camp was little higher than the North Col of Everest, so that problems of acclimatization above 23,000 feet were not encountered. On the other hand they were able, through acclimatization to that altitude, to do arduous work in tunnelling through ice and in excavating ice-caves; the technical difficulties between Camps VI and X had been far greater than below Everest's North Col; but, as on Everest, the route from 23,000 feet appeared to offer no insuperable difficulties. Norton had reached 28,126 feet on Everest without oxygen. There appeared no reason to believe that the summit of Kangchenjunga at 28,146 feet was unattainable.

In 1930 Professor G. O. Dyhrenfurth brought out a more elaborate expedition to the mountain with the object of attacking it from the north-west, as suggested by Freshfield in 1899. Originally German it became a rather makeshift international party composed of five Germans, three British, two Swiss, and one Austrian—Professor and Mrs. Dyhrenfurth, H. Richter, U. Wieland, and H. Hoerlin; F. S. Smythe, G. Wood-Johnson, and J. S. Hannah, of the Himalayan Club, who joined in India; Marcel Kurz and C. Duvanel; and E. Schneider. The approach to the north-west quadrant from Darjeeling is longer and more troublesome than the direct route to the Zemu glacier, since it means crossing the Kang La and other passes, entirely with coolie transport. Between 400 and 500 coolies were required and this host had to make the journey in three parties early in the year.

Base camp was pitched on 26 April at 16,570 feet, a little west of Pangperma, on the upper Kangchenjunga glacier opposite the tremendous north-west face of the mountain and about eight miles from the summit. Probably every member of the expedition, like Freshfield, was deceived by the scale, since none at that time had experience of the high Himalaya. A careful plan was drawn up: Camp I was to be pitched farther up the glacier, Camp II in the névé-basin under the North Col between the Twins and the summit, Camp III on the first ice-terrace, at the top of a steep ice-wall. While the route up the ice-wall was being prepared, a great mass of the hanging glacier broke away from the terrace and formed an ice-avalanche. Chettan, one of the best known and most skilful of the Sherpa porters, was killed. The disaster led to the abandonment of this route and, after a reconnaissance of the north-west ridge between the summit and Kangbachen (25,782) had revealed no alternative, the attempt was abandoned. The party set off for less ambitious peaks, and made the first ascents of Jongsong (24,344), Nepal Peak (23,560), Dodang

Nyima (23,620), and Ramthang (23,310), as well as a number of lower ones.[1]

Bauer returned to the attack in 1931, using his old base camp on the Zemu glacier. Five of his former party went with him—Allwein, Aufschnaiter, Brenner, Fendt, and Leupold. To these he added four younger men, H. Hartmann, H. Pircher, H. Schaller, and Karl Wien. By reason of the experience gained, it was a strong party, composed of men who had all climbed together. Tobin and Shebbeare once more helped them off from Darjeeling, the latter leading the first part of the expedition to the Base Camp. On 13 July, seven weeks after leaving Munich, Camp IV was re-established at the eastern end of the north-east spur. This was about six weeks earlier than in 1929, but the monsoon was in full force, and they were greeted by the thunder of avalanches on all sides.

The attempt began the following day. The 650-foot ice-fall to the upper Zemu glacier was quickly overcome, but the route to the Eagle's Eyrie (19,128) was raked by rocks loosened by the warmth of the monsoon, and was only safe daily before 8 a.m. With careful observation and every precaution, Camp VII was re-established. It became the advanced base for the next two months.

Beyond this point rock gradually disappears from the ridge, which thereafter is covered with ice-bosses and ribbed with ice and frozen snow. By traversing the ribs it was possible to avoid some of the heavier work on the ridge, which was reached on 22 July. Routemaking was more difficult and dangerous than in 1929 and a temporary shelter was made on the ridge to enable the forward party to work early. On 9 August Hermann Schaller and two porters were moving up to this camp when the snow gave way under Pasang, the second on the rope, and both he and Schaller fell to their death 1750 feet below.

The whole expedition withdrew from the ridge to bury their comrades on the rock island above the ice-fall of the Zemu glacier. Then on 24 August, fifteen days after the accident, four climbers, Bauer, Hartmann, Pircher, and Wien once more reached Camp VIII above the place where Schaller fell. In the interval the old route had been wrecked by the warm weather, and the bosses, ribs, and cornices

Page 274. The heights of Dodang Nyima and Ramthang are approximate.

had become treacherous with rotten snow. The porters also had become nervous and unreliable. Only three, Karmi, Kitar Dorje, and Pemba could be induced to go higher.[1] Progress along the ridge became very slow, and it took eight days to prepare the route to Camp IX (21,550). By 10 September Camp X was established at 22,980 feet,[2] and on the 12th the camp was occupied by six climbers, Allwein, Aufschnaiter, Bauer, Hartmann, Pircher, Wien, and the three porters. Four days later, a small ice-cave, Camp XI, was carved out of the ridge at 24,150 feet by Hartmann and Wien. On the 17th they reached the highest point of the crest at 25,263 feet, before the ridge sinks to a small depression and then rises again to meet the north ridge of Kangchenjunga at 25,500 feet. A layer of dangerous powder-snow, some twenty inches deep, lay loosely on the ice, and the party retired to Camp XI.

On the 18th Allwein, Pircher, and Wien re-examined this slope and agreed that it was unsafe to proceed. Possibly this dangerous state was only temporary, but it would have been folly to remain at this altitude on the off-chance. The danger of a heavy snowfall, such as had hampered the retreat in 1929, was too great a risk, and the strain at this altitude of carrying loads and of ice-work over the long period had begun to tell on their reserves of strength. On 20 September the last two members of the party, Hartmann and Wien, withdrew after four nights at Camp XI, and the whole party returned safely to Camp VI on the 24th.

On the journey back through Sikkim, Allwein, Pircher, and three porters crossed the Simvu Saddle on 1 October and descended the difficult Passanram valley, which had never yet been trodden by a European. For seven days they had to cut their way through ten miles of pathless virgin jungle. Wien remained for a time on the Zemu glacier to complete his photogrammetric survey.

On this expedition, as on his first, Bauer showed outstanding qualities of leadership. Though it would be wrong to say that the accident robbed the expedition of success, it undoubtedly made success

[1] Karmi (No. 117) was later on the 1936 Everest Expedition. He was killed in the avalanche which destroyed the German expedition to Nanga Parbat on 14 June 1937. Kitar Dorje is not the same man as Kitar who was with Bauer in 1929.

[2] The heights of Camps X and XI given here are from Wien's photogrammetric survey, and replace the aneroid measurements of the earlier accounts.

impossible. The demoralizing effect of it on the less experienced porters, the fortnight's delay, the need for remaking the route in the most exacting conditions at a high altitude with only three porters, rendered the task of the remaining six climbers wellnigh impossible before winter conditions set in. For the greater part of two months climbers and porters had been roped and anchored to the ice-pinnacled ridge, rarely able to relax except at night, and even then there was the ever-present peril of blizzard and tempest. When checked at the end by the misfortune of dangerous snow, deterioration of their powers of endurance, after so much strain, though they may not have realized it, must soon have forced them to retreat, especially as several had suffered from fever and chills.

Oxygen was not used, though a small supply had been taken for emergency use. Bauer strained his heart on 16 September between Camps X and XI and had to return. With the greatest difficulty he regained the ice-cave at Camp X, where he barely survived the night, without sleeping-bag or blanket, with the aid of the drug Kardiazol. It took him the whole of the following day to drag himself down to Camp IX. Fortunately Kangchenjunga, in an unwonted spirit of kindness, forbore to strike.

# 2. Kamet (25,447) and Nanda Devi (25,645)

No fewer than eight expeditions, all on a small scale, visited Kamet between 1907 and 1930. In the course of these, four serious attempts had been made on the mountain: by Slingsby and by Meade from the west, by Meade and by Kellas and Morshead from the east. Twice the col at 23,500 feet between Kamet and Abi Gamin had been reached; Meade had spent a night on it in June 1913; Kellas and Morshead, because of the excessive cold, had been unable to persuade their local Bhotia porters to pitch a tent there in September 1920. All three felt that the summit could be reached by a fit party from here in the day.

In 1931 the summit was reached by a strong party led by Frank Smythe. Five other climbers took part: Wing-Commander E. B. Beauman, R. Holdsworth, Dr. Raymond Greene, Eric Shipton, and Captain E. St. J. Birnie. All except Birnie had considerable Alpine experience, Smythe had been on Dyhrenfurth's Kangchenjunga expedition in 1930, Shipton had climbed Mount Kenya. Birnie, the only Hindustani-speaking member, was responsible for the all-important transport arrangements and for the welfare of the porters. It was partly the failure of the porters that had previously defeated Kellas.

For this reason ten Sherpas who had had experience, mostly on Everest or Kangchenjunga, were enlisted for Kamet by Tobin at Darjeeling. They were Lewa (No. 46), Kusang Siter Pasang (No. 20), Wangdi Nurbu (No. 25), sometimes known as Ongdi, Nullu Nurbu (No. 27), Kitar Dorje (No. 35), Ang Tsering I (No. 36), known then as 'Achung,' Nima Dorje I, Nima Sherpa, and Ang Nurbu.[1] Lewa, the most experienced, was put in charge of them. They were supplemented by men from villages near the Tibetan frontier, of whom six of the best were selected for work at the higher camps. Two

[1] Most porters enlisted in the early days had their names spelt according to fancy. On registration later efforts were made to spell them correctly and to give them numbers. The last three were unnumbered.

lance-naiks, Randoj Kan and Budibal Guru, were lent by the 3rd Gurkha Rifles (map page 119).

The expedition was a model of careful organization.[1] By 8 June the party was assembled at the base on the moraine below the junction of the Purbi Kamet and Raikana glaciers at about 15,350 feet. Successive camps were established, Camps I (16,800) and II (18,600) on the north side of the Purbi Kamet glacier, Camp III (20,700) on the upper shelf of the glacier, which was connected with Camp II by a steep snow gully. The difficult part of the climb was a 1000-foot rock wall above this camp up which a route had to be made safe for laden porters. Above it on 17 June Smythe, Shipton, and Lewa cut steps up the ice-dome and on the following day established Camp IV at about 22,000 feet, the rest of the party with the fittest of the porters carrying up provisions from Camp III. On the 20th Smythe, Shipton, and Holdsworth reconnoitred the route to Meade's col and set up Camp V just below it on a large snowfield at 23,300 feet.

On the 21st Smythe, Shipton, Holdsworth, Lewa, and Nima Dorje set out for the summit from this camp, while Beauman, Greene, and Birnie, with the two Gurkhas and five porters moved up to it in support. Smythe chose the north-east edge of the north face for his attack. Good progress was made to within 400 feet of the summit ridge, where the slope steepened and there was a thin layer of snow on ice. At this point, just below 25,000 feet, the porter Nima Dorje, who was carrying the cine-camera, was too exhausted to continue. The remaining four, taking turns to cut steps, reached the summit at 4.15 p.m. after a climb of more than eight hours, half of which was spent on the last five hundred feet.

After staying on the summit for twenty minutes the party descended to Camp V, much of the way through snow softened by the sun. On arrival Lewa's feet were found to be severely frostbitten and he was evacuated to lower camps the following day. Two days after the first success, Greene, Birnie, and the local porter Kesar Singh, a Bhotia from Gamsali, near Niti, repeated the climb to the summit. By the 27th the whole expedition was back at their base.

[1] Smythe's detailed account of this expedition is given in his book *Kamet Conquered* (London, 1932).

Kamet was the highest summit to be reached up to this time, though camps had been placed higher on Everest. Though some of the porters had been unable to reach the highest camp, some share of the success is due both to the Sherpas and to the local men. Properly trained and well led, the best of the local men would compare favourably with the Sherpa. An interesting innovation on this expedition was the use of ski by Holdsworth between Camps IV and V, that is between 22,000 and 23,500 feet. He was also able, in spite of slightly frostbitten feet, by using ski, to cover the eight miles back from Camp III to the base in one day.

Lewa's frostbitten feet recovered in hospital, though the tops of some of his toes had to be amputated; his mountaineering career was by no means ended.

At the end of this successful campaign the whole party, still with a month to spare, crossed from Gamsali by the route Mumm, Longstaff, and Bruce had taken in 1907 over the Bhiundhar Khal to Hanuman Chatti in the Alaknanda valley.[1] They followed the Alaknanda to Ghastoli and explored the head glaciers of the Arwa valley, crossing the main watershed into the head of the Chaturangi glacier. Birnie's sketch-map was an improvement on the old reconnaissance map made sixty years earlier, but has since been superseded by the modern half-inch surveys of 1935–7 (map page 265)[2].

★   ★   ★

Hugh Ruttledge with R. C. Wilson and T. H. Somervell had begun the post-war campaign against Nanda Devi in 1926, when they reconnoitred the mountain ring from the north-east. After his retirement Ruttledge in 1932 returned again to the Nanda Devi problem. With the guide Emile Rey of Courmayeur and six Sherpa porters recruited in Darjeeling, he reached the head of the Sundardhunga valley towards the end of May; they examined the southern section of the ring-wall east of Maiktoli (22,320) and especially where this drops to a saddle, the Sundardhunga Khal (18,110). An ice-terrace about 200 feet thick, rather similar to that on the north-west face of Kangchenjunga, was shedding large masses of serac to

[1] Page 118.
[2] H.J. iv (1932) 35. Survey of India Map 53 N/NW (1946).

sweep the approach. Ruttledge and Rey agreed that it might be climbed, but that it would involve continual danger during three days. After studying the face they agreed that, though a route might be found, it would be impossible for laden porters[1] (map page 116). At the end of May and in early June 1933 P. R. Oliver and D. Campbell made a reconnaissance of Dunagiri (23,184) on the northern ring-wall from the Tolma glen, but could find no route to its south-west arête and made no serious attempt to climb it, Oliver then crossed the Lata pass into the lower Rishiganga and by Longstaff's route of 1907 made the second ascent of Trisul (23,360). The remarkable feature of this climb was that Oliver was unaccompanied by professional Alpine guides or trained Sherpas, and relied entirely on Bhotia men recruited from the villages near Niti. Two of them, Kesar Singh and Kallu, had been on Smythe's expedition to Kamet in 1931 and Kesar Singh had been with Birnie and Greene to the summit. He now was Oliver's sole companion to the top of Trisul.[2]

In 1934, a few months after returning from the Everest expedition of the year before,[3] Eric Shipton and H. W. Tilman took up the Nanda Devi problem with a small lightly laden party, which included three Sherpa porters, Ang Tharkay, Pasang Bhutia, and Kusang Namgay. All three had been to Everest in 1933, Ang Tharkay and Pasang having helped to establish Camp VI at 27,400 feet.[4] They were among the first to receive the coveted 'Tiger's Badge' of the Himalayan Club. Ang Tharkay had also been with Bauer on Kangchenjunga in 1931; he was now about twenty-four years of age.

Shipton and Tilman determined to take Longstaff's advice and force a route up the Rishiganga gorge into the 'inner sanctuary' of Nanda Devi, if it were humanly possible, reconnoitre the mountain from close quarters, and discover whether there was a practicable route to the summit. It was fully realized that the party was too small to attempt the climb.[5]

[1] *H.J.* v (1933) 28.       [2] *H.J.* vi (1934) 91.
[3] See page 211 ff.
[4] Ang Tharkay (No. 19); Pasang Bhutia (No. 39); Kusang Namgay (No. 9).
[5] *H.J.* vii (1935) 1. For the full account of this exploration see Shipton's fascinating book, *Nanda Devi* (London, 1936).

Joshimath on the Dhauli river was reached on 20 May. The following day the party left with eleven Dhotial porters from Baijnath, all lightly laden, with forty days' supplies for themselves and ten days' food for the Dhotials. Eight days later they reached Longstaff's farthest point of 1907, and paid off the last of the Dhotials. The reconnaissance of the upper gorge began on 30 May. By 8 June this small strong party had forced its way through the two miles of gorge and established a camp at the snout of the main northern glacier, since named the Uttari Rishi Gal.

During the next three weeks they explored and mapped the whole of this northern glacier, reached four points on the mountain ring from the inside of it, including a col close to that seen by Ruttledge in 1926, a peak of about 21,000 feet, and a col at about 20,500 feet overlooking the Bagani (or Bagini) glacier.[1] They also examined the great north faces of Nanda Devi and Nanda Devi East and the precipitous rock wall between them. There was no feasible route to the summit from the north.

The first signs of the monsoon appeared on 23 June; survey and further reconnaissance became impossible and the party withdrew, by the way they had entered, to Joshimath, exactly six weeks after leaving it. After a week's rest they went north up the Alaknanda to Mana and explored the Bhagirath Kharak glacier in the hope of finding a pass into the head of the Gangotri glacier. Unsuccessful in this, they crossed the watershed northwards to one of the Arwa glaciers, explored by the Kamet expedition in 1931, crossed Birnie's pass, and followed the Chaturangi glacier down to its junction with the Gangotri glacier. They then returned to Arwa and Badrinath to explore the Satopanth glacier, which descends from the eastern face of the great Chaukhamba group of peaks. Throughout much of this period, during July and the first half of August, the monsoon affected the Badrinath–Kedarnath watershed severely, though the Arwa and Chaturangi glaciers were sheltered from it to some extent.

By 26 August they were back at Joshimath, and on 8 September they reached their old base camp in the inner sanctuary of Nanda Devi. They now completed the exploration and survey of the

[1] This glacier, formerly spelt *Bagini*, is shown on the modern survey as *Bāgani*. The old Bhagat Kharak has become Bhagirath Kharak.

southern basin, during which they climbed Maiktoli or East Trisul (22,320) and reconnoitred the serrated south rock ridge of Nanda Devi, which they climbed to a height of about 20,500 feet. Satisfied that this offered the best route to the summit after seeing the mountain from all angles, the party made its exit over the ring-wall by the Sundardhunga Khal which Ruttledge and Emile Rey had examined from the south in 1932, though they agreed that a crossing in the reverse direction was impossible.

The whole of this brilliant and successful reconnaissance had been well planned. The party travelled light and shared the loads with their porters; comforts were cut to a minimum. The expedition re-set the fashion in Himalayan mountaineering of the small compact party. Both Tilman and Shipton paid a high tribute to their Sherpa porters, particularly to Ang Tharkay, to whose cheerful co-operation they owed so much.

For nearly five months [wrote Tilman] we had lived and climbed together, and the more we saw of them the more we liked and respected them. That they can climb and carry loads is now taken for granted; but even more valuable assets to our small self-contained party were their cheerful grins, their willing work in camp and on the march, their complete lack of selfishness, their devotion to our service. To be their companion was a delight; to lead them, an honour.

And surely, though they forgot to mention it, great credit is due to Tilman and Shipton themselves.

\*   \*   \*

In 1936 Nanda Devi was climbed to the summit. The party for this venture was organized by T. Graham Brown, Professor of Physiology in the University of Wales, and the American Charles Houston. They had intended to make an attempt on Kangchenjunga, but were unable to get permission. It was composed of four Americans: W. F. Loomis, Charles Houston, Arthur Emmons, and Adams Carter, and four British: Graham Brown, N. E. Odell, H. W. Tilman, and Peter Lloyd. Emmons did not intend to climb high, since both his feet had been severely frostbitten on Minya Gongkar (c. 24,900) in Chinese Sikang in 1932. It was a strong party: Graham Brown was a veteran mountaineer with a high reputation;

Odell had been to Everest in 1924 and Tilman to the Nanda Devi basin two years before. Six Sherpas were engaged, but because of the requirements of the Everest expeditions and the casualties on Nanga Parbat in 1934, few good men were available. Five had been to Everest, but of these Da Namgyal (No. 33), now forty-one years of age, Pasang Phuttar (No. 79), and Nima Tsering III (No. 129) were past their best. Pasang Kikuli (No. 8) had been on all three Kangchenjunga expeditions, 1929, 1930, and 1931, on Everest in 1933, and was a survivor of the Nanga Parbat disaster of 1934; he was one of the first to wear the 'Tiger's Badge' and was still first-class. Kitar Dorje, with Everest 1924 and 1933, and Nanga Parbat 1934 to his credit, was also good; the sixth, Nuri, was a novice to climbing.

While awaiting the other members, Tilman and Loomis with two Sherpas carried an advance dump of supplies to a cave in the Rishi gorge before the monsoon and then returned to Ranikhet to meet the others. On 21 July the party left Joshimath with thirty-seven Dhotial porters, ten Mana Bhotias, and the six Sherpas, all with heavy loads, but the Dhotials would not face the upper Rishi gorge and had to be paid off. Great difficulty was experienced in forcing the gorge with the remainder, the Rishi being in monsoon flood, but by 2 August a base camp was established at about 15,500 feet, a mile above the snout of the south-east glacier (Dakkni Nanda Devi). The Mana men were paid off, and from here all subsequent carrying was done by the climbers and Sherpas.

The south ('Coxcomb') ridge, reconnoitred in 1934, was chosen for the attempt. Considerable trouble was encountered by blizzards during the ascent, but fortunately none lasted long. Camp I was placed on the ridge at 19,200 feet; Camp II, 'the Gîte,' on a ledge crowning a rock buttress at 20,400 feet. It was now 12 August. The Sherpas were already depleted in strength. Da Namgyal, with a bad cough, had gone back with the Mana men; Nima Tsering, and Kitar Dorje were sick at the base; Pasang Phuttar succumbed at Camp I; Pasang Kikuli and Nima carried loads thrice to Camp II, but then Nima sickened, Pasang Kikuli became snow-blind, and after resting in Camp II for a week they returned to the base. Above Camp II all carrying was done by the seven climbers.

On 18 August Camp III was placed under the shelter of a steep snow bank at 21,000 feet; on the 24th Camp IV on the top of a snow saddle at 21,700 feet. On this day five climbers, Odell, Houston, Loomis, Lloyd, and Tilman were in Camp IV, with Graham Brown and Carter in support in Camp III. The plan was for the five to carry a bivouac as high as possible on the 25th; Odell and Houston were to make a bid for the summit from here on the 26th, with the other three in support at Camp IV, where they would be joined by Graham Brown and Carter. Two of the five would then make a second attempt.

All went well at first. The bivouac was established at 23,500 feet and Loomis, Lloyd, and Tilman returned to Camp IV. On the 26th Odell and Houston reconnoitred to 24,000 feet, but found the distance to the summit too great and returned to the bivouac intending to place it higher. That night, however, Houston became mountain-sick with stomach trouble, and next morning was too ill to go on. Tilman and Lloyd joined Odell at the bivouac while Graham Brown and Carter brought the sick man down.

On the 28th the bivouac was carried up to 24,000 feet, Lloyd returning to Camp IV. The next day Tilman and Odell, starting from the high bivouac at 6 a.m., reached the summit, 25,645 feet, at 3 p.m., an average speed of a little under 200 feet an hour. This was good going over unreconnoitred and difficult ground at this altitude. Both climbers seem to have become fully acclimatized to 23,000 feet before the final climb. It was the joint effort of all the climbers in carrying above 20,400 feet, which made success possible.

It would have been of considerable physiological interest if Graham Brown and Lloyd had made a second climb to the summit with Tilman and Odell in support; and more convincing in the evidence of what a small compact party can do. They would probably have reached the top; and if four out of seven had reached the summit of Nanda Devi, it could have been convincingly argued that two out of seven might get to the top of Everest. As the evidence stood after this climb, it must be remembered that Nanda Devi is little higher than Camp V on Everest, and that neither the weather, though bad, nor the wind ever drove them back: Houston fell sick, Carter and Loomis both were slightly frostbitten, and one more casualty might have put the summit beyond their reach. The hardships of the gorge passage told considerably on the small number of porters and were partly responsible for the failure of the older men; and Kitar Dorje died of dysentery at the Base Camp. It was a difficult climb under difficult conditions, and the margin between success and failure was very small.

Not content with their achievement, while the main part of the expedition returned by the Rishi gorge, Tilman, Houston, and the Sherpa Pasang Kikuli climbed out of the basin by the col south of Nanda Devi East which Longstaff with the two Brocherels had reached in 1905 from the Lawan Gad.

# 3. Everest 1933–1938

LATE in August 1932 the Tibetan Government sanctioned another attempt to climb Everest. For eight years the Everest Committee in England had sought permission in vain. There was now little time to prepare, but the Committee had kept in touch with improvements in technical equipment. None of the most experienced climbers of the earlier expeditions could get away, but a younger generation of keen climbers had arisen. It was early decided to take a large party, partly because individual powers of acclimatization were not known, partly so that there would be a wider choice of men for the final assault. It was also felt that if the first attempts failed it might be possible to try again during or after the monsoon.

Ten men, each technically capable of reaching the summit, in addition to the leader, transport officer, doctor, and wireless operators, were chosen. Hugh Ruttledge, aged forty-eight, who had climbed in the Kumaun Himalaya six times since 1925, was selected to lead. He spoke the language and well knew the capabilities of Sherpa and Bhotia porters. The team comprised E. O. Shebbeare (forty-seven) and C. G. Crawford (forty-two), who had each been once to Everest in the twenties; Smythe (thirty-two), Birnie (thirty-two), Greene (thirty-one), and Shipton (twenty-five), who had reached the top of Kamet (25,447) in 1931; J. E. H. Boustead (thirty-seven), who had climbed in Sikkim in 1926; G. Wood-Johnson, who had been with Smythe to Kangchenjunga in 1930; P. Wyn Harris (twenty-nine), L. R. Wager (twenty-eight), J. L. Longland (twenty-seven), and T. A. Brocklebank (twenty-four), of established Alpine reputation; and W. Maclean, second medical officer to Greene. Nine of the fourteen had experience of the Himalaya, but neither Ruttledge nor Shebbeare were expected to go higher than the North Col, and the latter's duties were mainly to deal with transport problems. The average age of those from whom the assault members would be chosen was thirty.

Equipment had been much improved since 1924. A new double-skinned tent, a modification of the Central Asian *yurt* combined with an Arctic type, offering more protection from blizzards in the lower camps, had been designed. Much attention had been devoted to wind-proof clothing and tents for the high camps and to the scientific preparation of food for high altitudes. A lighter and improved oxygen apparatus had been tested. Ruttledge who studied every aspect of the earlier expeditions with the greatest care, superintended every detail.[1]

The strategy of the campaign was based on gradual acclimatization to 23,000 feet, involving an early start, short and comfortable marches across Tibet to the Base Camp, deliberate and successive establishment of Camps I, II, and III on the East Rongbuk glacier, each to be capable of being held against storm and blizzard, however violent. Camp IV on the North Col was then to be established methodically while the men and porters acclimatized to that altitude. From there the advance would be speeded up before deterioration set in (map page 158).

It was hoped that this plan would bring two and possibly three assault parties at the top of their form to Camp IV with sufficient porters to set up Camps V, VI, and if necessary VII above the col, so that the final climb, now known to be difficult, would be as short as possible. The assaults were planned for the second half of May. A wireless transmitting and receiving set had been financed privately by Mr. D. S. Richards, and Lieuts. E. C. Thompson and W. R. Smijth-Windham of the Royal Corps of Signals, accompanied the expedition to receive weather reports.

Hopes were high when the expedition established its Base Camp on 17 April 1933, twelve days earlier than its predecessors, and when on 6 May twelve climbers occupied Camp III at 21,000 feet at the foot of the col. The porters also were in good heart, in spite of storms which had buffeted the lower camps.

The North Col slopes had changed much in nine years and had become more difficult. In very bad weather, whenever there was a lull, eight of the party strove to open a route to the col. Only on 15 May was Camp IV set up on a ledge about 250 feet below it,

[1] Ruttledge: *Everest 1933* (London, 1934).

where it was hoped some shelter would be obtained from the bitter blasts of the west wind.

This was the second stage of the plan successfully completed, though with difficulty and with the expenditure of great effort. But there was no time to lose. A weather report received on 12 May recorded that the monsoon was active off Ceylon, ahead of time. Meanwhile the expedition was still being battered by storms from the west. The period of comparative calm before the monsoon broke was likely to be short.

On this day, 15 May, Smythe, Shipton, Wyn Harris, Longland, Birnie, and Boustead occupied Camp IV with fifteen porters. The tactical plan was now to acclimatize to this altitude while stocking the camp, and then to establish Camps V and VI, and make the assault in three successive days, culminating probably on the 23rd.

Unfortunately an even more violent storm than usual imprisoned the party at Camp IV for four days and prevented all movement between III and IV. Not until the 20th was any active progress possible. On that day a party with porters tried to establish Camp V but reached no higher than 24,500 feet. Meanwhile supplies were brought up to Camp IV at high pressure. The final day for the assault was put off to the 25th.

On 21 May Ruttledge went up to the col to direct the climb. He had received a further message on the 19th saying that the monsoon was active in the Bay of Bengal. He found climbers and porters in excellent health and spirits. The 22nd broke windless and sunny; four or five calm days might now be expected before the monsoon gained control. A fine effort by Wyn Harris, Greene, Birnie, and Boustead with twenty porters on that day established Camp V at 25,700 feet, with Wager and Longland in support. Unfortunately Greene, who had only had one day at Camp IV to acclimatize, strained his heart and had to return with Longland to the col. Twelve of the porters also returned, leaving Wyn Harris, Birnie, Boustead, and Wager with eight porters in Camp V. Of these Wyn Harris and Wager were to go on the following day to set up Camp VI.

Once again the weather intervened, western disturbances driving back the weak monsoon currents. During the night of the 22nd a violent blizzard struck Camp V and prevented a start the next morning. It lasted through the 23rd and 24th, reaching hurricane force, and on the 25th the party was forced back to Camp IV, which, because of the heavy snow, had now become dangerous. Two of the arctic tents were now moved on to the col itself, one to be occupied by Smythe, Shipton, Wyn Harris, Wager and Longland, the other by a fresh body of porters. The rest moved down to Camp III.

It now became a matter of a dash for the summit on the first opportunity. On the 28th the weather improved. Wyn Harris, Wager, Birnie, and Longland with eight porters, re-established Camp V at 25,700 feet, and spent the night there. The 29th also dawned fine. Wyn Harris, Wager, Longland, and the porters took up one small tent to 27,400 feet, where they established Camp VI on a tiny sloping ledge on Everest's north face some 250 feet below the north-east arête. It was a superb feat. Here, 600 feet higher than ever before, Wyn Harris and Wager spent the night. Longland brought the porters down. Their names were Ang Tharkay, Dawa Tsering, Nima Dorje II, Ang Tsering, Kipa Lama, Pasang Bhutia, Tsering Tharkay, and Ringsing Bhutia.[1]

On the way down Longland's party was caught by one of the sudden blizzards that come tearing out of the west without warning, and it was only Longland's brilliant leadership and skill which shepherded the exhausted porters down to safety.

The storm died down in the evening. On the 30th Smythe and Shipton moved up to Camp VI, while Wyn Harris and Wager delivered the first assault. The route to the summit was still undecided. Norton had reached the great couloir in 1934 by a diagonal traverse of the yellow band well below the arête; Mallory had favoured the crest of the arête, including a direct assault of the two steps. It was part of the task of Wager and Wyn Harris to see whether these steps were possible to climb, so that the difficult rocks of the couloir

[1] Ang Tharkay (No. 19) and Ringsing Bhutia (No. 32) both later received the Tiger's Badge of the Himalayan Club. Like them Pasang Bhutia (No. 39) and Tsering Tharkay (No. 50) went on three or four Everest expeditions. There were two Ang Tserings, I (No. 36) and II (No. 15), and two Nima Dorjes, I and II, on the 1933 Everest expedition. It was probably Ang Tsering I who went to Camp VI. The two Nima Dorjes, Dawa Tsering Sherpa, and Kipa Lama do not appear to have registered Himalayan Club numbers.

could be avoided. About 200 yards east of the first step and sixty feet below the crest, they came upon an ice-axe, belonging to either Mallory or Irvine, where it must have lain for nine years. In all probability it marked the site of the fatal slip, when one climber placed his axe on the slabs to check with both hands the fall of his companion.

Wyn Harris and Wager found it easy to turn the first step but at once saw that a frontal attack on the second, such as Mallory had proposed, would almost certainly fail. They traversed below it in the hope of reaching the arête beyond, but were unable to climb the smooth face of the black band of rock which outcropped at the second step. Much time was lost over this necessary exploration and when they continued their traverse and eventually reached the point from which Norton turned back beyond the couloir it was too late to attempt a final assault. They also found the snow of the consistency of castor sugar, giving no support for the feet. They did not deem the climb impossible, but calculated four hours at least would be required to reach the summit, nearly 900 feet higher, and it was now 12.30. They would then have to return on this difficult route in the dark with a certainty of being benighted. They wisely decided to turn back. During the return Wager dragged himself up to the arête east of the first step and looked down the colossal east face into the Karma valley. He is the only man to have done so.

They told their story to Smythe and Shipton at Camp VI and descended to the North Col. Meanwhile another gale blew up, followed by a heavy fall of snow which plastered the dangerous outward-sloping slabs of the face and in effect destroyed all chance of success. The storm imprisoned Smythe and Shipton throughout the 31st, and when they set out at 7.30 a.m. on a forlorn hope on 1 June, Shipton had had two sleepless nights, and his condition was deteriorating. He soon realized that he was too weak and exhausted to reach the great couloir. Smythe persevered alone, reached the same point as Norton, Wyn Harris, and Wager, with time in hand to attempt the climb, but found the condition of the snow too dangerous. The storm of the day before had put an end to any hope of reaching the summit and he was forced to return.

At Camp VI, Shipton decided to descend, and Smythe spent his third night here at 27,400 feet, where he contrived to sleep soundly for thirteen hours, oblivious of a gale. Next day he descended 4,400 feet to the North Col through a storm which nearly blew him off the mountain.

The whole party now returned to rest at the base, while the monsoon took charge. Camp III was again occupied on 15 June, but any attempt to reach the col was now out of the question. The rumble and thunder of avalanches made further attempts impossible.

So ended the fourth expedition. It was robbed of success primarily by the fact that there was no lull, no calm spell between the western blizzards and the establishment of the monsoon. The weather was in fact unfavourable throughout. Mallory once put the odds against success by a particular party in a given year at fifty to one. A first-class party, first-class organization and a substantial amount of luck are the three essentials. Ruttledge added that, when four consecutive days of fine weather synchronized with the perfect simultaneous acclimatization and training of six first-class climbers, perhaps two of them might reach the summit.

He was unshaken in his opinion that the best period for the assault is between 7 May and 15 June, and that after the first heavy monsoon snow falls on the north face the season is over. The best route to the summit had been proved to be Norton's traverse; Mallory's route by the arête was impracticable at the 'second step.' Oxygen he thought might be necessary for the last 1000 feet; further improvements in food and equipment could be made. Ruttledge also stressed the point that every member of the climbing party must have a long record of guideless climbing, and sufficient years of practice 'to give the unconscious balanced adaptation to angle, which will enable him to move with economy of effort at high altitudes.' This economy is essential if the last difficult pitch is to be climbed.[1]

Oxygen was not used by the climbers, though it saved life in a case of pneumonia and the hands of a frostbitten porter.

An interesting event unconnected with the climb occurred this year, when two Westland aeroplanes fitted with Pegasus engines on

[1] In 1954, after returning from his successful climb, Sir Edmund Hillary assured Ruttledge that, looking down from the summit at the northern route, he formed the opinion that the last 900 feet were unclimbable.

two occasions in April flew over Everest. They were piloted by the Marquis of Douglas and Clydesdale and Flight Lieutenant D. F. MacIntyre. The first plane to fly over the Himalaya had been in 1925, and the first to cross the Himalaya was a flight of five Wapitis, under Squadron Leader S. B. Harris, which landed at Gilgit on 30 March 1931, two and a quarter hours after leaving Risalpur 248 miles distant. The planes also made a circuit of Nanga Parbat (26,620). In 1933 the altitude record was held by the United States Air Corps at over 40,000 feet, but such heights had not yet been reached over the Himalaya. Considerable courage was required to fly headlong into the heart of Everest's icy plume, and the worth of the Pegasus engines that stood the test was fully proved. The first flight emphasized the extraordinary difficulty of recognizing and photographing peaks in this tangle of mountains. When the first batch of photographs was published in *The Times* of 24 April, and in the *Illustrated London News* of 29 April, there was a good deal of thunder about 'Nature's Last Terrestrial Secret Revealed.' Unfortunately the magnificent photograph purporting to show 'the awe-inspiring summit of Everest as seen slightly from the north-west' is actually of Makalu, and that of 'the amazing cliffs of black rock and terrific ice-slopes' of the 'north-east slopes of Everest looking along the climber's path,' is of a much lower mountain about 22,500 feet and some distance from Everest, though at first sight it bears a superficial resemblance to it.

In fact the air-photographs, excellent though they were, did little to solve the Everest problem, which was now one of strategy. Not everyone was convinced by Ruttledge's sound arguments. While he stated that the only possible period for the assault was between 7 May and 15 June, there was a school of thought, arguing from the German attacks on Kangchenjunga, that the monsoon and post-monsoon periods had been ruled out too hastily. The difficulties of the last thousand feet as encountered by Norton, Wyn Harris, Wager, and Smythe, so much greater than expected, led some to think that perhaps an attempt by the west ridge might succeed in spite of the verdict of Mallory and Bullock in 1921.

In the spring of 1935 the Tibetan Government sanctioned another expedition covering the year from June 1935 to June 1936. This gave the Everest Committee time to send out a reconnaissance expedition in 1935 to examine these problems, while preparing for another assault in 1936.

Eric Shipton who led this reconnaissance had six tasks to perform:

(1) to collect data about monsoon snow conditions at high altitudes, and to investigate the possibility of a monsoon or post-monsoon attempt;

(2) to re-examine the western ridge of Everest and the unknown 'Western Cwm,' but without entering Nepal;

(3) to report on ice-formations on the North Col and advise on any special equipment to deal with them;

(4) to try out new men for the 1936 expedition, especially with regard to their powers of acclimatization;

(5) to investigate food and equipment problems;

(6) to make a photogrammetric survey, improving and extending the survey of 1921.

Shipton's party comprised five other experienced mountaineers: Tilman, who had been with him in the Nanda Devi basin in 1934, L. V. Bryant—a New Zealander, Dr. Charles Warren, E. G. H. Kempson, E. H. L. Wigram, and Michael Spender, the last a good photographer and surveyor. The party travelled light, lived a good deal off the country, thereby saving much in transport, and reached Rongbuk on 4 July.

With them were only fifteen selected porters, including four of those who had been to Camp VI in 1933: Ang Tharkay, Pasang Bhutia, Ringsing Bhutia, and Tsering Tharkay. Forty local Tibetans helped them up the East Rongbuk glacier and Camp III was established rapidly by 8 July. The monsoon, which had not broken until 26 June, nearly three weeks later than in 1933, did not hamper them; but by now there was a considerable amount of new snow on the upper reaches of the mountain.

Fully realizing the danger of the North Col slopes during the monsoon, every section was examined carefully and tested before Camp IV was set up in the 12th, and occupied by Shipton, Kempson, and Warren. With nine porters and food for fifteen days they now proposed to acclimatize to that altitude before going higher to examine the snow conditions on the slabs.

Though it was no part of Shipton's plan to make an assault, once again Everest struck at the critical moment. The weather broke on the 13th and the party was imprisoned for four days in Camp IV. A short reconnaissance showed that the north-east ridge was impossible, and it was decided to descend to Camp III and carry out the rest of the programme. On the way down they were surprised to find that an enormous avalanche had broken away on their line of ascent, which only five days earlier they had considered perfectly safe. This was irrefutable evidence, added to that of 1922, that a monsoon attack on the mountain was out of the question. The avalanche danger was too great, the snow too unpredictable.

For the rest of July and August the party made a number of successful climbs on mountains up to 23,000 feet, but found the snow unfavourable above that altitude on every occasion. Tilman and Wigram re-examined the Lho La and the western arête, and came to the same conclusion as Mallory and Bullock had reached in 1921. Shipton and Bryant climbed three 21,000-foot peaks in the vicinity of the watershed and camped for two nights on the crest of a saddle from which they looked into the Sola Khumbu country of Nepal. Shipton said of the views he had of the Western Cwm: 'As far as we could see, the route up it did not look impossible, and I should very much like to have the opportunity one day of exploring it.' It was then out of the question since it would involve a base in Nepal. This was the first occasion that the Nepal route was seriously mentioned as giving a chance of success.

Shipton's reconnaissance had answered all the questions put to him and Spender completed the photography for a valuable map. Because of the speed with which he reached Camp IV Shipton's views regarding the superiority of a light mobile party over 'heavy cumbersome organizations' became very strong. He advocated a party of not more than six Europeans in the future. When he added that this view was borne out by the fact that 'no expedition consisting of a greater number of Europeans than this has ever achieved its object in the Himalaya,' he forgot that no party of six or less had succeeded so far in climbing a peak of over 26,000 feet. In the very next year, 1936, it required a party of eight to climb Nanda Devi, seven of whom had to do all the carrying from 20,000 feet, and two only of the eight reached the top. Nor did the experience of the Germans on Kangchenjunga support Shipton's views. Nine Germans on the 1929 expedition, ten in 1931, had been required to reach their highest camps, even when much of their transport arrangements had been assisted by Tobin in its earlier stages. These Germans were fully occupied all the time in preparing the routes from Camp VI onwards. Fewer would not have reached so far. All the experience of Everest expeditions had gone to show that at least six fit first-class climbers were required on the North Col of Everest, at 23,000 feet, fully and simultaneously acclimatized, and with their attention solely directed on the summit. To get them there and supply them for the high camps, skilled and acclimatized porters are necessary. These must be properly cared for; some will almost certainly fail and have to be brought down and cared for in lower camps, while the six climbers are still intent on the summit. Above all, the problem of simultaneous acclimatization of a number of men is one which can only be solved on the spot. Some acclimatize rapidly, and deterioration then sets in; others, for instance Odell in 1924, acclimatize slowly but surely, and deterioration is delayed. Some, probably most, acclimatize more quickly on their second visit to high altitudes than on their first; and there is some evidence that a young man generally acclimatizes quicker than an older man. Of six climbers, equally acclimatized to 23,000 feet at the right moment, two may reach the summit under favourable conditions; more than six are required to make certain of the six and to bring them back in safety. A climb is successful only when the party has returned. Dead men spell failure even if the summit is reached.

Ruttledge's party for 1936 comprised eight climbers potentially capable of reaching the summit of Everest, besides himself and three others. These three were G. N. Humphreys, doctor, W. R. Smijth-Windham, wireless operator, C. J. Morris, transport officer. The eight climbers were Smythe, Shipton, Wyn Harris, Kempson, Warren, Wigram, and two new-comers to Everest, P. R. Oliver, who had climbed Trisul in 1933, and J. M. L. Gavin, whose report from the R.A.F. medical board indicated that he had exceptional staying powers. By some strange mischance, Tilman and Bryant, who had been with Shipton in 1935, were ruled out on the grounds that they acclimatized too slowly and incompletely. In view of later events it is interesting also to record that a young climber, John Hunt, then aged twenty-six, who had with James Waller made a determined but unsuccessful assault on Saltoro Kangri (25,400) in the Karakoram in 1935, and had been selected by Ruttledge, was not passed by the R.A.F. board. Tilman consoled himself in 1936 by climbing to the top of Nanda Devi. These examples show how complex is the problem of selection.

Ruttledge's expedition of 1936 had less fortune than any other that ever went to Everest.[1] Carefully prepared to the last detail, with a first-class and united party sharing all the duties, Camp III was fully established on 7 and 8 May. Everest had shown a black rock-face when seen on the journey, but had now been white for some days, apparently because of western disturbances. The condition of the party was so good that it was decided to advance the programme. The slopes of the North Col though changed since 1935 were made safe for the porters; Camp IV was established on the 14th, and the next day Smythe and Shipton, who were to make the first assault, occupied this camp with thirty-six porters. Among them was a young porter aged nineteen, Tenzing Khumjung Bhutia (No. 48), now on his first big expedition. Unfortunately the mild conditions which had enabled this programme to be carried out were unfavourable on the upper part of the mountain. The west wind was absent, and the snow lay too deep for progress. On the 18th Smythe and Shipton decided that to establish the higher camps in these conditions would only lead to the premature exhaustion of the porters, and that a wait in Camp IV would mean deterioration. Camp IV was left fully stocked, the party descended to Camp III, and as most of the expedition had now spent eleven days at 21,000 feet or over, Ruttledge wisely withdrew every-one to the base.

Here, on the 19th, a disturbing wireless message was received that the monsoon had appeared off Ceylon. This was early, but in a nor-mal year a fortnight could still be counted upon before Everest would be affected. The expedition hurried back to Camp III by the 24th.

But the long absence of the west wind was a portent. With nothing to check it the monsoon swept up the Bay of Bengal into the

1 Ruttledge: *Everest: The Unfinished Adventure* (London, 1937).

Himalaya and struck the Everest region within four days. The North Col at once became highly dangerous and remained so until the end. A desperate attempt was made on 5 June by the eight climbers with porters to reach the col, but they realized it would be madness to go on, and they brought the porters down. The next day Wyn Harris and Shipton made one last effort. On reaching the long traverse Shipton led out across it; Wyn Harris was about to follow, when the whole slope avalanched, breaking up into the ice-blocks characteristic of wind-slab. Shipton was upset and carried away, partly submerged. Wyn Harris leapt back, jammed his axe in deep; his left hand was crushed against its head. He too was thrown on his back but managed to fix his axe deeper into the snow with the rope around it and to throw his weight on it. The strain came and the rope sang. Slowly the axe was being dragged from its anchorage; and then by a miracle the avalanche slowed down and stopped within a few feet of the edge of a four-hundred-foot ice-precipice, and the two climbers were saved. This was the end of the attempt. No incident on Everest, except perhaps Longland's descent with the porters from Camp VI in 1934, proved more conclusively that only climbers of the very highest technical skill and with the power of instinctively doing the right thing are fit to battle with Everest.

Before returning, the party explored the head of the Rongbuk glacier and examined the western slopes of the North Col. Though this had never been completely ruled out by Mallory and Bullock in 1921, it had been generally accepted as impracticable. The climbers now agreed that, though difficult, it was not impossible, and that it would probably be a safer line of descent for a party caught above the North Col after the advent of the monsoon than that to the East Rongbuk glacier.

The problem of Everest was now reduced largely to one of weather. One more attempt, in 1938, was made before World War II. Tilman, who had been successful on Nanda Devi in 1936, was chosen as leader. Holding much the same views as Shipton, he chose a small party of seven, including himself: Smythe, Shipton, Odell, Warren, Oliver, and Peter Lloyd, the last-named a new-comer to Everest, but with a high reputation.[1]

[1] Tilman: *Mount Everest 1938* (London, 1939).

This party with thirty-one porters under Ang Tharkay established Camp III by 26 April, but severe cold, sore throats and high temperatures ruled out an attempt to reach the North Col, and they crossed the Lhakpa La to the Kharta valley to recover. When they returned to Camp III on 18 May the weather was following much the same course as in 1936, with a white snow-face to Everest. The col was reached and Camp IV occupied on the 28th by Tilman, Odell, Oliver, and Warren. Two days later three of them, using oxygen, reached 24,500 feet, through deep snow. The North Col became dangerous and the party descended to recuperate.

Camp was now moved to the main Rongbuk glacier to attempt the col from the west side, and on 5 June they regained it. For two days the monsoon had weakened and snow had been blowing from the face of Everest. On the 6th, Smythe, Shipton, Lloyd, and Tilman, with seven porters, including Ang Tharkay, left the col and pitched Camp V at 25,800 feet, the last two returning to Camp IV. Two days later Smythe, Shipton, and the porters for the first time since 1933 set up Camp VI at 27,200 feet and the porters descended safely under Ang Tharkay. The next morning Smythe and Shipton struck out diagonally upwards but, after wallowing in deep powder-snow for some time, returned to Camp VI and descended to the col. Tilman and Lloyd made a second attempt after spending the night of the 9th in Camp VI, and came to the same conclusion. It is quite impossible to climb the last 2000 feet of the north face with deep snow on the rocks. The lesson had been learnt before, and was now rubbed in. Once the monsoon has broken, the season is ended for a large party or a small.

On this expedition two types of oxygen apparatus were used, the older 'open' type and a new 'closed' type. Of these the former was preferred, and Lloyd benefited by its use when going high with Tilman at the end. But once again the weather had been, as so often before, the deciding factor. Tilman maintained that the small party run on modest lines had proved itself as likely to get to the top as a large expensive one. This was too optimistic a claim. Rather, if proof were needed, it would be more correct to say that it is cheaper to lose the summit with a small party than with a large one. The weather prevented proof of anything else. There were more ailments, coughs, colds, influenza, than on previous expeditions, and all the climbers suffered from these on various occasions; but these also may be attributed to the weather and not to organization or numbers.

One factor apart from expense should be taken into account when comparing Tilman's expedition with earlier ones. Many of the porters now were much more reliable and more highly trained in ice-work; Ang Tharkay's list of travels included Kangchenjunga 1931, Everest 1933, 1936, and 1938, Nanda Devi basin 1934, the Kumaun Himalaya with Osmaston 1936, and the Karakoram with Shipton in 1937. He was still only twenty-eight years old. Pasang Bhutia had been four times to Everest, Wangdi Nurbu thrice. It was under such men as these and by the example and care of such men as Smythe, Shipton, Ruttledge, Tilman, and the rest that the younger generation of Sherpas and Bhotias served their apprenticeship. Nor must the lessons of the German expeditions to Kangchenjunga and Nanga Parbat be forgotten.

# 4. Nanga Parbat 1932, 1934

NANGA PARBAT is in some ways comparable topographically with Everest.[1] There is one impossible face, falling precipitously to the Rupal Gah like the fearsome east face of Everest: there is a western approach by the Diamirai glacier, explored by Mummery in 1895, which takes the place of the Western Cwm; and there is the Rakhiot glacier about eight miles long, on the north, in place of the main Rongbuk glacier, though it has no convenient eastern branch like the East Rongbuk glacier (maps pages 108, 158).

The face of the north ridge of Nanga Parbat as seen by Collie and Hastings when anxiously waiting for Mummery in August 1895 is as impossible to climb as the face of the west ridge of Everest from the north. If there is one weak spot in the defences it is the col on the north-east ridge between the Rakhiot Peak and the shoulder, the 'Silver Saddle'; this col is at about 22,800 feet, much the same as the North Col of Everest, between Changtse and the north-east shoulder. From the col to the top of Nanga Parbat at 26,620 feet the difference in height is rather less than that from the North Col to Everest's Camp VI where Norton and Somervell, Mallory and Irvine had all spent a night in June 1924.

It would seem that the problem of Nanga Parbat in 1932 was a comparatively simple one, especially as it was known that man could, from the physiological aspect, sleep at the top of it, and that the monsoon is not so active in the Punjab Himalaya as in Nepal. But there are contrasts as well as superficial similarities; and every mountain has its individual features and defences. Unlike Everest's north face, which is swept clear of ice and snow by the terrible blasts of the west wind, the north face of Nanga Parbat is draped with glaciers and ice-terraces, from which huge unstable masses break away by day and by night, and thunder down the slopes. Whereas the route from the snout of the Rongbuk glacier at 16,400 feet to the foot of

[1] For the topography of Nanga Parbat, see page 106 ff.

the North Col at 21,000 feet is easy, the Rakhiot glacier descends to 10,400 feet[1] and difficulties begin at the first ice-fall at about 17,500 feet; the glacier is then broken up by ice-blocks and crevasses and is within reach of ice-avalanches. The ascent from here to its col, on the ridge west of Rakhiot Peak may be likened to that to the North Col of Everest, twice as high, twice as broken and difficult, three times as dangerous, and four times as long. Whereas Everest's North Col can be reached on a fine day from its foot, at least three intermediate camps are required on Nanga Parbat. No camp directly beneath it is safe from avalanches in summer. A long ascent to the north of Rakhiot Peak is necessary, and a long traverse south to reach the col. The siting of the camps and the route between them are problems which beset the Germans, four times in the thirties: in 1932, 1934, 1937, and 1938.

The expedition in 1932 was led by Willy Merkl, aged thirty-two, an Alpinist of the first rank with much experience in the Alps, Caucasus, and Elburz. There were seven other first-class climbers: Peter Aschenbrenner, Fritz Bechtold, Hugo Hamberger, H. Kunigk, F. Simon, Fritz Wiessner, and an American—Rand Herron. Hamberger was doctor as well as climber. It will be noted that there was no separate transport officer, and none had knowledge of the language or previous experience of the Himalaya. It was a great pity that Bauer was not consulted. No member of Bauer's teams which had been to Kangchenjunga was included; the Himalayan Club was not notified or asked to assist or advise in the selection of porters, and no Sherpas or Bhotias were enlisted. This was to some extent remedied on arrival in Srinagar by Ernest Neve and Kenneth Hadow, the local secretaries of the Club, but it was too late to do anything about the porter problem.

The party crossed the Burzil pass at the end of May and were met at Astor by Captain R. N. D. Frier from the Gilgit garrison, who thereafter helped them with the porters, though it took time. The Rakhiot glacier was reached by the tiresome track from Doian on the Gilgit road in the Astor valley over the Lichar, Buldar, and Rakhiot ridges and camp was pitched at the end of June at 10,820 feet

[1] The heights given in these accounts are from Finsterwalder's large-scale photogrammetric survey of 1934; they differ considerably from those of the early accounts.

on the lovely alp of 'Märchenwiese,' near the snout of the Rakhiot glacier. Here the party bought their first experience. When they checked their baggage, they found that ten loads—warm clothing for forty porters—had been stolen on the march through Kashmir. It was a disastrous start and in fact it prejudiced success.

The approach began on 30 June, when Camp I was set up below a large serac on the glacier at about 14,660 feet. That night an ice-avalanche fell in its neighbourhood and the blast from it wrecked the tent and naturally scared the porters. Camp II was established at about 17,550 feet on the first terrace: three tents pitched in a depression among ice-blocks with a roomy cave cut out of the ice for additional accommodation. Here again they were just beyond the reach of a great avalanche which fell before they left it. Merkl's party found ice-caves less satisfactory than had Bauer on Kangchenjunga, because of the difference of temperature in the daytime. On this section of the glacier he records that in July and August it was so hot in the sun that work after eleven o'clock was exhausting, yet it was icy cold within the cave.

Camp III at 19,350 feet was set up on 5 July; Camp IV, at about 20,290 feet on the broad second terrace, some 300 feet below the crest of the ridge between the South Chongra and Rakhiot peaks, was established on the 8th. This terrace appeared to be exceptionally favourable for an advanced base and ten days were spent in stocking it. During this period the climbers were acclimatizing, and on the 18th Aschenbrenner and Kunigk climbed Rakhiot Peak (23,210).

On the 18th the assault party of six climbers were gathered in Camp IV, when the weather broke. It had been uninterruptedly fine for over a fortnight. It now snowed for three days. Kunigk, who was ill with an inflamed appendix had to be taken down by Hamberger; the porters had also succumbed to sickness and were unfit to go farther. The remaining four, Merkl, Aschenbrenner, Bechtold, and Herron made a long traverse below Rakhiot Peak in the freshly fallen snow and set up Camp V at 20,330 feet. It was difficult and heavy going over avalanche debris for laden climbers. Beyond this camp was the most difficult part of the climb. The proposed route led across a wide steep ice-trough, the 'Mulde,' cut deeply in the slopes and filled with recent snow, an obvious path for avalanches sweeping down to the vicinity of Camp II. A moderately safe track was made across it, but the party was reduced to three, Aschenbrenner having to retire with incipient frostbite.

The rib beyond the 'Mulde' was reached on 25 July and Camp VI was set up at 21,650 feet. Four days later, on the col west of Rakhiot Peak at 22,820 feet, a small tent (Camp VII) was pitched. Herron and Simon, who had come up to reinforce the attack, had to return with strained hearts, and Merkl, Bechtold, and Wiessner reached the col alone.

It was all in vain. On the 30th thick banks of heavy cloud enveloped the mountain. The three went forward but were driven back by a snowstorm, first to Camp VII, then to VI where their upward tracks had been obliterated and on 1 August across the dangerous traverse to Camp V, where Frier met them with four porters. Continued snow drove them down to the terrace at Camp IV and here they waited. It was not till 14 August that the weather cleared; they returned to the base to plan another assault; but in the deep fresh snow they only regained Camp IV with great difficulty, and the route beyond was out of the question.

As a reconnaissance this attempt was successful. A practicable route had been found. It had been rather too ambitious to expect victory at the first attempt. The need for careful planning and preparation and the scale of the difficulties were perhaps underestimated. A responsible transport officer on the march through Kashmir would have checked the loads and prevented loss. It was this which contributed to the failure of the untrained porters. Too great a strain fell on the members of the assault party, who had to make the route and carry loads in deep fresh snow. Neither the break in the weather nor the porters deserve all the blame. Only three out of eight climbers reached 22,800 feet; without porters they could not have reached the summit even in fine weather. This is no reflection on Merkl or his friends, but the fruit of Himalayan inexperience, and of too small an expedition run on too modest lines. In order to save expense no oxygen was taken.

Merkl took most of these lessons to heart, but he still underestimated the difficulties. The long spell of fine weather was the rare feature, not its break; he had been lucky, not unlucky. He was not 'within a day or two of the top,' for physiological reasons, and knew nothing yet of deterioration above 23,000 feet. Some of this knowledge had already been learnt on Everest in 1922, and emphasized in 1924, when the assault parties were reduced from four members to two.

On Nanga Parbat, as on Everest, it can be fine in one camp while a raging blizzard may make all movement impossible in another. Close support between camps is therefore essential for safety. Merkl wisely withdrew from Camp VII when the weather broke. There was no one in support nearer than Camp IV. Tracks had been obliterated; the descent was difficult, dangerous, and exhausting. Nanga Parbat had in fact given a fair warning.

Merkl returned to the attack in 1934. Besides himself he had eight experienced climbers all technically able to reach the summit: Aschenbrenner and Bechtold, who had been with him in 1932; U. Wieland and E. Schneider, who had been to Kangchenjunga in 1930; A. Drexel, W. Welzenbach, P. Müllritter, and W. Bernard, who was also the doctor. A survey group comprised Richard Finsterwalder, W. Raechl, and the geologist P. Misch. The Indian Government attached Captains R. N. D. Frier and R. A. K. Sangster to help with transport problems.

The Himalayan Club helped by enlisting thirty-five Sherpa and Bhotia porters under the experienced Lewa, fifteen of whom had been to Camp V on Everest in 1933. They included Nima Thondup, now thirty-nine years old, who had been four times to Everest and twice to Kangchenjunga; Pasang Kikuli, three times to Kangchenjunga and once to Everest; Nima Dorje I, twice to Everest and twice to Kangchenjunga; and Nima Dorje II who had carried a load to Camp VI at 27,400 feet on Everest.

At Märchenwiese, reached on 18 May, local porters were paid off and the Darjeeling men were strengthened by forty Baltis. Camps I, II, and III were established by 6 June approximately at the same heights as in 1932, at 14,660, 17,550, and 19,360 feet, but under more difficult weather conditions. At this point Drexel, who was suffering from a severe chill, had to return. He developed pneumonia and died of congestion of the lungs on the night of the 8th.

This tragedy and other troubles delayed the advance, but by 30 June Camp IV (20,290), again to be the advanced base, was fully stocked, a new Camp V (21,950) on the north-east ridge at the northern foot of Rakhiot Peak had been set up, and the assault parties and porters were gathered in Camp IV. It was planned to force a route from Camp V over a high shoulder of Rakhiot Peak and from there traverse direct to the col beyond, thus avoiding the dangerous crossing of the avalanche-swept 'Mulde.' Two groups, the first with four climbers, the second with three, would make separate attacks, with two days' interval between them.

The way over the Rakhiot Peak was long and arduous. Steps had to be cut in the steep ice-slope and ropes fixed to steady the laden porters for more than 400 feet of the climb. The second group had to assist the first, and it was four days before Camp VI on the col was extablished on 4 July, approximately in the same position as the Camp VII of 1932.

Müllritter returned from here with a sick porter to Camp IV on the 5th, with instructions to take up supplies to Camp VI, but the weather worsened at Camp IV and he waited for it to clear. On the same day the climbing party followed the narrow ridge in deep snow for about a thousand yards and set up Camp VII (23,130) at the point where it steepens for the ascent to the 'Silver Saddle' at 24,450 feet. The following morning Bechtold left this camp and returned to Camp IV with two porters who were down with mountain sickness and exhaustion. When he left, it was a magnificent clear morning, much like those of the previous week, though there was a snowstorm at Camp IV when he arrived. Here he found Müllritter and Bernard and learnt that the blizzard had prevented them from stocking Camp VI.

Meanwhile on the same day the five climbers, Merkl, Aschenbrenner, Schneider, Welzenbach, and Wieland with eleven porters, reached the Silver Saddle. Aschenbrenner and Schneider, who prepared the track, went on across the plateau south-westwards towards the summit and reached an altitude of about 25,280 feet. They believed that they were four or five hours from the highest point. The other three climbers with the laden porters took longer to reach the Saddle, and it was then, at 2 p.m., too late to go on, and Camp VIII was pitched at 24,560 feet. The eleven porters were Pasang Nurbu (No. 29), Nima Dorje II, Pintso (or Pinju) Nurbu, Kitar (No. 35),

Pasang Kikuli (No. 8), Dawa Thondup (No. 49), Nima Tashi, Nima Nurbu, Ang Tsering I (No. 36), Gaylay, and Dakshi.[1]

Nanga Parbat now struck back. The wind rose in the afternoon and during the night became a raging hurricane. Tents were damaged and dense clouds of wind-driven snow imprisoned the party throughout the day and night of the 7th. It was impossible to prepare the simplest meals. The assault had failed.

On the 8th the retreat began in two groups. The storm still raged. All were weakened by the altitude. Under such conditions the mind suffers and judgement may become faulty.

Aschenbrenner, Schneider, and the porters Pasang Nurbu, Nima Dorje II, and Pintso Nurbu went first to prepare the track; Merkl, Welzenbach, and Wieland were to follow with the remaining eight. The blizzard swept across the steep descent below the saddle, Nima Dorje was dragged from his steps and held with the greatest difficulty on the rope by Pasang and Aschenbrenner; his load, a precious sleeping-bag, was torn from his back and lost. As they neared Camp VII, Aschenbrenner and Schneider unroped in order to save time in preparing the route. Through a break in the storm they saw the second party descending from the Saddle.

In the evening Schneider and Aschenbrenner, completely exhausted and clad with ice from head to foot, reached Camp IV. In the storm they had lost sight of their porters, but believed them to be close behind. They waited anxiously through the night for them and for Merkl's party.

The three porters had, however, sheltered in Camp VII at the foot of the Silver Saddle and so lost touch with their two climbers. Merkl's party was in an even worse plight. Physical deterioration after the violent storm was taking a deadly toll. Merkl and Wieland in helping the porters down became frostbitten, and with their eight porters had to bivouac in the snow before reaching Camp VII. Here the blizzard raged on through the night, and the porter Nima Nurbu died before morning.

Early on the 9th the three climbers with four porters continued the descent. Ang Tsering stayed behind in the snow bivouac above with Gaylay and Dakshi, who were partly snow-blind and ill. Wieland

[1] Porters had not yet been given registered numbers.

died before reaching Camp VII. Merkl and Welzenbach reached it exhausted and sent their four remaining porters, Kitar, Dawa Thondup, Nima Tashi, and Pasang Kikuli on along the crest towards Camp VI; they failed to reach it and were forced to spend another night in the snow, close to the three porters of the first group, who were also benighted.

On the 10th these seven porters joined up, reached the shoulder of the Rakhiot Peak, and started down the ice-wall, where they were seen in the afternoon by the watchers in Camp IV. But they were in desperate straits. Nima Tashi and Nima Dorje II died from exposure and exhaustion floundering in the snow amid the ropes of the descent, Pintso Nurbu outside Camp V. Pasang Kikuli, Pasang Nurbu, Kitar, and Dawa Thondup struggled on into Camp IV, more dead than alive, with badly frostbitten hands and feet.

Meanwhile Merkl and Welzenbach were still in Camp VII, Ang Tsering, Dakshi, and Gaylay on the slopes of the Silver Saddle above. Dakshi died during the night of the 11th, and on the morning of the 12th Ang Tsering and Gaylay reached Camp VII. Here Welzenbach died during the night of the 13th, and the next morning the three survivors, Ang Tsering, Gaylay, and Merkl, set out for Camp VI. Before reaching it Merkl collapsed and the two porters dug a small ice-cave to shelter him. Gaylay stayed with Merkl, though he might have saved himself, while Ang Tsering fought his way down for help.

From below in Camp IV [writes Bechtold] a man was seen pressing forward along the level saddle. Now and again the storm bore down a cry for help. The lone figure reached and came down over the Rakhiot Peak. It was Ang Tsering, Willy Merkl's second orderly, who at length, completely exhausted and suffering from terrible frostbite, found refuge in Camp IV. With almost superhuman endurance he had fought his way down through storm and snow, a hero at every step. Since he brought no letter from Merkl or Gaylay, his simple tale was the last news of the heroic struggle of our comrades and their faithful porters high on the ridge above.

Throughout this period of five days repeated attempts to reach Camp VI were made by Bechtold and the others in Camp IV. Storm and deep snow prevented them from getting farther than Camp V; they were engulfed in the flood of freshly fallen snow.

So ended this attempt—in the greatest mountain disaster of our time. It is easy to look back and criticize. But it must be realized how little was known at that time about the rapid deterioration of strength above 23,000 feet, especially under storm conditions. There was also no oxygen. As events turned out it would have been wiser to have had two assault parties as originally planned—one in Camp VI or VII, while the other set out for Camp VIII; the porters should have gone down on the afternoon of the 6th. There were too many eager men too high, and no one in support between Camps IV and VIII, a distance of over three miles and more than 4000 feet in height. Had there been two fit climbers in Camp VI or VII to keep the route open the terrible nights spent in the intermediate bivouacs would have been avoided.[1] But there was also great heroism. Climbers and porters alike freely gave of their lives for one another. Gaylay died with his master. Ang Tsering's achievement won for him the Medal of Honour of the German Red Cross, and he went to Everest two years later; Dawa Thondup and Pasang Nurbu received the same decoration, and went again to Nanga Parbat in 1937 and to Masherbrum in 1938. Pasang Kikuli, also decorated with the Medal of Honour, survived his terrible frostbite, and sacrificed himself on K2 in 1939.

[1] The storm was caused by strong penetration of the monsoon, which was active in the outer Punjab Himalaya throughout the first week of July. An analysis of the weather during the period was made by A. Wagner and appears in *Mitteilungen des D. u. O.A.V.* (1934) 276. A summary is given in *H.J.* viii (1936) 78.

# 5. Nanga Parbat 1937, 1938, 1939

GERMAN mountaineering now came under the 'Sportsführer' of the German Reich. Under his patronage the Deutsche Himalaja Stiftung was founded. But as Paul Bauer said: 'the catastrophe of 1934 had destroyed everything and we had to begin again.' The survivors of the Kangchenjunga and Nanga Parbat parties gradually built up the Himalayan Fund by lectures, articles, books, photographs, and films. The real founders were Bauer and his Kangchenjunga team, and Bechtold. All were determined to return to the assault. In 1936 Paul Bauer took a small party of three other climbers to Sikkim, not for another attack on Kangchenjunga, but to pass on his own experience to younger men and to knit them together. The three were Karl Wien, who had been to Kangchenjunga in 1931, A. Göttner, and G. Hepp. They climbed Siniolchu (22,600) and Simvu North (21,473), both difficult first ascents and fine achievements.[1] These three formed the nucleus of a new expedition to Nanga Parbat in 1937. Wien took over the leadership and made up a party of experienced climbing friends. Besides himself, Göttner and Hepp, there were five other climbers: Müllritter, a survivor from 1934; Hans Hartmann, who had been on the north-east spur of Kangchenjunga in 1931, a keen physiologist who took with him his assistant, Ulrich Luft; P. Fankhauser and M. Pfeffer. Professor Troll was attached for geographical work in the neighbourhood of the mountain, and Lieutenant D. M. B. Smart of the Gilgit Scouts went to help with transport matters. Twelve experienced porters were enlisted at Darjeeling, and were supplemented as before by selected Baltis for work in the lower camps.

All went well at the start and Camp II was established above the ice-fall of the Lower Rakhiot glacier by 24 May. Two days later a great mass of ice from high up on the mountain broke away in an avalanche; its blast tore down two tents, smashed the tent-poles and

[1] See below, page 275.

threw men and loads to the ground, but no one was hurt. The weather was unsettled, however, and it was thought advisable to retire to the base.

On 3 June the weather had cleared sufficiently for Camp II to be regained and by the 7th Camp IV was dug into a hollow at 20,280 feet, in much the same position as in 1934. In succeeding days this camp was stocked as the assault base and on 11 June was fully occupied. Heavy snow fell at intervals in the next three days and though the site of Camp V was reached it was considered inadvisable to occupy it.

On the morning of the 14th Smart left Camp IV bringing down porters to the base, leaving Wien, Hartmann, Hepp, Göttner, Fankhauser, Pfeffer, and Müllritter and nine Sherpas in the Camp.[1] Four climbers with some porters were then leaving for Camp V, but were later seen from below to be returning. It was hoped to establish Camp VI within three days.

On the 17th Luft started up from the base with five fresh porters carrying stores to Camp II. At mid-day on the 18th he reached the site of Camp IV to find the whole camp buried under a gigantic avalanche. Of the tents and their occupants there was no sign. All had been destroyed.

The avalanche was more than two days old and the ice-blocks had formed a rigid mass. Three rucksacks were found, but without tools it was impossible to dig out the tents. Luft raced back to the base the same night, Smart sent runners to Chilas and Gilgit and from these two places officers and men of the Gilgit Scouts hurried to the mountain to help.

When the first rumours of the disaster were confirmed in Germany, Bauer, Bechtold, and Kraus immediately flew out to India. At Lahore an R.A.F. plane flew them to Gilgit. The base was reached on 8 July. Bad weather and fallen ice-blocks at Camp II had delayed the relief party and only on 15 July did they all reach the scene of the disaster. The avalanche area was 1300 feet long and 500 feet wide.

[1] Pasang Nurbu, 'Picture' (No. 29), Jigmay Sherpa (No. 23), Gyalgen III Monjo (No. 58), Chong Karma (No. 104), Ang Tsering II (No. 15), Mingma Tsering (No. 68), Karmi Sherpa (No. 117), Nima Tsering I (No. 17), Nima Tsering II (No. 110). Ang Tsering II is not the man who survived the disaster of 1934.

In bad weather at over 20,000 feet it was four days' heavy work before the first signs of the camp were struck—a porter's ice-axe. Two more days of tunnelling and trenching followed. In one tent were the porters—at the request of Nursang, the Sherpa sirdar, they were left where they had met their fate. Two out of the three climbers' tents were found. In the first were Hartmann, Pfeffer, and Hepp; in the second Wien and Fankhauser; the third with Müllritter and Göttner was never found, though the ice was trenched ten feet deep in all directions.

Diaries had been written up on the evening of 14 June. Watches had stopped soon after 12 o'clock; the avalanche fell just after midnight. Sixteen men were overwhelmed in their sleep. Nanga Parbat is pitiless.

\*   \*   \*

Eleven Germans and fifteen porters now lay dead in the shadow of the mountain, many of them the most fitted to reach the summit. Bauer, undeterred and with grim determination to avenge his friends, set out once more in 1938. He had with him Bechtold and Luft, survivors of 1934 and 1937, and five younger men: Chlingensperg, Rebitsch, Ruths, Schmaderer, and Zuck. A radio technician, Ebermann, was also taken, so that camps could keep in touch with one another; and Luft had an assistant for his physiological work in Dr. Balke. They had also the help of an aeroplane, piloted by Alexander Thoenes, which it was hoped would drop supplies to the high camps and so save porterage. Two British members of the Himalayan Club were also invited to join the expedition, Kenneth Hadow and Flight Lieutenant McKenna. There were thus twelve members in addition to Thoenes whose plane was based on Srinagar.

Planning on the weather reports of earlier expeditions, which had all encountered heavy snowfalls in the last half of May, Bauer hoped to establish his base on 1 June and to reach Camp IV about the middle of the month. The last half of June had generally been fine, and this seemed the most favourable period for the assault.

The route, however, between Camps I and IV had become more difficult and bad weather in the first part of June delayed the establishment of the camps. On 25 June Camp IV was set up, and on this day

Thoenes dropped loads in its vicinity, though all were not recovered. Bad weather then broke communications between Camps III and IV and not until 1 July did the weather turn fine. The slopes beyond were thus too deep in snow to be tackled, the assault had to be postponed, and the climbers were brought down to rest at the base.

On 12 July a fresh start was made. Camp IV was reoccupied on the 15th and the next day Camp V was pitched rather lower than that of 1934. Bad weather again set in and in the following days attempts to climb the ice-wall of Rakhiot Peak failed. Near the old Camp V was found the dead body of Pintso Nurbu, who had lain there for four years.

Bauer and Rebitsch now reconnoitred the traverse below the Rakhiot Peak and across the Mulde which had been taken by Merkl on his first expedition in 1932, and found it better than the storm-swept face on which ropes had been placed in 1934. On the 22nd Bauer led a small party, Luft, Bechtold, Zuck, and four porters across this traverse and up to the ridge where Camp VI had stood. There they found the bodies of Merkl and Gaylay. In Merkl's pocket was a letter written by him and Welzenbach in Camp VII on 12 July 1934.

During the days which followed attempts were made to reach the Silver Saddle by Luft, Rebitsch, Schmaderer, Zuck, and Ruths, supported by Bauer from Camp V, but the fair weather broke up on the 25th. Of the porters only one remained fit in Camp VI, the rest had been evacuated, and three only were in Camp IV. Physical deterioration was already setting in. Fearing a repetition of 1934 Bauer wisely gave the order to retire. On the 27th the whole party regained its base.

One more effort was made. Tempted by fine weather at the base, Camp IV was reoccupied on 1 August, and Camp V, in deep fresh snow, two days later, but the traverse across the Mulde was now impossible, and the party once more withdrew.

Bauer led his expedition with wisdom and caution. The weather in 1938 was as unfavourable on Nanga Parbat as it was on Everest. Throughout the route from Camp I to IV there was continual danger from collapsing seracs and ice-avalanches during the monsoon incursions; between Camps IV and VI the traverse of the Rakhiot Peak and of the Mulde are equally dangerous in bad weather. From

Camp VI to the summit and back is over seven miles. The spirit of kindness which Mallory had asked of Everest had been entirely missing on Nanga Parbat.

In view of these dangers Bauer at the end of his expedition sent Luft and Zuck to the Diamirai side of the mountain to get a close-up view of the face which had defeated Mummery in 1895. Their reports and photographs seemed to warrant a further investigation, and Peter Aufschnaiter, who had been with Bauer on Kangchenjunga in 1931, formed a small party to reconnoitre the Diamirai face in 1939. Like Karl Wien in 1935, the year before his ill-fated expedition, Aufschnaiter came over to England in 1938 to get permission and discuss his plans; he was staying with me in Oxford at the time of the Munich crisis.

Aufschnaiter's party was composed of three other first-class climbers, Heinrich Harrer of Graz, one of the team that had climbed the north face of the Eiger, L. Chicken, and H. Lobenhoffer. They took the Khagan route over the Babusar pass to Chilas, and after crossing the Indus followed a path through the Diamirai gorge; they pitched a base camp at about 13,450 feet on the right side of the Diamirai glacier on 1 June. From here, after making some minor ascents to examine the face, they selected a route, by piecing together various practicable sections, by which they hoped to reach a prominent rock outcrop (the 'pulpit'), forming the edge of an ice-terrace. Behind this a steep slope of ice and snow appeared to lead up to the snowfield below the 'Bazin Gap,' which had been the aim of Mummery. From this point, at about 25,630 feet, the route would turn south along the crest of the north ridge to the summit, a distance of nearly a mile.

It is uncertain how much of this route in its early stages is identical with that taken by Mummery, but it was found to be more difficult than had been expected, because of rotten rock. Harrer and Aufschnaiter made the first attempt with two porters, reached a height of about 19,350 feet, but it was no place for laden porters and they came down. Aufschnaiter and Chicken on a second attempt reached a higher point but were brought up against treacherous rock and had to give up. A final effort by all four climbers was more successful, Harrer and Lobenhoffer reaching the ridge of the 'pulpit' where they pitched a small tent at about 20,000 feet. According to Harrer, the rock above them appeared to be practicable, but the party was obviously not strong enough to continue.

Aufschnaiter concluded that the technical difficulties of this route are probably akin to some of the more difficult climbs in the Alps.

A team of mountaineers [he wrote] skilled and experienced in tackling ice and rock of this kind might prefer the Diamir face to the Rakhiot side. A party of at least seven climbers would be required, as some would have to prepare the way in order to leave a reserve for the final assault. The climbers would have to do a lot of load-carrying in addition, as few porters would be willing or capable of such steep and exposed rock and ice.

Up to the end of July the weather had been favourable, with only a few spells of really bad weather. But the higher reaches of the mountain were shrouded in mist almost every afternoon, probably causing snowfalls on the mountain; and this is the crux of the climb.

Early in August Aufschnaiter visited the Political Agent of Gilgit to discuss plans for an expedition in 1940. These were foiled by the outbreak of war, and the party was interned.

# 6. Karakoram Exploration

MUCH exploration and scientific work was carried out in the Karakoram before World War II. The first Italian expedition to follow in the tradition of the Duke of the Abruzzi and Filippo De Filippi was sponsored by the Milan section of the Italian Alpine Club and the Royal Italian Geographical Society, and was led by the Duke of Spoleto. Its objects were primarily the exploration of the head of the Baltoro glacier and of the blanks in our map of the middle Shaksgam, the survey of as much of the Baltoro as possible by stereophotogrammetry, and an extension of the geological survey of the region. The Duke hoped to make a circuit of K2 by crossing the Karakoram watershed north of Broad Peak or east of Baltoro Kangri (Conway's 'Golden Throne'), by descending the Gasherbrum or Urdok glaciers to the Shaksgam, and by returning over Younghusband's Muztagh pass of 1887.

I was privileged to go over the Duke's plans with him before he started. In the summer of 1928 he took a small advanced party to form a supply depot at Askole, the last village up the Braldoh. He was thus able to start early in 1929, cross the passes lightly laden, and his expedition was concentrated at Urdukas, seventeen miles up the Baltoro by the middle of May. This was essential to his plan, since by the middle of July flood-water in the Shaksgam makes the river very difficult to ford (map page 134).

At Urdukas the expedition divided. One party under the Duke ascended the Baltoro to 'Concordia,' and from there explored a saddle at its head east of Baltoro Kangri, at an altitude of over 21,000 feet, but found that it led to the head of either the Kondus or the Siachen glaciers southwards and not across the main watershed to the Urdok.

The other party under Umberto Balestreri and including the mountaineer and geologist Ardito Desio, with V. Ponti and an Italian guide, made the first crossing of the East Muztagh pass,

19,030 feet, since Younghusband's famous journey in 1887. They descended the Sarpo Laggo glacier to the Shaksgam and followed the valley up to the Urdok glacier. The Gasherbrum glacier, which they had to cross two miles above its snout, completely blocked the valley. The Urdok glacier was ascended for thirteen miles to a height of about 16,700 feet and its topography was sketched as far as the watershed. Meanwhile Desio made a rapid route reconnaissance up the Shaksgam, passing between the snout of the Staghar glacier and the valley-wall opposite, and over the difficult Singhi glacier which also blocked the valley. He reached the western side of the Kyagar glacier, which had held me up in 1926, did not cross it, but tied his route-map on to my stations on the hill the other side.[1]

This reconnaissance party returned to the Baltoro by the Muztagh pass. Before leaving the region Desio explored the Trango glacier, the second lowest of the northern side-branches of the Baltoro, and also the Panmah glacier, of which he made a map. Besides the reconnaissance maps of Desio, pairs of photographs were taken on the Baltoro from which large-scale maps were made by stereophotogrammetry on their return.

Another Italian expedition of interest was made on the southern flanks of the Great Karakoram in 1930 by Professor Giotto Dainelli, who had been geographer and geologist on De Filippi's expedition of 1913–14. With a light caravan he was on the Siachen glacier on 9 June, two months after leaving Florence and before the flood-water in the Nubra rose sufficiently to stop him. With fifty-seven coolies and one companion, Miss Ellen Kalau, who, like himself, was an expert skier, he spent two months on the glacier and made a geological and botanical survey of the whole of it from its snout to its head. He then ascended the branch glacier, the Teram Shehr, and made a pass over its head at about 20,100 feet to the Rimo glacier, which had been surveyed on the De Filippi expedition in 1914. About forty of his permanent porters were Ladakhis from the villages of Timis (Timosgam) and Tia, who have a reputation for reliability.

The Vissers made a third journey of exploration covering the years 1929 and 1930. Once again they had with them the guide Franz Lochmatter and Khan Sahib Afraz Gul Khan, lent by the

[1] Page 181.

Surveyor General. They also had with them Dr. R. Wyss, a geologist, and A. Sillem, an ornithologist. In order to reach the Siachen glacier at the head of the Nubra before the river became unfordable, they crossed the Zoji La on 7 May and the Khardung La north of Leh on the 31st. Even so, they had some difficulty with the Nubra fords.

Major M. L. A. Gompertz, who had joined me for a short time in 1926, and had reconnoitred the Mamostong glacier near the Saser pass, had suggested that there was a large unknown glacier beyond it which flowed into the Nubra.[1] Longstaff commented on this as follows: 'When it is desired to survey this unknown corner, will the party please proceed five miles up the Siachen glacier and take the first turning on their right?'[2] This good advice was taken by the Vissers and in consequence they discovered the two Terong glaciers and the Shelkar-Chorten glacier, which were unknown till then. These were surveyed in detail by the Khan Sahib during June.

The expedition then crossed the Saser pass, and surveyed the first two right-bank tributaries of the upper Shyok south of Saser Brangsa. In August they crossed the Depsang and surveyed the extreme northeast corner of Ladakh, east of the Karakoram pass, after which the Khan Sahib returned to India and the Vissers went on to winter in Yarkand.

The following year they left Yarkand in May and returned to Ladakh by the Karakoram pass. In the upper Shyok they made further explorations of the side-valleys, which were surveyed by Muhammad Akram, who was lent to them by the Survey of India for the purpose.

A fourth journey was made by the Vissers in 1935. They again had with them Dr. Wyss and both Khan Sahib Afraz Gul and Muhammad Akram. After completing the survey of the southern end of the Great Karakoram between the Nubra and upper Shyok, they took my route of 1926 into the head of the Shaksgam, and followed it down to the Kyagar glacier. Here they found the glacier still blocking the valley, but the whole of the eastern half had retreated, so that the glacier was only half as wide at its snout as in 1926; the surface of the remainder was about eighty feet lower,

---

[1] *G.J.* lxix (1927) 319.  [2] *Ib.* 330.

though the lake, the Kyagar Tso, dammed by it, was rather larger.[1] They found and used our old boat which we had laid up in a side-valley. Wyss spent three days in reconnoitring the glacier, before he found a way across it; the crossing took a further three days, so that Minchinton's estimate of 1926 that we might take a week to find a way and cross with our camp was not far out.

The Khan Sahib and Muhammad Akram were now sent down the Shaksgam with light camps. They cut a passage through the ice-pinnacles near the snout, crossed on 18 July, and then divided up the survey work, the Khan Sahib taking the section from the Kyagar to the Urdok, and Muhammad Akram working below the Urdok. Great difficulty was experienced with the flooded river between now and 15 August when they regained the Kyagar; on two occasions men were swept away when fording it and only saved by miracles (map page 134). The survey of the valley was completed as far as Younghusband's Durbin Jangal, including all the side-glaciers descending from the Great Karakoram watershed: Singhi (eighteen miles), Staghar (eleven miles), Urdok (fifteen miles), Gasherbrum (twelve miles), and Skyang Lungpa (seven miles). Muhammad Akram, though he just failed to reach Durbin Jangal, on account of the volume of water in the river, thought that the Zug-Shaksgam did not enter the Shaksgam, but must continue north into the Yarkand river.[2] On their return across the Kyagar glacier they found their route near the snout impassable and ascended the left moraine, crossed the glacier six miles from the snout, and came down a long medial moraine to the right bank. The Kyagar Tso during the summer had increased to a length of over five miles and near the glacier was over a hundred feet deep. A long and difficult traverse along the face of the cliffs on the southern shore had to be made.

This work was of particular interest to me, partly because the Khan Sahib's plane-table survey checked my long-distance stereo-photogrammetric survey, some of which had been photographed at a distance of thirty miles, and partly because several of my old Ladakhi porters of 1926 went down the valley with the Khan Sahib and did

[1] Ph. C. Visser & J. Visser-Hooft: *Karakoram*, Brill, Leiden. (1938), Vol. II, page 168, fig. 83.
[2] See page 182.

excellent work. They sent greetings to me in Oxford from the Singhi glacier![1]

The blank on the Karakoram map was now growing smaller, but it caught the eye of those two restless explorers Shipton and Tilman and they planned an expedition for 1937. Little could be gained now unless they returned with a good map of unknown country and they took with them Michael Spender, who had been surveyor to the Everest reconnaissance of 1935, and J. B. Auden of the Geological Survey of India, who also had much Himalayan experience. Their plan was to cross from the Baltoro glacier by the Muztagh or some other pass to the Sarpo Laggo glacier and from a base there to survey the middle Shaksgam as far as Durbin Jangal, Younghusband's Aghil route, and the northern side of K2. The worst feature of this plan is the unreliability of the local porters of the upper Braldoh.

To compensate for these expected delinquents, Shipton engaged seven Sherpas from Darjeeling: Ang Tharkay (No. 19), Ang Tenzing II (No. 3), Lhakpa Tenzing (No. 30), and Sonam (or Sen) Tenzing (No. 75) were all first-class and experienced men, the first three wearing the Tiger's Badge; Aila Sherpa (No. 61), Nukka (No. 70), and Lobsang Sherpa II (No. 144) were new to the work.[2]

Askole was reached on 24 May. Instead of taking the Muztagh pass they ascended the Trango glacier, following a suggestion by Desio that there appeared to be a practicable pass at its head. After camping at 17,000 feet on 1 June they managed to get their local porters up to 18,000 feet, when the bulk of them had had enough. Here a dump was made, eighty-three of the local men were paid off and sent back and the rest of the party with twenty Baltis crossed the pass, 18,650 feet, to the Sarpo Laggo glacier. It took them twelve days to relay the whole of their stores and equipment to a depot near the snout of the glacier near Suget Jangal.

---

[1] The full accounts of the Vissers first three expeditions are published in German, in *Karakoram*, Vol. I (Brockhaus, Leipzig, 1935); Vol. II (Brill, Leiden, 1938). The second volume is mainly concerned with the glaciological results of all four expeditions. No detailed account of the Shaksgam work of the two surveyors was published. The above summary is from private letters from the Khan Sahib written to me from the Shaksgam at the time.

[2] Aila and Lobsang both earned the Tiger's badge later. Nukka died of malaria in Bhutan in 1939.

Only four of the local porters were now retained, and the party travelled light. They reached Younghusband's Aghil pass on 19 June and separated into three parties. Shipton and Tilman with Ang Tharkay and Lobsang crossed a saddle (c. 19,500) into the Zug-Shaksgam, traced it up to the point reached by my party in 1926, and connected their survey to my points. With some difficulty they then followed the river down to its junction with the Surukwat, and so solved the problem that had puzzled us.[1] Meanwhile Spender and Auden, each with light parties, surveyed the whole basin of the Surukwat.

After regaining the main depot near Suget Jangal, Spender spent a week linking up his surveys of the Aghil and Sarpo Laggo and extending the latter, while the rest explored and mapped the glaciers descending from the stupendous north face of K2 which rises sheer from its northern glacier in one continuous sweep of 12,000 feet.

On 17 July they were back at the main depot, and the whole party explored and surveyed the Skamri glacier (Younghusband's 'Crevasse glacier'), which drains the northern flanks of the Panmah Muztagh. Its stream enters the Sarpo Laggo a short distance above Suget Jangal. Some three weeks were spent on the Skamri glacier, since loads had to be relayed to its head, and possible passes explored. On 11 August Auden left the party, crossed a pass into the Nobande-Sobande head of the Panmah and returned to Askole. Tilman crossed into the head of the Braldu glacier, which flows north from the Panmah Muztagh and drains eventually into the Shaksgam; from here he crossed into the head of the Biafo glacier (Conway's 'Snow Lake') and then cleared up the incorrect topography of the 'Cornice glacier' as recorded by the Workmans in 1903.

Shipton and Spender left the Skamri glacier by another new pass, the Wesm-i-Dur (18,930), descended into the valley of that name and followed it down to its junction with the Braldu near its terminal moraine. Spender writes: 'From one of our stations we saw more of this Karakoram country than from any other station I visited that summer. As far as we could see there was a turbulent ocean of peaks without so much as a glimpse of earth in repose. It hardly seemed possible that there should be so much of so disturbed a landscape;

[1] Page 182.

K2, now more than forty miles distant, towered over the ranges to the south-east, and to the west and south-west the Kanjuts and Disteghil showed as excellent fixed points for checking the map.'

On 26 August Shipton and Spender turned south up the Braldu glacier and spent four days climbing, exploring and surveying to its head, and tying their work on to fixed points of the Survey of India. Having completed all and more of their admirable programme they came down again, crossed the Shimshal pass and travelled back to India through Shimshal, Hunza, and Gilgit.[1]

As a result of Shipton's travels a large amount of new survey was added to the map of the Karakoram. There are a few blanks left. The Aghil mountains west of the Surukwat basin and in the great bend of the Shaksgam are still unmapped, as is the country on the left bank of the Shaksgam below the Sarpo Laggo junction. The former can best be penetrated from the north by one of the valleys near the junction of the Shaksgam (Oprang) and Yarkand (Raskam) rivers. There are scattered semi-nomadic people here. There is also an area north of Wood's 'Valley J' and west of Khufelang, which can be entered from the head of that valley. The political difficulties are likely to be even greater in the future than they were in the past.

Shipton returned in 1939 with a strong mountaineering party. After surveying and correcting the existing map of the Hispar-Biafo region he intended to winter in the Shimshal and complete the survey of the lower Shaksgam and Aghil mountains in the early spring of 1940, before the rivers rose. For the work south of the watershed he had five other mountaineers besides himself: R. Scott Russell (plant physiologist), E. C. Fountaine (doctor), P. Mott (surveyor), A. F. Betterton, and R. Campbell Secord. The Surveyor General attached two experienced mountain surveyors, Fazl Elahi and Inayat Khan; nine porters under the redoubtable Ang Tharkay were brought over from Darjeeling.[2]

Four months were spent among the Hispar, Biafo, Panmah, and Chogo Lungma glaciers, their branches and tributaries, and a detailed

---

[1] Eric Shipton: *Blank on the Map* (London, 1938); see also Michael Spender and J. B. Auden in *H.J.* x (1938) 22, 40.

[2] Four of the other eight were Lobsang Sherpa II (No. 144), Lhakpa Tenzing (No. 30), Gyalgen II Mikchen (No. 57), and Kusang Namgay (No. 9). The names of the others are not recorded.

map made of most of the area. Passes were crossed at the heads of the Nobande-Sobande and Choktoi glaciers of the Panmah complex into the 'Snow-Lake' (renamed Lukpe Lawo), and this area also was mapped. The whole was based on a series of minor triangulation up the Hispar and starting from the geodetic series of the Indo-Russian triangulation observed in 1913, but an unfortunate accident to the theodolite prevented a rigidly accurate connexion to the peaks fixed on the east. The outbreak of war prevented Shipton from carrying out the second half of his programme, and his winter and spring plans had to be abandoned.

# 7. Gasherbrum, Saltoro, Masherbrum, and Rakaposhi

THE attempts to climb Everest, Kangchenjunga, and Nanga Parbat set the pace in Himalayan climbing. Mountaineers in Europe began to look for something large and difficult, perhaps forgetting sometimes that an apprenticeship is as necessary to Himalayan problems as it is to any other great endeavour.

Professor G. O. Dyhrenfurth, who had already in 1930 led an international expedition to Kangchenjunga, turned his abilities to the Karakoram and organized another international expedition in 1934. There were two groups, one for mountaineering, the other for filming, with professional actor, actress, and operators. Perhaps this was necessary to subsidize the climbing, but Gasherbrum I (26,470) is hardly a suitable stage on which eleven men and two women of five nationalities should perform, and it is difficult to believe that any serious mountaineer of the party really enjoyed the outing.[1]

The party relied on local Balti porters, presumably from Askole and neighbourhood, and none of the party had had previous experience of handling them. These untrained men are not the type to use on steep, exposed, and difficult Karakoram ridges. Fortunately the climbing party had not gone far along the south-east ridge of Gasherbrum—they still had six miles to go—when on 6 July they were struck by the same break in the weather that destroyed Merkl's party on Nanga Parbat, and after five days of misery they returned.

Some serious mountaineering was accomplished when the film party withdrew from the Baltoro to more congenial altitudes. On 3 August André Roch, Belaieff, Ghiglione, and Winzeler reached the eastern summit of Baltoro Kangri, to which was assigned the height of 23,786 feet by aneroid. On the same day Dyhrenfurth, his

[1] Gasherbrum I is the old K5. Gasherbrum II, III, and IV were K4, K3a, and K3 respectively.

wife, Ertl Höcht, and two local porters climbed the western summit of Sia Kangri in a snowstorm.[1]

In 1936 a French expedition sponsored by the French Alpine Club and organized on a national scale joined in the assault on Gasherbrum I. It comprised seven climbers and four additional members: MM. de Ségogne (leader), Allain, Charignon, Leininger, Neltner, Deudon, and Carle (climbers), Arlaud (doctor), Captain N. R. Streatfeild (liaison and transport officer), MM. Ichac (photographer), and Azèmar (secretary). The climbers had considerable experience of the Alps and elsewhere, but none had visited the Himalaya. Streatfeild was therefore an important and integral member of the expedition. Thirty-five Sherpas and Bhotias were engaged by Mr. J. W. Kydd, the local Honorary Secretary of the Himalayan Club at Darjeeling, but most of them were new and inexperienced men because of the already organized Everest expedition. Equipment and stores were very carefully prepared in France before the start, and the expedition arrived in good heart at its base depot on the upper Baltoro glacier, at about 16,500 feet on 26 May. Here twenty of the best Baltis, who had brought the loads to this spot, were retained and the rest paid off and sent back. The expedition, now reduced to eleven Europeans, thirty-five Sherpas, twenty Baltis and five Kashmiris, had supplies for a campaign of about six weeks.

Dyhrenfurth had suggested that the best route was by a difficult rock- and ice-ridge which leads to the foot of the final pyramid. André Roch and Ertl, who had attempted it in 1934, had been unable to take their untrained Baltis more than a short distance, but had themselves reached about 20,600 feet and considered it would be

---

[1] Sia Kangri is the highest mountain of the Sia Group, called by the Workmans unofficially and without authority 'Queen Mary.' The highest point triangulated is 24,350 feet. The western summit is considerably lower, and almost certainly not more than 23,500 feet; but until a detailed topographical survey is carried out, its precise height will not be known. It is extremely improbable that there is a peak here higher than 25,000 feet, as Dyhrenfurth suggests, and that it would have been missed by the early triangulators, by the Duke of the Abruzzi's surveyors in 1909, by Collins in 1911, by Grant Peterkin in 1912, and by the photogrammetric survey of the Duke of Spoleto in 1929. For a discussion on the problem, see *H.J.* vii (1935) 145 ff. Marcel Kurz, who was included in Dyhrenfurth's party as topographer, unfortunately had a riding accident on the outward journey, so no survey was made. It cannot be emphasized too often that aneroid heights have very little precision.

practicable for porters with the aid of pitons and ropes. De Ségogne seems to have adopted this general plan.

The first part of this route is mostly on rock at an average slope of about forty-five degrees and leads to a great southern shoulder at about 23,200 feet, whence there appears, both from below and from the Duke of Spoleto's map, to be a comparatively gentle ascent along an ice-ridge for about a mile, and then a steeper climb to a second shoulder or peak at about 24,600 feet. The long seven-mile south-east ridge is joined soon afterwards and then comes the climb on the summit pyramid, about 1700 feet at an angle of one in three.

The expedition wasted no time. The Baltis were set to establish Camp I at the foot of the ridge as an advanced base, and on 30 May the reconnoitring of the ridge was begun. The climbing was more difficult than had been anticipated because of rotten rock; great care had to be exercised, and in many places ropes were fixed to assist the laden Sherpas. Progress was steady in fine weather to a site of Camp VI at about 23,000 feet, ropes having to be fixed the entire distance between here and Camp V. Probably Camp VII would have been placed on the shoulder, and the most difficult section of the climb from a technical aspect would have been over. From 26 May until 21 June the weather had been favourable. At this stage it broke up, and for ten days and nights snow fell almost continuously. Climbers and porters were unable to move either up or down from the high camps. It says much for the tents, made of fine balloon fabric, that they withstood the storm.

This bad weather lasted until 1 July. At the end of it, during the descent two Sherpas had a remarkable escape. In trying to take a short cut between Camps III and II they started a small avalanche which carried them down 1800 feet to the glacier below; by a miracle the accident was seen by a party and they were dug out, bruised and suffering from concussion, but with no broken bones.

It was impossible with the supplies at the disposal of the expedition to make a second serious attempt by this route, which undoubtedly is very long. Difficult though it is, it is probably the most practicable, and by it the mountain will one day be climbed. It may be that ropes will have to be fixed in difficult places over the first four thousand feet during the fine period of one year and the ascent of the ridge made during the fine weather of the next.

But the war put an end to the Gasherbrum campaigns and the assaults have not yet been renewed.

★ ★ ★

Three Lesser Karakoram mountains received the attention of climbers during this period: Saltoro Kangri (25,400) in 1935, Masherbrum (25,660) and Rakaposhi (25,550) in 1938. Very few details were then known of the approaches or of the summit ridges of any of them, and the three expeditions had much in common: the object of each was primarily to reconnoitre the best route rather than to press home an assault, though every party contains its optimists; each expedition was of modest size, and was paid for almost entirely by the members themselves, which necessitated economy and few comforts.

Saltoro Kangri is the old K10, triangulated at the same time as K2; its position and height are well fixed. It stands on the Lesser Karakoram at the head of a branch of the Kondus valley, on the Kondus–Siachen divide, about six miles west of the Saltoro pass which was crossed by Longstaff, Slingsby and Neve in 1909. The only details, and those very scanty, were contained in the Workmans' book, *Two Summers in the Ice-Wilds of the Karakoram*.

The party that reconnoitred it in 1935 comprised four officers on leave: James Waller of the Royal Artillery, John Hunt of the 60th Rifles, Rowland Brotherhood, and Dr. J. S. Carslaw of the Royal Air Force. They had with them two reliable Sherpas, Dawa Thondup (No. 49) and Palden (No. 54). Both had been on Ruttledge's 1933 Everest expedition and with Merkl on Nanga Parbat in 1934, Dawa Thondup being one of the badly frostbitten survivors of Camp VIII. For financial reasons more Sherpas could not be taken and local men from Korkondus had to be engaged to help.

After reaching the Kondus valley from Khapalu on the lower Shyok about the middle of May, six days were spent on a close reconnaissance of the west and south faces of the mountain from the Dong Dong and Likah glaciers. The party then forced a passage over the col at the head of the latter, a very difficult and arduous undertaking, mostly in vile weather, and gradually transferred an advanced base to the eastern side of the watershed. On 14 June they began an assault on the east face of the mountain and by the 19th had placed camps up to 22,200 feet. On the next day they reached the crest of the ridge about 2500 feet above the camp, but the lateness of the hour, exhaustion, and the necessity of getting down in worsening weather forced them to give up. Storms and avalanches impeded the return, but the party returned without loss having found a possible, and probably the only, route to the summit.

The expedition to Masherbrum in 1938 was also of modest dimensions, and comprised James Waller—who had been tempted to the mountain by a view of it when on the expedition just described—T. Graham Brown, who organized the successful party to Nanda Devi in 1936, J. O. M. Roberts, J. B. Harrison, and R. A. Hodgkin.[1] They had with them five first-class Sherpas from Darjeeling: Dawa Thondup (No. 49), Pasang Sherpa[2] (No. 139), Nima Tsering III (No. 129), Pasang Phuttar (No. 79), and Dawa Tsering. Dr. G. A. J. Teasdale and his wife accompanied the party to the Base Camp to be available in case of illness or accident—a wise precaution, as it happened. Teasdale was also an authority on diet problems at high altitudes.

The Masherbrum range is directly north-west of the Saltoro range and forms the southern barrier wall of the Baltoro glacier. Expeditions passing up this glacier have been intent on K2 and other giant peaks at its head. Masherbrum's twin peaks, neither reaching 26,000 feet, had been photographed but otherwise ignored. The two groups of the range, Masherbrum and Chogolisa,[3] are still not yet fully explored, and no detailed modern survey has yet been made of their southern flanks or of the glaciers which feed the two

[1] Hodgkin, as an undergraduate at Oxford reading geography, had recently distinguished himself by climbing the Radcliffe Camera on the moonlit eve of the Coronation (without the encouragement of his professor) and placing a Union Jack on the summit. This, I believe, was his first 'first ascent!'

[2] Pasang Sherpa, known sometimes as Pasang Dawa Lama; Nima Tsering I and Nima Tsering II had both died in the avalanche on Nanga Parbat in 1937. I presume Dawa Tsering Bhutia (No. 53) was with the Masherbrum party, since Dawa Tsering Sherpa was on the 1938 Everest expedition.

[3] Masherbrum's twin peaks were triangulated as K1E and K1W; Chogolisa (Conway's 'Bride Peak') is the old K6.

southward-flowing torrents, the Hushe and the Kondus. The latter, far downstream, becomes the Saltoro, and joins the Hushe; about five miles below the junction the combined drainage of both the Masherbrum and Saltoro ranges pours into the right bank of the lower Shyok river a few miles above Khapalu.

This place, Khapalu, is the base for all mountain exploration to the north and east. From it in 1935 Waller's party had ascended the Saltoro, Kondus, and Korkondus to attack Saltoro Kangri. In 1938 his party with Graham Brown and the others took the Hushe valley from Khapalu and on the 17 May pitched a base camp for the reconnaissance about twenty-four miles up it, three miles beyond the village of Hushe, and at the junction of two torrents which come down from the Masherbrum and Khondokoro (or Chundugero) glaciers.

Apart from the early Survey of India topographers, who do not seem to have gone beyond this point, the only previous explorers from this direction were Dr. H. Sillem in 1903 who left no account of his work and died soon after it, and the Workmans who in 1911 made some minor corrections to the topography, but no reliable survey. Sportsmen in search of game may have visited it, though there is no record. The 1938 party had therefore to make a preliminary reconnaissance before they could get to grips with the mountain at all. Both the Masherbrum and Khondokoro glaciers were carefully explored before it was decided to attack the mountain's south-east face.

Masherbrum has twin summits, Masherbrum East (25,660) being about a quarter of a mile north-east of Masherbrum West (25,610). They were called the north and south peaks by this expedition and are so shown on fig. 15. The west or south peak has an apparently impossible south-west face and a difficult south-east rockridge. The east or north peak has a steep and rocky east ridge. Between these two ridges is the steep, broken and crevassed southeast face of the twin summits. The problem was to find a way to the ice-plateau, at about 22,000 feet at the foot of this face, and then to reach the summit by climbing either the face or one of the two ridges.

The reconnaissance showed that the plateau could probably be reached by following the edge of a steep and crevassed branch of the main Masherbrum glacier, and then by traversing its head at about 17,500 feet and climbing a snow-covered dome (20,875). The route

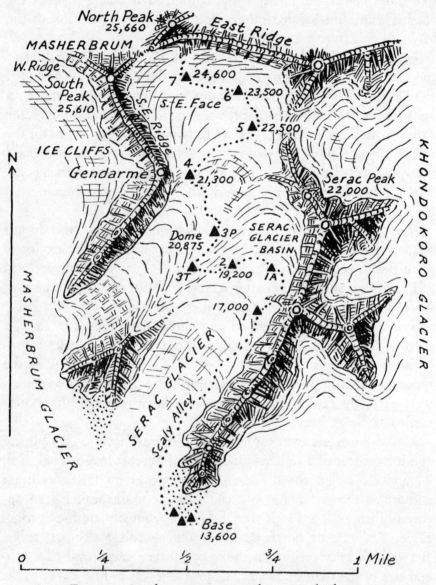

FIG. 15. *South-eastern approach to Masherbrum.*

was long, and because of the small number of porters it took from 30 May until 11 June before Camp IV, at 21,300 feet, was pitched on the glacier beyond the dome at the foot of the south-east ridge. The weather had not been good and much snow had fallen. During the night of the 12th there was a blizzard, but with the weather clearing on the morning of the 14th Harrison and Hodgkin, with Pasang Phuttar and Dawa Tsering, climbed the lower slopes of the face and set up Camp V at 22,500 feet; the next day they established Camp VI a thousand feet higher.

The 16th was an almost perfect day. Leaving Pasang Phuttar who was unwell in Camp VI, the other three climbed through the deep snow of the face and pitched a small tent (Camp VII) at about 24,600 feet; Dawa Tsering then returned to Camp VI. On the same day the supporting party occupied Camp V and stocked it. The 17th was a fair day and the two climbers in Camp VII reached the rocks of the east ridge, ploughing through waist-deep snow. These rocks were glazed and difficult, and after reaching a height of about 25,000 feet a high wind and exhaustion forced them to return to Camp VII, which they reached tired and partly frostbitten. On the same day Waller and the other Sherpas occupied Camp VI.

On the night of the 17th there was another snowstorm, and at 4 a.m. the tent at Camp VII was buried by a small snow-slide. The two climbers struggled out and decided to abandon it and get down to Camp VI. During the day the blizzard increased in intensity, visibility was reduced to nil, and they sheltered in a crevasse in the vain hope of the weather clearing. At about 5 p.m. Waller in Camp VI heard shouts, and with the Sherpas started to search for the two climbers, but failing to find them returned to Camp VI. Harrison and Hodgkin spent the night in a crevasse; they had sleeping-bags but no tent. The following morning they regained Camp VI; both were very badly frostbitten in hands and feet, and were in a bad way.

The climb now had to be abandoned, and every effort made to get the two climbers down. Every ounce of unnecessary equipment had to be left behind. The descent from Camp VI began on the 20th, but because of deep snow it was not till the 23rd that the party reached the Base Camp. Teasdale had come up to help. The frostbites were serious. Harrison, whose extremities were septic with wet gangrene, had to be carried in a litter back to Srinagar, and during the journey lost all his toes and most of his fingers. There is little doubt that the prompt decision to withdraw and the presence of the Teasdales and their skill and care saved the two men's lives. Teasdale himself ascribes the health of the party throughout and the survival of Harrison and Hodgkin to the balanced diet planned for the party beforehand. It was this he claimed which caused them to recover their health.[1]

\*　　\*　　\*

Rakaposhi (25,550) is perhaps, after K2, the best known of the Karakoram giants. On the road from Gilgit to Hunza, as the traveller approaches Chalt and turns his head, he is suddenly aware of the stupendous beauty of this mountain rising up from the conglomerate terraces of the left bank of the Hunza river. The Hunza-Nagar campaign of 1891 was fought on its northern skirts, but it is seen best in all its glory from Aliabad or Hunza farther up the river, where it is known as Dumani. Officers of the Gilgit garrison had shot game in its lower valleys, but no serious reconnaissance had been made of its upper reaches until in 1938 Campbell Secord and Michael Vyvyan were lured off the beaten track. Crossing the Hunza river by a rope-bridge they ascended the Jaglot nala and from its upper part examined the north-west and south-west ridges which descend from the summit pyramid. They were not equipped to press home an attack, but climbed to the north-west ridge; on 19 July from this ridge the summit of the north-west peak of the mountain at about 22,500 feet was reached. They were of the opinion that Rakaposhi might be climbed from here by a stronger party.

[1] *H.J.* xi (1939) 42 ff., 57 ff.

# 8. K2

REMOTE though it is, K2 was by 1938 one of the best known of the Karakoram giants. Its approaches were well mapped, the southern and south-eastern sides had been surveyed stereo-photogrammetrically; the Duke of Spoleto's map showed it on a scale of 1:25,000. Photographs of it from all sides could be examined microscopically. Yet no one had attempted to climb it since the Duke of the Abruzzi's expedition in 1909. His examination of three sides of it with experienced Italian guides had given little hope of climbing it from the Baltoro. Shipton and Tilman in 1937 ruled out the northern face as impracticable.

Mountaineers are rarely satisfied with the *dicta* of their predecessors, and the younger generation are ever hopeful and daring, as they ought to be. As a result, a very fine reconnaissance by Charles Houston in 1938 put the whole problem in a new setting. Houston had been with Graham Brown, Tilman, and Odell on Nanda Devi in 1936, and had then been to well over 24,000 feet. His expedition in 1938 was sponsored by the American Alpine Club, and was modelled on the idea that a small self-contained party was more likely to succeed than one highly organized with separate members to do the staff-work of transport, wireless, doctoring, and so on.

The other members of Houston's party were R. H. Bates, veteran of many Alaskan climbs, R. Burdsall, one of the two who had reached the top of Minya Gongkar (24,900) in 1931, W. P. House and P. Petzoldt, both fine mountaineers, and Captain N. R. Streatfeild, the only British member, who had been with de Ségogne's French expedition to Gasherbrum in 1936. Six Sherpas from Darjeeling were enlisted; but only one was experienced: Pasang Kikuli had been to Kangchenjunga, to Everest, and to Nanda Devi; he was one of the gallant but badly frostbitten survivors of Camp VIII on Nanga Parbat in 1934, and he had been awarded the Tiger's Badge and the Medal of Honour of the German Red Cross.[1]

The party thus comprised six climbers and six Sherpas. Houston intended to re-examine Abruzzi's three alternatives, the north-west ridge from the Savoia Col, the north-east ridge from Windy Gap, and the cut-off south-east 'Abruzzi' ridge which falls steeply from the shoulder at 25,354 feet to the Godwin-Austen glacier at its foot. The route by the Negrotto Col and the south-west ridge was never considered possible (map page 134).

The party reached 'Concordia' by 12 June, established a depot, and from a camp at the head of the Savoia glacier examined the approach to the Savoia Col. From Spoleto's map the altitude of the col is at about 21,850 feet. Houston and House on the 17 June reached 20,000 feet but decided that even if they cut a route to the col, they could not take laden porters. Immediately afterwards the north-east route was examined and this was also rejected. One party reached an altitude of about 20,000 feet, but soft dangerous snow turned them back. The next reconnaissance of the south-east ridge leading to the shoulder also gave little hope but appeared the best of the three.

Camp I was now placed at 17,500 feet at the base of the 'Abruzzi Ridge' and during the last stormy days of June it was stocked with supplies for a further advance. By 5 July the climbers were established in Camp II, 19,000 feet, and a successful reconnaissance showed a way to Camp III (20,700). The height to be climbed to the shoulder from the foot was about 7850 feet; Camp III was not yet half-way. After another short spell of bad weather and high winds, Houston and Petzoldt climbed a thousand feet higher and found an exposed shoulder for Camp IV at 21,500 feet. It was now considered too dangerous for all the climbers to be working on the ridge at one time because of the rotten and loose state of the rocks above. Burdsall, Streatfeild, and the three least experienced porters therefore returned to Camp I.

---

[1] Pasang Kikuli (No. 8). Four of the other Sherpas were Pintso Sherpa (No. 141), Pemba Kitar (No. 147), Tse Tendrup or Thondup (No. 38), and Ang Pemba. I have been unable to find the name of the sixth. All five were novices except Tse Tendrup, who had been on one previous expedition to Gasherbrum with the French.

Houston, Petzoldt, House, and Bates with Pasang Kikuli and two other Sherpas were established in Camp III on 12 July, with food for twenty days. The intermittent storms of late June and early July gave way to settled weather. Bates and House placed Camp IV (21,500) and reconnoitred the route to Camp V. This is one of the most difficult parts of the climb and involves the ascent of a steep buttress of red rock, about 150 feet high. Many pitons and several hundred feet of rope were needed before the site of Camp V was reached, only five hundred feet above Camp IV. Meanwhile Camp IV was stocked and on the 16th the four climbers were established in Camp V (22,000).

A brief but violent storm kept the party to their tents for most of the 17 July. Roughly two weeks' food remained; they realized that they must keep at least ten days' food in hand for the return, lest bad weather should confine them in one or other of these camps. This meant that they had four days for the 6250 feet from Camp V to the summit. All therefore now depended on the weather.

The 18th broke brilliantly clear and calm. Camp VI at 23,300 feet was set up; on the 19th the great shoulder at 25,354 feet was reached, the last two hundred yards being a delicate traverse across a bare green ice-slope at an angle of forty-five degrees. Camp VII was put here on the 20th, Petzoldt and Houston stayed in it, and the rest descended to Camp VI, there to remain in support.

An all-out attack was out of the question; only one day was left for the party of two to go as high as possible. Houston and Petzoldt climbed slowly but steadily through the deep snow, and shortly after noon reached a broad shoulder, rising gently to the base of the summit cone and littered with fragments broken away from the ice-cliffs two thousand feet above. At the far end of this dangerous stretch the two climbers found a large protected flat rock, safe for a possible Camp VIII, probably at about 26,100 feet. Beyond there seemed to be a route to the summit, with no technical difficulties greater than those already surmounted. Gambling on fine weather they could have gone higher and might just possibly have reached the summit but they would never have returned and they wisely withdrew to Camp VII.

On 25 July the whole party returned to the base. The same day clouds closed in on the upper part of the mountain; they did not lift for a week. There is little doubt that a party on the mountain would have had great difficulty in coming down during the storms between 24 July and 2 August, by which date their food would have been exhausted. Houston's decision on the 24th was wise. A great mountaineer, he knew when to turn back.

There are some features of this successful reconnaissance not unlike the ascent of Nanda Devi in 1936. The ascent of the Abruzzi ridge of K2 from 17,500 feet to the shoulder at 25,354 is comparable with that from 17,500 feet to the summit of Nanda Devi at 25,645 by the Coxcomb ridge. Both are difficult climbs, to some extent on crumbling rock, with icy couloir traverses between the ribs. Houston's party had done what Tilman and Odell had done, and in addition had reconnoitred a possible route for nearly another 3000 feet. Houston also gave a clear warning against the dangers of a descent in bad weather and stressed the necessity of a safety margin of time and of food.

Houston's reconnaissance was the basis of an assault on K2 by an American party led by Fritz Wiessner in 1939. Wiessner had been a member of Willy Merkl's first Nanga Parbat expedition in 1932. Besides himself there were five climbers—C. Cranmer, D. Wolfe, E. Cromwell, G. Sheldon, and J. Durrance—and nine Sherpa porters from Darjeeling, including the two experienced men Pasang Kikuli and Dawa Thondup, and two others who had been with Houston to K2 the year before, Pintso Sherpa and Tse Tendrup.[1] G. S. C. Trench, R.A. was transport officer.

All went well at the start. By 14 June Camp I (18,500) and Camp II (19,300) were set up on the Abruzzi ridge. The party suffered from bad weather, but in spite of it Camps IV (21,500) and V (22,000) were established by 6 July. This was only four days longer than in 1938. It now took five days to set up Camp VI at 23,400 feet, an exhausting task for both climbers and porters. On 11 July there were only three climbers and seven Sherpas fit to go on. All these were in Camp IV, except Wolfe who had gone up to Camp V.

[1] Pasang Kikuli (No. 8), Dawa Thondup (No. 49), Pintso Sherpa (No. 141), Tse Tendrup (No. 38). Others were Pasang Dawa Lama (Pasang Sherpa) (No. 139), who had been to Masherbrum; Sonam Sherpa (No. 143), Pasang Kitar, Dawa, and Tsering, four new men.

The following day all moved up to Camp VI, and there Durrance fell sick. He was brought down with difficulty by Pasang Kikuli, who was slightly frostbitten, and Dawa, to Camp II on the 14th and to the base three days later.

When he left Camp VI, only Wiessner, Wolfe, and five Sherpas remained to establish the high camps, keep open the difficult communications on the mountain and make a bid for the summit. This party was far too weak for safety, but on 14 July Camp VIII was pitched just below the shoulder at 25,234 feet. Pasang Dawa Lama remained here with the two climbers; Pasang Kitar and Tse Tendrup returned to Camp VII; Pintso Sherpa and Tsering were in Camp VI. Here they were all imprisoned by storm until the 17th, and on that morning Wolfe fell ill.

Wiessner now made the fatal and almost inconceivable decision to go on, regardless of the consequences. Leaving the sick Wolfe in Camp VIII he roamed on the mountain above with Pasang Dawa Lama for five days, sleeping in a light tent above the shoulder and making two abortive attempts to climb the mountain. Only on the 22nd did he return to Camp VIII to replenish his supplies. Here he found Wolfe, already short of food. No one had visited him from below for a week.

The three descended to Camp VII. It was empty, one of the tents had been torn by the storm and there was little food, but they were forced by the late hour to halt for the night. On the 23rd Wolfe was left in Camp VII while Wiessner and his Sherpa descended to Camp II, finding each camp successively evacuated and devoid of supplies. On the 24th they reached the base, meeting on the way a search party led by Cromwell, which had been examining the glacier below the mountain for any signs of an accident.

The Sherpas were in no way to blame. After the storm the two men in Camp VII, Pasang Kitar and Tse Tendrup, inexperienced and leaderless, had descended on the 17th to Camp VI, where they found Pintso Sherpa and Tsering equally bewildered and without instructions. They went on down to Camp IV, but found it empty. No one was in support.

It was the frostbitten Pasang Kikuli, alone in Camp II who was the first to act. Nervous for the safety of the party above, he climbed alone to Camp IV on the 18th and sent Pasang Kitar and Tse Tendrup up to Camp VI with orders to get supplies up to Camp VIII. These two reached Camp VI on the 19th and the next day with Pintso Sherpa reached Camp VII. Finding this empty they plodded on towards Camp VIII, but with their loads were too exhausted to reach it. They were within earshot and shouted. Receiving no reply they assumed that it too was empty. It must be emphasized that no word or sign of life had been received from above for six days, though at this moment Wolfe was lying sick in Camp VIII and Wiessner and Pasang Dawa Lama were resting in the tent above the shoulder. The three Sherpas concluded that there must have been an accident.

During the next three days the Sherpas evacuated the mountain. They reached the base on the 23rd, one day before Wiessner arrived with Pasang Dawa Lama. Another extraordinary decision was now made. Durrance, still far from well, was to start up on the 25th with three Sherpas to bring Wolfe down from Camp VII, and Wiessner with two Sherpas would follow two days later to make another bid for the summit!

It was inconceivable folly. Durrance started according to plan, but the weather worsened and he could get no farther than Camp IV, whence he and Dawa, both sick, returned. In storm and blizzard Pasang Kitar and Pintso Sherpa struggled on to Camp VI. On the evening of the 27th Durrance reached the base, where at last the idea of danger seems to have dawned. But it was again Pasang Kikuli who volunteered to act. On 28 July with Tsering he accomplished the amazing feat of reaching Camp VI in a single day. On the 29th leaving Tsering behind, he took Pintso Sherpa and Pasang Kitar to Camp VII. Wolfe had eaten nothing for several days; he staggered to his feet, but declared he was too weak to descend. The porters repitched his tent, brewed him some tea, but were unable to persuade him to come down. With no sleeping-bags themselves they had to descend to Camp VI for the night, intending to return the next day.

Throughout the 30th a storm raged over the mountain. With some improvement in the weather the three Sherpas again set out for Camp VII on the 31st. They were not seen again. Tsering waited anxiously for two nights in Camp VI, unable to search alone; knowing that they could not survive without food or sleeping-bags, he made his way back alone to the base, which he reached on the evening of 2 August. The glacier was again searched for signs of an accident; none were found. Wiessner and two porters reached Camp II on the 4th, but in view of their poor condition could go no farther.

It is difficult to record in temperate language the folly of this enterprise. From 11 July until the end of the month each day added to the errors of judgement. The weather was never to blame. The one redeeming feature was the heroism of Pasang Kikuli, Pasang Kitar, and Pintso Sherpa.

# 9. Kumaun Himalaya

THE re-survey of the Himalaya which began in Kashmir in 1910, and which was curtailed during and after World War I, came to an end temporarily in 1924 when only the Lesser Himalaya in the Kumaun division had been completed. It was realized that the maps of the Great Himalaya were unsatisfactory, and some had urged the Surveyor General to restart the survey. But during the years of the financial depression the survey budget was cut to the bone and, except on the north-west frontier, mountain surveys almost ceased.[1]

Longstaff's and Ruttledge's explorations in the Nanda Devi region; Longstaff's, Meade's, Slingsby's, and Morshead's reconnaissances round Kamet; Smythe's, Birnie's, and Pallis' sketch-maps of the upper Arwa glaciers and of the Gangotri glacier—all showed how very faulty were the existing maps of the uninhabited and glaciated regions of the Great Himalaya in the Kumaun division. But it was not until 1935 that the necessary funds were forthcoming for the survey to be taken up again.

The work began in September 1935 and from early 1936 was under the direction of Major Gordon Osmaston. By the end of 1938 the whole area from the Sutlej watershed on the west to the western boundary of Nepal on the east had been rigidly surveyed as far north as the Tibetan border, on the scale of three inches to four miles; it was based on an extension of the Indian triangulation and a great many newly fixed peaks. The detailed topographical survey covered the whole of the upper Bhagirathi basin, including the Gangotri glacier, all its branches, and the various mountain groups surrounding it—Srikanta, Jaonli, Kedarnath, Satopanth, Chaukhamba; the glaciers draining the Bhagirathi watershed eastwards to the Alaknanda; the Kamet group and the glaciers and upper tribu-

---

[1] These surveys from 1927 to 1930, under the direction of Colonel C. G. Lewis, covered Dir, Swat, Chitral, and the Hindu Kush west of Hunza State. They are outside the area dealt with in this book.

taries of the Dhauli; the Nanda Devi basin and its mountain ring; and the northern part of the Almora district, including the Panch Chuli group and a number of previously unknown glaciers and groups near the Tibetan border (map page 24).

Osmaston's party comprised two other officers, ten surveyors, fifty Garhwali *khalasis*, and some 120 local coolies. One of his first problems was to fix additional points up the Gangotri glacier in

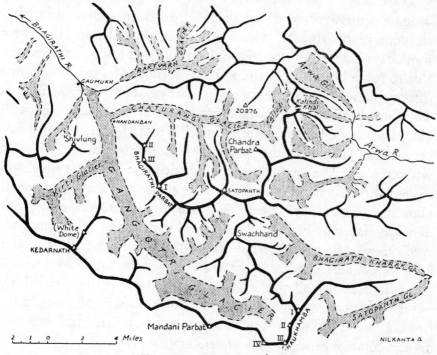

FIG. 16. *Gangotri glacier.*

order that the surveyors could make a complete survey of it. Several journeys had shown that the topography was much at fault. A reconnaissance led by Marco Pallis, with F. E. Hicks, C. F. Kirkus, R. C. Nicholson, and Dr. Charles Warren had in 1933 reconnoitred the lower eight miles of the Gangotri and the two large northern feeders, Raktvarn and Chaturangi,[1] and various members of the party had made climbs to over 20,000 feet. J. B. Auden of the

---

[1] The names here given are from Osmaston's survey. They are glaciers 1 and 2 of Pallis' account in *H.J.* vi (1934) 106.

Geological Survey had also worked in the lower reaches of the glacier in 1935.[1] In May 1936 Osmaston took a triangulation series up both the Gangotri and Chaturangi glaciers, and fixed a large number of peaks for the surveyors; his highest station of observation was 20,976 feet near the head of the Chaturangi.[2] This triangulation was a notable achievement, as was the subsequent detailed survey of this difficult area.

There were some narrow escapes. Fazl Elahi, an experienced mountain surveyor, was caught by an early monsoon blizzard in the same year, 1936, at the head of the Gangotri glacier. He was for some days completely snowbound and his supply-coolies were unable to reach him from Gaumukh, at the snout of the glacier, some fifteen miles away. After running short of fuel and food he was forced to abandon his tents and with four survey *khalasis*, each with two blankets, he started down the glacier, ploughing through waist-deep snow. They spent the first night huddled together in the snow without food. The next day they discarded one blanket apiece, and struggled on for three more miles in deep snow. After their second night they abandoned their last blanket, and it was only with difficulty that Fazl Elahi could shepherd them along. Towards dusk when they were utterly exhausted and it seemed that they would have to face a third night in the snow, they were found by a search party. Fazl Elahi and one *khalasi* reached base on their own legs, but the others collapsed and had to be carried down. All were badly frostbitten and had to have their boots cut away. Fazl Elahi with the highest courage brought in his plane-table survey.

During the survey a number of new passes were made by officers and surveyors. One, the Gupt Khal (18,990), at the head of the Bankund Gal (Banke glacier), leading to the Alaknanda, had been suspected by Mumm in 1907 and had been sought for in vain by Smythe's party in 1931.[3] It was first crossed by R. C. A. Edge and R. Gardiner in 1937; it was used later the same year by Smythe and Oliver when climbing Mana (23,860), which is about two miles north-east of it.

The survey of the difficult Nanda Devi basin was assisted by Eric

---

[1] *H.J.* viii (1936) 96.           [2] *H.J.* xi (1939) 128.
[3] Pages 118, 204 (map page 119).

Shipton, who after the Everest expedition of 1936 guided Osmaston through the Rishi gorge to the 'inner sanctuary' and helped him to select suitable stations.[1] Shipton took the opportunity to climb a number of mountains on his own and with Ang Tharkay to attempt Dunagiri (map page 116). The survey was carried out by stereo-photogrammetry, photographs being taken by a Wild photo-theodolite and by a Watts-Leica instrument. For this particular region Osmaston had with him six of the Sherpas who had already been to Everest earlier in the year: Ang Tharkay (No. 19), Ringsing Bhutia (No. 32), Tenzing Bhutia (No. 48), Gyalgen V Bhutia (No. 125), Sonam (or Sen) Tenzing (No. 75), and Ang Dawa.[2] For most of the rest of the survey local men, preferably from the upper valleys, were employed.

Before the survey an interesting reconnaissance had been carried out in July 1929 when Hugh Ruttledge and his wife, while on settlement work near the Tibetan border of his Almora district, crossed from the Kuthi tributary of the Kali over the Lebong pass into the Darmaganga valley; then with Darma men he made the first reconnaissance of the eastern face of Panch Chuli (22,650), reaching an altitude of 18,000 feet on the Sona glacier. From here it appeared to him possible to reach the northern arête, but he was not equipped to prosecute a serious climb. The group was surveyed in detail in 1938 (map page 24).

The results of these surveys are published on the scale of two miles to the inch, and these maps are as interesting and attractive as any published by the Survey of India.[3]

The survey of the Kumaun Himalaya led to much activity in this region, even before it was completed. Frank Smythe, when not on Everest expeditions, made several happy journeys plant-collecting, photographing, and climbing among the mountains between the Dhauli and Alaknanda. J. B. Auden travelled in the extreme north of the Almora district and along the Tibetan frontier studying the

---

[1] *H.J.* ix (1937) 74.

[2] There were three Ang Dawas on the 1936 Everest expedition, Nos. 40, 41, and 42. It is not known which of the three accompanied Osmaston and Shipton to Nanda Devi.   Tenzing Bhutia is now famous as Tenzing Norkhay Sherpa, G.M.

[3] Sheets 53 I/SE, 53 J/NE, 53 M/SW, 53 N/NW, 53 N/NE, 53 N/SE, 62 B/NW, 62 B/SW, 62 B/SE.

geology, as did a small Swiss party comprising Arnold Heim and August Gansser in 1936.[1]

In the same year four young Japanese from the Rikkyo University Mountaineering Club, with the Olympic ski-runner Takebushi, made the first successful ascent of Nanda Kot (22,510). They reached Martoli on the Goriganga about 15 August, and by the Lawan Gad approached the mountain by the route explored by Longstaff to a height of 21,000 feet in 1905.[2] Most of September was spent in reconnoitring and placing the camps on the north-east ridge. The summit was reached on 5 October by the five Japanese: Takebushi, Hotta, Yamagata, Yuasa, Hamano, and the porter Ang Tsering.[3] After this successful climb, the party crossed Traill's pass to the Pindari glacier, led by Dewan Singh of Martoli, who had crossed it with the Ruttledges and Wilson in 1926 (map page 116).[4]

An Austro-German party under Professor R. Schwarzgruber in 1938 added much to mountaineering knowledge of the Gangotri region. With him were four other climbers and a doctor, Rudolf Jonas. Before starting he was fortunate in obtaining an advance proof of Osmaston's new survey and it is therefore easier to follow his activities than those of his predecessors. He appears to have had about six Sherpas with him.[5] The post-monsoon period was chosen for the expedition and an early end to the monsoon made the journey to the Gangotri more pleasant than it would otherwise have been.

Base camp was set up at Nandanban (14,230) at the junction of the Chaturangi and Gangotri glaciers. First ascents were made of Bhagirathi II (21,364) on 9 September, Chandra Parbat (22,073) on 11 September, Mandani Parbat (20,320) on 20 September, Swachhand (22,050) on 23 September, and Sri Kailas (22,742) on the northern watershed on 16 October. As an illustration of the muddled topography of earlier days Bhagirathi II was believed by

---

[1] *H.J.* ix (1937) 38.  [2] Page 115.

[3] Probably Ang Tsering III (No. 51).

[4] *H.J.* x (1938) 71. For the Ruttledges' crossing of Traill's pass see page 187.

[5] Their names are not recorded in Schwarzgruber's account in *H.J.* xi (1939), but from other sources they appear to have been: Wangdi Nurbu (No. 25), Ang Dawa III (No. 42), Aila Sherpa (No. 61), Pasang Urgen (No. 98), Pasang Sherpa II (No. 127), and Pemba Nurbu (No. 150). All except Wangdi Nurbu were comparatively new men.

Pallis to be in the Satopanth group, and Chandra Parbat was thought by Birnie to be Satopanth itself; it was not their fault.

This expedition reconnoitred Satopanth (23,213) from the north, attempting without success to climb it by both the north-east and north-west ridges. Their view was that it might be climbed by a team of four or six climbers using the north-east ridge before the monsoon.

The great Chaukhamba group (23,420) was also thoroughly reconnoitred, first from the head of the Gangotri glacier, from which side they concluded it was unclimbable, and then, after crossing Birnie's pass into the Arwa, from the head of the Bhagirath Kharak glacier. From here they reached a height of about 19,000 feet during an attempt to reach the north-east ridge, but an ice-avalanche falling near them caused them to give up. They afterwards examined the eastern face, but found it quite impracticable. A whole month was spent on this reconnaissance.

In 1939 two other expeditions made successful climbs in the Kumaun Himalaya, one led by André Roch, the other by Adam Karpinski. Both were marred by tragedy.

Roch had with him two Swiss guides, Fritz Steuri of Grindelwald and David Zogg of Arosa, as well as a topographer, Ernst Huber, who was to make a photogrammetric survey of the Kosa glacier. He also engaged six Sherpas, none of whom had had much previous experience.[1] Roch planned his expedition with three climbing objectives, Dunagiri (23,184) on the northern ring-wall of Nanda Devi, the three peaks at the head of the Kosa glaciers, Hathi Parbat (22,070), Ghori Parbat (22,010) and Rataban (20,230), and Chaukhamba I (23,420), the great Badrinath peak at the head of the Gangotri mentioned above.

He approached Dunagiri by the Ramani glacier on its southern flank, and made the ascent by the well-reconnoitred south-west ridge, which had been first attempted by Graham in 1883, and later by Oliver in 1933. It had been climbed by Shipton and Ang Tharkay in 1936 to a height of about 22,000 feet and was reported by them to be practicable, though they had been forced by the late hour of the

---

[1] Ang Dawa I (No. 40), Gombu (No. 118), Nima II, Nima VI, Nuri, and Tillye.

day to return.[1] Roch's fine first ascent of this grand mountain is a good example of how in the Himalaya each attempt adds knowledge to the problem, and how by co-operation success comes at last. No mountain is the exclusive property of the nation that first reconnoitres it, and none should grudge the ultimate success. Roch, after one unsuccessful attempt, reached the summit with Zogg and Steuri on 5 July from a camp on the ridge at about 21,650 feet. He generously acknowledged the efforts of his predecessors.

Roch now turned his attention to the Kosa peaks, which, though not among the giants of the Himalaya, were unexpectedly difficult even to approach. Rataban was climbed by Huber and Nima VI and a local man, Mourcoulia of Lata, on 8 August, and Ghori Parbat by Roch, Steuri, and Zogg on 18 August.

The attempt on Chaukhamba ended in tragedy. Roch approached it from the north by way of the Bhagirath Kharak glacier, as recommended by Schwarzgruber in 1938. He set up a camp of three tents at about 18,800 feet, apparently at much the same spot reached by the previous party, and on a snow ridge that appeared absolutely safe from avalanches. On 10 September, an overcast and unpromising dawn followed a snowy night, and Roch decided to await better conditions. At noon when resting in their tents an avalanche fell from the slopes above, clouds of driven snow reached the camp, and all three tents, with their occupants inside them—though secured by guy-ropes to ice-axes anchored in the snow—were carried down the slope for a distance of about 1650 feet. Roch, Steuri, Zogg, Nuri, and Tillye were uninjured, but Ang Dawa was buried almost to the neck and Gombu and a Dhotial porter, Baly, appeared to be badly injured. Another local man, Ajitia, was never found. Ice-axes and other equipment had been lost, but enough was collected to fit out Zogg, Steuri, Nuri, and Tillye, who now descended for help, while Roch remained with the injured men. Gombu died during the night, but the next day with great difficulty Ang Dawa and Baly were brought down. Baly had suffered mainly from shock and bruises, but Ang Dawa's shoulder was broken in two places; both recovered.

As a result of this experience Roch considered this route too

[1] H.J. ix (1937) 79.

dangerous to be followed, and taking into account the reconnaissances of 1938 asserted that the sole remaining route to be tried is that by the complicated north-west arête. He paid a well-deserved tribute to both Sherpa and Dhotial porters.

The Polish Himalayan expedition in the same year also began with a successful ascent and ended in tragedy. The party consisted of four members of the Polish Mountaineering Club—A. Karpinski, J. Bujak, S. Bernadzikiewicz, and J. Klarner, with Major J. R. Foy and S. B. Blake of the Himalayan Club as transport and liaison officers. They also had with them six Sherpas and Bhotias: Palden (No. 54), Dawa Tsering Bhutia (No. 53), Injung Bhutia (No. 97) (all men with some experience), and three novices, Kipa, Nima (one of the many of that name), and Booktay (? Phu Tharkay, No. 153).

The party's first objective was Nanda Devi East (24,391), the southern ridge of which had been reconnoitred for a short distance by Longstaff in 1905 from the col he reached overlooking the Nanda Devi basin.[1]

Karpinski set up his base camp at Bhital Gwar at the head of the Lawan Gad, about two miles from the foot of the ascent to Longstaff's col (Nanda Devi Khal). The col was reached and the ascent made safe for laden porters, and camps were gradually laid out along the south ridge to the peak. Early in June after reaching about 21,000 feet the whole party was driven back to the base by bad weather, but on the 11th they were able to return to the assault.

On 21 June the first attempt to establish Camp V was made by Bernadzikiewicz and Klarner with Dawa Tsering and Injung. On reaching 22,800 feet they decided to put up their tent and send the two porters down. Almost at once the cornice under Injung broke away, but he was held on the rope by the steadiness of Dawa. Though not injured seriously, it was half an hour before he could be drawn up to the ridge and the shock and pressure caused by the rope during this time necessitated the return of the party to Camp IV and thence to the base.

A second attempt made by Karpinski and Bujak the following day failed through soft snow and a high wind. After further delay

[1] Page 115.

because Karpinski went sick with dysentery and had to be evacuated to the base, a third attempt was made. By 30 June the three remaining climbers and Dawa were concentrated once more in Camp V at 23,000 feet. The following day they were confined to their tents by wind and cloud.

On 2 July the summit was reached. Bujak and Dawa started on the first rope with Bernadzikiewicz and Klarner behind on a second. At about 23,550 feet Bernadzikiewicz had to give up, and Dawa brought him down. Bujak and Klarner went on and reached the summit at 5.20 p.m. After a rest of forty minutes they started back, and late that night, by the light of a full moon and in intense frost, they regained Camp V.

After returning to the base it was decided to follow the Goriganga valley northwards to Milam and from there to explore the head of the Milam glacier, which should be beyond the reach of the monsoon (map page 116). The glacier had been fully surveyed in 1938 but the mountains at its head had not been reconnoitred by climbers. The three highest summits have the collective name of Tirsuli— south peak (23,460), east peak (23,210) and north-west peak (23,080), all rising from a common base. Base camp was set up on 11 July on an alp named Rugus at about 13,500 feet. During the reconnaissance that followed, Karpinski and Bernadzikiewicz on 18 July relayed loads up to a camp between 20,000 and 21,000 feet on the east face of the east peak, where, having sent the porters down they spent the night. They had been unable to gain the south-east ridge as they had intended. The following morning Klarner and Bujak took more porters up to this camp and found it buried under an immense avalanche. Search was made in vain for the bodies for two days. The avalanche had been caused by a large mass of ice breaking from the face above; this had started a snow-avalanche of the wind-slab type and the whole had packed into a dense mass covering an area of about five acres, thirty feet deep in places. With the exception of two odd boots, a section of a tent-pole, a torn camera-case, and a single bag of stores, nothing was found.

These two tragedies emphasize the extraordinary difficulty encountered by the most experienced European climbers in judging snow and ice conditions in the Himalaya, particularly during the monsoon months. The Tirsuli avalanche had many features in common with that which destroyed Camp IV on Nanga Parbat in 1937. Both were caused by ice breaking away from high up and at an apparently safe distance; in doing so both started secondary avalanches of unconsolidated freshly fallen snow which carried them farther than seemed possible according to Alpine experience. In both cases the victims were overwhelmed in their sleep.

# 10. Sikkim and Assam Himalaya

THE Sikkim Himalaya became the mountain paradise of Bengal during the thirties and was the scene of great activity. Mountaineers of the Eastern Section of the Himalayan Club opened up new routes and passes, trained Darjeeling porters were becoming available in increasing numbers and hardly a year passed without some journey of interest. To describe all these in a short history would be a catalogue of names and places, but a few of the climbs on the high mountains must be chronicled.

After their disappointment in 1930 when they failed to find a practicable route to Kangchenjunga's summit, the members of Dyhrenfurth's 'International Expedition' consoled themselves handsomely by climbing three peaks above 23,000 feet (map page 38): Schneider climbed Nepal Peak (23,560), and with Hoerlin reached the top of Dodang Nyima (23,620), while no fewer than six made ascents of Jongsong (24,344).[1] Later the same year G. B. Gourlay and W. Eversden climbed Lhonak Peak (21,260), an imposing pyramid between Jongsong and Dodang Nyima, and opened up the attractions of climbing in the Lhonak district.[2]

In 1931 Allwein and Brenner during Bauer's expedition to Kangchenjunga climbed 'Sugarloaf' (21,128). Thereafter there is a succession of journeys to the Zemu, to Lhonak, and to the north-east of Sikkim by members of the Club, prominent among whom may be mentioned G. B. Gourlay, H. W. Tobin, E. O. Shebbeare, C. R. Cooke, Mrs. H. P. V. Townend and J. W. Kydd, who not only added to our knowledge, but spared no effort to help others to travel and climb.[3]

One of the most interesting of Sikkim climbs at this period was C. R. Cooke's winter ascent of Kabru (24,002) in 1935. Cooke held

[1] *H.J.* iii (1931) 77.    [2] *H.J.* iv (1932) 123.
[3] A fairly complete list of climbs in the Sikkim Himalaya up to 1936 is given in *H.J.* ix (1936) 167 ff.

the view that weather and snow conditions in October and November were more suitable for mountaineering than those in the shorter and more unsettled period before the monsoon. It was one of Shipton's tasks to test this theory on Everest during and after the monsoon of 1935, and it was with the same objective that Cooke chose November for his assault on Kabru.

Cooke was accompanied by G. Schoberth and six Darjeeling porters: Ang Tharkay (No. 19), Ang Tsering II (No. 15), Ang Thari (No. 13), Jigmay (No. 23), Kitar (No. 35), and Pasang Phuttar (No. 79). All except Ang Thari were experienced men. The difficult part of the climb is the ascent of the great ice-fall; from the southern face of the north peak and from the eastern face of the ridge between the two peaks of Kabru it drops 5,500 feet in about the same horizontal distance, a maze of ice-blocks, ice-walls, and crevasses. Cooke and Schoberth turned it by ascending from the east, under the slopes of the 'Dome,' on the south-east ridge of Kabru; but it took them from 28 October when they left their base until 18 November to find the way, lay out their camps, stock them, and reach the summit. Cooke finished the climb on the last day alone. Surely no one, after reading Cooke's account, can still believe that this was the mountain climbed by W. W. Graham in three days in 1883.

Cooke had fine weather throughout with no excessively cold temperatures—minus 11° F. was the lowest—and, until he reached the final ridge, no strong winds. Rubenson, a month earlier in 1907, recorded minus 27° F. and was less lucky with the weather. This fine climb by Cooke therefore seemed to bear out his theory about November climbing.[1]

In 1936 Paul Bauer took a small party to Sikkim, mainly to train for the expedition to Nanga Parbat the following year. With him were Karl Wien, A. Göttner, G. Hepp, and six Darjeeling porters: Hishey Bhutia (No. 111), Tewang (No. 12), Nima Tsering II (No. 110), Mingma Tsering (No. 68), Mingma Bhutia, and Purbu (or Phurba) Bhutia.[2] The party was established at its base camp

[1] H.J. (1936) 107.
[2] The first four, and possibly all six, had recently returned from the French expedition to Gasherbrum (page 249). I cannot identify the last two; probably they never registered at the Himalayan Club.

about the middle of August and first carried out an interesting piece of exploration at the head of the Zumtu glacier south-east of Siniolchu. During early September they made an unsuccessful attempt on the eastern of the 'Twins' (23,360, and then another by the south-west ridge on 'Tent Peak' (24,089). On this occasion they passed over the summit of Nepal Peak (23,560), but had to give up the ascent because of dangerous avalanches.

After being imprisoned in their base camp on the Zemu glacier the four climbers with Nima Tsering and Mingma Tsering set out on 19 September to climb Siniolchu (22,600) by its north-west ridge. An advanced camp was set up at the foot of Little Siniolchu at about 18,700 feet on the 21st, and, leaving the porters here, Bauer and his companions reached the ridge between Siniolchu and Little Siniolchu at 20,340 feet the next day. They spent the night on the ridge sitting in their tent-bags with their feet in their rucksacks, and with everything av...lable wrapped round their bodies. On the 23rd, at about 21,230 feet Bauer decided to halt with Hepp and remain in support while the other two unladen men made for the summit. Wien and Göttner reached it soon after 2 p.m. and then returned to their companions. A second night was spent on the ridge without tents, and the party regained their base camp on the 25th.[1]

Before leaving the region, Bauer, Göttner, and Hepp on 2 October climbed the western (21,473) of the two northern peaks of the Simvu massif and then crossed the northern watershed into Lhonak. Wien with two porters crossed the Simvu saddle and descended the Passanram glacier, hoping to extend his fine survey of the Zemu to the south of Siniolchu, and to connect it with the Zumtu glacier explored earlier in the season. An unfortunate accident to the photo-theodolite put an end to this project.

In the same year Shipton, Warren, Kempson, and Wigram returned from Everest by the Kongra La into Sikkim. From a camp on the Gordamah lake Shipton and Kempson reached the summit of Gordamah Peak (22,200).

In 1937 a German-Swiss expedition of three climbers Schmaderer, Paidar and Grob, spent about six weeks on the Zemu glacier

[1] Wien, Göttner, Hepp, Nima Tsering II, and Mingma Tsering were all killed by the avalanche on Nanga Parbat on 14 June 1937 (page 235).

investigating the approaches to Kangchenjunga, during the course of which they attempted the 'Tent Peak' and the 'Twins,' but, like Bauer's party, were driven off by soft and wind-slab snow. On 26 September they made the second ascent of Siniolchu.

Later the same year C. R. Cooke and John Hunt with Mrs. Hunt spent over a month on the Zemu glacier, from 18 October to 22 November. They had six Darjeeling porters.[1] Hunt and Cooke reached the Nepal Gap on 4 November and the former the south-west summit of Nepal Peak (23,440), but the west wind was so fierce on the ridge that it was almost impossible to stand up. After returning to their base, Cooke, with Pasang Kikuli and Dawa Thondup, reconnoitred the North Col (22,620) of Kangchenjunga. This col is at the head of the Twins glacier, and if practicable might offer a better route to the summit than the long and difficult route by the north-east spur climbed by Bauer's party in 1929 and 1931. Though Cooke just failed to reach the col, he thought that with more time and preparation it could be reached. This party suffered inconvenience from bad weather, but much of November seems to have been fine, especially during Cooke's exploration of the North Col from 14 to 19 November. The violent wind met by Hunt on the Tent Peak ridge would, however, at this season be equally devastating on the north ridge of Kangchenjunga, and would seem to rule out climbing at such extreme altitudes.

In 1939 the three climbers Schmaderer, Paidar, and Grob returned to Sikkim, and after a long-drawn-out struggle completed the ascent of Tent Peak. They took the same route as had been attempted by Bauer in 1936, and by themselves and by Hunt in 1937, over the top of Nepal Peak and by the corniced and difficult south-west ridge.

New ground was broken when F. Spencer Chapman in 1937 made the first big ascent in the Assam Himalaya. On his return from Lhasa, where he had spent six months as private secretary to the Political Officer in Sikkim, he had seen from the Tang La the great pyramid of Chomolhari (23,997) standing up to the east. In May

---

[1] Pasang Kikuli (No. 8); Dawa Thondup (No. 49); Pasang Dawa Lama (Pasang Sherpa, No. 139); Ringsing Bhutia (No. 32); Pasang Chikadi (No. 86); Hawang Sherpa (No. 142).

he returned to the Chumbi valley and with C. E. Crawford of Calcutta and three experienced porters, Nima Thondup (No. 67), Pasang Kikuli (No. 8), and Pasang Sherpa (No. 139), he made a thorough reconnaissance of the Bhutan approaches to the mountain. Phari was reached on 12 May and the party crossed the Sur La into the head tributaries of the Paro Chu. The existing quarter-inch map is only a compilation from various sources and has no pretensions to accuracy in the neighbourhood of the mountain.

Chapman chose one of the southern ridges of the mountain, which from his account appears to join the south-west ridge some distance from the summit. The ascent was difficult, and for a party of only five, all carrying loads, arduous in deep snow. Nima Thondup, who was forty-three years of age, was the first to drop out; Crawford, who had come direct from Calcutta and had had little time to acclimatize, returned from camp at 20,000 feet with Pasang Kikuli, who also was exhausted. On 21 May Chapman and Pasang Sherpa reached the summit after a difficult climb which involved much step-cutting.

The descent nearly ended in disaster. A slip by Pasang carried both down a distance of nearly four hundred feet, but was checked and finally stopped by Chapman. Both were very tired and when a blizzard came on and reduced visibility almost to nothing their upward tracks were soon covered. Four nights, from the 21st to 24th, were spent on the mountain before they reached the shelter of a yak-herd's hut, a brilliant performance on Chapman's part, since Pasang was in an exhausted state during most of the descent and both were partly frostbitten.[1]

The Assam Himalaya are still little known in detail, but although there was almost no climbing during the thirties, the journeys of Williamson, Kingdon Ward, Ludlow, and Sherriff added considerably to our knowledge of outlying parts. Mr. F. Williamson, the Political Officer in Sikkim, in 1933 travelled by Paro to Bumtang and then ascended the Chamka Chu northwards; he crossed the difficult glacier pass, Mon La Kar Chung La (17,442), over the Great Himalaya into Tibet, passing close to the Kulha Kangri massif, which rises to over 24,000 feet.

[1] H.J. x (1938) 126.

He was accompanied as far as Bumtang by F. Ludlow and G. Sherriff, who went on eastwards, bent on natural history exploration, to Trashiyangtse Dzong; they then worked in the northern parts of central Bhutan, where they added to our knowledge of the country gained by Claude White in 1906. In 1934 these two made a second journey, this time to eastern Bhutan and the Tibetan province of Monyul.

Most of Kingdon Ward's journeys of botanical exploration and plant-collecting during the last thirty years have been in the Mishmi hills east of the Tsangpo, in Tibet, or in northern Burma, and so fall outside the area here described. In 1935, however, he made an important journey from the Bhareli basin of the Lesser Himalaya in Assam, crossed the Great Himalaya east of Bhutan by the Tulung La (17,250) and Pen La (17,350) and explored the head basins of the Loro Chu and Tsari Chu on the Tibetan side of the range. These two rivers penetrate the main axis in gorges and unite the other side to form the Subansiri.[1]

In 1936 and again in 1938 Ludlow and Sherriff made extensive explorations north of the range, adding to Kingdon Ward's work in the Subansiri headwaters, and to our knowledge of the Siyom. Sherriff brought back an excellent sketch-map of their travels.[2]

[1] *H.J.* viii (1936) 125 ff.          [2] *H.J.* x (1938) 1 ff.; xii (1940) 1 ff.

# 11. The Inter-War Period

THE twenty years between the two wars brought great changes to the Himalaya. By the end of the thirties many laid more stress on the climbing of high mountains than on their scientific exploration and mapping. This change was illustrated not only by the later Everest expeditions themselves, but by each successive individual objective. It is partly to be explained by the better knowledge and better maps available, though there was still some uninformed criticism by those who understood little of the difficulties overcome by their predecessors.

The change was also caused to some extent by rivalry and a race for records. A curious brand of nationalism, quite out of place in the Himalaya, caused some to think that the honour of their country was at stake if they did not climb something larger and higher and more difficult than had been achieved by the climbers of some other country. This led some climbers to think that because they reconnoitred a mountain their country had some possessive right to climb it and that others should go elsewhere. This was a pity; for the climbing of a mountain should be a co-operative affair. Possibly the exclusively British expeditions to Everest were partly responsible for this attitude, though climbers in Britain or India never looked on Everest as theirs alone. Permission to enter Tibet to climb Everest was always so difficult to obtain that the Political Officer in Sikkim rarely found the Tibetan Government favourable to the project. The Everest Committee in England was disappointed time and again, and when permission arrived it had to seize the opportunity, however short the period for final preparations. Membership of the Himalayan Club was open to mountaineers of all countries, and the local secretaries and other members of the Club in India and England made it their business to assist all to obtain permission and to organize their transport.

Climbing technique and skill advanced greatly during these years, largely because of the increased number of guideless climbs in the

Alps and elsewhere. Many of the younger climbers were unable to afford the expense of professional guides and were thrown on their own resources. They brought their knowledge to the Himalaya and began to train the Himalayan porters, the best of whom were quick to learn, as Bruce had foretold. After 1920 it was rare for British climbers to employ professional guides from Europe, and even those who had never climbed in the Alps came to rely on their own judgement and on the loyalty and comradeship of their Sherpa and Bhotia porters. The debt owed to these men is fully realized by all Himalayan mountaineers. Much of the credit for their training goes to such men as Smythe and Shipton, who with Ruttledge and Tilman succeeded to the Himalayan mantles of Bruce and Longstaff. Bauer's expedition to Kangchenjunga also taught them much. But much credit is due to the members of the Eastern section of the Himalayan Club, who were guardians of their interests.

Equipment was much improved. Wind-proof tents and clothing, sleeping-bags of improved pattern and quality, boots, gloves, and almost every item of clothing and equipment had been redesigned for greater lightness, strength, and efficiency. Investigations into food-values, diet, cooking, endurance, all had a bearing on high-altitude problems, and enabled men to stay up higher and longer without serious deterioration. But it was still possible to enjoy journeys and climbs among the lesser hills without all the expense of special equipment, and many small parties whose doings are not recorded enjoyed the hills for their own sake.

In spite of all the knowledge gained there were still divergences of opinion as to fundamentals for the successful assault on the highest peaks. After the return of each of the seven expeditions to Everest, the knowledge gained was analysed and discussed. Planning, organization, equipment, strategy, and tactics were examined: the size of the party, the number of fully qualified technical climbers, the value of oxygen, type, design, and weight of the apparatus, time required for acclimatization, and many other problems. In 1935 it was still not quite certain whether the best season for Everest was before or after the monsoon, though many held strong views. Even at the end of 1938 there was divergence of opinion on many points among those who had taken part in the previous expeditions.

A most instructive discussion on these points followed Tilman's lecture to the Royal Geographical Society in 1938.[1] Among those who took part were Shipton, Smythe, Warren, Lloyd, Odell, and Raymond Greene, and their remarks showed how necessary was a close scientific analysis of the Everest problem. The accepted view from 1924 until 1937 had been to aim at having six fit men at Camp IV (22,900), acclimatized and ready to take advantage of a spell of fine weather. This had been considered the minimum for the safety and proper support of two of the six to reach the top and climb the mountain, in Mallory's words 'as mountaineers would have it climbed.' The problem was how small could the expedition be to get these six men there. Those who accepted the necessity for these six, and advocated a party of ten or twelve to make sure of them, were fully alive to the merits of a smaller party.

Neither the expedition of 1936 nor that of 1938 had thrown much light on this problem, since both were ruined by bad weather. Though the ascent of the mountain from the Nepal side raised different problems, it is interesting now to look back on this discussion, when so much more is known.

[1] G.J. xcii (1938) 490–8.

PART SIX

# 1939–1953

We have not journeyed across the centuries, across the oceans, across the mountains, across the prairies, because we were made of sugar candy.

WINSTON CHURCHILL

# 1. The Second World War and After

THE War was like a gigantic avalanche that sweeps everything before it. All were engulfed in the catastrophe. It was dark. There was only a glimmer of hope for mankind. Homes were shattered, families destroyed, Europe was devastated. The avalanche spread to Asia and the South Seas. Millions were wiped out. Nothing could ever be the same again.

India was never seriously threatened in World War I; she was protected by Britain at the gateways to the Indian Ocean and by the natural ramparts of her land frontiers; her soldiers served in France. In the second World War Indian troops also served abroad, but now it spread to Asia. It was not a trench-bound conflict like the first and there was greater scope for the individualistic qualities that come from mountaineering, especially in such operations as commando raids, and where in retreat men are left or dropped to harry communications.

Among Himalayans who distinguished themselves were Tilman, who, as a Gunner officer served in France and in the Western Desert of North Africa, and afterwards prosecuted war on his own for three years with the partisans of Albania and of Northern Italy; Spencer Chapman, of Arctic and Chomolhari fame, who trained commandos in Scotland and Australia, and survived the 'neutral' jungles of Malaya as a leader of guerilla warfare when most men would have succumbed; Eric Shipton, who found himself Consul-General at Kashgar from 1940 to 1942, on food control in Persia in 1943, and finished the war in Hungary; and Frank Smythe, who trained commandos, mountaineers, and ski-runners for service in any part of the world. And there were many others.

Nor was the spirit of resolution absent among the Himalayan adventurers of the continent. I had first met Peter Aufschnaiter in India as a member of Bauer's 1929 Kangchenjunga expedition, and he had stayed with me at Oxford when he was preparing for his expedition to Nanga Parbat in 1939. It was with some satisfaction that I learnt early in the war that he and his party had been interned in India and were, at any rate for the time being, behind barbed wire, and so were unlikely to be dropped by parachute into my back-garden to be met by pitchfork defiance. It was the height of British chivalry to put them at Dehra Dun within full view of the Himalaya and to give them Himalayan literature to read. I first heard of his and Harrer's escape when as penniless pilgrims and ragged mendicants they arrived in Lhasa and Peter wrote to me from there and asked me to let his mother and Harrer's people in Germany know that both were alive and well. I gladly carried out his request; they had been 'missing' for more than two years and had been 'presumed dead.' Peter sent me maps of his wanderings in Tibet. Their story is well told in Harrer's book.[1]

Of the three who climbed Tent Peak in Sikkim in 1939, E. Grob, of Swiss nationality, returned to his own country. His two companions, L. Schmaderer and H. Paidar, were interned in Dehra Dun, but they also managed to escape. They followed much the same route as Aufschnaiter and Harrer to Nelang and the Tibetan frontier, but were unable to travel east. In July 1945, when still wandering aimlessly and not knowing that the war was over, Schmaderer was brutally robbed and murdered at or near the little village of Tabo in Spiti. Paidar returned to Poo on the Sutlej and followed the river down to Saharan where he gave himself up and made a full report to the police. The murderers were arrested.

Among British Himalayan climbers who lost their lives during the war was Peter Oliver, who had climbed in the Baspa, the Dhaula Dhar, on Dunagiri, Trisul, and Mana; he was killed in Burma in 1945; another was Michael Spender, who, as a squadron leader in the Royal Air Force, was lost in an air accident in the same year.

These six years also saw the passing of several well-loved Himalayan pioneers of an older generation: Sir Francis Younghusband, 'the father of Karakoram exploration,' in 1942, Charles Bruce in 1939, and Norman Collie in 1942. Nanga Parbat was not climbed in their time, as Bruce had foretold years before.

[1] Heinrich Harrer: *Seven Years in Tibet* (London, 1953).

At the outbreak of war the stage was set for three crowning achievements, which waited on the weather: the ascents of Everest, K2, and Nanga Parbat. All had been thoroughly reconnoitred from all sides, except Everest, whose southern approach had been suspected but not seen from near at hand. The 'spirit of kindness' asked for by Mallory in 1922 had been absent from all of them. During the war there could be no great attempts. Short leave only was obtainable by British and American officers serving in India, but they could only go to the more accessible parts of the Himalaya. An Aircrew Mountain Centre was opened at Sonamarg in the Sind valley in Kashmir as a rehabilitation and physical training station. Mountain-climbing was among the health-giving activities of the Centre, and many mountains within a radius of twenty miles were climbed. A ski-ing centre was opened at Gulmarg in winter with the same objects in view, in collaboration with the Ski Club of India. The nearer mountains of the Pir Panjal, of Kashmir and Kulu, of the Beas and Chenab, came more into their own, and those who enjoyed these districts found plenty of interest on little-known ground.

The war brought revolutionary changes throughout the East. Nationalism had been fostered by the Japanese occupation of Southeast Asia and the whole of Asia was in a turmoil. Even before the end it was evident that the days of the British Raj in India were numbered. It is no part of this story to recite the agonies suffered by Moslems, Sikhs, and Hindus in the early days of 'partition,' but it will be long before the massacres and miseries are forgotten. They stained the beginning of a new era.

During the war the Himalayan Club was dormant. The annual journals which had recorded every aspect of Himalayan activity ceased to appear after 1940, since there was little to report and no leisure to seek material or to edit it. In 1946 the Club came to life again, but in the following year the emergence of India and Pakistan as separate States and the departure of many active members nearly killed it. Through the wisdom and enthusiasm of those who remained it survived to flourish again, largely because its headquarters were boldly transferred from Delhi to Calcutta where, among the civil community, more active British members were likely to remain.

By the end of 1948 the move to Calcutta was completed, active sections of the Club were established at Delhi, Karachi, and Bombay, and the Club Register of Members was gradually brought up to date. Many were scattered all over the world and had lost touch with the Club. Some were never traced, but by the efforts of those who remained the Club revived and by the end of 1950 membership was again over five hundred. The Darjeeling Register of Porters was brought up to date by Mr. L. Krenek, the local honorary secretary; and *The Himalayan Journal*, after two 'farewell volumes' edited under great difficulties by C. W. F. Noyce and Colonel H. W. Tobin, was once more well in its stride. A pleasing feature of the revival was the increased interest taken by Indians in mountaineering, and the Club welcomed them as members; several, especially officers in the services, have taken up climbing as a sport.

The difficulties of mountain travel increased greatly as a result of the war. All costs rose, and the higher charges for transport and porters made possible only the smaller type of expedition, unless heavily subsidized. Political troubles, particularly in Kashmir, were also responsible for many difficulties. Access to the Western parts of Kashmir is through Pakistan, much of the old Jhelum valley road by Murree and Kohala being within its sphere, while Eastern Kashmir is accessible only through India. For a time Gilgit and Hunza could be reached only by air, and permission to enter the old Gilgit Agency, except for officials, became almost impossible to obtain. Moreover, for climbs in the Pakistan sphere, the employment of porters recruited in Darjeeling, who were Indian subjects and non-Moslems, was frowned upon. On the other hand, Pakistan began to open up the Khagan valley as a holiday resort, and a rough motor-road was constructed from Abbottabad to the Babusar pass.

Restrictions were imposed on travel for non-Indians to other parts of the Himalaya. Permits became necessary to cross 'the inner line' in the Kumaun Himalaya, and even to enter northern Sikkim. Bhutan was, and is, completely closed to all travel. A ban was placed on the sale of Himalayan maps, their export was forbidden, and accredited agents in England have been unable to obtain modern editions. These are retrograde steps.

One great change for the better, and of immense importance to mountaineers, has been the opening up of Nepal. Changes in the

Nepal constitution, and perhaps the fear of Communist infiltration, were largely responsible. It was first evident in 1949 when a scientific expedition from the United States was allowed to visit the Nepalese foothills. With the new policy, vast regions of almost virgin mountain country await detailed reconnaissance and survey; none of the summits above 20,000 feet had yet been climbed, and among them were twenty-three over 25,000 feet.

In October 1950 Chinese Communist armies invaded Tibet, and once more a curtain falls over that secluded land. The Dalai Lama made a vain appeal to the United Nations for protection against aggression, and retired to the Chumbi valley. Without support from India and under promises made by China he returned to Lhasa. The promises have not been kept and the future of his country is dark.

The closing of Tibet and the opening of Nepal set new problems for the climbing of Everest. No longer was the distant approach through Tibet possible or necessary. Permission to use the shorter route through Nepal had been sought without success more than forty years before. Now at last it was to be granted. Mountaineers were not long in seizing the opportunity.

New difficulties and problems were also set for those who sought to climb Nanga Parbat, and the giants of the Karakoram.

The year 1947 marked the end of an era of Himalayan mountaineering and a new era began. In this new era Indians and Pakistanis are becoming more conscious of their mountains and of the pleasures of travel and climbing among them. Among British climbers left in India who have devoted their time to helping in this respect are Major-General H. Williams, who has encouraged and taken Indian army officers to the high hills, and J. T. M. Gibson, R. Greenwood, and J. Kempe who have encouraged and helped young Indians to take to mountaineering as a pastime.

Perhaps one who knew and loved the India of the past should end his story here. But the ascents of Everest, Nanga Parbat, and K2 are the crown of the past, however much they may set a pattern for the future. Moreover, the experience of the past is cumulative, and there seems to me—perhaps because I am growing old—a tendency to neglect some of the lessons of the past. Mallory's words quoted on page 164 are to my mind still the essence of mountaineering as a pastime: 'The party must keep a margin of safety. It is not to be a mad enterprise rashly pushed on regardless of danger. The ill-considered acceptance of any and every risk has no part in the essence of persevering courage.'

The great mountains are quick to kill or maim when mistakes are made. Surely a safe descent is as much a part of the climb as 'getting to the top.' Dead men are successful only when they have given their lives for others.

# 2. Punjab and Kumaun Himalaya

THE restrictions imposed on travel in the eastern Himalaya and the difficulties caused by the Kashmir problem focused attention on the Lesser Himalaya north of the eastern Punjab and of the United Provinces. There is still a great deal to be done by surveyors and mountaineers in Zaskar, Lahul, and Spiti.

Before the trouble arose over Kashmir, however, a useful reconnaissance was carried out by three army officers, R. Berry, T. S. Stobart, and R. James in the Nun Kun massif. At the end of May 1946, with three Sherpas, they ascended the Shafat glacier from the Suru river and made a close reconnaissance of the south side of Nun (23,410). Bad weather and shortage of time, coupled with avalanche conditions, prevented a serious attempt on the mountain, but they made some useful corrections to the Workmans' map.[1]

Nun was eventually climbed in 1953 by a French party led by Bernard Pierre. They travelled by Jammu and Kishtwar and pitched their base in the upper Fariabad valley. The party comprised Bernard Pierre, Michel Desorbay, J. Guillemin, Madame Claude Kogan, Pierre Vittos (a Swiss missionary working in Ladakh), and two Indian officers, Flight Lieutenant Nalni D. Jayal and Captain K. C. Johorey. They had with them six Sherpas, led by Ang Tharkay. Three camps at 18,000, 19,800, and 21,400 feet were placed on the west ridge of Nun (map page 110).

The assault party, comprising Madame Kogan and Vittos on one rope, and Bernard Pierre with the Sherpa Pemba Nurbu (No. 150) on another left Camp III at 21,400 feet at 7.30 a.m. on 28 August. During the ascent Bernard Pierre had to give up, but Madame Kogan and Pierre Vittos reached the summit at three o'clock. The three highest summits of the massif have now all been climbed: Pinnacle Peak (22,810) by the Workmans in 1906, Kun (23,250) by Calciati in 1914, and Nun (23,410) by this party in 1953.

[1] H.J. xiv (1947) 19.

South-east of the Nun Kun massif very little is yet known of the peaks and glaciers of the Great Himalaya, and the watershed has never been properly surveyed. There are some scattered peaks fixed by triangulation, but not yet enough. The survey of Kishtwar was unfinished in 1921 and then ceased, so that except for the general line of a few routes and passes much of the country between the Chandra-Bhaga (upper Chenab) and Zaskar is virtually blank, except for the main valley routes and a few passes.

In 1946 F. Kolb and L. Krenek drew attention to these deficiencies by a short but interesting piece of exploration up the Bhut tributary of the Chenab, during which they corrected the topography of the streams and glaciers of the Bhazun. There are some fine peaks, the highest being 21,570 feet, waiting to be climbed. They also corrected the map in the neighbourhood of the Muni La. There is great scope in this region for an expedition of mountain surveyors.[1]

Much the same applies to the Pir Panjal to the south-east between Kulu and Lahul, and in Spiti. Kulu is well known and fairly well surveyed as far as the Beas–Chandra watershed, though some of the glaciers are still only roughly sketched, and excepting Deo Tibba's two summits (19,687 and 20,410), little has been attempted. Bruce and his Gurkhas made some early reconnaissances here in and about 1912, and a few have been there since, generally helped by Major H. M. Banon, who has spent most of his life as a fruit-grower in Kulu and who knows the country better than anyone. L. C. Lind attempted Deo Tibba in 1940, E. H. Peck and C. R. Patterson in 1950, R. C. Evans, A. G. Trower, and E. Ker in 1951. The lower summit was climbed by a party led by J. de V. Graaff in 1952.[2]

Restrictions of the 'Inner Line' in Kumaun were responsible for the breaking of fresh ground at the head of the Parbati, the largest of the eastern tributaries of the Beas in Kulu. In 1941 J. O. M. Roberts had visited the Tos Nal and climbed 'White Sail' Peak, 21,148 feet.[3] In 1952 a party comprising K. Snelson, J. de V. Graaff, and E. A. Schelpe explored the Dibibokri basin, its four glaciers, and the Great Himalayan watershed, where there are three peaks of 21,000 feet or more. From Pulga, the uppermost hamlet of the

[1] H.J. xiv (1947) 33.  [2] H.J. xvii (1953) 118; Mountain World (1954) 220.
[3] A.J. liii (1941-2) 323.

Parbati, they and their five Sherpas did all their own carrying, and though they climbed only one summit over 20,000 feet, they made three passes over the main watershed and looked into the unexplored head of the Parahio tributary of the Spiti river.[1]

Beyond the watershed the whole of Lahul in the Chandra-Bhaga district is very sketchily surveyed. J. de V. Graaff in 1951 attempted a peak over 20,000 feet north of the Chhota Shigri. In 1953 A. E. Gunther and J. Kempe explored the Bara Shigri glacier and much of the country east of the elbow of the Chandra river. Their sketch-map shows how much remains to be explored in this area.[2]

Another region still awaiting detailed mapping is at the head of the Tons river in Tehri Garhwal, particularly on the north side of Bandarpunch (20,720). The south and east approaches appear to have been well surveyed under Osmaston in 1936, and routes to its summit were reconnoitred from this side by R. D. Leakey and others in 1942 and 1946. In 1950 J. T. M. Gibson made the first ascent with a party of young climbers and since then has almost yearly taken boys from the Doon School to its glaciers. Among other valleys visited was the lovely Harki Doon which lies between Surgnalin and Bandarpunch, where the boys have been initiated into the delights of climbing and ski-ing.[3]

The mountains bordering the Gangotri glacier and its tributary the Chaturangi, well surveyed by Osmaston's party, have been the scene of considerable recent activity, though there was a hiatus between 1948 and 1951. Almost the last expedition under British rule in India was a Swiss expedition, which took place here in 1947. It was sponsored by the *Schweizerische Stiftung für Alpine Forschüngen* and comprised Mme. Annelies Lohner, André Roch, Alfred Sutter, René Dittert, and Alexandre Graven. The party flew out to India from Switzerland in May and, after leaving Mussoorie on the 26th of that month, pitched their base at Nandanban at the junction of the Gangotri and Chaturangi on 11 June. T. H. Braham, later the energetic honorary secretary of the Himalayan Club, went with them and there were eight Darjeeling porters: Sirdar Wangdi Nurbu (No. 25), Ajeeba (No. 10), Ang Dawa I (No. 40), Tenzing Khumjung Bhutia

*H.J.* xviii (1954) 110.           [2] *A.J.* lix (1954) 288.

[3] *H.J.* xviii (1954) 93.

(No. 48), Dawa Thondup (No. 49), Pasang Urgen (No. 98), Ang Tsering IV (No. 101), and Ang Nurbu.[1] It was a strong and experienced team (map page 265).

A first attempt on Kedarnath (22,770), at the head of the Kirti glacier nearly ended in tragedy. On 25 June, when the party were traversing the narrow north-east ice-ridge between the 'White Dome' (22,410) and the summit, Wangdi Nurbu, who was on the last of the three ropes, fell and dragged Sutter with him. The two fell about 700 feet. With great difficulty the other five, Roch, Graven, Dittert, Ang Dawa, and Ang Nurbu, climbed down to them. Sutter was only slightly hurt, but Wangdi's left ankle was broken, his right knee injured and his skull bleeding. Night came on before they could get him down and they sheltered in a crevasse. Early the next morning all except Wangdi went down to get help, but the search party failed to find him and only on the 27th, after he had spent a second night out, did the rescue party reach him and bring him down to safety. He was transported to hospital at Dehra Dun and by a miracle survived his ordeal.

This was the last of Wangdi Nurbu's Himalayan expeditions. He was now about forty years old. He had been on climbs almost continuously since 1929, except for the war years: to Kangchenjunga in 1929 and 1930, to Kamet in 1931, to Everest in 1933, 1936, and 1938, to Nanga Parbat in 1934, and to the Gangotri glacier with Schwarzgruber late in 1938. He was in Garhwal with Smythe in 1937 and in Assam with Tilman in 1939.

Undeterred by this reverse the party returned to the assault early in July, and on the 11th Roch, Dittert, Graven, Sutter, and Tenzing reached the summit.

After this success the party made the first ascent of Satopanth (23,213) on 1 August, and, after crossing the Kalindi Khal into the Arwa valley followed the Alaknanda valley down to Joshimath. From here they crossed the Kuari pass and reached Sutol, the last hamlet in the Nandakini valley, and climbed Nanda Ghunti (20,700), the western outlier of the Trisul trident (map page 116).

[1] Dawa Thondup and Ang Tsering IV are called 'Thundu' and 'Angtensing' in the account in *The Himalayan Journal*. The names given in the text above are from the Himalayan Register. I am not sure which is correct.

The topography at the head of this valley had been first cleared up by Longstaff in 1907, but there was no serious attempt to climb it until B. R. Goodfellow and J. Buzzard tried the south face in 1944 and found it impracticable. The brothers P. L. and J. Wood with R. H. Sams and three good Dhotial porters tried again in 1945. After crossing a col from the south side of the Nanda Ghunti glacier, a tributary of the Ronti glacier which descends from Trisul, they climbed a col on the ridge between Nanda Ghunti and Ronti peaks, intending to reach the top of Nanda Ghunti by its north ridge. Shortage of time and threatening weather caused them to give up the attempt. Their view was that the route from the col to the summit was practicable.

A small expedition led by J. B. Tyson of Oxford University, visited the Gangotri peaks in 1952. The objects were primarily scientific, but they had with them four Sherpas and they succeeded in climbing Gangotri I (21,890) and III (21,578).[1]

In the same year V. Russenberger and L. Georges, members of a French expedition, reached the summit of Chaukhamba I (23,420), the highest of the great group at the head of the Gangotri glacier. Four camps were established on the mountain with the help of Sherpas led by Gyalgen II Mikchen (No. 57). Other expeditions have gone to this area in recent years, notably to Nilkanta (21,640), the beautiful peak that rises about five miles west of Badrinath; it is still unclimbed. It was attempted by Frank Smythe and Peter Oliver in 1937—Smythe described it as second in beauty only to Siniolchu; by a party led by C. G. Wylie in May 1947; by André Roch's Swiss party later in the same year; by a New Zealand party comprising E. P. Hillary, H. E. Riddiford, W. G. Lowe, and F. M. Cotter in 1951; and by a party led by T. H. Tilly in 1952.

The New Zealand party, after leaving Nilkanta, went up the Saraswati valley and reconnoitred both the Pachhmi Kamet and Dakkhni Chamrao approaches to Mukut Parbat (23,760), before deciding on the latter glacier for their attempt on this peak. It was climbed on 11 July by Riddiford, Cotter, and the Sherpa Pasang Dawa Lama (No. 139).[2] The party also explored the Uttari Chamrao glacier, and climbed three more peaks over 20,000 feet.

[1] H.J. xviii (1954) 87.    [2] H.J. xvii (1952) 42 ff.

Mukut Parbat's history goes back to the time of Richard Strachey, who in 1848 first determined its approximate height with those of other peaks in the neighbourhood. It is the 'Western Ibi Gamin' of the Schlagintweits in 1855. This was the last of the four peaks of the group to be climbed. Kamet (25,447)—Central Ibi Gamin of the Schlagintweits—had been climbed by Smythe's party in 1931; Mana (23,860) by Smythe in 1937; Abi Gamin (24,130)—the old Eastern Ibi Gamin—on 22 August 1950 by a small Anglo-Swiss party comprising A. Tissières, K. Berril, G. Chevalley, and R. Dittert, with four Sherpas, from the Tibetan side, which has not yet been surveyed.[1]

In 1951 a French expedition, unable to obtain the necessary permission from the Pakistan Government to visit K2 or Nanga Parbat, fell back on the Kumaun Himalaya and resolved to attempt the traverse of the ridge between Nanda Devi and Nanda Devi East. The first had been climbed by Tilman and Odell in 1936, the eastern peak by the Poles in 1939. The party was led by Roger Duplat and comprised L. Gevril, A. Barbezat, L. Dubost, P. Gendre, J. Languepin, L. Payan, and G. Vignes. They had with them Major N. D. Jayal of the Indian Army as transport officer and eight Darjeeling porters under Tenzing (No. 48) as sirdar. It was a difficult project and ended in tragedy (map page 116).

Base Camp was set up in the 'sanctuary' on the 1936 site on 18 June; Camps I, II, and III were placed on the Coxcomb ridge and three tents were taken up to Longstaff's col from the Lawan Gad. On 28 June Duplat and Vignes passed up through Camp III and pitched a bivouac at about 23,700 feet. On the following morning they sent down the Sherpas with a scribbled message:

Expect to be on summit by noon—bivouac below eastern summit—tomorrow eastern summit noon—sleep at Col Longstaff . . . Clear camps by Sherpas down to Camp I the day after to-morrow, by coolies between I and Base. Bring back everything. Gil and I have severe headaches, but apart from that all goes well. Camp about 7500 m.—Roger.

On that day, the 29th, at about 2 p.m. Gevril caught sight of them below the main summit—two figures, soon after to be enclosed by

[1] H.J. xvii (1952) 80.

mist. They still had the long and difficult traverse before them. They were not seen again. Gevril and Barbezat in Camp III wisely had not cleared the camps and waited for news of the climbers. The 30th passed, and during the afternoon Languepin, Jayal, and Da Namgyal II (No. 157) joined them with two tents at Camp III. On the following morning Gevril and Da Namgyal searched the mountain above in vain.

Meanwhile the eastern party comprising Dubost, Payan, and three Sherpas had reached Longstaff's col. On 2 July Dubost and Tenzing cut a track toward the summit of Nanda Devi East. They could see several occupants in Camp III on the Coxcomb ridge and thought that perhaps Duplat and Vignes had returned. After a rest on the 3rd, Dubost and Tenzing reached the summit of Nanda Devi East on the 4th. On the following day at Longstaff's col they learnt that the two climbers had failed to return. The base of the mountain was searched, but no trace of the missing men was found.

Two ascents of Trisul were made in this year 1951. The first was organized by Gurdial Singh, and comprised R. D. Greenwood, Flight L:eutenant N. D. Jayal, Surendra Lal, and three Sherpas.[1] On 23 June Gurdial Singh, Greenwood, and the Sherpa Dawa Thondup reached the summit. The second was by the French doctor, R. Walter, of Pondicherry, who with one Sherpa, Nima Tenzing (No. 149), climbed it independently the following day.

Panch Chuli (22,650), in northern Kumaun, is another mountain which has received considerable attention in recent years, though it is now difficult to obtain permission to visit it. Ruttledge had taken a hasty look at it in 1929, but after then it seems to have been left alone until 1950. In that year W. H. Murray and three others of the Scottish Mountaineering Club, after a rapid visit to reconnoitre Bethartoli Himal (20,840) in the south of the Rishi gorge and a visit to the Lampak valley, made a circuit by the Girthi gorge to the Goriganga, crossed over to the east side of Panch Chuli and in August made a reconnaissance of the mountain from the Sona Gad.[2]

---

[1] Gurdial Singh and Roy Greenwood were on the staff of the Indian Military Academy at Dehra Dun. The Sherpas were Dawa Thondup (No. 49), aged forty-four, Gyalgen II Mikchen (No. 57), and Lhakpa Tsering. They were helped also by old Kesar Singh, the local veteran of Kamet and Trisul. (*H.J.* xviii (1952) 112).

[2] *H.J.* xvi (1950–1) 38.

Later the same year J. de V. Graaff and K. Snelson also examined the group from the Sona Gad but found no practicable route.[1]

In 1953, Heinrich Harrer, after his experiences in Lhasa, reconnoitred Panch Chuli from the western side. From the little hamlet of Mathkot in the Goriganga valley, he, with F. Thomas and two Sherpas, explored the Pyunsani Gad to its head, whence they made their attempt by the west ridge. They were unsuccessful, but certainly had an exciting time.[2]

[1] *H.J.* xvii (1952) 97.　　　　[2] *H.J.* xviii (1954) 171.

# 3. Karakoram

THERE are few expeditions to the Karakoram to record between the war years and 1953. It was too distant and expensive at first, and the political situation soon brought difficulties.

In 1946 J. O. M. Roberts and G. Lorimer with two Sherpas made a spirited reconnaissance of Saser Kangri (25,170), the giant of the Saser Muztagh, on the watershed between the Nubra and the upper Shyok. It had been photographed by Arthur Neve in 1899, visited in bad weather by Longstaff in 1909, and surveyed during the Vissers' explorations of the range in 1935. The curtailment of his leave and the size of his party left Roberts with little hope of making a decisive attempt to climb it; but he examined it closely from the head of both the north and the south Phukpo glaciers and also the other peaks of the group from the head of the Sakang glacier. While engaged on this last, Lorimer and the Sherpa Sonam reconnoitred its north-eastern side from the Chamshen tributary of the upper Shyok, which he reached after crossing the Saser pass. Roberts concluded that none of the group appeared climbable from the Nubra side, and that an assault from the east was more likely to succeed.[1]

In June 1947 a second attempt to climb Rakaposhi (25,550) in the great bend of the Hunza river north of Gilgit was made by H. W. Tilman, Campbell Secord, H. Gyr, and R. Kappeler. Secord had reached the north-west peak on the north-west ridge with Vyvyan in 1938, but they were not then equipped to go farther and in any case the route from here to the summit appeared to be too long.

The strong party of 1947 continued the reconnaissance from the west, first from the Biro glacier and then by the Kunti. From the latter they reached a point called Baraioshen, at about 20,340 feet, on the south-west spur, but were unable from here to gain the 'Monk's Head,' a snow eminence on the spur short of the south-west ridge,

[1] *H.J.* xiv (1947) 1.

which appeared to offer some chance of reaching the summit. A third attempt by Tilman and Gyr landed them on the north-west ridge of Rakaposhi between the north-west peak and the summit, but the climb from here, at between 19,000 and 20,000 feet, to the summit was deemed by them to be impossible.[1]

From here the party went to Chalt and explored the Bola Das or Tutu Uns valley on the right bank of the Hunza river. This had never been surveyed and the lightly sketched detail depended on a sportsman's report who had gone up the valley as far as Toltar in search of game.[2] It has long been known that the head, and indeed the greater part of this Tutu Uns is unsurveyed and it is shown as 'unexplored' on the map. It is indeed a pity that some party that has gone up this valley in the past has not taken a surveyor from the Survey of India, as did the Vissers when they explored and mapped the Batura glacier with the help of Khan Sahib Afraz Gul in 1925. The whole of the area between the Hunza valley and the Batura Muztagh is badly in need of an accurate survey.

With the isolation of the Gilgit agency in 1947 it became almost impossible for mountaineers to carry on the exploration of the Karakoram. At last in 1952, Houston, who had already pioneered the route by the Abruzzi ridge of K2 in 1938, obtained the consent of the Pakistan Government to lead another attempt on the summit in the following year.

He had with him six other Americans, all experienced climbers: R. Bates, who had been with him in 1938, G. Bell (twenty-seven), A. Gilkey (twenty-six), D. Molenaar, P. Schoening (twenty-six), and R. Craig (twenty-eight). Captain H. R. A. Streather (twenty-seven) of the Gloucestershire Regiment, who had served with the Chitral Scouts and who had been with the successful Norwegian party to the top of Tirich Mir (25,263) in Chitral in 1950, was invited by Houston to help with the transport arrangements and to be a member of the climbing party. Colonel M. Ata Ullah, an experienced Pakistani doctor, was attached as liaison officer.

---

[1] H. W. Tilman: *Two Mountains and a River* (Cambridge, 1948); *H.J.* xvii (1952) 101.

[2] The Karumbar valley to the west has, I believe, been surveyed but is not yet shown accurately on maps available to the public.

Nothing shows more clearly the changes that have come over the Karakoram than this expedition of Houston. There had been warfare in the mountains. Skardu, the base town on the Indus for all major expeditions to the Baltoro since Abruzzi's day, had seen much fighting in 1947 between the adherents of Pakistan and those of India, and had changed hands several times. Before the war it had a population of perhaps two thousand; now in 1950 it was a frontier town of Pakistan, with more than three times as many inhabitants, including a Pakistan Political Agent and a military garrison supplied by air. There was still strong feeling over the Kashmir problem, and it was unapproachable, even for peaceful mountaineers, by the old route through Srinagar and the Zoji La. Planes had been flying to Gilgit since Squadron Leader Harris's historic flight with Wapitis in 1931, but this was the first time that a major Himalayan expedition had been able to cut out by air travel to Skardu almost the whole of its approach march to the Karakoram.

Another sign of the times was the disinclination of Pakistan, understandable under existing conditions, to permit Darjeeling porters, who were Indian nationals, to accompany the expedition. In compensation, the Mir of Hunza had chosen some reliable men from his State. It had long been known that these men are in a class of their own as natural rock-climbers, and that with technical training and good leadership the best of them would develop into first-class climbers, but this was the first time they had been engaged on a major climbing expedition outside the boundaries of their State. All of them came from villages close to Baltit, the capital of Hunza, from where Rakaposhi (or as they call it in their villages *Dumani*, the Mother of Mist) is in full view: Khairul Hayat, Ghulam Mohamed, and Hayat Khan, all from Altit, Haji Beg and Walayat Shah from Aliabad, Mohamed Ali from Hini, opposite Minapin.

It was a strong party and deserved success. Coolies were engaged from Skardu and the lower villages of the Shigar—the best of them apparently from the Satpura valley south of Skardu—to carry the expedition to the upper Baltoro (map page 134).

The expedition reached its base camp at about 16,500 feet on the Godwin-Austen glacier on 19 June, and, having discharged the Balti porters from in and around Skardu, set up Camp I (17,600) in fine weather at the foot of the Abruzzi ridge. From now onwards there were only the six Hunza porters and the eight climbers to do all the carrying to the high camps, and it was considered unwise to use the untrained Hunza men above Camp III. Colonel Ata Ullah remained at the base and kept in touch with the climbers by radio.

Camps II (19,300), III (20,500), IV (22,000), V (22,500) and VI (23,400) were regularly established and stocked up the Abruzzi ridge much in the same positions as in 1938.[1] At Camp VI were found the remains of the old tents of Wiessner's ill-fated attempt, and in them the sleeping-bags neatly rolled up with a few personal belongings of Pasang Kikuli and his two gallant companions, who had sacrificed their lives in a vain attempt to bring Wolfe down the mountain.

During the establishing of Camp VI the weather deteriorated and above this point the ice formations below the shoulder had altered. It was impossible to find a good site for a permanent Camp VII and only one small tent was erected at 24,700 feet on a narrow ledge cut out of the snow. Camp VIII at about 25,500 feet was placed above the shoulder, but it meant that the difference of altitude between Camps VI and VIII, the two main camps where more than two men could stay, was over 2000 feet; and it was difficult ground.

By the evening of 1 August Camp VIII was stocked and six of the party were in it. The weather was still not too good, but the next day the party at Camp VIII came down to VII, carried further supplies up to Camp VIII, and the remaining two, Bates and Streather, carried loads up from VI to VIII. This day, which had dawned clear and sunny, deteriorated later, and the climb was completed in bad weather.

All eight climbers were now in Camp VIII, a strong, confident, well-knit and well-acclimatized party. They had food and fuel to last the eight of them for at least ten days, and they had a well-stocked line of camps down the ridge to the base, where Colonel Ata Ullah, with the six Hunza men, was in touch with them by wireless. Three or four fine days out of the next ten was at this time of year a

---

[1] It will be noted that these heights, which are from Streather's account in *H.J.* xviii (1954) differ from those given in the account of the 1938 attempt (page 258), sometimes by as much as 500 feet. I do not know which set of heights is the more accurate. Both sets are probably by aneroid.

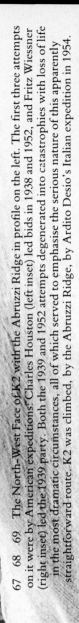

67  68  69   The North-West Face of K2 with the Abruzzi Ridge in profile on the left. The first three attempts on it were by American expeditions: Charles Houston (left inset) led bids in 1938 and 1952, and Fritz Wiessner (right inset) led the 1939 party. Both the 1939 and 1952 attempts degenerated into catastrophies with loss of life in the most dramatic circumstances, all of which served to emphasise the serious nature of this apparently straightforward route. K2 was climbed, by the Abruzzi Ridge, by Ardito Desio's Italian expedition in 1954.

70  71  Annapurna 1 was the first 26,000ft peak to be climbed. Maurice Herzog's French expedition made the ascent by a route up the North Face (above) in 1950 but at high cost – the summit team of Herzog (left) and Lachenal suffering terrible frostbite injuries culminating in multiple amputations carried out during the return march.

72  73  The final section of the Rakhiot route on Nanga Parbat (seen from Fore Peak) which was climbed in a remarkable solo effort by Hermann Buhl (inset), a member of Dr. Karl Herrligkoffer's 1953 Austro/German expedition.

74 75 Everest was finally climbed in 1953 by a route linking the Western Cwm with the South Col. Eric Shipton's reconnaissance of 1951 was followed by two Swiss attempts in 1952 which sorted out most of the route-finding problems. These prepared the way for John Hunt's successful Anglo/New Zealand bid the following year. The large photo shows the North Col and the line attempted by the seven pre-war attempts in profile on the left. The main features of the post-war route – the Khumbu Icefall, the Western Cwm, the Lhotse Face and the South Col – are all obvious on the right. The inset photo shows the typical mixed-climbing on the slopes above the South Col.

than here (1975) and presented a tricky technical obstacle for the summit party.

77 (above) Members of the 1953 team: George Band, Alfred Gregory, Michael Ward, Tom Stobart, George Lowe, Griffith Pugh, Edmund Hillary, John Hunt, Wilfrid Noyce, Tom Bourdillon, Tenzing Norgay, Charles Evans, Mike Westmacott and Charles Wylie.

78 (right) Tenzing on the summit of Everest – the final success after nine serious attempts during the previous thirty years.

79  80  Cho Oyu was the fifth peak above 26,000ft to be climbed. The experienced sherpa, Pasang Dawa Lama (inset) played a key role in the success of Dr. Herbert Tichy's small Austrian expedition in 1954.

81  82  Dhaulagiri established a reputation for difficulty following the Swiss (1953) and Argentinian (1954) attempts. Andre Roch's (inset) 1953 expedition worked out a route on the northern flank (below). This was later advanced by the Argentinians, led by Francisco Ibanez, but bad weather intervened and during the retreat Ibanez was severely frostbitten and eventually died of gangrene in Katmandu.

reasonable assumption, during which one of the four pairs could expect to reach the summit. It was planned to set up one more Camp (IX) from which to make the final bid.

Unfortunately the weather, which had deteriorated the previous afternoon, grew worse. Throughout the night the storm continued, in Streather's words, 'with unrelenting ferocity, and the wind seemed to have some personal malice' against them as though determined to blast them off the mountain. It raged throughout the 3rd and 4th, so fiercely that the stoves would not keep alight, nothing could be cooked or heated, and they were unable to get more than a cupful or two of liquid to drink.

On the morning of the 5th,[1] one of the four tents was destroyed. Houston and Bell crawled with their sleeping-bags for shelter into the other tents, and there were now eight men in three small tents. The same conditions continued throughout the 5th and 6th; there was no weakening in the storm or in the spirit of the climbers. During this period they had been in touch by radio with Colonel Ata Ullah, who had picked up special weather broadcasts by Radio Pakistan and relayed them to the climbers. Most of them reported continued storm.

On the morning of the 7th there appeared to be a break; the clouds were clearing and the sun shone, though the wind was still strong. For the first time in five days it was possible to take stock. Bell and Molenaar had been slightly frostbitten during the storm; it was decided that Bates and Streather should escort them down to Camp VII, whence they could reach VI, and that the escort should then, return to VIII with further supplies. Meanwhile Houston, Gilkey Schoening, and Craig would kick steps up towards the proposed Camp IX.

But the day brought fresh trouble. As Gilkey crawled from his tent he complained of cramp in his leg, and on trying to stand collapsed in a faint. Houston diagnosed phlebitis—blood clots had obstructed a vein in his left calf. All plans for the climb had now to be abandoned in an attempt to get Gilkey down the mountain; he had already been a week at 25,500 feet.

Wrapped in sleeping-bags and the torn tent, Gilkey was dragged

---

[1] According to Houston; Streather's account gives 4th.

by the party through the deep freshly-fallen snow. Within a hundred yards it was realized that the snow was in an avalanche condition and they had to drag him back to Camp VIII while Craig and Schoening reconnoitred for a better route. Late in the afternoon these two returned, having found a possible alternative route, though even here it would be extremely difficult to get Gilkey down to Camp VI.

Had the weather remained fine they might have succeeded. But it again deteriorated and once more the whole party was confined by storm in Camp VIII. On the 9th the situation had become so desperate and Gilkey's condition so bad—blood clots had lodged in his lung—that the decision to descend on the 10th at all costs was taken.

Once more he was wrapped in sleeping-bags and tent and in a raging blizzard dragged down through the snow and lowered down the steep ridge to the ice-slope below. After hours of exhausting work they had descended four hundred feet. It was certain now that they would get no farther than the single tent at Camp VII (24,700) and that some at least would have little if any shelter for the night.

They had just lowered Gilkey over a small vertical cliff, with Craig guarding the ropes and Schoening belayed, when Bell, who was hampered by frostbitten feet, slipped and dragged Streather with him. As they fell, their rope fouled that between Schoening and Gilkey, which checked their fall. The third rope with Houston and Bates became involved and they were thrown down the slope. Five of the climbers were falling—Houston, Bates, Molenaar, Streather, and Bell. By a miracle they were held by the firm belay of Schoening. 'The nylon stretched like a rubber band,' writes Houston, 'but did not break.'

When the fall of the five men stopped, they were precariously balanced above the abrupt cliff which forms the upper part of the Abruzzi ridge. By a second miracle none was badly injured. Bell had fallen about two hundred feet, the others rather less; Houston was unconscious with concussion, Bates hung on his rope upside down; Molenaar and Streather, bleeding and bruised, helped Bates who descended to Houston. Several loads had been lost, all were shaken and Bell had lost his axe and gloves.

Those who were able to do so made their way to Camp VII and erected a tiny bivouac tent beside the mountain tent and helped the casualties to shelter, an operation which took over half an hour. Streather, Bates, and Craig then went back for Gilkey, who had been firmly anchored to the slope by two ice-axes. He had vanished. During the short period an avalanche had fallen and swept him to his death.

Perhaps the mountain had been merciful. His seven companions would never have abandoned him; nor in the prevailing conditions and their own exhausted state could they now have brought him down alive. The night was spent in the two tiny tents—Houston delirious, Bell badly frostbitten in feet and hands, Schoening exhausted, the others making tea and passing it round for the rest to sip. None slept, the hours dragged on, but the wind dropped.

The next day they reached Camp VI with difficulty. Then the storm set in again and it was not till the night of the 14th that the party reached Camp II. The Hunza porters had heard the voices of the climbers above and bounded up the difficult rocks to help them into camp. The ordeal was ended.

It had been a Homeric struggle with a furious mountain.

# 4. Conquest of Nanga Parbat (26,620)

A WINTER visit in 1950 by three British mountaineers, J. W. Thornley, W. H. Crace, and R. M. W. Marsh, who had climbed together in Sikkim in 1947, added to the list of victims claimed by Nanga Parbat. They had come out to visit the Karakoram, but the Pakistan Government withdrew their permits after they arrived—possibly because they brought Sherpa porters with them—and rather than abandon their project altogether they planned to study winter conditions on the Rakhiot glacier. They did not intend to go high, and Marsh returned to their base on 16 November with frostbitten toes. Thornley and Crace were seen to pitch a tent at about 18,000 feet on 1 December. For three days the tent was visible from below, after which a heavy storm came on and neither the two men nor their tent were seen again. Marsh and two Sherpas searched for them without result and Pakistan planes hunted for them in vain.

Nanga Parbat was climbed to the summit on 3 July 1953, five weeks after Hunt's success on Everest. An Austro-German party returned to the assault after an interval of fourteen years. The expedition was led by Dr. Karl M. Herrligkoffer, who was also the chief medical officer. There were nine other members, eight of whom were considered potential climbers for the summit: Dr. Walter Frauenberger (deputy leader), Peter Aschenbrenner of Kufstein (leader of the climbers), Hermann Buhl and Kuno Rainer, both of Innsbrück, Hans Ertl, Albert Bitterling, a guide from Berchtesgaden, two younger men, Otto Kempter and Hermann Köllensperger, both aged twenty-seven, and Fritz Aumann of Munich, who was to be in charge of camp administration, radio, and photography. Aschenbrenner was the most experienced Himalayan climber, having already been to Nanga Parbat on Merkl's expeditions in 1932 and 1934. He had helped to pioneer both routes across the Rakhiot peak, which he had been the first to climb; he had been with Schneider when they reached an altitude of 25,280 feet in 1934; and he had survived the pitiless storm during the descent. Unfortunately he could only join the expedition for a short period of about six weeks and had to be back in Europe early in July.

The porter question caused some concern. Six Sherpas under Pasang Dawa Lama (No. 139) had been engaged, but were unable to enter Pakistan and had to return. Instead, the Mir of Hunza had again sent seventeen selected men from his State.[1]

The party arrived in India by sea and flew by Dakota from Rawalpindi to Gilgit; from there they started for Thelichi (Talichi), on the right bank of the Indus opposite the Astor confluence, by jeep, but after some breakdowns were glad of help from ponies and donkeys. A temporary base in the Rakhiot valley was established at 12,250 feet by 12 May, and they were here joined by Aschenbrenner who had flown out from Europe.

All went well. The weather was fine. The base at the foot of the great moraine was fully established by 24 May; by the 30th, Camp I, on the glacier and sheltered by a great rock, had been stocked, and the site for Camp II at 17,400 feet reached. Because of the shortage of porters it was decided to dispense with one camp, and to place Camp III on the upper terrace, where the old Camp IV had been destroyed in 1937. This Camp III was sited first at about 20,350 feet, but because of its exposure, Aschenbrenner moved it to a more sheltered and safer spot at 20,170 feet.

The advance was deliberate to allow the climbers to acclimatize. Most of the party had to carry light loads. By 10 June a strong group was in Camp III ready to tackle the Rakhiot traverse. On the 12th, 13th, and 14th there was a break in the weather and much snow fell; the 16th and 17th were fine, the 18th dull and threatening; but on this day a site for Camp IV was dug in the snow at the foot of Rakhiot Peak, with the aid of four Hunza porters.

At this point Rainer had to drop out. He caught a chill on the 18th, and developed phlebitis at Camp IV (21,950). He was evacuated with difficulty to Camp III on the 22nd and to the base on the 27th. Fortunately the weather remained fine throughout most of

[1] The names of only the four best are given in the preliminary account of this expedition; they all traversed the Rakhiot Peak; Madi, the sirdar, Ali Mahad, Haji Beg, and Hidayat Khan.

this time, though there was heavy snow throughout the 22nd and 23rd.

On the 25th news was received that the monsoon was expected in Rawalpindi within three days. The barometer was falling and it was felt that an attempt should be pressed on at once.

Aschenbrenner also now had to leave the party, since his time with the expedition was nearly up. The remainder were well placed for the first attempt, though some, notably Buhl, seemed to have acclimatized slowly.

On 27 June an assault party comprising Frauenberger, Kempter, Buhl, and Köllensperger reached Camp IV, and the following day made the difficult traverse of the Rakhiot Peak. At one point Köllensperger slipped and fell thirty feet but was held on the rope by Buhl. Soon afterwards the weather worsened, snow fell, and the party decided to withdraw to Camp IV and wait for more settled weather.

By the morning of 30 June the mountain was buried deep in snow. All camps were well stocked as far as Camp IV. But the four climbers of the first attempt were tired and depressed, the Hunza porters were unwilling to carry loads over the Rakhiot traverse, the weather was still bad, and all needed a rest. The higher camps were in touch by wireless with the base; it was decided to withdraw all climbers from Camp III and above. Köllensperger, in particular, was exhausted and he went down.

Suddenly, without warning, the weather cleared at mid-day and Frauenberger, the deputy leader, received permission to keep the climbers at Camp III. The first of July dawned in brilliant weather. Everyone's spirits rose. Frauenberger, Buhl, and Ertl with three Hunza men went up to Camp IV. It was proposed to take a camp to the 'Moor's Head' beyond the Rakhiot Peak on the 2nd, if the weather held, and to rush for the summit on the following day.

It was still perfect on 2 July. Kempter, with Madi, the Hunza sirdar, reached Camp IV. Frauenberger had persuaded the other three Hunza men to make a start, and personally adjusted their crampons and took them on his rope. All eight men made good time and Camp V was placed on the arête beyond the 'Moor's Head' at about 22,780 feet. Kempter and Buhl remained here while Frauenberger and Ertl escorted the porters back to Camp IV at sunset. All depended now on the weather.

A storm came on during the night of the 2nd. The two climbers at Camp V spent an uneasy evening, anchoring their tent more firmly. At 1 a.m. Buhl roused Kempter, but started alone at 2.30, leaving Kempter to catch him up later. The wind dropped and a perfect day dawned. By 7 a.m. Buhl was over the Silver Saddle (24,450). Kempter, who only started at 3 a.m. was still suffering from the exhaustion of his first attempt, during which he had done most of the step-cutting, but he also passed the Silver Saddle about an hour after Buhl. Both climbers report that it was now blazing hot in the sun on the great snow plateau. After a rest, Kempter started off again in at attempt to reach Buhl, now only a distant dot a mile ahead. While taking another rest, he fell asleep for about an hour, at the end of which he was too lethargic and exhausted by the heat to go on. Buhl had disappeared. Kempter waited for him at this altitude, about 25,000 feet, until five o'clock and then turned back, descended from the Silver Saddle and regained Camp V.

Meanwhile Frauenberger, having from Camp IV seen the two climbers reach the Silver Saddle, had gone up alone past the Rakhiot Peak to Camp V where he and Kempter spent an anxious night waiting for Buhl's return. Fortunately the 4th dawned fine and Frauenberger signalled Ertl at Camp IV to bring up another tent, light wireless, oxygen, and further supplies. This he did with the help of the Hunza porters, who were now going strongly.

Having dumped their loads Kempter escorted them back to Camp IV, while Frauenberger and Ertl prepared to go on to the Silver Saddle to search for Buhl. They were erecting a memorial tablet, inscribed with the names of Merkl and his lost companions, on the Moor's Head, when Buhl was seen to be descending the slope of the Silver Saddle. Nanga Parbat had at last been climbed.

In the fine weather of 3 July Buhl had pushed on over the wind-ribbed snow-plateau steadily gaining height, but with frequent rests. It was hot and there was no wind. On reaching the rocks of the fore peak (25,950) he discarded his rucksack with food and pullover, cached them, and traversed the peak to the Bazin Gap. This depression in the last rock ridge, at about 25,630 feet, had been Mummery's objective from the Diamirai side in 1895. Buhl had hoped to be on the summit by noon; it was now 3 p.m., he had still a thousand feet to climb, alone and along the narrow arête. Here he took two Pervitine tablets, the drug used by German airmen to keep them going on exhausting flights during the war.

This last arête was difficult. Sometimes clambering up smooth rock, sometimes over sun-softened slabs of snow, often traversing the south side of the arête with the great southern precipice falling 14,000 feet almost sheer to the Rupal nala below, he came to the last gendarme, overhanging the ridge and about forty feet high. This he traversed by its face, and regained the ridge by a crack.

Buhl crawled to the summit on all fours just before seven o'clock, having been climbing for over sixteen hours. The sun disappeared and at once the temperature began to fall. The rocks, however, retained some of the warmth of the day, and he started down; after going a short distance he bivouacked on the ridge, taking two tablets of Padutine as a deterrent to frostbite when his feet began to go dead. He continued descending at 4 a.m. on the 4th, and, moving with extreme caution, passed the Bazin Gap. By traversing the fore peak he reached the Diamir Gap (25,300) by noon, weak through lack of food. His right foot was frostbitten and he suffered from thirst and the illusion that he was accompanied by a second climber. Only with the greatest difficulty and with the aid of another Pervitine tablet did he reach the Silver Saddle at six o'clock. He was helped into Camp V by Ertl. The weather had fortunately been kind throughout the two days of his ordeal.

It is interesting to compare this success with the attempt of Schneider and Aschenbrenner on 6 July 1934 when they reached a height of 25,280 feet and thought that they were within four or five hours of the summit. This distance took Buhl ten hours. Had they then gone on they would have been caught by the storm on the ridge beyond the Bazin Gap, and nothing could have saved them during the days that followed. They would have added two more to the toll of thirty-one lives claimed by this vengeful mountain before the summit was reached.

Another point of interest is the fact that Buhl had been a slow acclimatizer. On the first attempt he suffered from altitude before reaching Camp IV and on 28 June during the traverse of the Rakhiot Peak carried no load and did little step-cutting. Yet on the all-important two days, 3 and 4 July, he showed the greatest endurance, after a short night with little sleep. He was on the move from about half-past two on the morning of the 3rd until seven o'clock on the evening of the 4th, with an almost sleepless night of six hours in his ridge bivouac at 26,000 feet. His reaction to altitude seems to have been very similar to that of Odell on Everest in 1924.

It is strange that Rainer should have developed phlebitis on Nanga Parbat, much as Gilkey had done on K2 in 1953. It has been suggested that Wolfe in 1939 suffered from the same complaint, though there was no one to diagnose it. Fortunately the return from Camp IV on Nanga Parbat is a different proposition from that down the precipitous slopes of the Abruzzi ridge.

These expeditions to K2 and Nanga Parbat both had to manage without the aid of trained Sherpa porters. On both attempts the Hunza men proved themselves reliable and capable when well led. 'If these people are properly handled,' writes Frauenberger, 'they will do anything.'[1]

---

[1] The above summary is compiled from the first accounts, supplemented by the general narrative in *The Mountain World* (1954), edited by Marcel Kurz, pp. 93 ff.; and Buhl's account in *H.J.* xviii (1954) 130 ff. Clock times and heights are not always consistent; as far as possible the latter have been adjusted to those given on Finsterwalder's map. Paul Bauer's *Das Ringen um den Nanga Parbat, 1856–1953* gives the story of the mountain over nearly a hundred years, but reached me too late to help. An English translation is in preparation under the title of *The Siege of Nanga Parbat.*

# 5. Nepal: Dhaulagiri (26,795) and Annapurna (26,492)

NEPAL had now opened her boundaries to mountaineers. A foretaste of coming events occurred in 1949 when a Swiss expedition, which had been refused permission to enter Nepal to reconnoitre Dhaulagiri, obtained the consent of the Nepalese Government to visit the extreme north-east corner of the country. It comprised René Dittert, Madame Lohner, and A. Sutter, all of whom had been on the 1947 expedition to Gangotri, Dr. Wyss-Dunant and two professional guides from Geneva, J. Pargätzi and A. Rubi.

The party entered Nepal by the well-known track by Dzongri and the Kang La and then followed Freshfield's route in the opposite direction to Kangbachen. They had with them a number of Sherpa porters, most of them untrained, for crossing the Kang La, but amongst them were five experienced men for high altitude climbing: Dawa Thondup (No. 49), Ajeeba (No. 10), Ang Dawa IV (No. 152), Pasang Dawa Lama (No. 139), and Gyalgen II Mikchen (No. 57).

A very useful reconnaissance of this corner of Nepal was carried out. Kangbachen (25,782) was reconnoitred, but without much prospect of a successful ascent, and the western wall of the great ridge running north from Kangchenjunga where it forms the head of the west Langpo glacier. Here the summit ridge of the Pyramid Peak (c. 23,400) on the Nepal-Sikkim border was climbed, by way of 'the Sphinx,' by Dittert, Sutter, Gyalgen, Ajeeba, and Dawa Thondup on 6 June. This peak had been attempted unsuccessfully from bases on the Sikkim side by C. R. Cooke, Spencer Chapman, and Harrison in 1936 and by Paidar, Schmaderer, and Grob in 1939.

The party also examined Drohmo (c. 23,300) on the western side of the Ginsang glacier, but finding no practicable route consoled themselves with an outlier which they named Tang Kongma (c. 20,500). Next they explored the unknown head of the Tsitsima nala, crossed the Chabuk La into Tibet and attempted Nupchu (c. 23,160) from the north. The map all along the watershed on the Tibetan side is quite unreliable, and it is not surprising that in the short time available they did not succeed. It is to be hoped that they brought back useful sketch-maps of this region.[1]

Tilman was also quickly on the scene the moment there was a chance of exploring the Great Himalaya in Nepal. He had visited Bogda Ola in the Tien Shan and Muztagh Ata on the Pamirs with Shipton since the war, and now in 1949 obtained permission to visit the headwaters of the Trisuli Gandaki in Central Nepal (map page 32). He had with him Peter Lloyd, who had been to Everest with him in 1938, O. Polunin, and H. Scott, all three scientists, and four Sherpas under Tenzing (No. 48). The Trisuli Gandaki[2] breaks through the Great Himalaya at the old frontier fort of Rasua Garhi, about fifteen miles from the Tibetan town of Kyirong, where Peter Aufschnaiter and Harrer had spent several months after their escape from the Dehra Dun internment camp. During their stay here Aufschnaiter had made a sketch-map of the Tibetan side of the frontier. Tilman's explorations were mostly in the Langtang Khola, which enters the Trisuli Gandaki about twelve miles below Rasua Garhi. The Indian surveyors in 1925 had shown the Langtang Khola as hemmed in by the Langtang Himal and the great mountain Gosainthan (26,291) standing well to the north of the watershed. Tilman's and Lloyd's explorations show that in all probability the Langtang Khola is fed by a large glacier which descends direct from Gosainthan, and that the watershed, and the boundary between Tibet and Nepal, are both farther north than expected. No high peaks were seriously attempted on this expedition, but a number of lesser points were reached for reconnaissance and photography, and Paldor (19,451) was climbed during an exploration of the Chilime Khola. Apart from topographical results, considerable collections were made by the scientific members of the party.[3]

Tilman was off again into Nepal in 1950. This time he obtained

[1] *H.J.* xvi (1950–1) 25.

[2] Like several other large rivers crossing into Nepal from Tibet, it is here known as the *Bhote Kosi*.

[3] *A.J.* lvii (1950) 305; *G.J.* cxvi (1950) 172.

permission to visit the western part of the Gandaki section of the Nepal Himalaya. He chose the region where the Marsyandi river breaks through the Great Himalaya with the Lamjung and Annapurna Himals on the west and the mountain massifs of Himal Chuli (25,801) and Manaslu (26,658) standing up to the east. He was persuaded to take five other mountaineers, in order to begin building up a nucleus of climbers with Himalayan experience. D. G. Lowndes, botanist, and J. O. M. Roberts already had some; R. C. Evans, J. H. Emlyn Jones, and W. P. Packard—a New Zealand Rhodes Scholar at Oxford, had none.

Because of unforeseen delays the party reached the Marsyandi a little later than planned and set up their camp at Thonje, north of the Great Himalaya, where the Marsyandi is joined by a large tributary, the Dudh Khola, draining the north slopes of Manaslu. This mountain was reconnoitred from the Dudh Khola, but Tilman did not feel justified in attempting it with an untrained party. He therefore ascended the Marsyandi to the village of Manangbhot, and examined the northern side of the Annapurna Himal, selecting Annapurna IV (24,688), as the one most suitable for his purpose. They had with them four Sherpas, among whom were Gyalgen Mikchen II (No. 57) and Da Namgyal II (No. 157).

Manangbhot is at about 11,500 feet. On 7 June, after relaying loads, Camp I was set up at 18,000 feet. Above this a thousand feet of moderately steep snow led to an ice-step about eighty feet high, up which a staircase had to be cut and fixed with ropes. Camp II was pitched above it and on the 13th Camp III was established and occupied at about 21,000 feet on the main ridge. So far the weather had been moderately good; but it now became more unsettled, though Camp IV was set up at about 22,500 feet on the 15th.

On 17 June Packard and Evans made a first attempt, and after two and a half hours' climbing were below the final shoulder, which is at about 24,000 feet; they had to turn back because of threatening weather, which later turned into a storm. A second attempt was made the following day, but Roberts and Gyalgen turned back on account of numbed feet. On a third attempt on the 19th, the shoulder was passed but at about six hundred feet from the summit the party had to give up from exhaustion.

After this attempt some interesting exploration was carried out north of the Marsyandi on the Tibetan frontier where two new passes were crossed into the basin of the Kali Gandaki; the return journey being by the pilgrim centre of Muktinath.

The last month of this expedition was mostly spent reconnoitring the approaches to Manaslu and Himal Chuli.[1]

The Himalayan Committee of the French Alpine Club, under the presidency of M. Lucien Devies, was also fortunate to obtain a permit to visit the mountains of Central Nepal in 1950. The French chose the mountains on either side of the gorge of the Kali Gandaki, immediately to the west of the region explored by Tilman. This was to be entirely a climbing venture, a 'do-or-die' affair for the 'honour of France.' Two alternative objectives were chosen: Dhaulagiri I (26,795) and Annapurna I (26,492), both over eight thousand metres, a factor in their choice. They are the culminating summits of the Himals on either side of the gorge. Their approaches were unknown, since the Indians engaged on the Nepal reconnaissance in 1925–7 did not visit the inner glaciers of the Great Himalaya. It is a curious trait among some mountaineers who set out to explore new ground that they expect to have a map of it accurate in detail; they like to have it both ways: to be the first there and to have had surveyors there before them.

A strong comparatively small party of nine was assembled by the Committee under the capable leadership of Maurice Herzog. It comprised Jean Couzy, Marcel Schatz, Louis Lachenal, Lionel Terray, and Gaston Rébuffat, several of whom were professional guides, Marcel Ichac, camera-man and reporter, Jacques Oudet, surgeon, and Francis de Noyelle, liaison officer and interpreter. Eight experienced Sherpas were brought from Darjeeling: Ang Tharkay (No. 19), Dawa Thondup (No. 49), Ang Dawa IV (No. 152), Ang Tsering III ('Pansy', No. 51), Ajeeba (No. 10), Aila (No. 61), Sarki (No. 151), and Phu Tharkey (No. 153).

The party flew out to India by air and entered Nepal from the metre-gauge railhead at Nautanwa, crossed the Terai to Butwal and followed the Kali Gandaki to Tukucha, which was reached on

[1] Tilman's later travels this year with the Houston party to the Sola Khumbu district are mentioned later (page 325).

21 April. Here the river breaks through the Great Himalaya, and the last part of the journey was along the pilgrim route to Muktinath, one of the main trade-routes between Nepal and Tibet.

Three weeks were allotted to the exploration of the two massifs, the first half of this period being devoted to the east and north-east sides of Dhaulagiri, the second half to the approaches to Annapurna.

Dhaulagiri, as the result of the reconnaissance, was found to have a long south ridge, a short north-west spur and a high short east ridge breaking at a rock shoulder into north-east and south-east ridges. The north-east ridge forms a barrier to approach from the east and terminates at the Tukucha Peak (c. 22,687). Attempts were made to reach the north-east and south-east ridges, and two longer reconnaissances were made by the Dambush Khola, over a col on the north-east ridge of Tukucha Peak; neither party was able to reach the northern foot of Dhaulagiri, and it was decided to concentrate on Annapurna, which offered better prospects of success.

Between 7 and 14 May Herzog, Ichac and Rébuffat explored the branch valley which enters the Kali Gandaki near Thinigaon, followed it over a pass to Manangbhot in the Marsyandi, but found themselves cut off from Annapurna I by a mountain barrier. It now became obvious that if any success was to be won a way must be found into the head of the Miristi Khola by a route partially explored at the end of April. The Miristi Khola is a large tributary of the Kali Gandaki which it reaches at Tatopani, some twenty miles below Tukucha, after passing through deep and difficult gorges.

The attempt now became a race against time. The problem here is largely one of weather, with conditions not unlike those of Everest. In a normal year, if there is such a thing, the best season for climbing would appear to be between 15 May and 15 June; but there is always a danger of an early monsoon.

By 18 May a base camp had been set up near the snout of the north Annapurna glacier. The last four days had been unsettled. A first attempt was made to climb the mountain by the north-west spur, but after two nights on its ridge it was judged to be too long and difficult.

Base Camp was now moved up the north Annapurna glacier and pitched on its north side below an ice-fall. From above this camp a possible route was seen across the upper part of the glacier to an ice-terrace at the foot of the broken north face of the mountain. Above this terrace it appeared that a way could be found across the face to an ice-wall, which formed the edge of a sickle-shaped summit ice-cap, up which there appeared to be no technical difficulties. The main uncertainties of the route lay between 19,500 feet and 23,000 feet, which was all steep ice and snow, with danger from avalanches at places, and at the points of junction with the 'Sickle.'

Camps I (c. 16,750) and II (c. 19,350) were quickly set up, and a message was sent to the base party at Tukucha to bring up all personnel and equipment for the assault. Camp III (c. 21,650) was pitched in a crevasse blocked by powder-snow. Camp IV (c. 23,500) was carried up by Herzog and two Sherpas, Dawa Thondup and Ang Dawa. Herzog in his account is rather critical of Dawa Thondup's unsteadiness; but this Sherpa had reached this altitude from 8000 feet without a day's rest, carrying loads each day—not by any means an inconsiderable achievement for a Sherpa who was now forty-three years of age.[1]

By 31 May all camps were ready as far as Camp IV. Terray, Rébuffat and the two Sherpas, Ang Tsering and Aila, having spent an exhausting day improving the track to Camp IV, where they spent a bad night, returned on this day to Camp II, meeting Herzog on the way up to Camp III with Lachenal, Ang Tharkay, and Sarki. The weather had been favourable during the placing of the camp, but most of the Frenchmen had felt the altitude severely and had acclimatized so slowly that they had had to go down to Camp II to recover. It was now a race with the monsoon, which was said to have arrived in Calcutta and was therefore expected within three or four days. Herzog determined to go all out for the summit within this short period.

[1] It is difficult to understand what Herzog means by Dawa Thondup's 'inexperience' on snow and ice. This Sherpa was on Everest in 1933 and 1936, on Nanga Parbat in 1934, on Saltoro Kangri in 1935, with Cooke in Sikkim in 1937, on Masherbrum in 1938 and on K2 in 1939. He had received the Order of the German Red Cross for good work on Nanga Parbat, and wore the Tiger's badge. Since the war he had been on several expeditions, and later this year (1950) he reached the summit of Abi Gamin (24,180). Herzog is also very much mistaken in saying that it was the first time Ang Tharkay and Sarki had done any climbing on ice and been obliged to get up vertical walls.

On 1 June, after a restful night at Camp III, Herzog, Lachenal, Ang Tharkay, and Sarki went on rapidly to Camp IV, struck one of the tents there and carried it on to the edge of the Sickle; here at Camp IVA the two Frenchmen spent the night, while Ang Tharkay and Sarki returned to Camp IV; the others in Camps II and III were getting ready to move up in support.

The next day Ang Tharkay and Sarki struck the tent at Camp IV, carried it up to IVA and with Herzog and Lachenal traversed and climbed the Sickle as high as 24,600 feet. Here one tent was set up for Herzog and Lachenal, and the two Sherpas, their task accomplished, went back. Schatz and Couzy with Ang Dawa and Phu Tharkay moved up from Camp III to IV, while Terray and Rébuffat with Ang Tsering and Aila carried supplies to Camp III, struck a tent there and brought it up to Camp IV. The two climbers at Camp V were now well supported.

On the 3rd Herzog and Lachenal, after a stormy night, started for the summit at six o'clock in brilliantly fine but very cold weather. They reached it at 2 p.m.

All had gone well to this point. Soon, however, the sky became overcast, and perhaps they delayed too long before starting down. They became separated, and Herzog, who lost his gloves, reached Camp V with difficulty and with badly frostbitten hands. Lachenal missed the camp and went past it in the storm that was now blowing up. Fortunately Terray and Rébuffat had moved up with a second tent from Camp IV in support during the day, found him and brought him in to Camp V.

The descent the following day was difficult and dangerous. Falling snow covered the tracks and reduced visibility. In their frostbitten condition progress was slow, and they lost the way. At nightfall Lachenal fell through a crevasse; the rest climbed down to him and here they spent the night. They had only one sleeping-bag between them; it was shared by Terray and Lachenal; all huddled together for warmth. In the morning snow from an avalanche half buried them in their crevasse, Rébuffat and Terray were snow-blind, Lachenal and Herzog so badly frostbitten that they could not put on their boots.

In this condition they were found by Schatz who guided them into Camp IVA, and from there they descended with the utmost difficulty to Camp IV which the Sherpas had re-established. Fortunately the weather remained fine. From here they went on down with the aid of the Sherpas, Herzog and Lachenal both terribly frostbitten. At one place Herzog and his two Sherpas, Aila and 'Pansy', were carried down five hundred feet by an avalanche; but they survived it by a miracle and with the help of Phu Tharkay and Ang Dawa, who came up to meet them, they reached Camp II, where all came under the care of the surgeon.

Annapurna I was the first mountain over eight thousand metres to be climbed to the summit. It was a fine achievement, especially since it was both reconnoitred and climbed during the first attempt. The organization and equipment had been prepared with great fore-thought and care. Success was due primarily to the determination of Herzog, but credit for the achievement is shared by all members of the party. There was very little margin of safety, and Herzog quite frankly states he was prepared to reach the summit or die in the attempt. He would have died but for the close support of his friends and of the Sherpas. Fortunately the monsoon, expected on 5 June, did not reach the area until some days after the party had reached its base.[1] But a heavy price was paid in fingers and toes, several of which had to be amputated in the weeks that followed.[2]

Climbing reconnaissances and attempts have multiplied since 1951. Tilman's visit to Annapurna IV and Manaslu in 1950 was followed by a Japanese reconnaissance party of six, including two scientists and a doctor.[3] It was led by Dr. K. Imanishi, and flew out from Tokyo to Calcutta on 25 August 1952. From there they flew to Darjeeling, where they engaged six Sherpas,[4] and then flew on, via Patna, to Katmandu. The party reached Tilman's old base camp in the Marsy-andi valley on 5 October. An attempt on Annapurna IV was foiled by heavy fresh snow and lack of acclimatization, and the party gave up the attempt at about 19,000 feet.

---

[1] As mentioned above, Tilman's party was on Annapurna IV at 23,000 feet or over on 17, 18, and 19 June (page 314).

[2] Maurice Herzog: *Annapurna* (London, 1952).

[3] Dr. K. Imanishi (aged fifty-nine), J. Taguchi (thirty-nine), M. Takagi (thirty-nine), K. Hayashi (twenty-six), S. Nakao, and S. Takebushi (forty-five).

[4] Gyalgen II Mikchen (No. 57), Ang Tsering III (No. 51), Sarki (No. 151), Ang Tsering IV (No. 101), Anno, and Dakko.

The main objective of the reconnaissance was Manaslu (26,658). This was now examined from the Dudh Khola; its south-western, western, and north-western flanks were ruled out as impracticable, a conclusion reached by Tilman in 1950. The party then crossed the Larkya Bhanjyang pass (17,102) to the head of the Buri Gandaki (Buriganga), and camp was set up on the Larkya glacier. Reconnaissances from here and from the Manaslu glacier, which drains towards Sama on the Buri Gandaki, showed that a possible route could be found at the head of the Manaslu glacier to the North Col (c. 23,300), between the main summit and its north peak, whence the summit might be reached.

A full-scale expedition was organized by the Himalayan Committee of the Japanese Alpine Club for the pre-monsoon period of 1953. It was well equipped and comprised fifteen members: Y. Mita (leader, aged fifty-two), M. Takagi (leader of the climbing party, aged forty), J. Taguchi (forty), H. Kato (forty-one), K. Kato (thirty-one), M. Murayama (thirty-four), J. Yamada (thirty), J. Muraki (twenty-nine), J. Ishizaka (twenty-four), S. Takebushi (forty-six), Dr. H. Tatsunuma (doctor, thirty-seven), Dr. H. Yamazaki (assistant doctor, twenty-eight), S. Nakao (botanist), Professor J. Kawakita (geographer, thirty-two), and T. Yoda (thirty-six). The party was large for the purpose of climbing, but scientific work and mapping were included in the programme, and it was also hoped to gain Himalayan experience for the future, Fifteen Sherpas were engaged.

Base camp was set up on the north bank of the Manaslu glacier at 12,625 feet and the attack began on 21 April. Camps I (15,100), II (16,400), III (17,700), and IV, at the Naike Col (18,400), between the Manaslu and Larkya glaciers, were established by 3 May. The ice-fall of the upper Manaslu glacier was now tackled; three camps were sited on it: Camp V (19,350), Camp VI (20,350), and Camp VII beyond the seracs (21,650). On 15 May the North Col was reached and Camp VIII (23,300) established.

The first attempt from here was begun on 17 May by Takagi, K. Kato, and Yamada with four Sherpas, but in unsettled weather they only reached 24,300 feet. Camp VIII was insufficiently stocked for a protracted stay in stormy weather and the party returned to rest. High wind and bad weather drove them back to Camp IV.

A second assault began in fine weather on 26 May, Camp VIII on the col was reached on the 28th, and on the 30th Camp IX (24,600) was occupied by K. Kato, Yamada, and Ishizaka, with Yamazaki and five Sherpas in support at Camp VIII. On 31 May, which was fine and windless, the three climbers set out for the summit at 7 a.m., but after reaching 25,400 feet in five hours, they realized that they were too far from the summit to reach it, they wisely withdrew, and the attempt was abandoned.

Dr. Takagi says that neither technical difficulties, bad weather, nor insufficient acclimatization were to blame; their failure was caused by lack of supplies and fuel in the high camps, due to an underestimate of the distance to be traversed.[1]

A short but valuable reconnaissance of the Annapurna Himal by B. R. Goodfellow, Honorary Secretary of the Alpine Club, and F. Yates was made at the end of March 1953. It was possible now to fly to Pokhara, the chief town of this central Nepalese province. In a little over a fortnight a close reconnaissance of the upper gorges south of the Annapurna Himal was not possible, but the geographical notes made of the approaches are well worth studying by any future expedition. There would appear to be problems here comparable with those of the penetration of the Rishiganga gorge to the sanctuary of Nanda Devi.[2]

An exhaustive reconnaissance of Dhaulagiri was made by a Swiss party in the same year. It was led by Bernhard Lauterburg, who, though sixty years of age, was physically strong and capable. It was a small party of seven, including André Roch, with great experience of the Himalaya, P. Braun, M. Eichelberg, R. Schatz, H. Huss, and R. Pfisterer as doctor. The party left Switzerland on 15 March, reached Bombay by sea and Pokhara in Nepal by air on 13 April, having collected six Sherpas under the experienced Ang Tharkay on the way.

Progress now slowed down. Leaving Pokhara with seventy ponies they crossed the Kali Gandaki at Beni and from there onwards up the Mayangdi valley were dependent on local porters.

[1] *The Mountain World* (1954), page 63; *H.J.* xviii (1954) 176.
[2] *H.J.* xviii (1954) 81.

The Mayangdi Khola is the great right-bank tributary which joins the Kali Gandaki at Beni; it drains the southern flanks of the Dhaulagiri Himal, and has a source in the glacier hidden behind the northern flanks of Dhaulagiri I. From Muri, the last village up the Mayangdi, it was unknown trackless country even to the locals, and a way had to be cut through the thick bamboo bush. It is indeed surprising that the existing map is as good as it is, considering the difficulties. At last on 2 May a base camp was set up below the tongue of the Mayangdi glacier, all but six of the local men were paid off, and henceforth all relaying of camps and stores had to be done by these six (three of whom soon decided that they had had enough), the Sherpas and the Swiss.

A reconnaissance from the slopes on the north side of the glacier, which gave a complete view of the north face of the mountain, showed a difficult but possible route by which to attack it. Camp I was set up at 14,750 feet; but it was a two-days' march from the base and ninety loads had to be transported by relays. On 13 May Camp II (16,730) was sited and all Sherpas were employed until the 17th establishing and stocking it. By the 19th a site for Camp IV at 19,700 feet had been found and Camp III had been stocked. It was arduous work which was beginning to tell on the climbers, but the weather was usually fine for the first half of the day. Eichelberg and Schatz turned back at noon on the 21st, having reached 20,700 feet in loose powder-snow. Huss and Schatz now had to go down to Camp I for a rest, but on the 23rd Roch, Eichelberg, and Braun established Camp V at about 21,500 feet more or less hanging it to the face just before the first rock ledges; from here on the 27th Roch and Eichelberg reached an altitude of 23,400 feet before turning back because of the difficulties of the ascent at that altitude.

Everything now depended on being able to find a camp-site higher than Camp V. On 28 May Braun and Schatz, with three Sherpas, Gyalgen II, Ila Tenzing, and Kamin, reached Camp V. Lauterburg went with them to 21,000 feet, a fine achievement for one of sixty, and then returned to Camp IV.

The five spent the evening in two small tents, and started at 2 a.m. on the 19th. Ila Tenzing and his two Sherpas with the heavy oxygen apparatus led at first, but at about 23,000 feet it was decided to send the Sherpas down. The Swiss took over their loads. The rock-climbing here was extremely difficult; loose powder-snow lay on the steep slaty slabs; it was very slippery. There were no holds, the rock was unweathered, smooth, and without joints in which pitons could be driven. They reached an altitude of about 25,000 feet before turning back.

The adventure was not quite over. While the three Sherpas were descending to Camp V, one of them slipped and all three fell in a cloud of snow, a distance of 1600 feet. By a miracle they came to rest above the seracs of the ice-wall, below the level of Camp IV. Preparations were being made at Camp IV to rescue them, when they picked themselves up and started for Camp IV on their own. Except for scratches and bruises they were unhurt.

Before leaving the area, two additional reconnaissances were made: one to the North Col, on the north-east ridge between Dhaulagiri and the Tukucha Peak, which had been attempted by the French from the east in 1950, the other to the South Col on the south-west ridge, from which the great southern face could be seen. The north-east ridge from the North Col was considered extremely difficult, and the aspect of the south face of Dhaulagiri was described by Schatz as 'one of the most horrifying we had ever seen.' All sides of Dhaulagiri have now been examined.

Roch sums up the reconnaissance by saying that the party tried 'the only apparently practicable route. The climbing of Dhaulagiri will demand a new technique for the Himalaya, such as the dynamiting of a camp-site, which at the present time seems far-fetched, but in fifty years' time may perhaps be accepted as commonplace by all climbers.' Shades of Mummery! I hope such sacrilegious methods will never be used, nor that an atom bomb will be used to demolish it![1]

One other piece of exploration deserves mention. In 1953 W. H. Murray, who had led the Scottish expedition to Kumaun in 1950, and had been with Shipton to the south side of Everest in 1951, together with J. B. Tyson, who had climbed Gangotri I and III in 1952, reconnoitred the northern approaches to Api (23,399) and

---

[1] This summary of the Swiss expedition is compiled from Roch's brief account in *H.J.* xviii (1954) 118 ff. and Schatz's in *The Mountain World* (1954), pages 71–81.

Nampa (22,162) in the extreme north-west of Nepal. They were joined by Bentley Beetham, a veteran of Everest 1924. The approaches had first been looked at by Longstaff in 1905, but Murray had to gain access by the Nepal side of the Kali, because of restrictions to travel in Kumaun. Delays occurred in obtaining permission from Nepal and they were hampered by rain in the last half of June. But they saw enough to appreciate the difficulties of attempting the mountain from the north.[1]

[1] No detailed account of this expedition has I believe yet been published. A general account appeared in *Blackwood's Magazine*, April 1954.

## 5. The Ascent of Everest

THE post-war and final phase of the epic of Everest begins in 1950, when the American, Oscar R. Houston, in the late spring of that year unexpectedly obtained permission to travel through eastern Nepal to the southern side of the mountain. Since the war the joint Himalayan Committee of the Alpine Club and Royal Geographical Society, successor to the old Mount Everest Committee, had sought permission for an expedition to enter Tibet and Nepal in vain. It is beyond my power, and would be unwise, to attempt to describe in great detail the events of the four adventurous years which led to the final achievement (map page 158).

There were milestones on the journey to the summit. First, the unprepared reconnaissance of Charles Houston and H. W. Tilman at the end of 1950. Second, the brilliant reconnaissance of Eric Shipton's party after the monsoon in 1951. Third, the two Swiss attempts, before and after the monsoon in 1952, and Shipton's expedition to Cho Oyu, which gathered physiological and other data of great importance. And last, the achievement of John Hunt's incomparable team.

The Houston party set out primarily to visit the district of Sola Khumbu, but it included Oscar Houston's son Charles, who had been joint organizer of the Nanda Devi climb in 1936 and who had successfully reconnoitred the Abruzzi ridge on K2 in 1938. Tilman, leader of the 1938 Everest expedition, companion of Charles Houston on Nanda Devi, and with great Himalayan experience, was also invited. These two, Tilman and Houston, after the party had reached Namche Bazar, the centre of the Sola Khumbu country, the home of the Sherpas, went ahead up the Imja Khola and pitched a camp on the Khumbu glacier in order to examine the approach to the Western Cwm, first seen by Mallory in 1921. In the short time at their disposal their reconnaissance was inconclusive. The great ice-fall that poured from the Cwm between the precipices of the western ridge of Everest and those of Nuptse could, they felt, be forced, though its passage would offer many hazards and obstacles to laden porters. They were unable in the time at their disposal to see the slopes below the South Col. An interesting observation was the absence of snow on the summit of Everest in the middle of November. Houston, as a result, suggested that conditions for climbing might possibly be better at this period than in May or June, though the high wind, great cold, and short daylight hours might make the climb impossible. There is little doubt that the winter snowfall in the Sola Khumbu villages is much less than that at the same altitude in the western Himalaya, which are more affected by western depressions.

The inception of the 1951 reconnaissance was due to W. H. Murray, Michael Ward, and Campbell Secord, who put forward the proposition for an autumn reconnaissance to the Himalayan Committee. They chose as leader Eric Shipton, whose experience of Everest, and of the Himalaya, was second to none.

The party comprised Shipton, Murray, Ward, T. Bourdillon, and two New Zealanders—E. Hillary and E. Riddiford, who had been climbing during the summer in the Kumaun Himalaya.[1] As in the previous year, the party entered eastern Nepal from the railhead at Jogbani (map page 34). Ang Tharkay with fourteen Sherpas joined them here on 25 August, and after slow progress through Nepal during the monsoon they reached Namche Bazar on 22 September and their base camp at about 18,000 feet on the Khumbu glacier at the foot of Pumo-ri a week later.

The members of this expedition made a complete reconnaissance of the ice-fall entrance to the Western Cwm. They had set out to find the answers to four questions. Could a way be found up the ice-fall entrance to the Western Cwm, which would be safe for laden porters? Were the slopes leading from the Cwm to the South Col climbable? Was the south-east ridge from the col as easy as it appeared from air-photographs? Were the autumn conditions likely to be more favourable than those in spring?

As they faced the ice-fall from the Khumbu glacier the left-hand side was covered by avalanche debris fallen from the west ridge of Everest, and it was considered too dangerous a route for laden

[1] Page 295.

porters. A way was found, more difficult, but safer, through the maze of seracs and crevasses to the right of this danger zone. On the first reconnaissance early in September some members were insufficiently acclimatized for the strenuous work between 19,000 and 20,000 feet, but after spending more than two weeks exploring and climbing in the districts west and south-east of Everest, the party returned on 20 October to try again. A great change had occurred in the condition of the ice-fall. Over a large area the seracs had collapsed and the ice was still in movement and dangerous.

With great difficulty a way was pioneered through this ice-maze, and by the end of the month the party reached its top at over 20,000 feet. Beyond this point they were held up by an enormous crevasse which could only be turned by traversing the danger area to the left. They had, however, seen enough to answer the first of their four questions and to give a fair estimate of the others.

Before leaving the area a considerable amount of subsidiary exploration was carried out to the west of Everest. New passes were made and the mountains, ridges, and glaciers as far west as Gauri Sankar (23,440) were explored, all of which added greatly to our knowledge of the Nepal Himalaya.

There was little doubt after this fine exploration by Shipton's party that this southern route to Everest held several important advantages over the old northern route through Tibet. On the old route the technical difficulties begin with the climbing of the North Col, from about 21,000 feet to 23,000 feet, after which, in the absence of high wind and storm, there are no serious problems until about 25,500 feet. Then comes the exhausting—and, in conditions of unconsolidated powder-snow and high wind, the dangerous— traverse of the down-tilted slabs to the couloir at about 28,000 feet. The final climb of a thousand feet by rib or couloir to the summit is technically extremely difficult and perhaps impossible at that altitude.

By the Khumbu route, on the other hand, the problems are set at different altitudes. The difficult ice-fall, from about 18,200 feet to 20,000 feet, had been climbed and the route to the foot of Lhotse at about 22,000 feet appeared to be straightforward. As far as could be seen, it appeared possible to reach the South Col at about 25,850 feet; technical difficulties should be more easily surmountable below that altitude than above it. From the col to the summit the strata are favourable for climbing, and on a fine day sunshine makes an early start and a longer climbing day possible.

This expedition of 1951 was the eighth expedition to Everest sponsored by the Royal Geographical Society and Alpine Club. It had been intended as a prelude to an assault in 1952, but it was found that the Swiss Foundation for Alpine Research had already obtained the consent of the Nepal Government to make an attempt, and the two sponsoring bodies agreed that the Swiss should go in 1952 and the British in 1953. In the meanwhile the Himalayan Committee wisely decided to send an expedition to the neighbouring mountain Cho Oyu, to try out members for the following year and to gain further experience and more physiological data.

The Swiss made two attempts in 1952, the first before the monsoon, the second after. There were twelve members in the first party: Dr. E. Wyss-Dunant (leader), René Dittert, André Roch, Raymond Lambert, Dr. Gabriel Chevalley, René Aubert, Léon Flory, Jean-Jacques Asper, Ernest Hofstetter, Professor A. Lombard (geologist), A. Zimmermann (botanist), and Mme. Lobsiger-Dellenbach (ethnologist). Of these twelve, eight only were effectives for the assault.

The party flew from Switzerland to Bombay in two sections, on 13 and 20 March. They reached New Delhi by air on the 22nd, and Katmandu on the 24th. Three days later they started again and reached Namche Bazar on 13 April. Base Camp was established on the lower Khumbu glacier at 16,570 feet a week later.

Camp I was established on the glacier at 17,225 feet[1] on 25 April, none too early in view of the long distance to be reconnoitred and climbed before the end of May. There had been little time to acclimatize. The first attempt to climb the ice-fall was unsuccessful, but by placing a Camp II (18,374) half-way up, and using the avalanche couloir to the left, close under Everest's west ridge, they

[1] The heights given here are from the summary account given in *The Mountain World* (1953) (edited by Marcel Kurz). There are considerable discrepancies between them and those of the expeditions of 1951 and 1953. In the absence of a precise survey all must be considered approximate. The heights of Hunt's camps in 1953 as given by him are II, 19,400; III, 20,200; IV, 21,200; V, 22,000.

reached the top of the ice-fall on 4 May and occupied Camp III (19,358) two days later.

The strenuous work of stocking this camp was carried on by the Sherpas for the next ten days while the climbers went forward, establishing Camp IV (21,162) in the middle of the Western Cwm on 9 May, and Camp V (22,639) at its eastern end on the 11th.

The north-west face of Lhotse is draped by a broad glacier which descends to the Cwm. An icy couloir leads up to the South Col at 25,854 feet, edged on its north side at its upper end by a rocky outcrop, now known as the Geneva Spur. Stores for the assault were carried up from Camp V and dumped near the foot of this spur, ropes being fixed between this point and Camp V to ease the task, but no camp was pitched.

Dittert, who was leader of the climbing party, decided that the camps were sufficiently stocked to begin the assault from Camp V on 24 May. There was still 6000 feet of unreconnoitred ascent above 23,000 feet before them. The plan was to place Camp VI on the South Col, roughly half-way between Camp V and the summit, and one more, Camp VII, at 27,500 feet, or higher if possible, on the south-east ridge. The base for the assault was Camp V. The first attempt was to be made by Lambert, Flory, Aubert, and the seven Sherpas, Tenzing (No. 48), Da Namgyal II (No. 157), Pasang Phuttar II, Phu Tharkay (No. 153), Ang Nurbu, Mingma Dorje, and Ajeeba (No. 10).[1]

Up till now the weather had been favourable. The assault party started up from Camp V at 9 a.m. on the 24th, but before long it was overtaken by bad weather and driven back to camp. The 25th dawned fine and the party again set out, with the Sherpas lightly laden. One of them, Ajeeba, was unwell and had to return before reaching the dump at the Geneva Spur. The rest reached the dump, picked up the loads, and resumed the climb at about 12.30. They were now carrying heavy loads and altitude began to tell. In the afternoon, at about 25,300 feet, Ang Nurbu and Mingma Dorje had

---

[1] Da Namgyal was twenty-seven, Pasang Phuttar II, a new man, twenty-one, Phu Tharkay thirty, Mingma Dorje twenty-five, and Ajeeba a comparative veteran of forty-one. Tenzing, the sirdar, was at this time thirty-five according to Himalayan Club records, thirty-eight according to Sir John Hunt.

to descend because of incipient frostbite, and their loads had to be taken over by the three Swiss. Altitude and the heavy loads much reduced the rate of climbing, and the seven men failed to reach the col before dark. Platforms for two tents were cut in the icy slope and here they spent the night.

On the 26th Camp VI was set up in a high wind on the col, but the day was spent in bringing up more supplies from the dump. This arduous work was too much for the porters, and on the 27th Da Namgyal, Pasang Phuttar, and Phu Tharkay were too exhausted to continue and had to go down.

This was fatal to success. The three Swiss and Tenzing could no longer hope to carry tents, sleeping-bags, and supplies for a high camp on the ridge. A great effort was made on the 27th to carry enough up to form a dump for a second assault. At 27,560 feet Tenzing proposed that he and Lambert should spend a night in the single tent at that spot and go for the summit the next day, while Flory and Aubert returned to the col.

This bold suggestion was approved, but it was a forlorn hope. Lambert and Tenzing spent a dreadful night, without sleeping-bags, with little food, and only a small quantity of snow melted by candle-flame to drink; neither dared to sleep for fear of frostbite, against which they fought by thumping and rubbing their limbs throughout the long hours.

That they had the will to start upwards again at six o'clock on the 28th is astounding. The ascent was not difficult, but the weather worsened; at about 28,200 feet they could go no farther. It had taken them five and a half hours to climb 650 feet.

Both were in a state of mental and physical exhaustion, and deterioration was increasing with every hour. Only with the utmost determination did they regain the col in the evening.

The four at the col had now shot their bolt. On their way down to Camp V on the 29th they met Dittert, Roch, Asper, Chevalley, and Hofstetter ascending with Sherpas for the second attempt. These reached the col, but, for one reason or another, partly because of the fierce wind, partly from altitude and exhaustion, could go no farther, and on 1 June the climb was abandoned.

The Swiss Foundation now sent a second expedition to attempt the climb in the post-monsoon period. Two only of the earlier party were included, Chevalley and Lambert. There were four others: E. Reiss, G. Gross, A. Spöhel, and Professor Dyhrenfurth. The last joined the party at the end of October, so that there were only seven effective climbers. Tenzing again commanded the Sherpa contingent.

The expedition left Katmandu on 10 September. The ice-fall was found to be easier and safer than in the spring, and Camp V at the foot of Lhotse was occupied by 26 October. The next three days were spent in opening up the route towards the South Col. On the 31st a large mass of ice broke away from high up on the Lhotse face and shot down the couloir. Two ropes of three Sherpas and one rope with Chevalley and two Sherpas were in the direct line of the fall. Mingma Dorje was struck on the head and killed, and one rope of three Sherpas lost their footing and slid six hundred feet to the Cwm. One broke his collar bone, the rest escaped with minor injuries, but all were shaken and more or less put out of action.

After the accident a new and safer route was reconnoitred. It was longer than the old and ascended the face of the Lhotse glacier. Two camps, VI and VII, were placed on the glacier and the Geneva Spur and couloir were avoided. But it was not until 19 November that Camp VIII was pitched on the South Col by Lambert, Reiss, Tenzing, and seven Sherpas. The following day an attempt was made to ascend the south-east ridge. The wind harried them and the cold was intense, and the party was forced to turn back at about 26,500 feet. There was no chance of the wind and cold abating and the attempt was abandoned.[1]

These two Swiss expeditions brought success within reach. It was now known that the ascent to the col was possible for laden Sherpas and that the south-east ridge was climbable to within a thousand feet of the summit. It was not the failure or failings of the porters that prevented success, so much as the failure to realize that laden porters have their limits of endurance, as have other men. They also require rests and acclimatization. The endurance of Lambert and Tenzing, men of great courage and determination, was exceptional. A much bigger reserve of porters was needed to establish and provision a camp on the col. It is also probable that the intense

[1] *The Mountain World* (1953), pages 39–136.

physiological strain of climbing above 25,000 feet and the rapid rate of deterioration which follows exhaustion and lack of liquid to drink were underestimated.

Shipton's expedition to Cho Oyu in 1952 was to serve several important purposes: (i) to test the ability of selected mountaineers to climb at great heights and to provide a nucleus of the best of them for 1953; (ii) to experiment with the use of oxygen; (iii) to study exactly the physiological problems of high altitude climbing, such as acclimatization and deterioration, diet and liquid consumption; and (iv) to test new clothing and equipment.

Cho Oyu (26,750), about twenty miles west of Everest at the head of the Dudh Kosi, had been visited by Shipton and Ward the year before, and they had seen what appeared to be a practicable route from the south-west. Eight other climbers were invited to join the expedition: Bourdillon, Riddiford, and Hillary, who had been on the 1951 Everest expedition, Campbell Secord, G. Lowe, R. C. Evans, A. Gregory, and R. Colledge. Dr. Griffith Pugh, of the Medical Research Council, was attached to study the physiological problems.

A close inspection of Cho Oyu's south-west ridge was made, but it was at once realized that this was impossible. By climbing a 21,000-foot peak above the Nangpa La, Hillary and Lowe thought that the west face might be climbed, but since this meant that a base would have to be established beyond the Tibetan border the project had to be abandoned. The rest of the time at the disposal of the expedition was devoted to exploration and to the climbing of a number of peaks and passes, both in the region west of Everest at the head of the Bhote Kosi and Dudh Kosi and in that at the head of the Barun glacier, between the Everest and Makalu groups.[1]

\* \* \*

The achievement of John Hunt and his team in 1953 is so recent and so indelibly stamped on our minds as a truly Elizabethan feat that it is almost presumptuous for a chronicler to attempt to describe it. The leader's own account stresses the indispensable part played by every member throughout the expedition, and so much careful

[1] G.J. cxix (1953) 129 ff.

preparation and attention to detail led up to the ultimate success that it is difficult to pick out the salient features.[1]

Hunt's strategy was based on a detailed appreciation of the ideas and experience of previous Everest expeditions and on the technical advice, sometimes conflicting, of many experts. His own Himalayan experience gave weight to his fundamental decisions regarding the size of the party, number of porters, quality, quantity, and type of equipment and food, which were reached from a close analysis of many factors, such as the earliest date for the first assault, the period of preparation, possible weather interruptions, delays from sickness or casualties, and physiological matters, such as acclimatization and deterioration.[2]

In order to plan three possible attempts to follow in quick succession during the short climbing season, above 26,000 feet, before the monsoon, Hunt calculated that he must have a climbing party of ten. In addition, he required a doctor who, though an experienced climber, would take no part in the assault, a physiologist, and a 'camera-man' to film the expedition. The last was taken partly because it was felt that a film would be the best way of telling the story afterwards, and partly to help pay for the cost of the expedition. These made a total of thirteen. Later, in Katmandu, Tenzing was invited to become a member of the climbing party, making fourteen in all. Though not included as members of the expedition, there were also James Morris, *The Times* correspondent, who joined the party later at the base and relieved the leader of much despatch-writing, and Major James Roberts, who brought up the rear with additional oxygen cylinders, which were not ready at the time the rest of the baggage left England.

The names and ages of the climbing party were: John Hunt (forty-two), Charles Evans (thirty-three), Tom Bourdillon (twenty-eight), Alfred Gregory (thirty-nine), Edmund Hillary (thirty-three), George Lowe (twenty-eight), Charles Wylie (thirty-two), Michael Westmacott (twenty-seven), George Band (twenty-three), and Wilfrid Noyce (thirty-four). According to Hunt, Tenzing was

---

[1] John Hunt: *The Ascent of Everest* (London, 1953).

[2] The physiological problems are summarized by Griffith Pugh and Michael Ward in Appendix VII of Sir John Hunt's book.

thirty-nine, though in Himalayan Club records he was only thirty-six. The average age was between thirty-two and thirty-three. Griffith Pugh, the mountain physiologist, who had been with Shipton to Cho Oyu in 1952, Michael Ward, the doctor, who had been to Everest in 1951, and Tom Stobart, a widely travelled photographer, completed the team.

They were all drawn from the British Commonwealth, not for nationalistic but mainly for psychological reasons. As is well known, on such expeditions stresses and strains between individuals are apt to be considerable. It is not a case of fifty-fifty, but, as Bruce once said, of giving ninety-nine and taking one. Complete selflessness is essential for success, and men brought up in the same traditions, whatever their nation, combine better because of those traditions. Moreover, the closeness of understanding between men with Himalayan experience and Sherpa porters who had already climbed with them, was also important.

Hunt planned to establish and stock his camps as far as the South Col by 15 May, ready for his first assault party of two men to seize the first opportunity after that date. This party was to be followed by a second and third party in quick succession, acting in support of each other and taking over the attempt from their predecessors in case of failure. This entailed a period of methodical stockpiling of supplies, equipment and oxygen at camps above the base as far as the South Col, that is, between about 18,000 and 26,000 feet. An estimate of this period had to be made and of the number of porters required for working in relays, allowing for delays caused by bad weather, sickness, and casualties. At this point the acclimatization and deterioration at the critical altitude of 23,000 feet entered the problem. Hunt's solution was to reach the area as early as possible, acclimatize to 19,000 or 20,000 feet before attacking the ice-fall, and half-way through the stockpiling period to break off and give the whole team a rest of three or four days at Lobuje, a comparatively attractive camp low down the Khumbu glacier. After the rest, the stockpiling above an advanced base in the Cwm was to be speeded up and the assaults launched from the South Col before serious deterioration set in. If possible an advanced bivouac would be placed above the South Col.

The whole expedition assembled at Katmandu on 8 March and reached Namche Bazar a fortnight later. A temporary base was set up at Thyangboche on the 27th and acclimatization was begun. Parties of climbers and Sherpas under Hunt, Evans, and Hillary went off into the neighbouring valleys to practise and climb together, to try out and get used to the two types of oxygen apparatus, and to train the Sherpas. During the second part of this period Hillary's party, which included Lowe, Band, and Westmacott, set up camp on the Khumbu glacier at 17,900 feet on 12 April and began the reconnaissance of the ice-fall the following day. It should be remembered that ice problems differ greatly from year to year, and to a less extent from day to day; the ice is always in movement as it passes over the lip of the Western Cwm and changes to a greater slope. The choice of a route up the ice-fall and the making of it safe by bridging the crevasses and fixing ropes at difficult pitches were the first problems of the climb, even though they had been solved in 1951 and 1952.

This first obstacle was overcome by Hillary's 'ice-fall party.' By 15 April Camp II at 19,400 feet, half-way up the ice-fall, had been set up. By the 22nd, when the base on the glacier below the ice-fall was fully established and stocked, Camp III was set up at the top of it at about 20,000 feet and the whole expedition was assembled and acclimatized for the operation of stockpiling an advanced base in the Cwm.

This date, 22 April, should be compared with 4 May 1952 when the partly acclimatized smaller Swiss party was established at about the same point. It may also be held to correspond roughly with the position of Ruttledge's fully acclimatized party at the head of the East Rongbuk glacier (21,000) on 6 May 1934, though the horizontal distance between Camp III on the north side to the summit was considerably less than that from Camp III above the ice-fall, and the route was better known. Hunt's party was not only at the top of the ice-fall twelve days ahead of the Swiss, but it was more fully acclimatized, had worked together in various combinations for some three weeks, and because of the Swiss expeditions it had a better knowledge of the problems ahead.

The systematic build-up period began on 24 April and was

divided into two parts: during the first week three parties, each of seven Sherpas with two climbers, lifted loads from the base up the ice-fall to Camp III, while another party of seven, under Gregory and Noyce, carried the loads to 21,200 feet, the site of the old Swiss Camp IV, half-way along the Cwm, the route having been reconnoitred already by Hunt, Evans, Hillary, and Tenzing. These so-called 'ferries' ran with clockwork regularity, in spite of bad weather and of snowfalls which daily obliterated the tracks, making diversions necessary. When Camp IV, the advanced base, was finally established on 1 May, some ninety loads had been lifted over the ice-fall route, and half of these had been carried on to Camp IV.

A halt was now called and the carrying parties retired to Lobuje on 2 May for a three-day rest. The next major obstacle, the Lhotse face, had now to be tackled and Hunt went forward with Evans and Bourdillon for a first reconnaissance. They reached 22,500 feet; the weather was particularly bad, and Hunt decided against pressing the reconnaissance farther. He had already chosen the general line of the route taken by the Swiss in their second attempt after the monsoon of 1952, in preference to the spring route by the Geneva Spur, and proposed to place two Camps, VI and VII, at altitudes of 23,000 and 24,000 feet on the face. Leaving Bourdillon and Evans, with Ward and Wylie moving up in support, to carry on the reconnaissance, he returned to base.

The conquest of the Lhotse face took longer than expected. Bad weather and high winds, coupled with the altitude, were the enemies. Not until 10 May was Camp VI fully established by Lowe, and it was only on the 17th that Lowe and Noyce set up Camp VII, with a safe route behind them. Meanwhile the 'ferrying' of supplies went on uninterruptedly from below, and everything necessary for the assault was now at Camp IV or higher. The last 'low-level lift' to Camp IV was on the 18th. Two days later Noyce with eight laden Sherpas for Camp VII took over from Lowe, Ward and Sherpa Da Tenzing, and on the 21st Noyce and Annullu, watched from below, completed the route to the South Col. When Lowe came down on the 20th, he had been on the Lhotse face for eleven days, mostly at 23,000 feet or over. These were great achievements.

Hunt's tactical plan for the attempt had been slightly modified by circumstances. He now decided to make two instead of three successive assaults, the first using the lighter but more experimental 'closed' oxygen apparatus, the second the 'open' type. The first pair were to make for the South Summit and to reach the top if possible, but in view of the unknown difficulties, they were not to press the attack to the extent of compromising the second assault. The two pairs chosen were Bourdillon and Evans, and Hillary and Tenzing, and it was largely to spare them for this final effort that the arduous and exhausting work on the Lhotse face had been shared by the others.

The preliminary moves of this plan were being made when Noyce completed the route to the South Col on the 21st. On the same date parties of Sherpas were on the move carrying loads up the face. On this day Wylie reached Camp VII with seven laden Sherpas and on the 22nd, with Hillary and Tenzing leading, Wylie reached the col with fourteen laden men, dumped their loads and returned. The weather had turned fine on the 15th, and though the wind was still strong, especially on the col, prospects were good.

These performances on the Lhotse face paved the way to success, if success were possible. The achievement of Noyce and Annullu on the 21st lit the flame of confidence at Camp VII, so that the great body of Sherpas under Wylie there were able to reach the col the next day. Hillary and Tenzing had gone up from Camp IV to Camp VII on the 21st, led the party to the col on the 22nd, and returned the same night to Camp IV. It was on this wave of confidence that the assaults began.

On 24 May the first assault party—Bourdillon and Evans, with Hunt, Da Namgyal, and Ang Tenzing in support—reached the South Col and in a fierce wind erected the tents that had been brought up on the 22nd. They rested on the 25th, partly to establish the camp and re-arrange the equipment, partly to allow the second assault party to close up to Camp VII, and partly to ensure that their oxygen equipment was in perfect working order.

The first assault from the col took place on the 26th. Evans and Bourdillon were successful in reaching their limited objective, the South Summit (c. 28,700), but trouble with Evans' oxygen apparatus had delayed the start, the problem of selecting the route at this

337

extreme altitude, beyond the point reached by Lambert and Tenzing the year before, slowed the rate of climbing, and when the two reached the South Summit at one o'clock they had insufficient oxygen for what was now seen to be the difficult final climb of the summit ridge and for their descent to the col. They wisely decided to return.

Meanwhile Hunt and Da Namgyal, following up in support, had carried loads of about fifty pounds—tent, food, kerosine, and oxygen bottles—to between 27,300 and 27,500 feet to save the energies of the second assault party. All returned safely but exhausted to the col, and were able to describe their efforts to the second assault party which arrived from Camp VII the same day. With Hillary and Tenzing and their supports—Gregory, Lowe, Ang Temba, and Ang Nyima—had come five more Sherpas, the elderly Dawa Thondup, Annullu who had already done fine work with Noyce on the Lhotse face, Topkie, Ang Nurbu, and Da Tenzing, all carrying extra loads.

The following night at the crowded Camp VIII was terrible. The wind rose to gale force, and none slept. The 27th dawned with a raging wind and the second assault had to be postponed. The first assault party went down to Camp VII during the day, utterly exhausted after their three nights at Camp VIII and their efforts above it; at Camp VII they were looked after by Noyce and Ward. The latter escorted Evans to Camp IV later in the day and Hunt reached it on the 28th.

All now depended on the weather. Camp VIII was well stocked, but most of the Sherpas had shot their bolt; some had already carried loads to the col at least twice. On the other hand, Hillary, Tenzing, Gregory, Lowe, and the Sherpa Ang Nyima were ready at the col, with supplies and oxygen; Noyce was moving up in support. All the planning of the last six months had been directed to this climax. It was the apex of a great pyramid of effort.

Throughout the 27th the second assault party waited at the col while the wind raged. Preparations were made for a start on the morrow, since any prolonged stay at this altitude increased deterioration. After another wild night, the wind eased at 8 a.m. on the 18th. Lowe, Gregory, and Ang Nyima started soon after, to be followed by Hillary and Tenzing. They passed the point where Lambert and

Tenzing had spent the night of 27 May 1952, picked up the loads dumped by Hunt's party on the first assault, and at about 27,900 feet Lowe, Gregory, and Ang Nyima dumped their loads and returned to the col. Hillary and Tenzing built a small platform and pitched the tiny tent. They had sufficient oxygen for four hours each during the night at the rate of one litre a minute, and just enough for the climb—about 1100 feet—the following day. Both of them had some sleep.

The wind dropped during the night and the 29th dawned fine. At 6.30 the two men started. Mounting steadily and with frequent changes of lead they reached the South Summit at 9 o'clock—eight hundred feet in two and a half hours; they rested and examined the last difficult ridge, heavily corniced above the east face on one side and with steep rocks dropping to the precipices above the Western Cwm on the other. After an hour's going they reached and overcame the most difficult part of the climb, a great rock step forty feet in height. Progress was now extremely slow—a foot a minute—and seemed slower. At half-past eleven they reached the summit.

Throughout this climb Hillary was able to calculate the amount of oxygen he and Tenzing were using, and how much would be required for the descent. On the summit he took photographs, again checked the oxygen and worked out the rate of supply for the descent. After fifteen minutes' rest they started down. They were back at their bivouac of the night before by two o'clock, changed on to the last two bottles of oxygen, shouldered their sleeping-bags, and tired but happy went on to the col to be met by Lowe, laden with hot soup and emergency oxygen. Just before reaching the tents Hillary's oxygen ran out. There had been enough, but none too much.

No bare record of this achievement by one who took no part can do it justice. Hunt's team had won success without a casualty. All came back. In England those of us who had followed the epic of Everest and the fortunes of each expedition since Howard-Bury's reconnaissance in 1921 had once more prayed for success and for the safety of our friends. As we moved to our seats at six o'clock on the morning of the Queen's Coronation, the great news spread among the crowds.

# 1954 and the Future

If the patient, persistent efforts of a few men, striving in unity to attain such a goal as Everest, fortified in the attainment of their ideal by many others, can result in victory, can we not equally apply this power to solving other problems, less lofty but more pressing, in this sorely troubled world?

SIR JOHN HUNT

# 1954 and the Future

THE year 1954 has hardly yet passed into history. In the Himalaya it has been a year of intense activity. There are tragedies to record as well as successes, and these tragedies are reminders that a Himalayan mountain is unforgiving and unforgetful. Full details are not yet available.

The most outstanding success was achieved by Ardito Desio, who was on the Duke of Spoleto's expedition of 1929, and who now led a successful party to K2 (28,250), the second highest mountain in the world. There were eleven climbers and six scientists. The summit was reached at about 6 p.m. on 31 July, after successive camps had been set up on the Abruzzi ridge, by A. Compagnoni and L. Lacedelli, from a camp at about 27,000 feet, which was regained in darkness. One of the climbers, Mario Puchoz, died of pneumonia at Camp II.

Rakaposhi (25,550) was visited by a German expedition led by Herr Rebitsch and comprising seven climbers and six scientists. Much scientific work and mapping was carried out in the neighbouring district, but one of the scientists, Karl Heckler, lost his life by drowning in the Hunza river. The mountain was also visited by a small British expedition of six, led by Dr. A. Tissières of Cambridge. The Monk's Head was climbed, but the party was then driven back by bad weather.

Nepal sanctioned several expeditions. On the west, an Italian expedition, led by Professor P. Ghiglione, a veteran of 71, went to Api (23,399). The summit was reached by G. Rosencrantz, J. Barenghi, and a Sherpa porter. On the descent they were caught by a blizzard, and only the Sherpa survived. Dr. R. Bignani, another member of the party, was drowned while crossing the river Kali.

Dr. Rudolf Jonas led an Austrian party to Saipal (23,079), east of the Api-Nampa group; he was unfortunate in losing one of his team, Karl Reiss, who died from pneumonia. Saipal was also visited by a small scientific party from Oxford University, the objects being mountain exploration and the study of botany, geology, and glaciology.

An Argentine expedition to Dhaulagiri I (26,795) was brought out by Francisco Ibanez. It had no member with Himalayan mountain experience, and it would have been wiser to have been less ambitious. The party reached a point within about a thousand feet of the summit, but most of the eleven climbers were severely frostbitten, and the attempt had to be abandoned. Ibanez himself unfortunately died as a result of gangrene following frostbite, after his feet had been amputated at Katmandu.

Raymond Lambert, of Everest fame, took a party to Gauri Sankar, west of Everest, but subsequently joined forces with Dr. Jonas's team from Saipal for an attempt on Cho Oyu (26,750). A fine achievement followed: The summit was reached on 19 October by Dr. H. Tichy, S. Joechler, and the Sherpa Pasang Dawa Lama (No. 139).

Several peaks above 20,000 feet were climbed in the Barun glacier area east of Everest by a New Zealand party led by Sir Edmund Hillary and sponsored by the New Zealand Alpine Club. The party of ten included Charles Evans and George Lowe, of the successful Everest team. Hillary, Shipton, Evans, and Lowe had visited the Barun glacier in 1952. It is fed from the Great Himalaya between Pethangtse (22,060) and Makalu (27,790) and was largely unexplored. In 1954 Pethangtse was climbed by Wilkins, Hardie, and Ball; Baruntse (23,560) by Lowe, Beaven, Harrow, and Todd. One member of the party, McFarlane, fell into a crevasse, but was rescued by Hillary.

Later a small French party went out to the same area to reconnoitre Makalu, as a preliminary to an all-out attempt before the monsoon of 1955. Makalu II (25,120) was climbed.

Still farther east a British expedition, organized and led by J. W. R. Kempe, of the Hyderabad Public School, reconnoitred the south-west face of Kangchenjunga from the Yalung glacier. This was the scene of Guillarmod's expedition in 1905 when Pache and three porters were killed, and it does not appear to have been examined since. The party comprised Kempe, T. H. Braham, J. W. Tucker, S. R. Jackson, G. C. Lewis, and D. S. Matthews. The key to an ascent from this side appears to be an ice-shelf across the face at an altitude of between 23,000 and 24,000 feet. A camp was placed at 21,000 feet and several unsuccessful attempts were made to reach the shelf, but snow and ice conditions rendered the route too hazardous to be followed farther. The whole of this quadrant of Kangchenjunga appears to be seriously menaced by avalanches, particularly after mid-day. Kangchenjunga is the third highest mountain in the world. It may well displace K2 and be in fact the second highest. It is certainly the highest unclimbed summit, and of those in the first ten probably the most difficult.

These incomplete notes, collected before the reports are written, must suffice. The new era of mountaineering in the Himalaya has begun, and the old days are gone. To-day men fly out from Europe, climb and fly back again within a month or two, and much of the charm of the lower hills is missed by them.

But there is still a boundless scope in these grandest of all mountains for the future traveller, scientist, and climber. Mountain and ski clubs are coming into being. The Mountain Institute at Darjeeling was opened in 1954, with Major N. D. Jayal as Director and Tenzing as chief instructor. Among the other instructors are several well-known Sherpas, including the indomitable Ang Tharkay. The Himalayan Club has celebrated its twenty-fifth birthday. Pakistan has its Karakoram Club, and The Ski and Mountaineering Club of Pakistan. As a result of expeditions to the Himalaya west of Nepal there is a growing number of local men with experience of high altitudes. They are hardy and self-reliant and are coming to enjoy life on the high hills.

\*　　　\*　　　\*

As the pilgrim grows old his mind recalls all the glories of Himachal, to whose divinest altars his footsteps marked a way, 'where the Ganges falls from the foot of Vishnu like the slender thread of the lotus flower.' The memory of them is imperishable and beyond price.

# Appendix A

## HIMALAYAN AND KARAKORAM PEAKS

### Positions and Heights of Peaks above 25,000 feet

| Order of Magnitude | Name and Early Designation | S. of I Pk. No. & Sheet | Height in feet | Latitude ° ′ ″ | Longitude ° ′ ″ | System | Section and Group |
|---|---|---|---|---|---|---|---|
| 1 | *Mount Everest (XV) | Pk. 37/72I | 29,002[1] | 27 59 16 | 86 55 40 | Nepal Himalaya | Kosi Section |
| 2 | *K2 | Pk. 13/52A | 28,250 | 35 52 55 | 76 30 51 | Great Karakoram | Baltoro Muztagh |
| 3 | †Kangchenjunga I (IX) | Pk. 10¹/78A | 28,146 | 27 42 09 | 88 09 00 | Sikkim Himalaya | Sikkim–Nepal W'shed |
| 4 | Lhotse (E1) | Sheet 72I | 27,890 | 27 57 43 | 86 56 10 | Nepal Himalaya | Kosi Section |
| 5 | Kangchenjunga II (VIII) | Pk. 10²/78A | 27,803 | 27 41 30 | 88 09 24 | Sikkim Himalaya | Sikkim–Nepal W'shed |
| 6 | †Makalu (XIII) | Pk. 2/72M | 27,790 | 27 53 23 | 87 05 29 | Nepal Himalaya | Kosi Section |
| 7 | †Dhaulagiri (XLII) | Pk. 9/62P | 26,795 | 28 41 48 | 83 29 42 | Nepal Himalaya | Karnali Section |
| 8 | *Cho Oyu | Pk. 5/71L | 26,750 | 28 05 32 | 86 39 51 | Nepal Himalaya | Kosi Section |
| 9 | †Manaslu (Kutang I) (XXX) | Pk. 14/71D | 26,658 | 28 33 00 | 84 33 43 | Nepal Himalaya | Gandaki Section |
| 10 | *Nanga Parbat I | Pk. 48/43I | 26,620 (26,660)[2] | 35 14 21 | 74 35 24 | Punjab Himalaya | |
| 11 | *Annapurna I (XXXIX) | Pk. 16/62P | 26,492 | 28 35 44 | 83 49 19 | Nepal Himalaya | Gandaki Section |
| 12 | †Gasherbrum I (K5) | Pk. 23/52A | 26,470 | 35 43 30 | 76 41 48 | Great Karakoram | Baltoro Muztagh |
| 13 | Broad Peak I | Pk. 16/52A | 26,414 | 35 48 35 | 76 34 25 | Great Karakoram | Baltoro Muztagh |
| 14 | Gasherbrum II (K4) | Pk. 21/52A | 26,360 | 35 45 31 | 76 39 15 | Great Karakoram | Baltoro Muztagh |
| 15 | Gosainthan (Shisha Pangma) (XXIII) | Pk. 46/71H | 26,291 | 28 21 07 | 85 46 55 | Nepal Himalaya | Gandaki Section |
| 16 | Gasherbrum III (K3a) | Pk. 20/52A | 26,090 | 35 45 36 | 76 38 33 | Great Karakoram | Baltoro Muztagh |
| 17 | Annapurna II (XXXIV) | Pk. 3/71D | 26,041 | 28 32 05 | 84 07 26 | Nepal Himalaya | Gandaki Section |
| 18 | Broad Peak II | Pk. 15/52A | 26,017 | 35 50 25 | 76 33 40 | Great Karakoram | Baltoro Muztagh |
| 19 | Gasherbrum IV (K3) | Pk. 19/52A | 26,000 | 35 45 38 | 76 37 02 | Great Karakoram | Baltoro Muztagh |
| 20 | Gyachung Kang (T57) | Pk. 3/71L | 25,990 | 28 05 52 | 86 44 41 | Nepal Himalaya | Kosi Section |
| 21 | Disteghil Sar I | Pk. 20/42P | 25,868 | 36 19 35 | 75 11 20 | Great Karakoram | Hispar Muztagh |
| 22 | Himal Chuli (XXVIII) | Pk. 19/71D | 25,801 | 28 26 03 | 84 38 34 | Nepal Himalaya | Gandaki Section |
| 23 | †Kangbachen | Pk. 9/78A | 25,782 | 27 42 59 | 88 06 47 | Sikkim Himalaya | Kangchenjunga Group |
| 24 | Ngojumba Kang | Pk. 2/71L | 25,730 | 28 06 24 | 86 41 15 | Nepal Himalaya | Kosi Section |
| 25 | Manaslu II (Kutang II) (XXIX) | Pk. 16/71D | 25,705 | 28 30 12 | 84 34 07 | Nepal Himalaya | Gandaki Section |
| 26 | Nuptse (E2) | Sheet 72I | 25,700 | 27 57 53 | 86 53 23 | Nepal Himalaya | Kosi Section |
| 27 | †Masherbrum East (K1E) | Pk. 7/52A | 25,660 | 35 38 36 | 76 18 31 | Lesser Karakoram | Masherbrum Range |

| No. | Peak | Designation | Latitude | Longitude | Height (ft) | Himalaya | Section/Group |
|---|---|---|---|---|---|---|---|
| 28 | Nanda Devi (LVIII) | Pk. 115/55IN | 30 22 32 | 79 58 22 | 25,645 | Kumaun Himalaya | Kosi Section |
| 29 | Chomo Lonzo | Pl. 1/72M | 27 55 47 | 87 06 44 | 25,640 | Nepal Himalaya | |
| 30 | Masherbrum West (K1W) | Pk. 8/52A | 35 38 29 | 76 18 23 | 25,610 | Lesser Karakoram | Masherbrum Range |
| 31 | Nanga Parbat II (North Peak) | Pk. 47/43I | 35 15 22 | 74 35 14 | 25,572[3] (25,620) | Punjab Himalaya | |
| 32 | †Rakaposhi (U49) | Pk. 27/42L | 36 08 39 | 74 29 22 | 25,550 | Lesser Karakoram | Rakaposhi Range |
| 33 | (Hunza-Kunji I) | Pk. 32/42L | 36 30 39 | 74 31 26 | 25,540 | Great Karakoram | Batura Muztagh |
| 34 | (Zemu Peak) | Sheet 78A | 27 41 13 | 88 10 32 | 25,526 | Sikkim Himalaya | Kangchenjunga Group |
| 35 | Kanjut Sar (Trans-Indus No. 4) | Pk. 12/42P | 36 12 21 | 75 25 03 | 25,460 | Great Karakoram | Hispar Muztagh |
| 36 | ★Kamet (LXVII) | Pk. 49/53N | 30 55 13 | 79 35 37 | 25,447 | Kumaun Himalaya | Kamet Group |
| 37 | Namcha Barwa | Pk. 5/82O | 29 37 51 | 95 03 31 | 25,445 | Assam Himalaya | |
| 38 | Dhaulagiri II (XLIII) | Pk. 5/62P | 28 45 45 | 83 23 25 | 25,429 | Nepal Himalaya | Gandaki-Karnali W'shed |
| 39 | †Saltoro Kangri I (K10) | Pk. 36/52A | 35 24 01 | 76 50 55 | 25,400 | Great Karakoram | Saltoro Range |
| 40 | Gurla Mandhata | Pk. 7/62F | 30 26 18 | 81 17 57 | 25,355 | Nepal Himalaya | Karnali Section (Zaskar range) |
| 41 | Janu (XI) | Pk. 13/78A | 27 40 56 | 88 02 47 | 25,294 | Nepal Himalaya | Kosi Section |
| 42 | (Hunza Kunji II) | Pk. 31/42L | 36 31 54 | 74 30 01 | 25,294 | Great Karakoram | Batura Muztagh |
| 43 | Saltoro Kangri II (K11) | Pk. 35/52A | 35 24 24 | 76 50 50 | 25,280 | Great Karakoram | Saltoro Range |
| 44 | Dhaulagiri III (XLIV) | Pk. 6/62P | 28 45 13 | 83 22 46 | 25,271 | Nepal Himalaya | Gandaki-Karnali W'shed |
| 45 | Disteghil Sar II | Pk. 5/42P | 36 19 09 | 75 13 10 | 25,250 | Great Karakoram | Hispar Muztagh |
| 46 | Saser Kangri (K22) | Pk. 29/52F | 34 52 00 | 77 45 13 | 25,170 | Great Karakoram | Saser Muztagh |
| 47 | Gosainthan II (B504) | Pk. 44/71H | 28 21 17 | 85 48 45 | 25,134 | Nepal Himalaya | Kosi Section |
| 48 | ★Makalu II | Sheet 72M | 27 54 58 | 87 04 54 | 25,120 | Nepal Himalaya | Kosi Section |
| 49 | †Chogolisa I (K6) | Pk. 25/52A | 35 36 44 | 76 34 23 | 25,110 | Lesser Karakoram | Masherbrum Range |
| 50 | Dhaulagiri IV (XLVI) | Pk. 7/62P | 28 44 07 | 83 18 53 | 25,064 | Nepal Himalaya | Gandaki-Karnali W'shed |

* Peaks climbed are marked with an asterisk. Those reconnoitred and attempted seriously are marked with a dagger†. With the exception of K2, the early observers' designations, shown in brackets, have been abandoned.

1 The latest (1954) provisional height of Everest, obtained from observations in Nepal is 29,028 feet. It is not yet known whether heights on maps are to be changed (See Appendix B).

2 26,620 feet is the officially accepted height of Nanga Parbat I, according to Burrard. On the latest Survey of India sheet 43I (1934) the height is shown as 26,660 feet, and this height was used by Professor R. Finsterwalder in 1936 for his map (scale 1:50,000) made by stereo-photogrammetry. The relative magnitude of Manaslu and Nanga Parbat I is in doubt.

3 25,572 feet is the official height of Nanga Parbat II according to Burrard. The height shown on the latest Survey of India quarter-inch map 43I is 25,620. Finsterwalder's 1:50,000 stereo-photogrammetric map gives twin North peak summits 7816 m. about 7785 m. about half a mile apart (c. 25,640 feet and 25,540 feet). The relative position of Masherbrum West and Nanga Parbat North in the list is therefore doubtful.

# Appendix B

## ON THE DETERMINATION OF HIMALAYAN HEIGHTS

The heights of Himalayan peaks have been obtained by theodolite observations to them made at distant stations of the Great Trigonometrical Survey. The base distance between two stations and their heights are known from previous observations, the angles between the base and the rays from each station to the peak are measured by theodolite, and the distances to the peak are calculated. If the angle of elevation to the peak is also measured at each station, the differences of height between them and the peak can be calculated. In plane trigonometry the difference of height is the distance multiplied by the tangent of the angle of elevation. If the observations are made at a number of stations, several determinations of height are obtained; they will not agree exactly, but a mean may be taken.

In practice there are many corrections to be made, and many complications: the curvature of the earth; terrestrial refraction which bends the ray of observation; deflection of the vertical, caused by inequalities of mass in the earth's crust, which throws the base-plate of the theodolite out of the spheroidal horizontal and varies from station to station. If the summit is rounded and snow-capped, there is doubt about the depth of snow, and it may vary at different seasons of the year; unless it is sharp-pointed the same spot on it may not be observed from all stations.

When all these doubts are resolved with the utmost care and patience by observers and computors, where is the base—casually referred to as 'mean sea-level'—above which we are measuring the height? For the earth's figure or 'geoid' is not a true spheroid, mean sea-level is not a spheroidal surface, and we do not know exactly where it is under a particular mountain of the Great Himalaya. In other words we can observe the top; we cannot observe the bottom.

One of Sir George Everest's contributions to science was the measurement of an arc of the meridian in India, from which was calculated the Everest spheroid; this is the mathematical figure which most nearly fitted the geoid in India as known in Everest's day, and on it the geodetic triangulation is calculated. Further observations then have to be made to calculate the separation of the geoid and spheroid, so that this correction can be applied to the height.

Refraction varies at different altitudes. It is greatest at low altitudes and with small angles of elevation, greater and more variable in the early morning than in the afternoon. On a long-distance ray from a low station to a high and distant peak, the correction for refraction may be as much as a thousand feet. The separation of the geoid from the spheroid may mean a correction of the order of a hundred feet. Variability of snow-depth, at the best only an estimate, is probably

348

not more than twenty feet at the most, and much less than this on wind-swept summits above 27,000 feet where the snow does not consolidate.

The first determination of the height of Everest, the mean of a number of observations from six stations in the Ganges plain, gave a value of 29,002 feet. It had been corrected for refraction, so far as scientific knowledge allowed, up to 1852. Within fifty years it was known that too great a correction had been applied. Much more has now been learnt about refraction, deflection of the vertical, and the geoid. In 1906 Sir Sidney Burrard, by applying better values for refraction and re-computing the old observations, obtained a provisional height of 29,141 feet above the spheroid, but advocated the retention of the old height of 29,002 feet until more was known. In 1922 Dr. de Graaff Hunter, F.R.S., calculated the height above the spheroid at 29,149 feet and a probable rise of the geoid above the spheroid at the base of Everest of seventy feet, bringing its height above mean sea-level to 29,079 feet. Others, working on the same lines and using Hunter's formulæ and tables, have suggested a larger separation and a lower height.[1]

The opening of Nepal since 1949 has for the first time given the observers of the Survey of India the opportunity of extending triangulation into that country; Everest has now been observed from higher stations; the rays to it are shorter; and subsidiary observations have enabled Mr. B. I. Gulatee, the present Director of the Geodetic Branch, to obtain a truer value of the separation of the two base surfaces. The important result is that the rise of the geoid above the spheroid works out at about 109 feet, bringing Burrard's and Hunter's spheroidal heights down to 29,032 and 29,040 feet above the geoid respectively. A slightly different position for the summit, which from a distance is not well defined, is found about eighteen yards south-west of the old position; but there is no reason to believe that the new fixing under less favourable weather conditions is better than the old, and any slight displacement of position will affect the height. From the recent observations Mr. B. L. Gulatee has found a new value of 29,028 feet for the new position of the summit at the time of minimum snow-cap, the observations having been made between December and March.[2] It must however be remembered that very little is known of the variation of snow-depth on the summit from day to day, season to season, and year to year. The fierce west wind clears the summit and faces of un-consolidated powder-particles very rapidly—witness Everest's famous 'plume'—and the mountain faces turn from white to black in a day. Probably the only season of the year when any snow consolidates on the summit is during the monsoon, but how much is lost by evaporation and melting is unknown. It may, however, now be confidently stated that Everest's height above mean sea-level is between 29,028 and 29,040 feet. It is a remarkable tribute to the accuracy of the

---

[1] de Graaff Hunter, J.: *S. of I. Geodetic Report I (1924)*; Bomford, G.: *S. of I. G.R. III* (1929).

[2] Gulatee, B. L.: *S. of I. Technical Paper*, No. 8 (1954). See also de Graaff Hunter, J.: 'Various determinations over a century of the height of Mount Everest' in *G.J.* cxxi (1955) 21.

old observations of a hundred years ago that they agree so closely with those now found after applying the modern corrections.

As with Everest, so with the other great mountains. The official height of Kangchenjunga for a hundred years has been 28,146 feet. De Graaff Hunter's calculations in 1922 showed that the height corrected for refraction was about 28,287 feet above the spheroid, less sixty-two feet for the rise of the geoid. This gives a height above mean sea-level of 28,225 feet, which is certainly nearer the truth than the old figure. Its rival is K2 (28,250) in the Karakoram. According to Hunter, its spheroidal height would not be sensibly altered by modern ideas of refraction, because the original observations were made from stations between 15,000 and 18,000 feet. But nothing is known of the separation of the geoid from the spheroid in these parts; and if the spheroid is higher than the geoid here, as is possible, K2 might be displaced from second place by Kangchenjunga. But it is only a possibility.

The same considerations apply to all the heights given in Appendix A, to a greater or less extent. Some, in fact most, have been well fixed for position, and the summits of some have been accurately observed for height from high stations; but little is yet known of the separation of the geoid and spheroid under the high Himalaya and Karakoram, so that no change should yet be made in the accepted official figures. In 1934 Dr. Finsterwalder, during the Nanga Parbat expedition, derived a height of 26,654 feet for that mountain. The latest Survey of India map gives the height as 26,660 feet; but the 'official height' remains 26,620 feet until such time as finality is reached.[1]

Mountaineers frequently carry with them aneroids which give them rough determinations of altitude. Heights obtained by this means can be most misleading. In comparing heights recorded for camps placed at the same spot I have constantly found differences of 500 feet or more obtained by different expeditions. I have known my own aneroid give heights for the same survey station differing from each other on successive mornings by 300 feet, and neither was within 200 feet of the correct height by triangulation. Aneroids may be useful in determining the difference in altitude climbed in a short time, if the atmospheric pressure remains constant and the weather fine, but they are of no use for exact determinations of altitude in the high Himalaya.

[1] For an elaboration of the problem see J. de Graaff Hunter's paper in *Occasional Notes*, Royal Astronomical Society, Vol. 3 (Oct. 1953).

# Appendix C

## CHRONOLOGICAL SUMMARY

(Pages are shown in brackets)

1624. Andrade and Marques cross Mana pass to Tsaparang (56).

1626. Cacella and Cabral cross Tang La to Shigatse (58).

1631. Azevedo reaches Leh by Mana pass and returns to India by Baralacha and Rohtang passes (57).

1661–62. Grueber and d'Orville reach India from Peking via Tibet and Nepal (58).

1714–15. Desideri crosses Zoji La and Tibet to Lhasa (58).

1735. D'Anville's *Atlas of China* published (60).

1767. Kinloch's visit to S. Nepal (60).

1774. Bogle's mission through Bhutan to Shigatse (61).

1782. Rennell's *Map of Hindoostan* first published (61).

1783. Turner's mission to Shigatse (61).

1792. Kirkpatrick's visit to Katmandu (61).

1801–03. Charles Crawford in Nepal; Robert Colebrooke, Surveyor General of Bengal (63).

1808. Webb, Raper and Hearsey explore upper Bhagirathi and Alaknanda. First observations to high Himalayan peaks (64).

1809. Metcalfe's treaty with Ranjit Singh of the Punjab (65).

1812. Moorcroft and Hearsey cross Niti pass to Manasarowar; Mir Izzet Ullah crosses Karakoram pass (66).

1814–16. Nepalese War: Nepal closed; Kumaun opened (67).

1817. Regular exploration of Kumaun begins (68). Gerard brothers explore Bashahr (69).

1817–35. Traill, Deputy Commissioner of Kumaun (69).

1820–25. Moorcroft's and Trebeck's travels in Ladakh (66, 69).

1823. George Everest becomes Superintendent of G.T.S. (71).

1830–43. George Everest, Surveyor General of India (71).

1830. Alexander Gardner crosses Karakoram to India (69).

1835–38. Vigne's travels in Kashmir (69).

1845. First Sikh War (74).

1846. Survey of India begins primary triangulation along foot of Himalaya (72).

1846–48. Boundary Commission travels of Alexander Cunningham, Thomas Thomson, Henry and Richard Strachey (80, 81).

1848. Annexation of the Punjab (74).

1848–49. Joseph Hooker's journeys in eastern Nepal and Sikkim (81).

1852. Discovery of height of Mount Everest (73).

1854–58. Travels of the three Schlagintweits (82).

1856. Regular triangulation and survey of Kashmir begin (74).

1858. Discovery of height of K2 (76).

1860. Survey of India *khalasi* fixes pole on Shilla (23,050 feet) (75).

1861. Reconnaissance surveys of Karakoram glaciers (77).

1862–71. Drew's travels in Kashmir (91).

1864. Completion of western Himalayan reconnaissance surveys (80).

1865–85. Pundit explorations (84–91). Survey of India reconnaissance surveys of Sikkim (90).

1869–71. Robert Shaw's travels to Central Asia (92).

1873–74. Forsyth's Second Yarkand Mission (92).

1883. Graham's climbs in Sikkim and in Nanda Devi region (93).

1887. Younghusband crosses the Muztagh pass (100).

1887–1906. Waddell and White in Sikkim and Bhutan (123).

1889. Gilgit Agency established (100). Younghusband's second Karakoram journey (101).

1891. Hunza-Nagir campaign (102).

1892. Conway's Karakoram expedition (103).

1892–93. Cockerill's explorations in Hunza (102).

1895. Mummery's attempt to climb Nanga Parbat (107).

1896. Pamir Boundary Commission (105).

1898. Bruce's exploration of Nun Kun group (110).

1899. Freshfield's reconnaissance of Kangchenjunga (124).

1902. Eckenstein's expedition to K2 (132). 

1903–04. Younghusband's Tibet Mission. Ryder's survey of the Tsangpo (125).

1905. Guillarmod's attempt to climb Kangchenjunga (126). Longstaff's first expedition to Nanda Devi 'ring' (114).

1907. Longstaff's first ascent of Trisul, 23,360 feet (117). Rubenson and Monrad Aas reach 23,900 feet on Kabru (126). Kellas begins his Sikkim climbs (128).

1909. Abruzzi's expedition to K2. He reaches 24,600 feet on Chogolisa (133). Longstaff discovers Teram Kangri and the upper Siachen glacier (137).

1909–13. Triangulation link between India and Russia completed (145).

1910. Survey of India begins the re-survey of the Himalaya (142). Kellas climbs Pauhunri (23,180) and Chomiomo (22,430) (129).

1911–13. Survey of India explorations in eastern Assam Himalaya (129).

1913. Meade camps at 23,420 feet on Kamet (120).

1913–14. De Filippi's Karakoram expedition (140).

1914. Calciati climbs Kun (23,250) (112).

1914–18. First World War (151).

1920. Kellas and Morshead attempt Kamet (25,447) (185).

1921. Everest: Howard-Bury's reconnaissance (154–63).

1922. Everest (Bruce): First Assault. Mallory, Somervell and Norton reach 26,800 feet without oxygen; Finch and J. G. Bruce 27,300 feet with oxygen. Highest camp 25,500 feet (164–71).

# APPENDIX C

1924. Everest (Bruce and Norton): Second Assault; Norton reaches 28,126 feet, Somervell 27,700 feet; death of Mallory and Irvine at c. 27,600 feet; highest camp 26,800 feet (172–6).

1925. Visser's Hunza Karakoram exploration (177).

1926. Mason's Shaksgam exploration (180).

1926, 1927. Ruttledge's explorations of Nanda Devi 'ring' (187).

1927–28. Founding of the Himalayan Club (189).

1929. Bauer's Kangchenjunga reconnaissance. Allwein and Kraus reach 24,250 feet (195). Spoleto's Baltoro glacier expedition (240).

1929–30. Visser's third Karakoram expedition (241).

1930. Dyhrenfurth's reconnaissance of Kangchenjunga (198). First ascent of Jongsong Peak (24,344) (274).

1931. Bauer's second Kangchenjunga expedition; Hartmann and Wien reach 25,263 feet; Schaller killed (199). Smythe's first ascent of Kamet (25,447) (202).

1932. First German Nanga Parbat expedition (Merkl) (226).

1933. Everest (Ruttledge): Third Assault; Wyn Harris, Wager, Smythe reach 28,126 (Norton's highest), Shipton c. 27,700; highest camp 27,400 feet (211). Houston-Everest flight (217). Second ascent of Trisul (Oliver) (205).

1934. Nanga Parbat: Second German attempt (Merkl). Aschenbrenner and Schneider reach 25,280 feet; death of four Germans and six porters (229). Shipton's and Tilman's Nanda Devi reconnaissance (205). Dyhrenfurth's Baltoro expedition (248).

1935. Everest (Shipton): Monsoon reconnaissance (218). Visser's fourth Karakoram expedition (242). Waller's attempt on Saltoro Kangri (251). Cooke's first ascent of Kabru (24,002) (275). Kingdon Ward's exploration of the upper Subansiri (279).

1935–38. Survey of India re-survey of Kumaun Himalaya (Osmaston) (264).

1936. Everest (Ruttledge): Fourth Assault ruined by weather (220). First ascent of Nanda Devi (25,645): Tilman and Odell (207). German party (Bauer) climbs Siniolchu (22,600) (276). Japanese party (Takebushi) climbs Nanda Kot (22,510) (268). French expedition (de Ségogne) attempts Gasherbrum I (26,470) (249).

1937. Nanga Parbat: Third German attempt; death of seven Germans and nine porters (234). Shipton's first Karakoram expedition (244). Spencer Chapman's first ascent of Chomolhari (23,997) (278).

1938. Everest (Tilman): Fifth Assault ruined by weather (222). Nanga Parbat (Bauer): Fourth German attempt (236). K2 (Houston): American reconnaissance to 26,100 feet (257). Austro-German expedition (Schwarzgruber) to Gangotri; Satopanth and Chaukhamba reconnoitred (268). Waller's attempt on Masherbrum (252). Campbell Secord and Vyvyan reconnoitre Rakaposhi (256).

1939. Nanga Parbat (Aufschnaiter): Diamirai face reconnaissance (239). K2 (Wiessner): First American attempt; death of Wolfe and three Sherpas (260). Shipton's second Karakoram expedition (246). Swiss expedition (Roch) climbs Dunagiri (23,184) and attempts Chaukhamba (269). Polish expedition (Karpinski) climbs Nanda Devi East (24,391) and attempts Tirsuli; death of

# APPENDIX C

Bernadzikiewicz and Karpinski (271). German party (Schmaderer) climbs Tent Peak (24,157) (277).

1939–45. Second World War (285).

1947. Swiss expedition (Roch) climbs Kedarnath (22,770) and Satopanth (23,170) (293). Second reconnaissance of Rakaposhi (Tilman & Gyr) (299). Partition of India into India and Pakistan, with independence (287).

1949. Opening of Nepal to exploration (288). Swiss expedition to N.E. Nepal; First ascent of Pyramid Peak (23,370) (312). Tilman's first expedition to Central Nepal (313).

1950. Chinese Comminust armies invade Tibet (289). Anglo-Swiss party climbs Abi Gamin, 24,130 feet (296). Tilman's second expedition to central Nepal; attempt on Annapurna IV (24,688); reconnaissance of Manaslu and Himal Chuli (314). French expedition reconnoitres Dhaulagiri I (26,795) and climbs Annapurna I (26,492) (315). Everest: Tilman and Houston reconnoitre Khumbu glacier (325).

1951. New Zealand party climbs Mukut Parbat (23,760) (295). French party attempts traverse from Nanda Devi to Nanda Devi East; Duplat and Vignes killed (296). Everest: Shipton's reconnaissance of the southern approach. Khumbu ice-fall climbed (326).

1952. French party (Russenberger and Georges) climbs Chaukhamba I (295). Japanese party (Imanishi) attempts Annapurna IV (24,688) and reconnoitres Manaslu (26,658) (319). Everest: Sixth and seventh assaults: Swiss attempts; Lambert and Tenzing reach c. 28,200 feet (328). Shipton's reconnaissance and training expedition to Cho Oyu (332).

1953. Japanese expedition (Mita) reaches 25,400 feet on Manaslu (320). Swiss expedition (Lauterburg) reaches c. 25,000 feet on Dhaulagiri I (26,795) (321). French expedition climbs Nun (23,410) (291). Austro-German expedition makes first ascent of Nanga Parbat (26,620) (306). K2: American attempt (Houston); death of Gilkey (300). Everest: Eighth assault: First ascent by Hillary and Tenzing of Hunt's expedition (332–9).

# Appendix D

## SHORT BIBLIOGRAPHY

THE literature of the Himalaya is vast. Much of the early history is scattered in periodicals and journals, in official departmental reports, in reports by commissions; some remains unpublished in Indian departmental files. A great deal appears in *Asiatic Researches; Journal of the Asiatic Society of Bengal* (*J.A.S.B.*); *Journal of the Royal Geographical Society* (*J.R.G.S.* and *G.J.*); *General Reports, Synoptical Volumes, Narrative Reports,* and *Records* of the Survey of India; *Alpine Journal* (*A.J.*), and *Himalayan Journal* (*H.J.*). References to the more important of these are given in footnotes to the text. Only the principal books on exploration and mountaineering in the Himalaya and Karakoram are given below. Technical and scientific publications are omitted. Unless otherwise stated the place of publication is London.

(a) TRAVELS AND EXPLORATION BEFORE 1885

Cunningham, A.: *Ladak: Physical, Statistical and Historical, &c.* (1854).
Dainelli, G.: *La Esplorazione della Regione fra l'Himalaja Occidentale e il Caracorum* (Bologna, 1934).
De Filippi, F.: *An Account of Tibet: The Travels of Ippolito Desideri of Pistoia, 1712–27* (1932).
Drew, F.: *The Jummoo and Kashmir Territories* (1875).
Forsyth, T. D.: *Report of a Mission to Yarkand in 1873* (Calcutta, 1875).
Gordon, T. E.: *The Roof of the World* (1876).
Hooker, J.: *Himalayan Journals,* 2 vols. (1854).
Markham, C. R.: *A Memoir on the Indian Survey* (2nd ed. Black) (1878).
Moorcroft, W. & Trebeck, G.: *Travels in the Himalayan Provinces of Hindustan and the Panjab, etc.* (ed. H. H. Wilson) (1841).
Phillimore, R. H.: *The Historical Records of the Survey of India.* Vol. I, 18th Century (1945); Vol. II, 1800–1815 (1950); Vol. III, 1815–1830 (1954); Vol. IV, 1830–1843: George Everest, in the press; Vol. V, 1844–1861, in preparation (Dehra Dun).
Schlagintweit, H. von: *Reisen in Indien und Hochasien,* 4 vols. (Jena, 1869–80).
Thomson, T.: *Western Himalaya and Tibet* (1852).
Vigne, G. T.: *Travels in Kashmir, etc.* (1852).
Wessels, C. J.: *Early Jesuit Travellers in Central Asia* (1603–1721) (The Hague, 1924).

(b) 1885-1918

Bruce, C. G.: *Twenty Years in the Himalaya* (1910); *Kulu and Lahoul* (1914); *Himalayan Wanderer* (1934).

Burrard, S. G. & Hayden, H. H.: *A Sketch of the Geography and Geology of the Himalaya Mountains and Tibet* (Dehra Dun, 1908); (revised ed. Burrard, Sir S. & Heron, A. M., Dehra Dun, 1933).

Collie, J. N.: *Climbing on the Himalaya* (Edinburgh 1902).

Conway, W. M.: *Climbing and Exploration in the Karakoram Himalayas* (1894).

De Filippi, F.: *Karakoram and Western Himalaya* (1912); *Himalaya, Karakoram and Eastern Turkistan (1913-14)* (1932).

Durand, A. G.: *The Making of a Frontier* (1900).

Eckenstein, O.: *The Karakorams and Kashmir* (1896).

Francke, A. H.: *A History of Western Tibet* (1907).

Fraser, D.: *The Marches of Hindustan* (1907).

Freshfield, D.: *Round Kangchenjunga* (1903).

Guillarmod, J. J.: *Six mois dans l'Himalaya, le Karakorum et l'Hindu-Kush* (Neuchâtel, n.d. ?1904).

Knight, E. F.: *Where Three Empires Meet* (1895).

Mason, K.: *Completion of the Link Connecting the Triangulations of India and Russia 1913* (Dehra Dun, 1914).

Meade, C. F.: *Approach to the Hills* (1940).

Mumm, A. L.: *Five Months in the Himalaya* (1909).

Neve, A.: *Thirty Years in Kashmir* (1913).

Neve, E.: *Beyond the Pir Panjal* (1914).

Rawling, C. G.: *The Great Plateau* (1905).

Sherring, C.: *Western Tibet and the British Borderlands* (1906).

Waddell, L. A.: *Among the Himalayas* (1899).

White, J. C.: *Sikkim and Bhutan: Twenty-one years on the North-east Frontier, 1887-1908* (1909).

Wood, H.: *Explorations in the Eastern Kara-koram and the Upper Yarkand Valley, 1914* (Dehra Dun, 1922).

Workman, W. H. & F. B.: *In the Ice-World of Himalaya* (1900); *Ice-bound Heights of the Mustagh* (1908); *Peaks and Glaciers of Nun Kun* (1909); *The Call of the Snowy Hispar* (1910); *Two Summers in the Ice-Wilds of Eastern Karakoram* (1917).

Younghusband, F. E.: *The Heart of a Continent* (1896).


(c) 1918-1928

Bruce, C. G.: *The Assault on Mount Everest 1922* (1923).

Howard-Bury, C. K.: *Mount Everest: The Reconnaissance 1921* (1922).

Longstaff, T.: *This is My Voyage* (1949).

Mason, K.: *The Exploration of the Shaksgam and Aghil Ranges 1926* (Dehra Dun, 1927).

Norton, E. F.: *The Fight for Everest 1924* (1925).

Visser-Hooft, J.: *Among the Kara-Korum Glaciers* (1926).

# APPENDIX D

*(d)* 1929–1939

Bauer, P.: *Im Kampf um den Himalaja* (Munich, 1931); *Um den Kantsch, 1931* (Munich, 1933); *Himalayan Campaign: The German Attack on Kangchenjunga* (trans. S. Austin) (Oxford, 1937); *Himalayan Quest* (trans. E. G. Hall) (1938).

Bechtold, F.: *Deutsche am Nanga Parbat: Der Angriff 1934* (Munich, 1935); *Nanga Parbat Adventure* (trans. H. E. G. Tyndale) (1935).

Bruce, C. G.: *Himalayan Wanderer* (1934).

Dyhrenfurth, G. O.: *Dämon Himalaya* (Basel, 1935).

Fellowes, P. F. M. and Blacker, L. V. S.: *First over Everest* (1933).

Ruttledge, H.: *Everest 1933* (1934); *Everest: The Unfinished Adventure* (1937).

Schomberg, R. C. F.: *Unknown Karakoram* (1936).

Scott Russell, R.: *Mountain Prospect* (1946).

Ségogne, H. de, and others: *Himalayan Assault* (trans. N. E. Morin) (1936).

Shipton, E.: *Nanda Devi* (1936); *Blank on the Map* (1938); *Upon that Mountain* (1943).

Smythe, F. S.: *The Kangchenjunga Adventure* (1932); *Kamet Conquered* (1932); *Camp Six: 1933 Mount Everest Expedition* (1937); *The Valley of Flowers* (1938).

Tilman, H. W.: *The Ascent of Nanda Devi* (Cambridge, 1937); *Mount Everest, 1938* (1939).

Visser, Ph. C. and Visser-Hooft, J.: *Karakoram*, Vol. I (Leipzig, 1935), Vol. II (Leiden, 1938).

Waller, J.: *The Everlasting Hills* (Edinburgh, 1939).

Younghusband, Sir F.: *Everest: The Challenge* (1936).

*(e)* 1940 AND AFTER

Bauer, P.: *Das Ringen um den Nanga Parbat 1856–1953* (Munich, 1955).

Harrer, H.: *Seven Years in Tibet* (1953).

Herzog, M.: *Annapurna* (trans. N. Morin & J. A. Smith) (1952).

Hunt, J.: *The Ascent of Everest* (1953).

Kurz, M. (ed.): *Berge der Welt* (annual volumes; since 1953 Eng. trans. *The Mountain World*).

Murray, W. H.: *The Scottish Himalayan Expedition* (1951); *The Story of Everest* (1953).

Noyce, W.: *Mountains and Men* (1947).

Seaver, G.: *Francis Younghusband, Explorer and Mystic* (1952).

Tilman, H. W.: *Two Mountains and a River* (1948).

357

# Index

Abbottabad, 12, 288
Abdul Subhan, 'the Munshi,' 87, 92-3
Abetti, Prof. G., 140-1
Abi Gamin (24,130), 23, 27, 82, 118, 120, 202; first ascent, 296
Abors, 43, 90, 129, 130
Abruzzi, Duke of the, 20, 50, 104, 133-6, 140, 151-2, 249, 257; Baltoro exped., 133-6; — ridge (K2), 55, 135, 258-63; 300-5
acclimatization, 152, 185-6, 212-13, 220, 281-2, 310-11, 332-3
Afghanistan, 99
Afraz Gul Khan, K. S., 89, 177-8, 180-3, 241-3
Aghil Mts., 9, 16, 100, 246; — P., 101, 245
Agra, 56, 57, 59
AK, see Kishen Singh
Aka tribes, 43
Aksai-chin plains, 82
Alaknanda, R., 5, 6, 22, 23, 57, 64, 66, 118-19, 204, 206, 264, 267, 294
Alampi La, 69
Alessandri, C., 140
Alessio, Com. A., 140-1
Allsup, W., 190-1
Allwein, E., 195-7, 199-200, 274
Almond, Capt. R. L., 153
Almora, 5, 25, 64, 115, 120; dist., 265, 267
Alpine Club, 154-5, 164, 325, 328
Alpine Journal, 189-90, 192
American Alpine Club, 257
Amo Chu (R.), 40, 42
Andes, 64
Andkhui, 67
Andrade, Antonio de, 25, 56-7
aneroid barometers, heights by, 72, 350
Anglo-Russian Boundary Commission, 99; — Agreement (1907), 143
Annapurna I (26,492), 5, 6, 7, 29, 33, 51, 125, 315-9, 346; first ascent, 316-9; — II (26,041), 29, 33, 346; — III (24,858), 33; — IV (24,688), 33, 314, 319; — Himal, 33, 314, 321
Antilli, A., 140-1
Api (23,399), 22, 25, 29, 30, 51, 115, 323-4, 343
Apsarasas, 17, 181
Arandu, 103, 131
Arun R., 29, 34, 35, 37, 159, 161
Arwa glaciers, 204, 206, 264, 269, 294
Aschenbrenner, P., 226-31, 306-8, 310
Asiatic Society of Bengal, 189
Askole, 17, 131, 240, 244, 248
Asper, J.-Jacques, 328-30
Assam Himalaya, 9, 89, 129, 277-9; defined, 10; described, 42-4; frontier tracts, 42; map, 8; monsoon, 46
Astor, 100; —, R., 69, 106
Ata Muhammad, 'the Mullah,' 87, 89
Atlas of China (d'Anville), 60
Attock, 66
Aubert, René, 328-30
Auden, J. B., 5, 27, 244-5, 265-8.
Aufschnaiter, Peter, 36, 195-7, 199-200, 238-9, 285-6, 313
Aumann, F., 306
avalanches, 52; — disasters: Everest, 171; Nanga Parbat, 109, 235-6; Chaukhamba, 270; Tirsuli, 172
Azevedo, Francisco de, 57, 58

Babusar P. (13,690), 12, 238, 288

Badrinath, 23, 56, 64, 119, 206
Bagani (Bagini) glac., 117, 206
Bagmati R., 63
Bagrot, 103
Baijnath, 14.
Bailey, F. M., 42, 44, 90, 129, 130
Baines, A. C., 135
Balestreri, Umberto, 240
Balipara (dist.), 42
Baltistan, 9, 10, 11, 17, 69, 81, 101; porters, 132, 234, 248, 301
Baltoro glac., 9, 16, 17, 19, 20, 77, 100, 104, 132-6, 240-1, 248-9, 252, 257, 301; map, 134; weather, 50; — Kangri, (23,390), 104, 139, 240, 248; — Muztagh, 19
Band, G., 333-9
Bandarpunch (20,720), 22, 27, 153; first ascent, 293
Banihal P. (8985), 14
Bankund (Banke) glac., 266
Banon, Maj. H. M., 292
Baralacha La (16,200), 13, 57, 69
Baramula, 12
Barbezat, A., 296-7
Barbung Khola (R.), 31
Barenghi, J., 343
Bareux, Ernest, 133
Bargaon, 87
Barhma Sakil (15,440), 14, 112
Barmal glac., 110-11
Barton, Rev. C. E., 15, 111
Barun glac., 36, 332, 344
Baruntse (23,560), 36; first ascent, 344
Bashahr, 11, 69
Baspa R., 12, 23, 69, 79
Bat Kol P. (14,370), 13
Bates, R. H., 257-9, 300-5
Batura glac., 16, 17, 179; — Muztagh, 19, 178, 300
Bauer, Paul, 39, 41, 124, 195-201, 226-7, 234-8, 275-6, 277, 281, 311; first (German) Kangchenjunga exped., 195-8; second, 199-201; 1938 Nanga Parbat exped., 236-8
Bazin Gap (c. 25,630), 238, 309-10
Beas R., 10, 11, 12, 13, 14, 287, 292
Beauman, W.-Com. E. B., 202-3
Bechtold, Fritz, 226-30, 232, 234-7
Beetham, Bentley, 172, 324
Beigel, E., 195-7
Bell, G., 300-5
Bell, Lieut. H. G., 144-5
Bell, Sir Charles, 155
Bellew, Dr. H., 92
Bernadzikiewicz, S., 26, 271-2; death, 272
Bernard, Dr. W., 229-30
Bernier, 14
Berril, K., 296
Betterton, A. F., 246
Bhagirath Kharak glac., 119, 206, 269-70
Bhagirathi R., 22, 23, 64, 68, 79, 264; — II (21,364), 26; first ascent, 268
Bhareli R., 43, 279
Bheri R., 31, 32
Bhiundhar Khal (P.) (16,700), 118-19, 204; — valley, 118
Bhote Kosi R., 34, 36, 332; see also Po Chu, Tamba Kosi, Dudh Kosi
Bhotias, 186, 202, 208
Bhutan, 42-3, 58, 61, 78, 84, 91, 123-4, 129, 278-9, 288; Deb Raja of, 61
Biafo glac., 16, 17, 20, 69, 77, 131, 245-6
Biddulph, Capt. J., 92, 99

Bir Singh, 66, 85
Birdwood, F.-M. Lord (C.-in-C. India), 189
Birehi R., 64
Birnie, Capt. E. St. J., 202-4, 211, 213-14, 264; —'s pass, 206, 269
Bitterling, Albert, 306
Blacker, Valentine (S. G. India 1823-6), 68
Blake, S. B., 271
Blanc, Pierre, 120
Bogle, George, 61, 89
Boss, Emil, 93, 114
Bourdillon, T. D., 326-7, 332, 333-9
Boustead, J. E. H., 211, 213
Braham, T. H., 293, 344
Brahmaputra R., 6, 9, 42, 43, 89, 129
Braldoh R., 17, 77, 131, 240
Braldu glac., 101, 245-6
Brantschen, Johann, 177
Braun, P., 321-3
Brenner, J., 195-7, 199, 274
Broad Peak (26,414), 19, 135, 240, 346; — II (26,017), 346
Brocherel, Alexis and Henri, 114, 117-19, 133; Emil, 133
Brocklebank, T. A., 211
Brotherhood, R., 251
Brown, Prof. T. Graham, 207-9, 252-3, 257
Bruce, Gen. the Hon. Charles G., 14, 15, 26, 55, 99, 101, 112-13, 114, 122, 132, 142, 145, 151-3, 154-5, 189-90, 281, 286, 292; (Conway) Baltoro, 103-4; (Mummery) Nanga Parbat, 107-9; Nun Kun, 110; Nanda Devi, 116-9; Everest (1922), 165-71; Everest (1924), 172
Bruce, J. G., 166, 169-70, 172-4
Bryant, L. V., 218-19, 220
Buhl, Hermann, 306-11
Bujak, Jakub, 26, 271-2
Bukhara, 66, 67, 89
Bullock, G. H., 155, 159-63, 222
Bumtang, 278-9; — Chu (R.), 42, 43
Bunar Gah, 106
Bunji, 89
Burdsall, R., 257-8
Buri Gandaki R. (Buriganga), 29, 32, 33, 85, 320
Burrard, Sir Sidney (S.G. 1910-19), ix, 9, 22, 37, 73, 74, 90, 142, 153, 349
Burzil P. (13,775), 6, 12, 19, 49, 50, 69, 103, 226
Butwal, 67
Byas Rikhi Himal, 29

Cabral, John, 58, 61
Cacella, Stephen, 58, 61
Calciati, Count, 15, 112
Campbell, D., 205
Cardew, Capt. E. B., 129, 153
Carslaw, Dr. J. S., 251
Carter, Adams, 207-9
Carter, Lieut. T. T., 82
Cave, Capt. F. O., 180-2
Cayley, Dr. H., 92
Chabrang, 58; see also Tsaparang
Chakrata, 25
Chalt, 102, 256, 300
Chamba, 11, 13
Chamoli, 23
Chandar Parbat (22,073), 26; first ascent, 268
Chandra-Bhaga R., 11, 12, 13, 14, 292-3
Chang La, 69, 141
Changabang (A21) (22,520), 93-4, 117

# INDEX

Chang-chenmo, 78
Changtse (24,730), 160
Chapman, Capt. E. F., 92
Chapman, F. Spencer, 39, 42, 277-8, 285
Chapursan R., 17, 103, 184
Chase, Maj. A. A., 153
Chaturangi glac., 204, 206, 265-6, 268, 293
Chaukhamba (23,420), 22, 23, 26, 114, 119, 206, 264, 269-70, 295; avalanches, 269, 270; first ascent, 295
Chayul Dzong, 43
Chenab R., 10, 11, 12, 287, 292
Chevalley, Dr. Gabriel, 296, 328-31
*choti barsat*, 48
Chhotkhaga P. (16,900), *see* Nela P.
Chilas, 12, 84, 100, 235, 238; campaign (1892), 107
China (hill-station), view from, 25
Chinese Turkestan (Sinkiang), 80, 84, 92, 99, 105
Chini, 11, 22
Chitral, 84, 99
Cho Oyu (26,750), 7, 29, 36, 159, 328, 332, 346; first ascent, 344
Chogolisa (25,110), 104, 135, 136, 252, 347; — saddle, 136
Chogo Lungma glac., 70, 77, 131, 132, 246
Chomiomo (22,430), first ascent, 129
Chomo Lonzo (25,640), 347
Chomo Lungma, 73
Chomolhari (23,997), 42, 43, 277-8
Chong Kumdan glac., 17, 138
Choten Nyima La, 123, 128
Christian church (Tibet), 25, 57-8
Chumbi valley, 40, 42, 43, 58, 61, 125, 156, 278, 289
Chungthang (Tsungtang), 40
Churen Himal (24,158), 31
Clifford, Maj. R. C., 180-3
Cockerill, Sir George K., 20, 102-3, 145, 177-8
Colebrooke, Robert H., (S.G. Bengal 1794-1808), 63-5, 71
Colledge, R., 332
Collie, Prof. J. Norman, 80, 94, 99, 107-9, 190, 286
Collins, V. D. B., 139, 144-5, 153, 249
Compagnoni, A., 343
Concordia, 135, 240, 258
Conway, Sir W. Martin (Lord Conway of Allington), 20, 55, 94, 99, 111, 190; Karakoram exped., 103-5
Cooke, C. R., 39, 51, 274-5, 277
Corbett, Sir Geoffrey, 189-92
Coresma, Nuno, 58
Correa, Ambrosio, 58
Corry, Maj. J. B., 113, 142, 153
Cotter, F. M., 295
Couzy, Jean, 315-8
Cowie, Capt. H. McC., 125
Coxcomb Ridge (Nanda Devi), 207-9, 260, 296
Crace, W. H., 306 (death)
Craig, R., 300-5
Crawford, C. E., 278
Crawford, C. G., 166, 170-1, 211
Crawford, Charles (S.G. Bengal, 1813-15), 63, 64, 67
Crowley, A. E., 126, 132
Cunningham, Alexander, 20, 80-1
cyclonic disturbances, 48

Daba Dzong, 66, 85
Daflas, 43, 78, 130
Dainelli, Prof. Giotto, 69, 140, 241
Dalai Lama, 155, 289
Dalhousie, 5; —, Lord, 74
d'Anville, J.-B. B., 60, 84; *Carte de l'Inde*, 61
Darjeeling, 5, 37, 78, 81, 94, 156, 195, 199; monsoon rainfall, 46
Darkot P., 92, 99, 144
De Filippi, Sir Filippo, 20, 133, 136, 179-82, 241; Karakoram Exped., 140-1
Deb (or Devi) Singh, 66, 84
Dehra Dun, 85, 111, 137, 140, 286

Delhi, 59; monsoon rainfall, 46
Dent, Clinton, 152
Deo Tibba (20,410), 13, 202; first ascent, 202
Depsang Plateau, 141, 181, 242
Desideri, Ippolito, 59, 60, 66
Desio, Prof. Ardito, 21, 240-1, 244, 343
*Deutsche Himalaja Stiftung*, 234
Devadhunga, 73
Devies, Lucien, 315
Dharmsala, 14
Dhaula Dhar, 11, 12, 14, 22, 23; described, 11; monsoon, 47
Dhaulagiri I (26,795), 5, 6, 29, 31, 51, 65, 67, 73, 315-16, 321-3, 344, 346; Webb's height, 64; — Group, 31, 347; — Himal, 31, 87, 125, 322
Dhauli R., 23, 26, 64, 66, 115, 117-18, 206, 265, 267
Dhauliganga R., 22
Dhotial porters, 206, 208, 271
Diamirai glac., 106-9, 225, 238-9
Dibang R., 129
Dibrugheta, 93, 117
Digar La, 66, 69
Dihang R., 9, 90, 129, 130
Disteghil Sar I (25,868), 19, 102, 145, 179, 346; — II (25,250), 347
Dittert, René, 39, 293-4, 296, 312, 328-30
Dodang Nyima (range), 40; — Pk., (23,620), 199, 274; first ascent, 274
Dogras, 99
Do-Kyong La (10,400), 43
Dongkya Ridge, 40; — La, 91
Dorah P., 99
Dorje Lakpa I (23,240), 36
d'Orville, Albert, 58-9
Douglas and Clydesdale, Marquis of, 217
Doya La, 161
Dras, 13; — rainfall, 47, 49
Drew, F., 91, 189
Drexel, A., 229
Drohmo (c. 23,300), 312
Duars, 42, 58
Dubost, L., 296-7
Dudh Khola (R.) (Marsyandi), 314, 320
Dudh Kosi R., (Bhote Kosi), 34, 122, 332
Dunagiri (23,184), 26, 93-4, 117, 205, 267, 269-70; first ascent, 270; — Gad (R.), 117
Dungri La (18,400), *see* Mana pass
Dunn, Prof. S. G., 142
Duplat, R., 296-7; death, 297
Durand, Sir Algernon, 100, 102
Durrance, J., 260-2
Duvanel, C., 198
Dyer, J., 79
Dyhrenfurth, Prof. G. O., and Mrs., 41, 198, 248-9, 274
Dzakar Chu, 159-60
Dzongka, 33
Dzongri, 93, 94, 123-4, 312

E61 (23,890), 80
Eckenstein, O., 103-4, 132, 133
Edge, Capt. R. C. A., 266
Eichelberg, M., 321-2
Emmons, Arthur, 207
equipment, 212, 281, 332
Ertl, H., 306-10
Evans, R. C., 292, 314, 332, 333-9, 344
Everest, Sir George (S.G. India 1830-43), 71-2, 74, 348; —'s spheroid, 71
Everest, Mount (29,002), 5, 6, 7, 29, 33, 36, 55, 87, 105, 116, 122, 125, 137, 151-2, 197-8, 287, 346; — Committee, 155, 165, 211, 217, 280, 325; — Flight, 216-17; height, 349; map, 158; monsoon, 47; name, 73, 76, 87; weather, 51; expeditions: (1921), 154-63; (1922), 164-71; (1924), 172-6; (1933), 211-16; (1935), 217-20; (1936), 220-2; (1938), 222-4; (1950), 325-6; (1951), 326-8; (1952), 328-31; (1953, Ascent), 332-9
Eversden, W., 274

Falconer, H., 69, 70

Fankhauser, P., 234-6
Farrar, J. P., 154
Fazl Elahi, 246, 266
Fendt, W., 195-7, 199
Ferber, A. C., 133
Field, Capt. J. A., 44, 130, 153
Finch, George I., 155, 166-70, 187-8
Finsterwalder, Prof. Richard, 37, 183, 226, 229, 350
Flory, Léon, 328-30
food, 212
Forked Peak (20,340), 94, 126
Forsyth, Sir Douglas, 92
Fountaine, E. C., 246
Foy, Major, J. R., 271
Frauenberger, Dr. W., 306-9, 311
French Alpine Club, 315
Freshfield, Douglas, 41, 55, 80, 99, 122, 154, 190; Kangchenjunga exped., 124-5
Frier, Capt. R. N. D., 226, 228-9

Gandaki R., 6, 10, 29, 32; — Section, Nepal Himalaya, 314; described, 32-3; map, 32
Ganesh Himal (24,299), 29, 33
Ganges R., 6, 7, 10, 22; sources, 63
Gangotri, 64; — glac., 22, 26, 206, 264-5, 268-9, 293-5; map, 265; triangulation, 266; — peaks: I (21,890), 27, 295 (first ascent); III (21,578), 27, 295 (first ascent)
Gangtok, 40
Garbyang, 29, 115
Gardiner, Capt. R., 266
Gardner, Alexander, 19, 69
Garstin, John, (S.G. Bengal 1808-13), 65
Gartok, 66, 115, 125
Garwood, Prof., 37, 55, 94, 124-5
Gasherbrum I (26,490), 16, 17, 19, 21, 104, 135, 182; attempts, 248-51; group, 248; heights, 346; — glac., 101, 240-1, 243
Gaumukh, 23, 64, 68, 266
Gauri Sankar (23,440), 36, 73, 125, 327
Gavin, J. M. L., 220
Gawler, Col. J. C., 82
Gendre, P., 296
Genghis Khan, 13
Geological Survey of India, 121, 266
George V., H. M. King, 155
Georges, L., 295
Gerard, Capt. Alexander and Dr. J. G., 68
Gerard, John, 61, 68
Gevril, L., 296-7
Ghiglione, Prof. P., 343
Ghori Parbat (22,010), 23, 26, 269-70; first ascent, 270
Ghujerab R., 177-8, 184
Gibson, J. T. M., 27, 289, 293
Gilgit, 12, 19, 69, 84, 99-103, 131, 144, 145, 178, 217, 235, 256, 288, 301; rainfall, 47; wind, 50; — road, 12, 102, 226; — Scouts, 234-5
Gilkey, A., 300-05, 311; death, 305
Ginori Marchese, 140
Godwin-Austen, H. H., 20, 55, 76-8, 80, 104; — glac., 104, 132, 135, 301
Goes, Benedict de, 56
Gogra R., 22
Goodfellow, B. R., 295, 321
Gor, 15
Gordamah (22,200), 276; first ascent, 276
Goriganga R., 5, 6, 22, 69, 114-15, 272, 297-8
Gosainthan (26,291), 29, 33, 36, 313, 346; (25,134), 347
Göttner, Adolf, 39, 234-6, 275-6; death, 235
Gourlay, G. B., 190-1, 274
Government of India, 155-6, 180, 191, 229
Graaff, J. de V., 292-3, 298
Graham, W. W., 26, 39, 93-5, 114, 117, 123, 269, 275
Graven, Prof. J., 293-4
'Great Game in Asia,' 84, 86
Great Himalaya, 5, 6, 9, 11, 22, 29-36, 39, 40, 44, 47; defined, 5; section, 6; triangulation, 74

Great Karakoram, 20, 100, 101, 177–84, 240–7; defined, 19; monsoon, 47
Great Meridional Arc, 71, 74
Great Rangit R., 81
Great Trigonometrical Survey (G.T.S.), 70, 71, 73, 79, 80, 142, 145, 348
Greene, Dr. Raymond, 202–3, 211, 213
Greenwood, R. D., 289
Gregory, Alfred, 332, 333–9
Grob, E., 39, 276, 277
Grombchevsky, Capt., 101, 102
Grueber, Johann, 58–9
Guge (Tibet), 25, 57
Guicha La, 93, 123, 124
Gulab Singh, Maharajah, 9, 77, 80
Gulatee, B. L., 74, 349–50
Gulmarg, 15, 48, 77, 287
Gunter, Maj. C. P., 129
Gupt Khal (P.) (18,990), 266
Gurais, 12
Gurdial Singh, 297
Gurkhas, 15, 101, 103–5, 107–9, 110–13, 142, 145–6, 180, 188
Gurla Mandhata (25,355), 7, 30, 115, 136, 347
Gya, 57
Gyachung Kang (25,990), 36, 160, 346; — glac., 160; — Chu, 160
Gyala, 90
Gyala Peri (23,460), 44
Gyantse, 43, 61, 125
Gyr, Hans, 299–300

Hadow, Maj. Kenneth, 226, 236
Hamberger, Dr. Hugo, 226–7
Hanle, 57, 74
Hannah, J. S., 198
Haramosh Range, 19
Haramukh (16,872), 12, 76, 112, 119
Hari Ram, MH, 87, 156
Harkbir Thapa, Subadar, 104–5, 110–13
Harman, Capt. H. J., 89–91, 123
Harrer, Heinrich, 36, 238–9, 286, 298, 313
Harris, Sqd. Leader, S. B., 217, 301
Harrison, J. B., 15, 39, 252–6
Harsil, 22, 23
Hartmann, Hans, 199–200, 234–6
Hastings, G., 107–8
Hathi Parbat (22,070), 23, 269
Hayward, Lieut. G. W., 91–2, 99
Hazara, 66
Hazard, J. de V., 172, 173, 175
Hearsey, Hyder Young, 64–6, 67, 85
Heckler, K., 343
height observations, accuracy of, 72, 348–50
Henderson, G., 92
Henderson, J., 69
Hepp, G., 39, 234–6, 275–6; death, 235
Herbert, James D., 67–8, 71
Heron, Dr. A. M., 156, 159–61
Herrligkoffer, Dr. K. M., 306
Herron, Rand, 226–8
Herzog, Maurice, 31, 33, 51, 315–19
Hillary, Sir Edmund, 36, 192, 216, 295, 326–7, 332, 333–9, 344
Himal Chuli (25,801), 33, 314–15, 346
Himalaya, described, 3–10; meaning and pronunciation, 3
Himalayan Club, 151, 189–92, 195, 226, 229, 271, 274, 280–1, 287–8; Committee, 325–6, 328; founding of, 189–92
Himalayan Journal, The, 192, 288
Hindu Kush, 16, 99, 102–3
Hingston, Maj. R. W. G., 145–6, 152, 172, 180, 188
Hinks, Arthur, 183
Hispar glac., 9, 16, 17, 19, 20, 77, 103, 131–2, 246–7; — Muztagh, 19, 20, 178–9; — P., 104, 131
Hodgkin, R. A., 252–6
Hodgson, Brian, 73
Hodgson, John Anthony, (S.G. India, 1821–1823, 1826–9), 67, 68
Hoerlin, H., 39, 198, 274
Hofstetter, Ernest, 328–30

Holdich, Sir Thomas H., 92, 105
Holdsworth, R., 202–4
Honigmann, E., 133
Hoogly, 58
Hooker, Sir Joseph, 40, 81, 87
Hotta, Y., 26
House, W. P., 257–9
Houston, Dr. Charles, 20, 50, 136, 207–10, 325–6; (1938 K2), 257–60; (1953 K2), 300–5
Houston, Oscar R., 325
Howard-Bury, Col., 164, 190; (1921 Everest), 155–63
Huber, Ernst, 269–70
Huddleston, Capt. P. G., 130, 153
Hume, A. O., 92
Humla Karnali R., 29, 30, 31
Humphreys, Dr. G. N., 220
Hundes prov. (Tibet), 66
Hunt, Sir John, 51, 55, 221, 251–2, 277, 325, 340; ascent of Everest, 332–9
Hunter, Dr. J. de Graaff, 52, 72, 74, 140, 143–4, 349–50
Hunza, 17, 19, 99–103, 183–4, 246, 256, 288, 300; Mir of, 56, 301, 307; people, 17, 100; porters, 145, 301–5, 307–9, 311; weather, 50; — -Nagir Campaign, 102, 256; — R., 17, 19, 99, 144–5, 177–9
'Hurree Babu,' 86, 91
Hushe glac., and vall., 131, 253
Huss, H., 321–2

Ibanez, F., 344
Ibi Gamin, 82, 296
Ichac, Marcel, 249, 315–16
Imanishi, Dr. K., 319
Imboden, Joseph, 93
Imja Khola, 325
Inayat Khan, 246
Inderbinen, Moritz, 116
Indian Atlas, 83; — Mutiny, 77
Indira Col, 101
Indo-Russian triangulation, 143–7, 247
Indus R., 5, 6, 7, 11, 16, 17, 70, 125, 238
Irshad P., 99
Irvine, Andrew, 172, 174–6, 215
Irwin, Lord (Viceroy) (Earl of Halifax), 189
Ishizaka, J., 320–1
Ishkoman R., 16

Jacot-Guillarmod, Dr. J., 41, 126, 132–3, 135
James, Capt. Ralph, 111, 291
Jammu, 11, 12, 13, 14
Jamna Prasad, 140–1
Janu (25,294), 37, 347
Jaonli, 264
Japanese Alpine Club, 320
Jayal, Flt. Lieut. Nalni D., 291, 297
Jayal, Maj. N. D., 296–7, 345
Jelep La (14,390), 40, 157
Jesuits, 25, 56–60
Jhelum R., 10, 11; — valley 'cart-road,' 14, 95, 288
Joechler, S., 344
Johnson, W. H., 79–80, 141, 189
Johorey, Capt. K. C., 291
Jonas, Rudolf, 268, 343–4
Jones, J. H. Emlyn, 314
Jongsong Peak (24,344), 39, 128, 198, 274; first ascent, 274; — La (20,080), 124, 128
Joshimath, 23, 64, 66, 93, 118, 206, 208, 294
Jubonu, 94
Jugal Himal, 34, 36
Jumna R., 10, 22, 79

Kali Gandaki R., 5, 6, 29, 31, 32, 33, 87, 88, 315–6, 321–2; — gorge, 29, 33
Kalian Singh, GK, 84, 86
Kamet (25,447), 7, 23, 26, 27, 66, 82, 114, 118–20, 157, 185–6, 202–4, 264, 296, 347; first ascent, 202–4
Kampa Dzong, 59, 123, 156–7, 159
Kamri P. (13,368), 12, 49
Kanawar, 69
Kang Chu (Tamba Kosi), 34; — La, 91, 93, 122–4, 198, 312
Kangbachen (hamlet) (13,150), 124, 312, 346; — (Pk.) (25,782), 37, 198, 312
Kangchenjau (22,700), 40, 129
Kangchenjunga I (28,146), 5, 6, 29, 35, 37, 41, 55, 73, 87, 90–1, 93, 122, 220, 234, 277, 312, 344–6; height, 350; map, 38; monsoon, 47; ridges, 37–8; (Freshfield, 1899), 124–5; (Bauer, 1929), 195–8; (Dyhrenfurth, 1930), 198–9; (Bauer, 1931), 199–201; — II (27,803), 37, 346; — glacier, 124–5; 128, 198; —, North Col, (22,620), 198, 277
Kangra, 11, 14
Kanjut Sar (25,460), 19, 179, 347
Kappeler, R., 299
Karakash R., 82, 91
Karakoram, 9, 92, 131–47, 177–184, 240–63, 299–305; described, 16–21; map, 18; monsoon, 47, 50; nomenclature, 18
Karakoram P. (18,605), 13, 16, 66, 69, 79, 81, 92, 101, 131, 138, 242
Karbir Burathoki, Subadar, 103–5, 110–13, 117–18
Karma Chu, 159, 161–2, 167, 215
Karnali R., 6, 10, 29, 31, 32; — section, Nepal Himalaya, described, 29–33; map, 30
Karnaprayag, 66
Karpinski, Adam, 26, 269, 271–2; death, 272
Karumbar R., 16, 144
Karun Pir (P.) (15,988), 179, 183
Kashgar, 66, 82, 92, 141
Kashmir, 11, 12, 15, 66, 74, 91; first survey, 74–80; re-survey (1910), 142–7
Kathgodam, 25, 186
Katmandu, 5, 28, 59, 67, 87, 319, 328, 331, 333, 335
Kato, H. and K., 319, 320–1
Kauffmann, Ulrich, 93, 114
Kedarnath (22,770), 22, 25, 264, 294; first ascent, 294
Kellas, Dr. A. M., 39, 40, 41, 120, 127–9, 152, 155–9, 175, 176, 185–6, 202; death, 157
Kempe, J. W. R., 289, 293, 344
Kempson, E. G. H., 218, 220, 276
Kempter, Otto, 306–9
Kero Lungma glac., 77
Kesar Singh (Bhotia), 203, 205, 297
Khagan, 12, 113, 119, 238
Khalatse, 13
Khapalu, 70, 137, 251, 253
Kharta Chu, 159, 161–3, 223
Khotan, 80
Khumbu glac., 35, 122, 161, 325–8
Khunjerab R., 17, 103, 177–8, 184; — P. (16,188), 178
Khurdopin glac., 102, 179
Kilik P., 99
Kinloch, Capt., 60
Kinthup, 90, 123, 130
Kipling's 'Kim,' 86
Kirkpatrick, William, 61, 68
Kirkus, C. F., 265
Kishen Singh, AK, 84, 86–9, 92, 114
Kishenganga R., 12, 113
Kishtwar, 11, 13, 292
Klarner, J., 271–2
Knowles, G., 132
Kogan, Mme. Claude, 15, 291
Koh-i-Nur (16,725), 12, 112
Kolahoi (17,799), 12, 112, 142
Kolb, F., 292
Köllensperger, H., 306–8

# INDEX

Kondus glac., 131, 139, 140, 240; — valley, 251
Kosi R., 6, 10, 29, 35, 63; — Section, Nepal Himalaya, described, 33–6; map, 34
Kraus, K. von., 195–7, 235
Krenek, L., 288, 292
Krishna Gandaki R., see Kali Gandaki
Kuari P. (12,140), 64, 115, 117, 294
Kulbahadur Gurung, 113, 118, 142
Kulha Kangri (24,784), 42, 43, 278
Kulu, 13, 14, 287, 292
Kumaun Himalaya, 9, 67, 68, 82, 91, 93, 114–21, 185–8, 264–73, 293–8; defined, 10; described, 22–7; maps, 6, 8, 24; monsoon, 47; re-survey, 264–7; triangulation, 74, 79; weather, 50
Kun (23,250), 15, 109–12; first ascent, 112
Kunigk, H., 226–7
Kungri La, 13
Kunhar R., 12, 113
Kurz, Marcel, 124, 198, 249, 311
Kyagar glac., 182, 241–3
Kydd, J. W., 249, 274
Kyetrak glac., 159, 161; — Chu, 160
Kyirong, 33, 36, 85, 313

Lacedelli, L., 343
Lachalung La (16,600), 13, 57
Lachen, 40, 159; — Chu (R.), 37, 40
Lachenal, Louis, 315–19
Lachung Chu (R.), 37, 40, 91
Ladakh, 9, 10, 11, 66, 69, 80–2, 131; people, 17; porters, 181; — Range, 9, 16, 19, 69, 141
Lahore, 59
Lahul, 13, 14, 291–3
Lambert, Raymond, 51, 328–31, 344
Lambo Chu (R.), 40
Lambton, William, 71
Lamjung Himal, 33, 314
Landour, view from, 25
Langpo Peak (22,800), 39, 128; first ascent, 128; — glac., 128
Langtang Himal, 36, 313; — Khola (R.), 313
Langtang Lirung (23,771), 36
Langu, R., 31
Languepin, J., 296–7
Lansdowne, 25
Lapche Kang, 34, 36
Larji, 11
Larkya Himal, 33
Lata P., 117, 205
Lauterburg, Bernhard, 321–2
Lawan (Lwanl) valley, 115, 210, 268, 271, 296
Lawrence, Sir John, 77
Leh, 13, 19, 57, 59, 66, 69, 92, 141, 242; rainfall, 47
Lenox-Conyngham, Sir Gerald, 144
Leo Pargial (22,280), 13
Lesser Himalaya, 4, 25, 32; defined, 4; monsoon, 46–7
Lesser Karakoram, 19, 251–6
Leupold, J., 195–7, 199
Lewis, Brig. Sir Clinton G., 130
Lhakpa La (22,200), 162–3, 223
Lhasa, 43, 59, 66, 84, 85, 88–91, 125, 277, 286, 289
Lho La (c. 19,250),160–1, 219
Lhobrak Chu (R.), 42, 43
Lhonak (dist.), 40, 123, 124, 128, 274; — Pk. (21,260), 274; first ascent, 274
Lhotse (27,890), 29, 33, 36, 162, 327, 329, 331, 336, 346
Lhuntse (dist.), 43
Lichar spur, 70, 226
Liddar R., 12, 142
Lingtren (21,730), 160
Lingzitang plains, 82
Lipu Lekh P. (16,750), 115, 187
Lloyd, Peter, 207–9, 222–3, 313
Lochmatter, Franz, 120, 177–9, 241
Logbahadur Gurung, 142
Lohner, Mme. A., 293, 312

Longland, J. L., 211, 213–4, 222
Longstaff, Dr. T. G., 20, 25, 30, 55, 75, 94, 95, 99, 114–20, 127, 133, 151–3, 154, 177, 186–8, 190, 205, 210, 242, 264, 268, 281, 295, 299; (Karakoram) exped., 136–9; (Kumaun Himalaya), 114–20; (1922 Everest), 165–7, 170–1; —'s Col, 115, 210, 271, 296–7
Loomis, W. F., 207–9
Lorimer, G., 299
Lowe, W. G., 295, 332, 333–9, 344
Lowndes, D. G., 314
Lucas, Major, F. G., 15, 110
Ludlow, F., 42, 43, 44, 278–9
Luft, Ulrich, 234–8
Luhit, R., 129
Luhri, 14
Lungnak La, 123

Macartney, Sir George, 102
McCormick, A. D., 103
McInnes, C. S., 139, 144–5
MacIntyre, Flt. Lieut. D. F., 217
McKay, Capt. H. M., 153
McKenna, Flt. Lieut., 236
Maclean, Dr. W., 211
McNair, William Watts, 93
Mahabharat Lekh, 5, 32, 37; monsoon, 47
Mahalungur Himal, 33, 36, 73
Maiktoli (22,320), 114, 207; first ascent, 207
Makalu I (27,790), 5, 6, 29, 36, 125, 162, 217, 332, 344, 346; — II (25,120), 162, 347
Malana R., 13
Mallory, G. L., 154–5, 159–63, 164–71, 172–6, 214–15, 216, 222, 289, 325; death of, 175
Malpichi, Stanislaus, 58
Mamostong Kangri (24,690), 177, 242
Mana (village), 206; — (peak) (23,860), 23, 26, 82, 266, 296; first ascent, 266; — (pass) (18,400), 23, 56–8, 119
Manangbhot, 314, 316
Manas R., 42
Manasarowar L., 7, 64, 66, 80, 85, 115, 125, 187
Manaslu I (26,658), 29, 314–15, 320, 346; — II (25,705), 33, 346; — glacier, 320
Mandakini R., 22
Mandani Parbat (20,320), 268
Mandi, 14
Mandir Parbat (21,520), 23
Mani Singh, GM, 84–6
Manners-Smith, Maj. J., V.C., 102, 122
Marang La (16,600), 13
Marinelli, O., 140
Markham, Sir Clements, 74
Marques, Manuel, 25, 56–8
Marsh, R. M. W., 306
Marsyandi R., 32, 33, 314, 319
Martoli, 69, 268
Masherbrum (E., 25,660; W., 25,610), 16, 21, 251–6, 346, 347; map, 254; — Range, 19, 252
Mason, Kenneth, 112, 142–6, 179–183
Mayandi Khola (R.), 321–2
Mazeno P. (17,640), 100, 106–7
Meade, C. F., 120, 171, 178, 202, 264; —'s Col (23,420), 120, 186
Meade, Maj. H. R. C., 43
Medical Research Council, 185, 332
Merkl, Willy, 49, 226–33; death, 231
Metcalfe, Charles, 65
Milàm, 66, 84, 85, 114, 187, 272; — glac., 26, 121, 272
Millais, G. W., 112
Minchinton, Maj. H. D., 180–2
Mintaka P. (15,450), 99, 101, 144
Mir Izzet Ullah, 66, 69
Miris, 43, 130
Mirza Shuja, 'the Mirza,' 87, 89
Misch, P., 229
Mishmi hills, 129, 279
Moguls, 14
Molenaar, D., 300–5

Momhil glac., 102
Mon La Kar Chung La (P.) (17,442), 43, 278
Monrad Aas, I., 39, 94, 126–7
Monserrate, Anthony, 56
monsoon, 45, 46, 47, 48, 49, 50; on Everest, 213, 216, 218, 221–2; on Nanga Parbat, 233; on Annapurna, 317
Montagnier, H. F., 145, 183–4
Montgomerie, Capt. T. G., 76–7, 84, 87, 89, 142
Moorcroft, William, 19, 65–7, 69, 85
Morris, C. John, 145, 166, 183–4, 220
Morris, James, 333
Morshead, Col. H. T., 44, 90, 129, 130, 155–7, 159, 161–3, 166–70, 185–6, 202, 264
Mott, P., 246
Mountain Club of India, 189–91
Mrigthuni (22,490), 114, 116
Mugu Karnali R., 30, 31
Muhammad Akram, 242–3
Muktinath, 33, 87, 315, 316; — pilgrimage, 33
Mukut Himal, 31
Mukut Parbat (23,760), 27, 82, 295–6; first ascent, 295
Müllritter, P., 229–30, 234–6
Mulungutti glac., 102, 145, 178–9
Mumm, A. L., 69, 116–19, 152, 154, 266
Mummery, A. F., 15, 49, 99, 107–9, 238; death, 109; —'s col, 108
Murchison, Sir Roderick, 73
Murray, W. H., 30, 51, 297, 323, 326–7
Murree, 5; monsoon rainfall, 46
Mussoorie, 5, 25; monsoon rainfall, 47
Muzaffarabad, 12
muz-tagh, 19
Muztagh P., 20, 100, 133, 240–1

Nag Tibba Ra., 25
Nagir State, 100, 103, 131; people, 17; porters, 103–4
Nain Singh, 'The Pundit,' 84–6, 88
Naini Tal, 5, 25, 94, 114, 120; monsoon rainfall, 46–7
Namcha Barwa (25,445), 5, 6, 9, 42, 44, 130, 347
Namche Bazar, 35, 325–6, 328, 335
Nampa (22,162), 22, 29, 324
Nanda Devi (25,645), 5, 6, 22, 25, 26, 27, 69, 93–4, 114–17, 187–8, 204–10, 219, 257, 260, 265–7, 267, 296–7, 347; first ascent, 207–10; map, 116; weather, 50; — East (24,391), 26, 27, 114–15, 206, 210, 271–2, 296–7; first ascent, 272; second, 297
Nanda Ghunti (20,700), 114, 294–5; first ascent, 294
Nandakini R., 64, 120, 188, 294
Nanda Kot (22,510), 22, 26, 69, 115, 187, 268; first ascent, 268
Nanga Parbat (26,620), 5–7, 11, 12, 15, 70, 217, 286–7, 346; Everest compared, 225; map, 108; monsoon, 47, 49; topography, 106, 225; weather, 49; (Mummery, 1895), 107–9; (Merkl, 1932), 226–8; (Merkl, 1934), 229–33; (Wien, 1937), 234–6; (Bauer, 1938), 236–8; (Aufschnaiter 1939), 238–9; first ascent, 306–11; — II (25,572), 106, 347
Nangpa La (19,050), 35, 332
Napoleon, 65
Natha Singh, 122
Negrotto, F., 133, 136
Nela P. (16,900), 23, 79
Nepal, 84, 85; policy of exclusion, 67–8, 84; opening of, 289; — survey of, 28, 68, 315; — Gap (20,670), 124, 128; first ascent, 128
Nepal Himalaya, 9, 122, 312–24; defined, 10; described, 28–36; maps, 6, 8, 30, 32, 34; monsoon, 46, 47; survey, accuracy of, 28; weather, 51

# INDEX

Nepal Peak (23,560), 39, 124, 128, 198, 274, 277; first ascent, 274
Nepalese War (1814-16), 67, 81; — boundary, 67
Nera La (15,966), 13
Neuville, C. J., 139
Neve, Dr. Arthur, 15, 99, 107, 111-12, 137-8, 142, 151-3, 177, 299
Neve, Dr. Ernest, 99, 112, 142, 151, 190, 226
Ngojumba Kang (25,730), 36, 159-60, 346
Nilgiri Parbat (21,240), 23, 118
Nilkanta (21,640), 295
Nilt, 102
Niti, 185-6; — P. (16,628), 23, 66, 118
No La (16,600); 85
Noel, Capt. J. B. L., 154, 166, 169, 172
North Col (Everest) (22,900), 160-3, 164, 166-71, 172, 197-8, 211-16, 218-20, 221-3, 327; avalanches, 171, 216, 219, 222
Norton, Gen. E. F., 51, 166-70, 172-6, 188, 190, 198, 214-15, 216, 217
Noyce, C. W. F., 288, 333-9
Nubra R., 17, 19, 69, 81, 138, 177, 241-2, 299
Nun (23,410), 15, 109-12, 291; first ascent, 291
Nun Kun, 11, 12, 13, 15, 109-12, 152, 291-2; map, 110; monsoon, 47
Nup La, 160
Nupchu (c. 23,100), 313
Nuptse (25,700), 161, 326, 346
Nushik La, 77, 103, 131
Nyenam, 34, 59, 87
Nyonno Ri (22,142), 35

Oakes, Capt. G. F. T., 44, 130, 153
Odell, N. E., 26, 51, 172-6, 207-9, 220, 222-3, 257, 260, 311
Oliver, Maj. D. G., 138, 141, 177
Oliver, Capt. P. R., 205, 220, 222-3, 266, 269, 286, 295; death, 286
Oliviera, John de, 57
Olon, 90
Oprang R. (see also Shaksgam R.), 100, 178-80
Osmaston, Maj. Gordon, 26, 264-7, 293
Oudet, Jacques, 315, 319
Oxus R., 92
oxygen, 117, 152, 167, 169-71, 172-4, 185, 187, 212, 216, 223, 281, 322, 332, 335-9

Pache, M., 126
Pachhu (Panchu) glac., 114
Packard, W. P., 314
Paidar, H., 39, 276, 277, 286
Pervitine tablets, 310
Pakistan, 287-8; Government, 300, 306
Pallis, Marco, 264-5, 269
Pamirs, 50, 89, 92, 144; Pamir Boundary Commission, 105
Panamik, 138, 181
Panch Chuli (22,650), 22, 114, 265, 267, 297-8
Pandim, 94, 123
Pandoh, 11
Pangong Tso (L.), 69, 78
Panmah glac., 17, 19, 77, 241, 245-6; — Muztagh, 101, 245
Parang La (18,300), 13
Parasing (15,040), 14, 113
Parbati R., 13, 14, 292-3
Pargätzi, J., 39, 312
Paro Dzong, 43, 58, 61, 278
Partition of India, 287; effects of, 288-9
Pashpati, 33
Passanram valley, 200, 276
Pasu glac., 178
Pathankot, 14
Pauhunri (23,180), 40, 43, 128-9; first ascent, 129
Payan, L., 296-7
Peking, 58-60
Pemakoi-chen, 90, 129, 130

Pemayangtse, 90, 91
Pen La (P.) (17,350), 279
Perren, Johann, 120, 178
Peterkin, Grant, 139-40, 141, 249
Pethangtse (22,060), 162, 344; first ascent, 344
Petigax, G., 140-1
Petigax, Joseph and Laurenzo, 131, 133
Petzoldt, Paul, 20, 257-9
Pfannl, H., 132-3
Pfeffer, M., 234-6
Phari, 157, 159
Phillimore, Col. R. H., 60
Phung Chu (R.), 29, 35, 87, 159-60
physiology, mountain, 104, 129, 146, 185-6, 332-3
Pickersgill, Joshua, 67
Pierre, Bernard, 291
Pin Parbati P., 14
Pindar R., 22, 64, 120
Pindari glac., 69, 121
Pinnacle Peak (22,810), 15, 109, 111
Pioneer Peak (22,600), 104
Pir Panjal, 11, 12, 13, 14, 77, 112, 287, 292; described, 13; monsoon, 47; — P., 14, 59
Pircher, H., 199-200
Plassey, Battle of, 61
Po Chu (R.) (Bhote Kosi), 29, 34, 59, 87
Pocock, I. S., 82
Pokhara, 321
Polunin, O., 313
Ponti, V., 240
Puchoz, M., 343
Pugh, Dr. L. Griffith, 332, 334
Pumo-ri (23,190), 160, 326
Punaka (5,200), 43, 51, 78; — Chu (Sankosh R.), 43
Punch R., 12
Pundit explorers, 84-91
Punjab, annexation of, 74
Punjab Himalaya, 9, 91, 106-13, 143, 225-39, 291-2; best climbing season, 49, 50; defined, 10; described, 11-15; maps, 6, 8, monsoon, 47
Putha Hiunchuli (23,750), 31
Pyramid Peak (23,400), 39, 124, 312; first ascent, 312

Raeburn, Harold, 94, 155, 159, 162-3
Raechl, W., 229
Raghobir Thapa, 107
Raidak R., 42, 58
Raikana glac., 118-20, 186
Rainer, K., 306-7, 311
rainfall, monsoon, 46-8; winter, 48-9
Raithal, 64, 68
Rakaposhi (25,550), 16, 21, 103, 251, 256, 299-300, 343, 347; monsoon, 47; weather, 50; — Range, 19, 103
Rakas Tal L., 7, 8, 64, 80, 115, 125
Rakhiot glac., 106, 108, 225-7, 234, 306; — Peak (23,210), 106, 225-7, 230, 237, 307-9, 311; first ascent, 227
Ramani glac., 93, 117
Ramganga R., 22, 65
Ramnagar, 25, 65
Ramthang (23,310), 199
Ranikhet, 5, 25, 208
Ranjit Singh of the Punjab, 65, 69, 74
Raper, Capt. Felix V., 64
Rapiu La, 167
Rasua Garhi, 33, 85, 313
Rataban (20,230), 23, 26, 118, 269-70; first ascent, 270
Rathong glac., 39, 126
Ravi R., 10, 11, 12, 14
Rawalpindi, monsoon rainfall, 46
Rawling, C. G., 66, 153, 154
Reading, Lord (Viceroy), 155
Rebitsch, 236-7, 343
Rébuffat, Gaston, 315-8
Regis, Baptiste, 60
Rennell, James, 60-2, 64; Map of Hindoostan, 61

Rey, Emile, 204-5
Richards, D. S., 212
Richter, H., 198
Rickmers, Rickmer, 195
Riddiford, H. E., 295, 326-7, 332
Ridi, 33
Rikkyo University, 268
Rimo glac., 17, 20, 141, 241
Rinzin Namgyal, RN, 91, 124
Rishiganga R., 25, 117-18, 188, 205; — gorge, 26, 93, 118, 206, 208, 210, 267
Robert, W., 91, 94
Roberts, J. O. M., 252, 292, 299, 314, 333
Robertson, Capt. C. L., 130
Roch, André, 26, 248-9, 269-71, 293-4, 295, 321-3, 328-30
Rohtang P. (13,050), 13, 57
Rongbuk, 160, 218; — glac., 160-1, 166, 222-3; West — glac., 160-1; East — glac., 161-2, 167, 218
Rosencrantz, G., 343
Roudebush, J. H., 103-4
Rowaling Himal, 36
Royal Geographical Society, 18, 78, 93, 103, 104, 154-6, 183, 185, 282, 325, 328
Rubenson, C. W., 39, 94, 126-7, 275
Rubi, A., 312
Rundall, J. W., 14
Rupal Gah, 106-7, 225
Rupshu, 11, 13, 69, 81
Russell, R. Scott, 246
Russenberger, V., 295
Russia, 84, 99, 101
Ruttledge, Hugh, and Mrs., xi, 26, 51, 69, 187-8, 190, 204-5, 206, 224, 264, 267-8, 281, 297; (1933 Everest), 211-16; (1936 Everest), 220-2
Ryall, E. C., 78, 82, 137-8
Ryder, Capt. C. H. D., 125, 156

Sadiya, 42, 129
St. Elmo's Fires, 52
Saipal (23,079), 29, 30, 343
Sakya Dzong, 87
Saltoro Kangri (25,400), 16, 21, 137, 139, 251-3, 347; — Range, 19, 252, 347; — P., 66, 70, 101, 137, 139, 251; — Vall., 70, 77, 253
Sams, R. H., 295
Sangster, Capt. R. A. K., 229
Sankosh R., 42, 43
Sapt. Kosi R., 35
Saraswati R. (Alaknanda), 23, 26, 57, 295
Sarat Chandra Das, SCD, 91
Sar-bulak (Russian h.s., 17,284), 145
Sarda R., 22
Sargaroin (20,370), 25
Sarpo Laggo glac., 100, 101, 241, 244-5
Saser Kangri (25,170), 138, 177, 299, 347; — Muztagh, 20, 177; — P. (17,480), 81, 177, 181, 242, 299
Satopanth (23,213), 22, 264, 269, 294; first ascent, 294; — glac., 119, 206
Sauwala (23,539), 31
Savoie, Albert, 133
Schaller, Hermann, 41, 199
Schatz, Marcel, 315-18
Schatz, R., 321-3
Schelpe, E. A., 292
Schlagintweits, 69, 73, 82, 85, 296
Schmaderer, L., 39, 236-7, 276, 277, 286; death, 286
Schneider, E., 39, 198, 229-31, 274, 310
Schoberth, G., 275
Schoening, P., 300-5
Schwarzgruber, Rudolf, 26, 268-9, 270
Scott, H., 313
Secord, R. Campbell, 50, 246, 256, 299, 326-7, 332
Ségogne, H. de, 249-50
Sella, Vittorio, 133, 136
Sentinel Peak (21,240), first ascent, 128
Seti Gandaki R., 32
Seti Karnali, R., 31, 32

Shahidulla, 91, 101
Shaksgam R. (*see also* Oprang R.), 9, 16, 100, 101, 137–40, 178–83, 240–3, 244–6
Shalshal P. (16,390), 115
Shaw, Robert, B., 92, 141
Shebbeare, E. O., 172, 191, 195, 199, 211, 274
Shelverton, G., 76, 79
Sher Ali, Amir of Afghanistan, 89
Sher Jang, 89, 130
Sherpas, 105, 127, 157, 162–3, 169–71, 188, 191–2, 203, 204, 207–8, 224, 271, 281, 288; porter register, 191–2, 288
Aila Sherpa (No. 61), 224, 268, 315, 317–9
Ajeeba (No. 10), 293, 312, 315, 329
Ang Dawa I (No. 40), 269, 293–4); — III (No. 42), 268; — IV (No. 152), 312, 315, 317–19
Ang Nurbu (No. 172), 202, 294, 329, 338
Ang Nyima (No. 1), 338–9
Ang Temba, 338
Ang Tenzing II (No. 3), 191, 244; — III (Balu), 337
Ang Tharkay (No. 19), 191, 205, 207, 214, 218, 223–4, 244–6, 267, 269, 275, 291, 315, 317–18, 321, 326, 345
Ang Tsering I (No. 36), 202, 214, 231–3; — II (No. 15), 214, 235, 275; death, 235; — III (Pansy) (No. 51), 191, 315, 317–19; — IV (No. 101), 294, 319
Annullu (No. 170), 336–8
Chettan (Sherpa), 41, 187–8, 196–8; death, 198
Da Namgyal I (No. 33), 208; — II (No. 157), 297, 314, 329–30, 337–8
Da Tenzing, 336; — II, 336, 338
Dawa Thondup (No. 49), 191, 231–3, 251, 252, 260–2, 277, 294, 297, 312, 315, 317, 338
Dawa Tsering Sherpa, 214; — Bhutia (No. 53), 252, 256, 271–3
Gaylay Sherpa, 231–3, 237; death, 233
Gyalgen II Mikchen (No. 57), 246, 295, 297, 312, 314, 319, 322–3
Jigmay (Jigmi) Sherpa (No. 23), 235, 275; death, 235
Karmi Sherpa (No. 117), 200, 235 (death)
Kitar Dorje (No. 35), 200, 202, 208, 210, 230–2, 275; death, 210
Lewa (Sherpa) (No. 46), 171, 188, 196–7, 202–4, 229
Mingma Tsering (No. 68), 235 (death), 275–6
Nima Dorje I, 202–3, 214, 229; — II, 214, 229–32; death, 232
Nima Thondup (No. 67), 229, 278
Nima Tsering I (No. 17), 235 (death); — II (No. 110), 235 (death), 275–6; — III (No. 129), 208, 252
Palden (No. 54), 251, 271
Pasang Bhutia (No. 39), 205, 214, 218, 224
Pasang Dawa Lama (Pasang Sherpa) (No. 139), 20, 42, 191, 252, 260–2, 277, 278, 295, 307, 312, 344
Pasang Kikuli (No. 8), 208, 210, 229–33, 257–9, 260–3, 277, 278, 302; death, 262–3
Pasang Kitar, 260–3; death, 262–3
Pasang Nurbu ('Picture') (No. 29), 230–3, 235 (death)
Pasang Phuttar (No. 79), 208, 252, 255, 275
Pasang Urgen (No. 98), 268, 294
Phu Tharkay (No. 153), 315, 318–19, 329–30
Pintso Nurbu Sherpa, 231–2, 237; death, 232
Pintso Sherpa (No. 141), 258, 260–3; death, 262–3
Ringsing Bhutia (No. 32), 214, 218, 267, 277
Sarki (No. 151), 315, 317–18, 319
Sonam (Sen) Tenzing (No. 75), 244, 267

Sherpas—*continued*
Tenzing Norkhay Sherpa, G.M. (Tenzing Bhutia, or Tenzing Khumjung) (No. 48), 51, 191, 221, 267, 293–4, 296–7, 329–30, 333–9, 345
Tse Tendrup (No. 38), 258, 260–2
Tsering Tharkay (No. 50), 214, 218
Wangdi Nurbu (Ongdi) (No. 25), 202, 224, 268, 293–4
Sherpur, 93
Sherriff, George, 42, 43, 44, 278–9
Sherring, C. A., 115, 187–8
Shib Lal, 140–1
Shigar R., 17, 77, 301
Shigatse, 58, 61, 84, 87, 88, 89, 125
Shilla (23,050), 13; first ascent, 75
Shimshal P., 101, 102, 184, 246; — porters, 184; — valley, 17, 102, 145, 177–9, 183; — vill., 178, 184
Shingo R., 109
Shipki, 11, 13, 125
Shipton, Eric E., 20, 26, 36, 50, 51, 101, 132, 145, 182, 202–3, 205–7, 211, 213–15, 220–4, 266–7, 269, 276, 281, 285, 313, 325; (1935 Everest), 218–20; (1937, 1939 Karakoram), 244–7; (1951 Everest), 326–7; (1952, Cho Oyu), 332
Shisha Pangma, *see* Gosainthan
Shyok R., 9, 16, 17, 19, 66, 69, 81, 137–9, 141, 242, 251, 299
Sia La (*c.* 18,700), 139; — Kangri (24,350), 249
Siachen glac., 9, 16, 17, 19, 81, 101, 131, 137–40, 240, 241, 251; — Muztagh, 181
Siebe, Gorman & Co., 152
Sikkim, 10, 81, 84, 91, 93, 123–5, 156–7, 288
Sikkim Himalaya, 10, 123–9, 274–7; defined, 10; described, 37–41; survey of, 90, 156; maps, 6, 8, 38; monsoon, 46, 47
Sillem, Dr. H., 15, 111, 253
Silver Saddle (Nanga Parbat) (24,464), 49, 225, 230–2, 237, 309–10
Simikot, 30
Simla, 5, 13, 14, 25, 69; monsoon rainfall, 46
Simon, F., 226, 228
Simvu (22,360), 37, 94, 123, 124, 128; — North Peak (21,473), 234, 276; first ascent, 276; — Saddle (18,110), 128, 200, 276
Sind R., 12, 142
Singalila ridge, 39, 87, 93, 122
Singhi glac., 182, 241, 243–4
Siniolchu (22,600), 37, 94, 234, 276; first ascent, 276
Siri, Dr. William, 36
Siwaliks, 4, 5, 6, 7, 12, 32, 42; defined, 4
Siyom R., 279
Skamri glac. (Crevasse glac.), 101, 245
Skardu, 19, 69, 70, 74, 131, 140, 301
Skoro La (16,644), 69, 77, 104, 131
Skyang Kangri (24,750), 135
Slingsby, Capt. A. M., 120, 137–8, 153, 202, 264
Smart, Lieut. D. M. B., 234–5
Smijth-Windham, W. R., 212, 220
Smyth, Maj. Edmund, 84, 119
Smythe, Frank S., 26, 27, 39, 198, 202–4, 211, 213–16, 217, 220–4, 264, 267, 281, 285, 295; Kamet exped., 202–4, 266
Snelson, K., 292, 298
snowfall, 49, 326
Sola Khumbu (dist.), 35, 219, 325–6
Somervell, Dr. T. Howard, 26, 166–71, 172–6, 187, 204
Sonamarg, 49, 287
Sousa, Gonzales de, 57
South Col (Everest), 162, 326–7, 329–31, 334, 336–9
Spender, Michael, 20, 132, 183, 218–19, 244–6, 286
Sphinx, 39, 312
Spin R., 13
Spiti, 13, 14, 69, 75, 286, 291–3

Spoleto, Duke of, 20, 183, 249, 257; Karakoram exped., 240–1
Spranger, A. J., 140–1
Squires, Capt. R. D., 113, 142, 153
Sri Kailas (22,742), 268
Srikanta (20,120), 22, 264
Srinagar (Alaknanda), 56
Srinagar (Kashmir), 12, 14, 56, 59; snowfall, 49
Staghar glac., 182, 241, 243
Stein, Sir Aurel, x, 80, 89, 177
stereo-photogrammetry, 146, 183, 200, 240–1, 267
Steuri, Fritz, 269–70
Stobart, T. S., 291, 334
Stolicza, Dr. F., 92
Strachey, Henry and Richard, 19, 80–2, 116, 119, 296
Streatfeild, Capt. N. R., 249, 257–8
Streather, Capt. H. R. A., 300–5
Strutt, Col. E. L., 166–70, 190
Subansiri R., 43, 130, 279
'Sugarloaf' (21,128), 274; first ascent, 274
Sun Kosi R., 29, 35
Sundardhunga, 120, 204; — Khal (P.) (18,110), 204–5, 207
Sunset Peak, 14, 112
Suru, 13, 109, 110, 291
Survey of India, 20, 25, 89, 90, 139, 140, 142–7, 154–6, 185, 264–7
Sutlej R., 7, 11, 13, 14, 22, 25, 65, 66, 79, 125
Sutter, Alfred, 293–4, 312
Swachhand (22,050), 268
Swat, 89
Swiss Foundation for Alpine Research, 293, 328, 330

Tagalaung La (17,500), 57
Taghdumbash Pamir, 101, 145–6, 178
Taguchi, J., 319, 320
Takagi, Dr. M., 319, 320–1
Takebushi, S., 268, 319, 320
Taklakot, 30, 115, 187
Talung R., 37; glac., 39, 41, 93, 123; Peak (23,082), 39
Tamba Kosi R. (Bhote Kosi), 34, 36
Tamur Kosi R., 34, 35, 37, 87
Tanakpur, 22
Tandy, Sir Edward A. (Surveyor General), 18, 189
Tang la (15,219), 43, 58, 61, 157, 159, 277
Tanner, Col. H. C. B., 90–1, 94, 123
Tapoban, 64, 115, 117
Tarshing, 107
Tatakuti (15,560), 14, 112
Teasdale, Dr. G. A. J. and Mrs., 252, 255–6
Tejbir (Gurkha), 169–70
Tengkye (Tinki) Dzong, 156, 159, — La, 159
Tengri Nor, 88
Tent Peak (24,089), 39, 124, 277; first ascent, 277
Tenzing, *see* Tenzing Norkhay, under Sherpas
Terai, 72, 81, 315
Teram Kangri I (24,489), 137–9, 144, 181; — II (24,300), — III (24,218), 139
Teram Shehr glac., 139, 241
Terray, Lionel, 315–18
Teshu Lama, 61
Thalayasagar (22,650), 22
*The Times*, 155
Thoenes, A., 195–7, 236–7
Thompson, E. C., 212
Thomson, Dr. Thomas, 20, 81
Thuli Bheri R., 31
thunderstorms, 52
Thyangboche, 335
Tibet: Government, 154–5, 172, 176, 211, 217, 280; Invasion by Communist China, 289; Jesuit journeys, 56–60; Pundit journeys, 56–60; Ruttledge and Wilson, 187; Sherriff, Ludlow and Kingdon Ward, 278–9; Sherring and Longstaff, 115; Younghusband Mission, 125;

# INDEX

Tichy, H., 344
Tilly, T. H., 295
Tilman, H. W., 20, 26, 33, 50, 51, 132, 205–10, 218–21, 244–5, 257, 260, 281, 285, 299–300, 313–14, 320, 325–6; 1938 Everest exped., 222–4
Timphu glac., 187
Tingri Dzong, 35, 59, 87, 159; — Maidan, 35
Tinkar Khola (R.), 30, 115
Tipta La (16,740), 87
Tirich Mir (25,263), 300
Tirsuli Peaks (23,460; 23,210; 23,080), 26, 272; avalanche, 272–3
Tissières, A., 296, 343
Tista R., 6, 10, 37, 40, 81, 91, 123
Tobin, Col. H. W., 41, 190–1, 195–6, 199, 274, 288
Tons, R., 22, 293
Torabaz Khan, 184
Townend, Mrs. H. P. V., 191, 274
Tra-dom (Tradun), 33, 85, 88
Traill, G. W., 69; —'s Pass, 69, 187, 268
Trango glac., 241, 244
Trashigong Dzong, 43
Trashi Yangtse (R.), 42, 43
Trashiyangtse Dzong, 279
Trebeck, George, 67, 69
Trench, G. S. C., 260
Trenchard, Capt. O. H. B., 130
triangulation, 71, 72; Indo-Russian, 143–7; Kashmir 74–6, 142
Trisul (23,360), 26, 114–18, 120, 127, 151, 188, 205; first ascent, 117–18; second, 205; third and fourth, 297; — glac., 117
Trisuli Gandaki R., 29, 32, 33, 36, 313; — gorge, 29, 33
Troll, Prof., 234
Trongsa Chu (R.), 42
Trotter, Capt. H., 92
Tsangpo R., 7, 9, 33, 44, 58, 84, 85, 125, 130, 156, 279; identification with Brahmaputra, 61, 89–90
Tsaparang, 25, 57–8
Tso Moriri (L.), 69
Tukucha, 315–7; — Pk. (22,688), 31, 316, 323
Tulung La (P.) (17,250), 279
Tumlong, 81
Tungan rebellion, 84
Turner, Samuel, 61, 84, 89

Tutu Uns, 300
Twins (23,360), 39, 128, 196, 198, 276, 277
Tyson, John B., 27, 30, 295, 323

Ugyen Gyatso, UG, 91
Ullah, Col. M. Ata, 300–3
Umasi La (17,370), 13
Urdok glac., 101, 137, 240–1, 243
Urdukas (Rdokass), 135, 240

Vigne, G. T., 19, 70; — glac., 104, 135
Vignes, G., 296–7; death, 297
Virjerab glac., 102, 179
Visser, Dr. Ph. C., and Mrs., 20, 145, 177–9, 241–2, 299
Vitços, Pierre, 15, 291
Vyvyan, Michael, 256, 299

Waddell, L. A., 90, 94, 95, 123–4
Wager, Prof. L. R., 176, 211, 213–15, 217
Wakefield, Dr. A. W., 166, 169–70
Wakhjir, P., 99
Walker, Gen. J. T., 78, 80, 84
Waller, Capt. James, 15, 221, 251–6
Walter, R., 297
Wangtu, 11
Ward, F. Kingdon, x, 42, 44, 88, 278–9
Ward, Michael, 326–7, 332, 334
Warren, Dr. Charles, 218, 220, 222–3, 265, 276
Warren Hastings, 60, 61
Warwan R., 12, 13, 110, 142
Waugh, Sir Andrew (S.G. India), 72–4
Wahab (Wauhope), Col. R. A., 105
weather, 45–52
Webb, Capt. William S., 63–7, 71
Welzenbach, W., 229–32, 237; death, 232
Wesseley, V., 132
westerly depressions, 48, 51
Western Cwm (Everest), 35, 218–19, 325–7, 329–31, 334–9
Westmacott, M., 333–9
Wheeler, Brig. Sir E. Oliver, 156, 159–63
White, Claude, 42, 43, 123–4, 279
Wieland, U., 198, 229–32; death, 231–2
Wien, Karl, 39, 49, 183, 199–200, 234–6, 237, 238, 275–6; death, 235
Wiessner, Fritz, 50, 226, 228, 260–3, 302
Wigram, E. H. L., 218–19, 220, 276

Wigram, Rev. M. E., 111
Williams, Gen. H., 289
Williamson, F., 42, 43, 278
Williamson, Noel, 129
Wilson, Gen. R. C., 26, 187, 204, 268
wind, prevailing, 45, 50
Windy Gap, 135, 258
wireless, 212
Wolfe, D., 260–2, 302, 311; death, 262
Wollaston, A. F. R., 155, 159, 161–3
Wong Chu (R.), 42
Wood, Capt. Henry, 80, 122, 125, 140–1, 179–82
Wood, P. L. and J., 295
Wood-Johnson, G., 39, 198, 211
Workman, Dr. and Mrs., 15, 111, 131–3, 139–40, 245, 253
World War I, 151–3; — II, 285–8
Wylie, C. G., 295, 333–9
Wyn Harris, Sir P., 176, 211, 213–15, 217, 220, 222
Wyss, Dr. R., 242–3
Wyss-Dunant, Dr. E., 312, 328–9

Yalung glac., 39, 91, 95, 122, 124, 344
Yamada, J., 320–1
Yarkand, 66, 69, 82, 84, 91, 92, 100, 141; — R., 9, 16, 66–7, 92, 100–1, 141, 180, 182, 246; — trade-route, 138
Yaru Chu (R.), 29, 35, 40, 159
Yasin, 92, 99, 144
Yazghil glac., 102, 179
yeti, 56
Young, G. Mackworth, 58, 190
Younghusband, Sir Francis E., 16, 20, 99–102, 104, 125, 135, 137, 154–5, 179–80, 190, 286; —'s Col, 101, 138; —'s Tibet Mission, 40, 43, 125

Zaskar, 11, 13, 81, 291; — Range, 11, 13, 23, 26, 29, 75, 81
Zemu glac., 37, 41, 123–4, 128, 183, 195–201, 274–7
Zemu Gap (19,275), 37, 124, 128, 196
Zogg, David, 269–70
Zoji La (11,578), 6, 12, 19, 47, 49, 59, 66, 140, 242, 301
Zorawar Singh, 9, 13
Zug-Shaksgam R., 182, 243, 245
Zurbriggen, Mattias, 103–5, 131

# A Publisher's Note of Correction

Trevor Braham brought the following information to our attention shortly before we went to press:

"In 1955 the Swiss geographer, Marcel Kurz, wrote an extensive (7-page) review for *The Journal of the Swiss Foundation for Alpine Research*, Zurich (Vol 1, No. 5). The comments were mostly of a complimentary nature but the last page contained a list of "errors" found by the reviewer. Having examined these minutely it is my opinion that, with five exceptions, they are justified on the basis of factual evidence."

Most of these concern details of continental expeditions and may well have resulted from inaccurate source material. We are confident that the author would have incorporated all of these if he carried out his own revision.

Page 12: The altitude of 23,050ft (7025m) for Shilla is certainly exaggerated as the note at the bottom of page 75 seems to suggest.

Page 15: The only ascent of Kun (7075m) is that of Piacenza, not Calciati (see page 112 – below).

Page 23: Among the satellites of Kamet should be added Mukut Parbat (7042m) previously called West Ibi Gamin. The author writes Goriganga but then G*h*ori Parbat.

Page 30: The footnote regarding the 1954 Ghiglione expedition is inaccurate.

Page 36 and index: Ro*l*waling not Rowaling.

Page 39: The expedition that climbed Pyramid Peak also included Alfred Sutter, its leader. Smythe climbed Jonsong Peak (6459m) with us on 8 June 1930. Wood-Johnson, who was unwell, did not go to the summit.

Page 41: The Jacot-Guillarmod Kangchenjunga expedition did not include any French climbers, the majority being Swiss.

Page 49: On the 1953 Nanga Parbat expedition the fine weather did not start until 1 July.

Page 111: Sillem explored Nun Kun in 1903 not 1905.

Page 112: Count Calciati should read Count Piacenza.

Page 124: The Sella brothers were not guides but photographers for Freshfield on his tour of Kangchenjunga. The guide was Angelo Maquignaz from Valtournanche.

Page 126: See page 41. There were no French climbers – De Righi was Italian.

Page 132, index and photo 12: Wessely not Wesseley (twice).

Page 143: The Eckenstein expedition had skis and Jacot-Guillarmod used them up to the foot of Windy Gap.

Page 160: The West Ridge of Everest does have a shoulder.

Page 187: 1925/26 not 1926/27.

Page 249 and index: Azéma not Azèmar. The route attempted by Ertl and Roch in 1934 is not the same as that used by the French on Hidden Peak in 1936 – there are two different spurs.

Page 291 and index: Shap'at and not Shafat. Vittoz and not Vittos (three times). Piacenza 1913 not Calciati 1914.

Page 294: The Sutter expedition (1947) also made the first ascent Balbala East (6418m).

Page 295: However this expedition never attempted Nilkanta.

Page 312: Pargätzi and Rubi are guides from the Oberland, not Geneva. It is thanks to the photographs taken by this expedition that we managed to complete the north-west corner of our 1:150,000 Sikkim map.

Page 331: The person concerned is Norman Dyhrenfurth, the son of Professor G. O. Dyhrenfurth.

Page 343: Ghiglione is an engineer not a teacher.

Page 344: The Cho Oyu entry gives the wrong impression – Dr Tichy (not Jonas) did not accept Lambert's collaboration.